# Law and Regulation of Mobile Payment Systems

D1322170

Over the last ten years, mobile payment systems have revolutionised banking in some countries in Africa. In Kenya, the introduction of M-Pesa, a new financial services model, has transformed the banking and financial services industry. Giving the unbanked majority access to the financial services market it has attracted over 18 million subscribers, which is remarkable given that fewer than 4 million people in Kenya have bank accounts.

This book addresses the legal and regulatory issues arising out of the introduction of M-Pesa in Kenya and its drive towards financial inclusion. It considers the interaction between regulation and technological innovation with a particular focus on the regulatory tools, institutional arrangements and government decisional processes through the examination as a whole of its regulatory capacity. This is done with a view to understanding the regulatory capacity of Kenya in addressing the vulnerabilities presented by technological innovation in the financial industry for consumers after financial inclusion. It also examines the way that mobile payments have been regulated by criticising the piecemeal approach that the Central Bank of Kenya has taken in addressing the legal and regulatory issues presented by mobile payments. The book argues there are significant gaps in the regulatory regime of mobile banking in Kenya.

**Joy Malala** is a lecturer at Strathmore University, Kenya.

# Routledge Research in Finance and Banking Law

For a full list of titles in this series, please visit www.routledge.com

# Law and Regulation of Mobile Payment Systems

Issues arising 'post' financial inclusion in Kenya

Joy Malala

Routledge
Taylor & Francis Group

LONDON AND NEW YORK

First published 2018 by Routledge

2 Park Square, Milton Park, Abingdon, Oxfordshire OX14 4RN

52 Vanderbilt Avenue, New York, NY 10017

*Routledge is an imprint of the Taylor & Francis Group, an informa business*

First issued in paperback 2019

*British Library Cataloguing-in-Publication Data*
A catalogue record for this book is available from the British Library

*Library of Congress Cataloging-in-Publication Data*
Names: Malala, Joy, author.
Title: Law and regulation of mobile payment systems : issues arising "post" financial inclusion in Kenya / Joy Malala.
Description: Abingdon, Oxon ; New York, NY : Routledge, 2017. | Series: Routledge research in finance and banking law | Based on author's thesis (doctoral—University of Warwick, England, 2014) issued under title: Mobile payments systems in Kenya : a new era or a false dawn? : an examination of the legal and regulatory issues arising 'post' financial inclusions. | Includes bibliographical references and index.
Identifiers: LCCN 2017035831 | ISBN 9781138739987 (hardback) | ISBN 9781351728584 (adobe reader) | ISBN 9781351728577 (epub) | ISBN 9781351728560 (mobipocket)
Subjects: LCSH: Electronic funds transfers—Law and legislation—Kenya. | Mobile commerce—Law and legislation—Kenya. | Financial services industry—Law and legislation—Kenya. | Payments—Kenya—Data processing.
Classification: LCC KSK902.5.E4 M35 2017 | DDC 346.6762/082178—dc23
LC record available at https://lccn.loc.gov/2017035831

ISBN: 978-1-138-73998-7 (hbk)
ISBN: 978-0-367-88735-3 (pbk)

Typeset in Galliard
by Apex CoVantage, LLC

# Contents

# Acknowledgements

My gratitude goes to God, my pillar and strength throughout this journey, without whom I would not have stayed the course. I would also like to acknowledge my family, my loving parents Florence and Rebman, whose constant love and support has been unwavering, unfaltering and unconditional. Their moral, emotional and financial support, constant commitment and dedication to the realization of my dreams has been both uplifting and humbling. I would also thank my darling husband Dr. Ronny Scholz for his support and pragmatism who always encourages me to pursue new heights. Additionally, thanks to my siblings, especially my sister Melisa and my brothers, Steve, Tony and Joseph in many ways; this achievement is as much theirs as it is mine.

This work could not have been completed without the support of my supervisor, Professor Dalvinder Singh. In addition to his incisive and direct academic criticism of my arguments and writing, he was a pillar of knowledge and basic common sense when it came to the completion of this thesis. During the many meetings when I had felt less than adequate and lacked the self-belief and confidence in my work, he never failed to reassure me of my capabilities. My journey through Warwick undeniably bears the positive impact of various individuals who, in their different ways, have their indelible influences woven into the fabric of this book. I would especially like to thank Helen Riley, the academic support librarian, who would respond to every single query I had about the library's resources with fervour and dedication that was insurmountable; every book and every article that I requested would be obtained for me with swiftness and accuracy, and for that I shall be eternally grateful.

Finally, there is no way I could finish without acknowledging my doctoral colleagues, especially one of my dearest friends, Rumana Islam, who has been my righteous soul sister, helper, confidant, consigliore and all round mentor; this journey would not be the same without her by my side, literally and figuratively. Thanks to the greater PhD community in Warwick. I would also like to acknowledge Marion and Francois, my surrogate family in France, for their long distance support and encouragement and Sylvie Nyamunga and her family, for being my constant prayer warriors, always supporting me and reminding me that the end was in sight and that it would all be worth it. Finally, thanks to all the people who have assisted me in ways that I know and ways that I would never even know. Lastly, thanks to Margaret Muchoki for her assistance and diligence in ensuring that the finished product is one of which I should be proud.

# 1 Problem and scope
## of the study
## Introduction

*'A country's payment system is what makes it real and financial markets work . . . when commodities are exchanged for cash, cheque, giro, credit card, or debit card payments rather than other commodities, trade expands as transaction costs fall and production specialisation increases.'*[1]

## 1.1 Background

In 2008, Kenya enjoyed stable growth within its banking sector, and it appeared to have avoided most of the ripple effects from the Global Financial Crisis.[2] However, despite the resilience of leading local retail banks in the preceding years, only 19 per cent of Kenya's 40 million people had bank accounts in 2009.[3] As is the case in many developing economies, banking is still widely considered to be the exclusive preserve of the rich, who can afford the regular and costly fees charged by banks whose branches were, and continue to be, few and far between.[4] Until recently, there had been very little incentive for banks to serve the 'unbanked' and 'under banked'[5] members of society, principally, due to the significant costs entailed in establishing a network of regional branches and the minimal margins associated with providing banking services to the 'poor'.[6] Consequently, the adoption of mobile financial services, and in particular mobile payments, has become an effective step in the evolution of payment schemes.[7] This has enabled the gap created by the lack of a broad financial infrastructure in Kenya to be narrowed.[8]

As a result, mobile payment systems have become commonplace in Kenya over the last 7 years[9] through the introduction of M-Pesa[10] by the leading mobile network operator (MNO) Safaricom Ltd.[11] M-Pesa, a new financial services model, has transformed the banking and financial services industry in Kenya by giving the unbanked majority access to the financial services market, and in the process, it has attracted over 18 million subscribers.[12] This is remarkable, given that fewer than 4 million people in Kenya have bank accounts. It has succeeded in transferring people from a cash economy to modern book entry systems. The annual deposit value stands at KSh. 93,273,000,000 billion ($932,730,000); withdrawals are KSh. 79,917,000,000 billion; and transfers are KSh. 84,882,000,000 billion, including KSh. 25,610,000,000 billion, from airtime values of KSh. 3,551,000,000 billion.[13] Therefore, the significance to the Kenyan economy cannot be underestimated. Simple payment and settlement functions have been made even more convenient and accessible by this technological innovation in the payments system. Mobile payments have, to a large extent, achieved the policy objectives of financial access and inclusion, which have been part of the overall landscape of financial services and delivery in developing countries such as Kenya. Therefore, in order to understand the importance of this new financial service, this thesis aims to address some legal regulatory issues that arise out of this innovation as they pertain to Kenya, post-financial inclusion. Financial inclusion or inclusive financing is the delivery of financial services at affordable costs to disadvantaged and low-income segments of society. This is in contrast to financial exclusion, where those services are not available or affordable. The term 'post-financial inclusion' in this thesis will be used to describe the subsequent phase when financial inclusion has been achieved, a period through which a large portion of the population has access to finance and financial services and the rate of inclusion as begun to plateau.

## 1.2 Problem statement

Innovation and technology present an intersection between growth and development, which is also an intermediary between the innovators, on the one hand, and those that use the innovations, on the other. Innovation has also been seen as both transformative and catalytic for the way that a country's most productive economic sectors develop. Innovation in this context will refer to both innovation in technology and in the financial products and services introduced. It should be clear that the concept of 'innovation' encompasses not only 'technological innovation', that is, the diffusion of new products and services of a technological nature into the economy.

However, it equally includes non-technological forms of innovation, such as 'organisation' innovations. It may be used interchangeably with the term 'technology', although clarification will be given as and when needed and in context.

This is particularly true in a developing country such as Kenya, a sub-Saharan African country whose private sector is still under-capitalised and under-developed.[14] Innovation is needed and should be encouraged, as the private sector is the main driver of economic growth,[15] a position adopted in development literature[16] as well as in Kenya's ambitious economic development plans, which seek to transform it into a middle-income economy by the year 2030.[17]

Furthermore, this thesis addresses the interaction between regulation and technological innovation from Kenya's perspective, with a particular focus on the regulatory tools, institutional arrangements and government decisional processes through the examination of its regulatory capacity as a whole. This is done with a view to understanding the regulatory capacity of Kenya in addressing the vulnerabilities presented by technological innovation in the financial industry for consumers after financial inclusion. It also examines the way that mobile payments have been regulated by criticising the piecemeal approach that the Central Bank of Kenya (CBK) has taken in addressing the legal and regulatory issues presented by mobile payments.

This focus is used because many of the major obstacles to technological innovations in developing countries are related to the institutional and regulatory environment.[18] Such obstacles are not fundamentally different from those experienced in the developed countries; however, they are exacerbated in developing countries and are more challenging to address, particularly because of the absence of a coherent regulatory system.[19]

## 1.3 Purpose

An effective payment system in which the transferability of claims is effected in full and on time is a prerequisite for any economy. Similarly, disruptions in the payment system result in disruptions in aggregate economic activity.[20] In general, payment systems can preserve or undermine the public trust and confidence in financial systems; thus, they are under close public policy scrutiny with a view to safeguarding financial stability and ensuring financial integrity.

Therefore, the purpose of this study is also to discuss the legal and regulatory issues that underpin mobile payments in Kenya by postulating that the protection of consumers and the stability of the financial system should be the main justification for government intervention by way of regulation. This is in response to the rapid adoption, speculation and optimism regarding the effects of mobile payments on economic development in Africa, where policy-makers have rightly touted the poverty eradicating potential of mobile payments due to their financial inclusivity.[21]

Since there is currently an increased focus on payments systems issues which reflect the political changes and economic development occurring around the world, this study aims to examine the legal and regulatory issues that mobile payments present.[22] Despite the existence of other payments systems, such as electronic payments,[23] there have not been any other advances in Kenya's payments system because it largely remained a cash dominant society and any other forms of payments systems had primarily been cheques, electronic funds transfers, automated teller machine (ATM) cards, and debit and credit cards until the introduction of mobile payments.[24]

A number of unique and country specific factors have contributed to the success and acceptance of mobile payments, and these will be discussed in Chapter 2.[25] Among these are the wide availability and heavy use of mobile phones[26] because the telecommunications regulatory environment enabled faster adoption of mobile phone usage. In 1997, over 75 per cent of countries in sub-Saharan Africa had no mobile phone network. By 2009, a mobile phone network existed in every country, with 49 per cent of markets fully liberalised, 25 per cent partially deregulated and 26 per cent as monopolies.[27] The most common reason given for this increase is the technology in the market and the willingness of consumers to embrace new payment systems via mobile devices. In Kenya, many people are completely unbanked and so have no access to traditional bank accounts and financial services, because they lack a sufficient income to qualify for such services.[28] Establishing an efficient payment system is essential for the efficient functioning of competitive money and capital markets as well as monetary control. These are the prerequisites for the creation of a well-developed market-based financial system. Hence, the stability and efficient working of the banking system is tied to the integrity and resilience of the payments system, and disruptions in the payments system result in disruptions in aggregate economic activity.[29] Additionally, instability that manifests itself in the payments system can be seen as more alarming than instability in deposits.[30] This fear is manifest in the larger volume of daily payments within the mobile financial services and the speedy movement of the funds, as well as the unfamiliarity with the clearing process.[31] Therefore, the payment system is one of the first places where financial stress is manifested, through the Herstatt Risk,[32] as firms in financial difficulty fail to meet their payment obligations.[33] Moreover, there are very few theoretical, and even fewer empirical, studies which look at the fragility and risks of mobile payments systems, much less the payment systems as a whole in developing countries, especially in those countries that are trying to restructure their banking and monetary systems.

The theoretical framework that underpins this thesis is that, since innovation in financial services always outpaces regulation,[34] developing countries that adopt innovative products and services should have the regulatory capacity to do so. In order to advance governments' financial inclusion agendas, regulators should have the capacity to regulate these innovative products and services in a way that protects those who might otherwise be left vulnerable in times of financial crises. This regulatory capacity[35] should be commensurate with their economic development, regulatory development and their regulatory objectives as a whole. This thesis asserts that regulatory authorities in Kenya should be equipped to provide appropriate and adequate regulation of technological innovation that takes into account the best approach that would justify and balance regulatory or state intervention. Further, this thesis will aim to discuss this adequate and appropriate approach by focusing on a risk-based and prudential approach to regulation. Such an approach focuses on the stability and integrity of the payments system and the financial system as a whole, and the conduct of the business approach to regulation which encompasses consumer protection issues and accountability of the regulators in their mandate of regulating mobile payments.

## 1.4  Research questions

### 1.4.1  Main questions

The general reflections in the preceding part suggest the existence of a dependence between the state of a country's economic development and the effectiveness of its payments system. Mobile payment systems have offered a viable, partial solution to a nation's ability to provide financial access to drive economic growth.

A fundamental policy question is, therefore, how can a country then protect those who were previously excluded against the risks that new technology poses, or the previously unbanked, through adequate and appropriate regulation[36] that does not stifle innovation? In essence, what legal and regulatory considerations must Kenya secure in order to ensure a robust and economically significant payments system that is financially inclusive and eventually leads to growth and better infrastructure in its financial system? Further, what would those considerations mean for a country's law and institutional development process? All these reflect the aim of this study, which highlights the weak implementation of previous regulatory frameworks for payments and the lack of enforcement action which have raised deficiencies in the regulatory capacity.

### 1.4.2 Secondary questions

In order to fully explore the main research question outlined above, the following secondary questions are pertinent.

### i  Why is a study of mobile payments important to Kenya?

The success of mobile payments in Kenya has offered an opportunity for discourse amongst developing countries in their efforts to modernise their payments systems. Kenya's economic policies have not always matched the policy recognition of the importance of financial inclusion, through innovative payment systems, to economic growth with commensurate public policy measures that translate such recognition into market practice. Development research illustrates that the historical mismatch between academic and policy recognition of that role is increasingly being bridged, as governments across the world pay closer attention to the determinants of financial inclusion. Further, Kenyan public policy since 2003, through Vision 2030, has been to increase and emphasise the instrumental role of Kenya's private sector in driving sustainable economic development, employment-led growth and wealth creation.[37]

These important documents are: the Economic Recovery Strategy (ERS) of 2003–2007, Vision 2030 of 2007 (Vision 2030),[38] the Private Sector Development Strategy (PSDS) 2006–2012,[39] and the Master Plan Study for Kenya's Industrial Development (MAPSKID) 2007.[40] This recognition mirrors global practice which has been reinforced by recent and ongoing governmental reactions to the 'Great Recession', or the banking crisis of 2007–2008.[41] This crisis caused governments around the world to directly channel huge amounts of public funds into private businesses to stem a drawn-out recession.[42] While laudable, the persisting fragmentation of the current regulatory regime exposes fundamental deficiencies in the institutional arrangements for regulating payments systems. Therefore, this thesis attempts to draw out the correlation between having an efficient regulatory framework that safeguards these governmental goals and one that enables financial inclusion.

Are laws and legal institutions really relevant to the growth of mobile payments in a developing country like Kenya? If so, what are the key emerging legal and regulatory issues?

This thesis argues that in a developing country context, legal and regulatory issues are likely to be more influential than macroeconomic factors in nurturing fortuitous environments for a prudential mobile payments system. In adopting this proposition, this thesis examines the regulatory framework that currently deals with mobile payments and whether this environment is equipped to regulate mobile payments. Therefore, the presence, rather than the absence, of law should be viewed here as an adequate 'enabler', hence the question of what can Kenya do to enable an adequate and appropriate regulatory framework that supports mobile payments is apposite. As discussed in detail in Chapter 2,[43] Kenya has a nascent payment system industry, and this suggests that it is still a new form of financial innovation.[44]

*ii   What are the risks created by mobile payments to the financial system in Kenya and, consequently, what are the specific risks to consumers as a result of a lack of an adequate regulatory framework?*

This second part of the question seeks to explore whether mobile payments have now become systemically important payment systems that need specific regulatory oversight. This thesis will argue that there should be a regulatory framework that considers the consumer protection mandate specific to mobile payments due to the systemic importance of MNOs in the payments system in Kenya. Additionally, it needs to be considered whether this specific oversight should be anchored in the law. It will also examine the extent to which the legal and regulatory issues raised by mobile payments are effectively resolved within the current regulatory framework.

*iii   What reforms should be implemented in the current regulatory framework to adequately oversee mobile payments?*

A discernible theme that arises from the literature, as far as developing countries and payments systems are concerned, is the notion that socio-economic environments, with particular emphasis on legal and regulatory conditions, are especially crucial to financial inclusion. This line of thinking argues that the drivers of economic and financial growth, including employment-led growth, are determined by the relative sophistication of regulatory and legal systems that seek to provide both a conducive, enabling environment and one that protects consumers. This line of inquiry will be used to present an appropriate regulatory framework for mobile payments systems. This study will propose an appropriate approach to regulating mobile payments.

## 1.5 Originality and contribution to knowledge

Originality in this thesis can be found in the discussion chapters: Chapters 3 through to 5. This thesis is also original in the sense that it is the first comprehensive study of the regulatory issues surrounding mobile payments in Kenya post-financial inclusion. As a contribution to knowledge, therefore, this thesis extends the frontiers of what we know about the challenges of regulators in adapting new financial services after the initial objectives have been met. It brings together the regulatory and statutory experience of mobile payments in Kenya, and this will allow for an understanding of how the various pieces of regulation and the regulators fit together; where inconsistencies in the law exist; where practice is incongruent with the law; where the law is vague or silent; and how mobile payments stakeholders have related to the laws and institutions supporting their businesses. As such, this study serves as a baseline for future academic endeavours and offers future studies a coherent basis upon which to extrapolate.

## 1.6 Literature review

The literature review in this study is based on a wide examination of primary sources, regulation and case studies of the law in action, as well as secondary sources, scholarly literature and policy documents. It includes a preliminary bibliography for both primary and secondary sources. It is important to note that, although the examination of the regulation of mobile payments is still growing, there has not yet been a thorough review of existing work.[45] Moreover, research so far seems fragmented and lacks a roadmap or an agenda that discusses post-financial inclusion issues. The pertinent issues that were noted in the literature review for mobile payments are that the literature tends to classify mobile financial services into three main categories: mobile banking, mobile transfers and mobile payments. However, in this thesis, 'mobile payments' will be used as an all-encompassing term for these three categories. Much of the literature on mobile payments is still in development; the literature has focused on 'mobile payments' in the developing world. This thesis has adopted the classical tools of legal inquiry. However, even this approach does not yield adequate results when the law is linked to development. Thus, from a methodological framework, the central line of inquiry will employ the following three alternative questions:

i   Do laws cause strong mobile financial services to develop?
ii  Does the development of mobile financial services serve as a catalyst for the emergence of strong payments systems law?
iii Would a developing economy that does not boast either strong laws or strong financial markets create both?

A practical evaluation may be useful when conducting value judgments using this methodology. A nascent financial market, it could be hypothesised, would demand supporting legal structures and, as these structures are operationalised, the markets expand and mature. With maturing markets and an enlightened set of market participants, the demand for even better law is made. This cyclical process between strengthened law and strengthened financial markets appears to be a continuous one.[46] This interpretation sits particularly well with the theoretical stance in this thesis: that the law and legal institutions are likely to play stronger roles vis-à-vis macroeconomic factors in the emergence of mobile payments systems in a developing or emerging market context which other developing and emerging states can adopt.

In addition, there is an important theoretical gap related to the central legal themes of mobile payments. An expansive portion focuses on issues such as adoption or market analysis, neglecting other relevant themes such as regulation and effective socio-economic impacts. Thus, it is clear that there is a gap, because although there are emerging mobile payments systems worldwide, academic research is still in its infancy. However, there are limitations in the existing literature, both in discussing mobile payments in general and discussing their regulatory issues in Kenya specifically. Much of the available literature examined has quite rightly only discussed payments systems and electronic payments generally. The paucity of the existing literature on mobile payments omits any comparative and legal analysis; it is not particularly domestic-focused and has mostly been prepared in isolation by the various institutional stakeholders involved.[47] This has often skewed the critical examination of the risks to consumers brought about by mobile payments, as the focus has tended to be on the system's successes and how it has brought the financially excluded into the financial realm.

The emerging dominance of the mobile payments system in Kenya and internationally requires an extended contemporary approach to the discussion and evaluation of regulatory issues and options as part of the quest for a more effective regulatory system. Therefore, there has been some disagreement over how a regulatory atmosphere should be approached to enable mobile payments to attain their full potential.[48] This is a gap in the current research which this thesis aims to address. In doing so, this thesis contributes with a critical analysis of consumer protection in mobile payments and a proposal for an adequate approach to regulation. This thesis has the potential to benefit stakeholders, policy-makers and research organisations that have a need for such legal analysis.

However, it is clear that, while the legal and regulatory structures are also important, they have not been investigated enough. In addition, this thesis will expand to take into account the complicated institutional and policy environment within which major payments system decisions take place.[49] These will constitute the analytical framework used by this study in making a case for better financial consumer protection legislation. This vacuum in the literature helps to explain why a service with such a large potential has not been disseminated worldwide.[50] The reasons for these failures include the fact that successful cases are not clearly understood and, as a result, are not being replicated in other developing countries.

In terms of particular sources, major works by authors have been taken into consideration, such as the work by Julia Black, John Braithwaite, Anthony Ogus, Michelle Yeung and Bronwen Morgan.[51] This study references a number of journal articles written by specialists in mobile payments markets, such as the discussion by Olga and Morawczynski[52] on the adoption and convergence of financial services and telecommunications from the Consultative Group to Assist the Poor.[53]

Changes in the legal and regulatory environment encompass evolving jurisprudence, regulations and other norms with requirements that need compliance.

Mobile payments research on these issues should examine the impact of regulations on the development and success of mobile payments services markets.[54] However, current research on legislation regarding mobile payments provides an informative description of the complexities and problems surrounding these topics, yet it does not provide adequate solutions to solve these issues. However, the importance of the literature cannot be underestimated, as it not only leads to a better understanding of the state of the research in the field but it also discerns patterns in the development of the field itself. This thesis aims to address these issues. Mobile payments research, like the technology itself, is very new, and research on its adoption across several countries is currently very limited. By providing a better understanding of some of the macro level factors, such as governmental regulation, multiple regulator coordination, competition policy and multi-stakeholder interests, this thesis offers some insights that can be utilised by stakeholders to advance mobile payments discourse in other developing countries or emerging markets that hope to adopt mobile payments into their payments systems infrastructure.

## 1.7 Outline of the thesis

The regulation of mobile payments is an important one, especially for a country like Kenya that is in continual need of more innovative ways to encourage and sustain access to finance while maintaining resilience in the financial system. The tensions between economists and lawyers over the regulatory determinants of mobile payments in the developing world are explored, yielding the proposition that underlies the main research question and which is summed up in the thesis statement. As it is a contested claim, this chapter lays the framework for an evaluation of the reality of the Kenyan mobile payments experience, enabling lessons to be learned that can inform future efforts to strengthen the framework for regulating mobile payments.

This thesis is divided into 6 chapters, including this chapter. Chapter 1 introduces the thesis by providing the background and the conceptual framework through which the legal and regulatory challenges of mobile payments can be tackled. It clarifies the contribution of the thesis and discusses the research questions. Having clarified the research problem and contextualised it within a specified legal context for investigation, and having explored various underlying concepts and issues, including an exposition of the varied terminology employed in describing the problem at hand, the rest of this thesis is organised as follows:

Chapter 2 is titled: 'Kenya's Payments System: An Exploratory and Explanatory Analysis', and it offers background information on the development of Kenya's payment system. This chapter will start by setting out the historical context of the payments system in Kenya. It will discuss the efforts of Kenya to modernise its payment system as a useful segue into a discussion on its regulatory capacity. It will then explore the introduction of mobile payments as part of Kenya's payments system framework. This will be done by discussing the 'telecommunications revolution'[55] in Kenya, which provided an environment that allowed the success of mobile payments and has consequently led to financial inclusion. It is hoped that examining the importance of a country's payments system in its economy and financial system will demonstrate the increased focus on mobile payments system issues that reflect both political changes and economic development in Kenya. This chapter also highlights the importance of a stable and resilient[56] payment system, as this allowed for the emergence of mobile payments as a preferred payment method in Kenya. It discusses the enabling environment, but more specifically the enabling legal environment, for the successful uptake of mobile payments as proof of its ubiquitous success in Kenya. This chapter is a preamble to a discussion on the risks that the payments system poses to consumers.

Chapter 3, titled 'Financial Stability and Integrity Post Financial Inclusion through Mobile Payments', explores the risks inherent in payment systems and then highlights the unique risks introduced by a mobile payments system to a post-financially inclusive Kenya. It will offer this discussion through the assertion that the use of mobile payments has resulted in the increase of public involvement in the formal financial system. Through this involvement, the expansion of savings accounts in the regulated financial intermediaries has converted widely distributed consumer risk, from the use of mobile payments, into a 'concentrated systemic risk', where the value of the 'items' in transit on 'deposit' through trustee accounts is no longer insignificant. These issues will be put forward, as they should be of great concern to regulators in Kenya, who are ultimately responsible for finding a balance between an enabling environment that is conducive to innovation and economic development and one that addresses consumer protection concerns. The chapter begins with the observation that failure in the payments system can produce a domino effect that is damaging to financial stability and integrity. This not only provides the main justification for regulatory intervention but also raises the question as to whether the central bank can perform better in its mandate to regulate and mitigate market failure as a result of a weak regulatory implementation of its prescribed payments system regulation. This chapter also discusses the legal, operational, security, and liquidity risks created by mobile payments as a justification for the reformation of the current regulatory framework and the implementation of an appropriate regulation.

Following the examination of the risks and regulatory challenges, Chapter 4 discusses the current regulatory framework for mobile payments. This chapter will consider how Kenya has dealt with the regulatory challenges that the mobile payments system has presented. It will highlight the fragmented, incomplete, ambiguous and often conflicting regulatory environment that mobile payments currently operate under. This chapter hopes to discuss the gaps in the current regulatory framework in an attempt to explore the regulatory capacity that the CBK has in its mandate. The focus in this chapter is to explore some of the main regulatory challenges that mobile payments present, for instance, the legal definition of 'mobile money' and 'deposit' in the context of mobile payments and whether pre-existing paper-based common law and contractual principles, such as those between a banker and a customer, have relevance and application to mobile payments. This chapter will also challenge the approach that the CBK has taken in prudentially regulating mobile payments as well as examining the adverse trend prevalent in the monitoring and enforcement capabilities established by the CBK's National Payments Act.[57] It is hoped that this critical analysis will uncover the gaps and complexities it presents for consumers and their protection.

Chapter 4, titled 'The Legal and Regulatory Challenges', discusses the consequences of the application of the current regulatory framework on the regulation of mobile payments and how it affects consumers. This chapter considers the justification for consumer protection by arguing that an appropriate regulatory framework for mobile payments should be established to ensure that consumers are adequately protected while still balancing the objectives of regulating mobile payments. The discussion in this chapter concerns the difficult and perhaps impossible role of the CBK as the principal adjudicator of mobile payments disputes between financial institutions and consumers. The Banking Act CAP 488 is also briefly reviewed to the extent that it relates, in small part, to the National Payment System Act 2011 and is also a self-regulating instrument. This chapter also examines the role and relevance of the legislative force of the Consumer Protection Act 2012 and its omission of payment systems from its content. Finally, it proposes the establishment of a separate consumer agency to deal with conduct of business requirements for consumer needs.

Chapter 5 describes what an adequate and appropriate regulatory framework should look like by stressing the accountability and the functions of the CBK in its mandate as the sole regulatory authority for the financial system in Kenya. This chapter offers a criticism of the current regulatory framework for mobile payments. It further argues that while the stability and integrity of payments systems are important, mobile payments deserve special attention because of their specific system design, and because through their creation of a systemically important institution in the MNO, this poses further systemic risk to the economic and financial system as a whole. This chapter also calls for a reform in the current regulatory framework, taking into account the objectives as stated throughout the thesis of stability, integrity and consumer protection.

Chapter 6 is the conclusion to this thesis. It draws on the summaries and conclusions made in the four analytical chapters and revisits the mobile payments system problems and debate in order to assess the contribution of the research. It offers possible regulatory solutions to the mobile payments system challenges in Kenya and offers areas for future research and exploration.

## Notes

1 David B. Humphrey, Lawrence B. Pulley and Jukka M. Vesala, 'Cash, Paper, and Electronic Payments: A Cross-country Analysis' (1996) 28(4) *Journal of Money, Credit and Banking* 914.
2 The Global Financial Crisis in 2007/2008 as defined in John Raymond LaBrosse, Rodrigo Olivares-Caminal and Dalvinder Singh, *Financial Crisis Containment and Government Guarantees* (Edward Elgar 2013).
3 Mark Pickens, David Porteous and Sarah Rotman, 'Banking the Poor via G2P Payments' (2009) 58 *Focus Note*.

4 Growth Commission, *Post-Crisis Growth in Developing Countries: A Special Report of the Commission on Growth and Development on the Implications of the 2008 Financial Crisis* (Washington DC: The World Bank 2010).

5 The terms 'unbanked' and 'under banked' will be used in this paper to refer to persons who do not have a bank account or who rely on alternative financial services. See, Federal Deposit Insurance Corporation (FDIC), 'Tapping the Unbanked Market' (Symposium) <www.fdic.gov/news/conferences/TUM_bio. html> accessed 3 September 2013.

6 Ignacio Mas and Daniel Radcliffe, 'Mobile Payments Go Viral: M-PESA in Kenya' (2011) 32 *Journal of Financial Transformation* 169; See Alliance for Financial Inclusion, 'Enabling Mobile Money Transfer' (*Youtube*, 24 May 2012) 'Enabling Mobile Money Transfer' <www.youtube.com/watch?v=LFXAX42WA6Q> accessed 3 September 2014.

7 Olga Morawczynski, 'Examining the Adoption, Usage and Outcomes of Mobile Money Services: the Case of M-PESA in Kenya' (PhD Thesis, University of Edinburgh 2011). This uptake will be explored in Chapter 2 when the thesis examines the enabling environment for mobile payments.

8 Stamatis Karnouskos and Fraunhofer Fokus, 'Mobile Payment: A Journey Through Existing Procedures and Standardization Initiatives' (2004) 6(4) *IEEE Communications Surveys* 24. 'Financial Infrastructures' is the set of institutions that enable effective operation of financial intermediaries. This includes such elements as payment systems, credit information bureaus and collateral registries. More broadly, financial infrastructure encompasses the existing legal and regulatory framework for financial sector operations.

9 This period is from 2008–2014.

10 M-Pesa (M for mobile, *Pesa* is Swahili for money) is a mobile phone-based money transfer and micro financing service for Safaricom and Vodacom, the largest mobile network operators in Kenya and, currently, the most developed mobile payment system in the world. M-Pesa allows users with a national ID card or passport to deposit, withdraw and transfer money easily with a mobile device. See Safaricom, <www.safaricom.co.ke/?id=257> accessed 3 September 2014.

11 Safaricom Ltd is a leading mobile network operator in Kenya. It was formed in 1997 as a fully owned subsidiary of Telkom Kenya. In May 2000, Vodafone Group Plc of the United Kingdom acquired a 40 per cent stake and management responsibility for the company.

12 Safaricom, 'MPESA Timeline' <www.safaricom.co.ke/mpesa_timeline/timeline. html#> accessed 3 September 2014.

13 Ibid.

14 Richard Kitchen, 'Venture Capital: Is It Appropriate for Developing Countries?' (1992) *Contributions in Economics and Economic History*

15 Klaus Fischer and George Papaioannou (eds), Hofstra University. Yochanan Shachmurove, 'An Introduction to the Special Issues on Financial Markets of the Middle East' (2004) 9(3) *International Journal of Business* 213.

16 Department for International Development (DfID), 'The Engine of Development: The Private Sector and Prosperity for Poor People' (DfID, 2011) <www.dfid.gov.uk/Documents/publications1/Private-sector-approach-paper-May2011.pdf> accessed 3 September 2014. See also, Asian Development Bank, 'Overview' (ADB, 2011) <www.adb.org/themes/private-sector-development/ overview> accessed 3 September 2013.

17 Government of Kenya, 'Vision 2030' <www.vision2030.go.ke/index.php/vision> accessed 3 September 2014

18 'Institutional environment' will be used here to mean the infrastructure in Kenya.

19 Jean Eric – Aurbert, 'Promoting Innovation in Developing Countries: A Conceptual Framework 2005' <http://info.worldbank.org/etools/docs/library/

137729/0-3097AubertPaper%5B1%5D.pdf.> World Bank Publications accessed 29 September 2013.

20 George J. Benston and George G. Kaufman, 'Is the Banking and Payments System Fragile?' (1995) 9 *Journal of Financial Services Research* 209.

21 Sara Corbett, 'Can the Cell Phone Help End Global Poverty?' *New York Times* (New York, 13 April 2008)

22 The Payments System Regulator (PSR) under the Financial Conduct Authority UK was recently created on 1 of April 2014 with a view to addressing the promotion of effective competition in the markets for payment systems, promoting innovation, and ensuring that they are developed with the interests of its users in mind.

23 Joyce Wangui Gikandi and Chris Bloor, 'Adoption and Effectiveness of Electronic Banking in Kenya' (2010) 9(4) *Electronic Commerce Research and Applications* 277.

24 Kevin P. Donovan, 'Mobile Money, More Freedom? The Impact of M-PESA's Network Power on Development as Freedom' (2012) 6 *International Journal of Communication* 2647. Other means of payment, though somewhat narrower in scope, include POS, microfinance institutions and SACCOs.

25 See Chapter 2 Section 2.4, "The Enabling Environment for Mobile Payments", pg. 29.

26 Olga Morawczynski, 'Exploring the Usage and Impact of "transformational" Mobile Financial Services: the Case of M-PESA in Kenya' (2009) 3(3) *Journal of Eastern African Studies* 509.

27 Jenny Aker and Isaac Mbiti, *Mobile Phones and Economic Development in Africa* (Center for Global Development Working Paper 211, 2010)

28 AJM Shafiul and Alam Bhuiyan, 'Peripheral View: Conceptualizing the Information Society as a Postcolonial Subject' (2008) 70(2) *International Communication Gazette* 99.

29 Hans J. Blommestein and Michael George Spencer, *The Role of Financial Institutions in the Transition to a Market Economy* (International Monetary Fund 1993)

30 International Competition Network (Antitrust Enforcement in Regulated Sectors Subgroup 1), 'An increasing role for competition in the regulation of banks' (June 2005) <www.internationalcompetitionnetwork.org/uploads/library/doc382.pdf> accessed 3 September 2014.

31 George J. Benston and George G. Kaufman, 'Is the Banking and Payments System Fragile?' (1995) 9(3–4) *Journal of Financial Services Research* 209.

32 Herstatt risk, also known as cross-currency settlement risk or foreign exchange risk, is the risk that a party to a trade fails to make payment even though it has been paid by its counterparty. See, George G. Kaufman and Kenneth E. Scott, 'What is Systemic Risk, and do Bank Regulators Retard or Contribute to it?' (2003) 7(3) *Independent Review* 371. Similarly, systemic risk has taken centre stage following the GFC, and regulators are now re-examining their approach to financial system stability in the context of their interconnectivity. See, David Bholat and Joanna Gray, 'Organizational Form as a Source of Systemic Risk' (2013) 7 *Economics: The Open-Access, Open-Assessment E-Journal.*

33 Bruce J. Summers, *The Payment System: Design, Management, and Supervision* (International Monetary Fund 1994)

34 It is suggested that complex financial markets innovate more quickly than regulators can adapt as was discussed in Anabtawi & Schwarcz, supra note 5, (manuscript at 40–41) Cf. Kathryn Judge, Fragmentation Nodes: A Study in Financial Innovation, Complexity and Systemic Risk 82 (14 December 2010) (unpublished manuscript; on file with author; explaining why market observers and regulators failed to observe the 'most pernicious forms of complexity' leading to the recent financial collapse). Additionally, it is due to the emergence of various payment systems and options that are enabled through advanced technology such as RFID, NFC, Bluetooth.

35 Regulatory capacity is defined as the combination of individual competence, organisational capabilities, assets and relationships that enable a political entity to formulate, monitor and enforce regulation. For further discussion on regulatory capacity. see Chapter 5, 'The Appropriate Regulatory Approach for Mobile Payments Systems'.

36 The adequate and appropriate regulatory approach to mobile payments will be extensively discussed in Chapter 5.

37 See Government of Kenya Budget Statement for Fiscal Year 2011–2012 focusing on tax and business regulatory reforms: Government of Kenya, 'Budget Statement for Fiscal Year 2011–2012' (Uhuru Muigai Kenyatta, Minister for Finance & Deputy Prime Minister, 8 June 2011) paras 10, 19, 22, 35 <http://statehousekenya.go.ke/publications/07-06-2011-12-BudgetSpeech-Distribution%20Final%20_MF.pdf> accessed 3 September 2014.

38 Government of Kenya (n 18).

39 Government of Kenya, 'The State of Kenya's Private Sector' (African Development Bank Group, 29 October 2013) <www.afdb.org/en/documents/document/the-state-of-kenyas-private-sector-34093/> accessed 3 September 2014.

40 Republic of Kenya, Ministry of Industrialisation (2011) <www.industrialization.go.ke/index.php/downloads> accessed 3 September 2014.

41 The Global Financial Crises, between the periods of 2007–2008 (n 2).

42 Masaaki Shirakawa, 'The International Policy Response to Financial Crises' (Federal Reserve Bank of Kansas City Symposium, 2009)<www.kansascityfed.org/publicat/sympos/2009/papers/Shirakawa.08.24.09.pdf> accessed 3 September 2014.

43 Chapter 2 will discuss the proliferation of mobile payments system with an analysis of its success, brought about by an enabling environment.

44 A financial innovation here is defined as running a new process that reduces costs, reduces risks, or provides an improved product/service/instrument that better satisfies financial system participants' demands. In this case, the cost to reaching out to unbanked markets is reduced through mobile payments

45 Jane Webster and Richard T. Watson, 'Analyzing the Past to Prepare for the Future: Writing a Literature Review' (2002) 26(2) *MIS Quarterly* xiii–xxiii

46 Mark J. Roe, 'Legal Origins, Politics, and Modern Stock Markets' (2006) 120 *Harvard Law Review* 460.

47 Most of the literature produced on mobile payments has been by donor agencies, such as the World Bank, the CGAP and the DfID

48 Simone Di Castri, 'Mobile Money: Enabling Regulatory Solutions' (GSMA, Mobile Money for the Unbanked) 8.

49 Meiling Pope and others, 'Mobile Payments: The Reality on the Ground in Selected Asian Countries and the United States' (2011) 6(2) *International Journal of Mobile Marketing* 88.

50 Eduardo Henrique Diniz, Joao Porto de Albuquerque and Adrian Kemmer Cernev, 'Mobile Money and Payment: A Literature Review Based on Academic and Practitioner-Oriented Publications (2001–2011)' 3 December 2011

51 Tomi Dahlberg, Niina Mallat, Jan Ondrus and Agneiszka Zmijewska, 'Mobile payment market and research – past, present and future' (Presentation at Helsinki Mobility Roundtable, Helsinki, Finland, 1–2 June 2006) <http://sprouts.aisnet.org/483/1/Mobile_Applications_3_1.pdf> accessed 3 September 2014.

52 Olga Morawczynski, 'Exploring the Usage and Impact of "Transformational" Mobile Financial Services: the Case of M-PESA in Kenya' (2009) 3(3) *Journal of Eastern African Studies* 509–525.

53 CGAP is an independent policy and research centre dedicated to advancing financial access to the world's poor (www.cgap.org) accessed 3 September 2014.

54 Ibid. at 54

55 This is the period during which telecommunications received great acceptance and uptake in Kenya.
56 Joanna Gray, 'Toward a More Resilient Financial System' (2012–2013) 36 Seattle U.l.Rev.799
57 National Payment System Act (No 39 of 2011).

## Bibliography

Aker, Jenny and Isaac Mbiti, *Mobile Phones and Economic Development in Africa*, Center for Global Development Working Paper 211 (2010).

Alliance for Financial Inclusion, 'Enabling Mobile Money Transfer' (*Youtube*, 24 May 2012) 'Enabling Mobile Money Transfer' <www.youtube.com/watch?v= LFXAX42WA6Q> accessed 3 September 2014.

Asian Development Bank, *Overview* (ADB, 2011) <www.adb.org/themes/private-sector-development/overview> accessed 3 September 2013.

Benston, George J. and George G. Kaufman, 'Is the Banking and Payments System Fragile?' (1995) 9 *Journal of Financial Services Research* 209.

Bholat, David and Joanna Gray, 'Organizational Form as a Source of Systemic Risk' (2013) 7 *Economics: The Open-Access*, Open-Assessment E-Journal.

Blommestein, Hans J. and Michael George Spencer, *The Role of Financial Institutions in the Transition to a Market Economy* (International Monetary Fund 1993)

'Budget Statement for Fiscal Year 2011–2012' (Uhuru Muigai Kenyatta, Minister for Finance & Deputy Prime Minister, 8 June 2011) paras 10, 19, 22, 35 <http://statehousekenya.go.ke/publications/07-06-2011-12-BudgetSpeech-Distribu tion%20Final%20_MF.pdf> accessed 3 September 2014.

Castri, Simone Di, 'Mobile Money: Enabling Regulatory Solutions' (GSMA, Mobile Money for the Unbanked) 8.

CGAP is an independent policy and research centre dedicated to advancing financial access to the world's poor <www.cgap.org> accessed 3 September 2014.

Corbett, Sara, 'Can the Cell Phone Help End Global Poverty?' *New York Times* (New York, 13 April 2008).

Dahlberg, Tomi, Niina Mallat, Jan Ondrus and Agneiszka Zmijewska, 'Mobile payment market and research – past, present and future' (Presentation at Helsinki Mobility Roundtable, Helsinki, Finland, 1–2 June 2006) <http://sprouts.aisnet.org/483/1/Mobile_Applications_3_1.pdf> accessed 3 September 2014.

Department for International Development (DfID), 'The Engine of Development: The Private Sector and Prosperity for Poor People' (DfID, 2011) <www.dfid.gov.uk/Documents/publications1/Private-sector-approach-paper-May2011.pdf> accessed 3 September 2014.

Diniz, Eduardo Henrique, Joao Porto de Albuquerque and Adrian Kemmer Cernev, 'Mobile Money and Payment: A Literature Review Based on Academic and Practitioner-Oriented Publications (2001–2011)' 3 December 2011.

Donovan, Kevin P., 'Mobile Money, More Freedom? The Impact of M-PESA's Network Power on Development as Freedom' (2012) 6 *International Journal of Communication* 2647.

Eric–Aurbert, Jean, *Promoting Innovation in Developing Countries: A Conceptual Framework 2005* (World Bank Publications) <http://info.worldbank.org/etools/docs/library/137729/0-3097AubertPaper%5B1%5D.pdf.> accessed 29 September 2013.

Federal Deposit Insurance Corporation (FDIC), 'Tapping the Unbanked Market' (Symposium) <www.fdic.gov/news/conferences/TUM_bio.html> accessed 3 September 2013.

Fischer, Klaus, and George J. Papaioannou (eds.), *Business Finance in Less Developed Capital Markets*. Hofstra University; Yochanan Shachmurove, 'An Introduction to the Special Issues on Financial Markets of the Middle East' (2004) 9(3) *International Journal of Business* 213.

Gikandi, Joyce Wangui and Chris Bloor, 'Adoption and Effectiveness of Electronic Banking in Kenya' (2010) 9(4) *Electronic Commerce Research and Applications* 277.

Government of Kenya, 'Vision 2030' <www.vision2030.go.ke/index.php/vision> accessed 3 September 2014.

Government of Kenya, *The State of Kenya's Private Sector* (African Development Bank Group, 29 October 2013) <www.afdb.org/en/documents/document/the-state-of-kenyas-private-sector-34093/> accessed 3 September 2014.

Gray, Joanna, 'Toward a More Resilient Financial System' (2012–2013) 36 *Seattle U.l.Rev.* 799.

Growth Commission, *Post-Crisis Growth in Developing Countries: A Special Report of the Commission on Growth and Development on the Implications of the 2008 Financial Crisis* (Washington DC: The World Bank (2010).

Humphrey, David B., Lawrence B. Pulley and Jukka M. Vesala, 'Cash, Paper, and Electronic Payments: A Cross-country Analysis' (1996) 28(4) *Journal of Money, Credit and Banking* 914.

International Competition Network (Antitrust Enforcement in Regulated Sectors Subgroup 1), 'An Increasing Role for Competition in the Regulation of Banks' (June 2005) <www.internationalcompetitionnetwork.org/uploads/library/doc382.pdf> accessed 3 September 2014.

Karnouskos, Stamatis and Fraunhofer Fokus, 'Mobile Payment: A Journey Through Existing Procedures and Standardization Initiatives' (2004) 6(4) *IEEE Communications Surveys* 24.

Kaufman, George G. and Kenneth E. Scott, 'What Is Systemic Risk, and Do Bank Regulators Retard or Contribute to It?' (2003) 7(3) *Independent Review* 371.

Kitchen, Richard, 'Venture Capital: Is It Appropriate for Developing Countries?' (1992) *Contributions in Economics and Economic History* 15.

LaBrosse, John Raymond, Rodrigo Olivares- Caminal and Dalvinder Singh, *Financial Crisis Containment and Government Guarantees* (Edward Elgar 2013).

Mas, Ignacio and Daniel Radcliffe, 'Mobile Payments Go Viral: M-PESA in Kenya' (2011) 32 *Journal of Financial Transformation* 169

Morawczynski, Olga, 'Examining the Adoption, Usage and Outcomes of Mobile Money Services: The Case of M-PESA in Kenya' (PhD Thesis, University of Edinburgh 2011).

Morawczynski, Olga, 'Exploring the Usage and Impact of "Transformational" Mobile Financial Services: The Case of M-PESA in Kenya' (2009) 3(3) *Journal of Eastern African Studies* 509–525.

Olga Morawczynski, 'Exploring the Usage and Impact of "transformational" Mobile Financial Services: The Case of M-PESA in Kenya' (2009) 3(3) *Journal of Eastern African Studies* 509.

Pickens, Mark, David Porteous and Sarah Rotman, 'Banking the Poor via G2P Payments' (2009) 58 *Focus Note*.

Pope, Meiling and others, 'Mobile Payments: The Reality on the Ground in Selected Asian Countries and the United States' (2011) 6(2) *International Journal of Mobile Marketing* 88.

Republic of Kenya, Ministry of Industrialisation (2011), <www.industrialization. go.ke/index.php/downloads> accessed 3 September 2014.

Roe, Mark J., 'Legal Origins, Politics, and Modern Stock Markets' (2006) 120 *Harvard Law Review* 460.

Safaricom <www.safaricom.co.ke/?id=257> accessed 3 September 2014.

Safaricom, 'MPESA Timeline' <www.safaricom.co.ke/mpesa_timeline/timeline. html#> accessed 3 September 2014.

Shafiul, A. J. M. and Alam Bhuiyan, 'Peripheral View: Conceptualizing the Information Society as a Postcolonial Subject' (2008) 70(2) *International Communication Gazette* 99.

Shirakawa, Masaaki, *The International Policy Response to Financial Crises* (Federal Reserve Bank of Kansas City Symposium, 2009) 22 <www.kansascityfed.org/publ icat/sympos/2009/papers/Shirakawa.08.24.09.pdf> accessed 3 September 2014.

Summers, Bruce J., *The Payment System: Design, Management, and Supervision* (International Monetary Fund 1994).

Webster, Jane and Richard T. Watson, 'Analyzing the Past to Prepare for the Future: Writing a Literature Review' (2002) 26(2) *MIS Quarterly* xiii–xxiii.

# 2 Introduction to the mobile payments system in Kenya
## Background and historical context

*'Banks are dinosaurs we shall by pass them.' Bill Gates*[1]

## 2.1 Introduction

The CBK has overall responsibility for maintaining financial stability in the financial sector, since central banks have to ensure that the payment systems are vital for the proper functioning of financial markets.[2] A well-functioning payment system is essential for both the growth of an efficient financial sector and confidence in the banking sector.[3] In this regard, the CBK is aware of the numerous benefits of an efficient payments system, especially in fulfilling its role in the effective implementation of the monetary policy operations and financial stability.[4] Efforts to modernise the payments system first began in 1993[5] when the CBK and the Kenya Bankers Association[6] began a collaboration. However, this modernisation was centered on addressing short-term challenges. This was a flaw in its approach, as the CBK mainly focused on the need to improve the system for clearing cheques; at the time, this was the only and most important non-cash payment instrument in use.

This meant that much of the Kenyan population remained principally cash dominant.[7] Furthermore, much of the Kenyan population still lacked a practical substitute for the cash economy and informal financial services.[8]

Financial inclusion[9] and access to finance[10] were never thought possible through payments systems, as old models that provided access to finance were minimal at best[11] and were still being explored, such as microfinance,[12] bank branches and ATM distribution in rural areas. All this changed with the introduction of mobile payments.[13] Over 80 per cent of the adult population in sub-Saharan Africa lacked a bank account in the early 2000s, which was above the world average of 50 per cent.[14]

The key hindrances to financial development were the lack of access by the disadvantaged to finance, as such access promotes economic growth at the broadest levels.[15]

A financial inclusion agenda[16] by governments, much less by the Kenyan government prior to mobile payments, did not include an examination of payments systems as an effective means of achieving inclusion.[17] This study will highlight this oversight. This chapter begins by tracing significant changes in the national payments system in Kenya as a way of providing background to the introduction of mobile payments. Mobile payments will be introduced by considering their metamorphosis from a microfinance instrument to their present-day highly visible, if sometimes controversial, market standing.[18] It will discuss the CBK's efforts to modernise the payments system as an important segue into its regulatory capacity.[19] It will further explore the introduction of mobile payments, in particular, Safaricom's[20] M-Pesa,[21] as part of Kenya's payments system framework by describing the telecommunications revolution in Kenya[22] and providing a brief background and analysis of the development of mobile phone usage, further answering the question of how mobile payments developed and emerged in the Kenyan context.

Furthermore, it highlights the role of public policy in shaping the growth of mobile payments in Kenya and the central role that the main regulator, the CBK, had in its advancement.[23] Through a review of its history and eventual success in Kenya, it is also possible to acquire an appreciation of why these public policy responses to its emergence have increasingly gained impetus around the world. This will be done by explaining how M-Pesa shifted from a microfinance product[24] to a national payment system and by highlighting the country specific factors that have remained unique to Kenya and have hampered the same success in other countries.[25] The enabling environment that ensured the success of mobile payments will also be discussed. Finally, financial inclusion will be shown as the resultant success.[26] It is hoped that examining the importance of a country's payment system in its economy and financial system will demonstrate the increased focus of mobile payment system issues which reflect both regulatory changes and economic development in Kenya.

This chapter also highlights the importance of a stable and efficient payment system as the central focus of the emergence of mobile payments as a preferred payment method in Kenya. It will present this discussion as a preamble to the risks that it poses to consumers who are included, as mobile payments have changed the face of banking through inadvertently seeking new markets through innovative financial services. It will also aim to show the impetus that M-Pesa has placed on local financial institutions to become innovative in the same way banks conduct their business. This chapter therefore and in general, offers a contextual background to the adoption, usage and scaling up of mobile payments in the Kenyan market in order to analyse its ubiquity and its success.

## 2.2 The development of a payments system in Kenya

### 2.2.1 Payments system definition

At its most basic level, a payments system is merely an agreed-upon way to transfer value between buyers and sellers in a transaction.[27] When coupled with rules and procedures, a payment system provides the infrastructure for transferring money from one entity in the economy to another. The goal of an efficient payments system is to allow instant confirmation of a transaction and to allow the buyer and seller to directly exchange the necessary information. It gives value to completing a transaction without third-party confirmation and does so within a secure environment.[28] A payments system is notable for the 'things'[29] that are used as money to transfer value in an economic exchange of goods or services.[30] As the economy develops, so too do these 'things': commodities, money, currency, cheques and, finally, the use of electronic means to transfer value.

In an advanced payments system, various procedures, rules, standards and instruments are used to exchange monetary value between parties in order to discharge an obligation.[31] With good and clear procedures, rules and standards, the payment instrument will be able to function efficiently and will allow mobilisation of financial resources at lower transaction costs, both of which promote economic growth.[32] Other features that are important for a payments system are the functions of clearing[33] and settlement.[34] All payments systems involve clearing and settlement functions in order to finalise the value transferred. The clearing function, which is composed of processing and collection, can be paper-based or electronic. Settlement finality can take place at the time of transaction or after a period of delay. Payments can carry immediate settlement when the funding can be validated before the transaction.[35]

Settlement after a period of delay usually occurs when some time is required to ensure the availability of funds.[36] Since an efficient and strong financial sector is one of the key requirements for a safe and sound financial system,[37]it would be right to say that payments systems are one of the crucial factors that determine this. Until recently, the issue of the development of payments systems has often been of secondary importance to financial sector reform. This is due to the view that a payment system is only a mechanical process and nothing more than a mechanisation of commercial banks' back-office function.[38] However, a different approach is now being taken as it has become clear that payments systems have operated on technological development in the last 20 years.

These technological developments have created risks that are capable of affecting the global economy.[39] It is also recognised that payments systems are an important element of financial stability for all countries, and the failure of payments systems may affect financial and economic stability.[40]

The World Bank holds the view that a payments system plays an important role in the process of developing a sound financial market.[41] It acknowledges that market economies rely on payments systems to enable trade and exchange among enterprises and consumers in product markets.[42] Concurrently, the payments system is also used to convert domestic and international savings into productive investments through financial markets.[43] The Bank for International Settlements (BIS) hosts the Committee on Payment and Settlement Systems (CPSS) and has carried out much work on retail payments systems.[44] While the development of new technology affects retail payments systems and their instruments, the application of modern technology has facilitated innovations in their instruments and services.[45] The CPSS acknowledges that new technologies not only lead to the emergence of new retail payments instruments, such as electronic money and mobile payments, but also to the development of new electronic payments delivery and processing, such as internet payments methods.[46]

A payments system is hence a composite 'network of instruments, institutions and services that facilitate the transfer of value between parties in a transaction'.[47] Similarly in many areas of economic activity, the organisational structure and the operations of payments systems are shaped by government policies and regulatory environments as well as by market forces.[48]

Payments systems enable the financial sector to serve the needs of the real economy. Their improvement is a priority in the transformation of wealth, development of banking systems and emerging money markets.[49] The development of the payments system has significant implications for the accounting and legal framework of any financial system. The telecommunications infrastructure, the institutional capacity of the central and commercial banks that are major providers and users of the payments systems, and the monetary instruments and management are also impacted by the payments system.[50] The characteristics of the payments systems depend on the payments services that are being offered in a particular country. Therefore, to date, mobile payments are becoming an increasingly important factor that affects the strategic competitiveness and future profitability of both private service providers in the system and business users. This is mainly due to the fact that new payments technologies have offered both lower costs and greater convenience to consumers who are the end users of these retail payments services.

Payments systems can therefore be broadly defined as the means of conducting transactions in an economy.[51] These transactions are a set of instruments, banking procedures and, typically,[52] interbank funds transfer systems that facilitate the circulation of money.[53] More precisely, a payments system is a mechanism, or a set of mechanisms which, coupled with rules and procedures, provide 'an infrastructure for transferring money from one entity in the economy to another'.[54] That infrastructure links together different banks, giro organisations and other financial institutions, payers and payees with banks, as well as a national bank with commercial banks. A simple payments system mechanism, that of exchanging currency for goods, represents direct real-time payments which, in the light of its straightforwardness and legal clarity, sets a standard of efficiency against which other payments systems may be compared.[55] Most of the other major payment mechanisms involve the transfer of deposits[56] or claims, which can be done on paper or electronically.[57] Notwithstanding the technical variations that differentiate paper-based and electronic payment systems for transferring where a similar outcome is expected money, the financial claim of the payer is reduced and the claim of the payee is increased.[58]

Therefore, the term 'payments system' has been used fairly widely to cover both clearing and settlement of payments. Clearing in a payments system involves the transmission of payment information between the payer and payee through intermediaries, that is, the transmission and recording of the instructions to make a payment.[59] Settlement, on the other hand, is the actual transfer of money to a payee's account based on payment instructions, that is, the actual transfer of some medium generally acceptable in fulfillment of the payment instruction. The act of settlement therefore, discharges an obligation in respect of funds or securities, between two or more parties.

### 2.2.2 *The modernisation of the payments system prior to mobile payments*

The modernisation of Kenya's payments system began with the automation of the Nairobi Clearing House in 1998. It began with the specific aim of improvement and 'the clearing of cheques between banks using Magnetic Ink Character Recognition (MICR) technology and electronic funds transfer (EFT) payments'.[60] This policy shift resulted in the reduction of the clearing time from a high of 14 days to the current three days.[61] Kenya also successfully launched The Kenya National Payments System Framework and Strategy Document in September 2004 and The Kenya Electronic Payments and Settlement System (KEPSS) in July 2005. KEPSS's implementation helped post-date and phase out the preceding paper-based interbank settlement system, completely transforming the management of liquidity in the banking industry.[62] In 2008, the CBK, in conjunction with the Kenya Bankers Association, as previously stated, initiated other modernisation programmes which are expected to come to fruition. These include value capping, cheque truncation, the GPay project and the failure to settle mechanism.[63]

All of these were aimed at mitigating various risks[64] and augmenting the efficiency and effectiveness of Kenya's payments system. While the introduction of the real-time gross settlement (RTGS) system was anticipated to reduce the systemic implication of the Automated Clearing House (ACH) and increase the stability and soundness of the payments system, there had been no major change in the volumes and values of payment instruments going through the ACH. Therefore, the ACH still remains a systemically important payment system (SIPS), as opposed to being a low risk retail payments system, although this changed upon the introduction of mobile payments. The modernisation process did not focus on alternative payments systems until the 'technology revolution',[65] when the convergence of the telecoms industry and the financial services industry began.

The 'technology revolution'[66] began in 1994 when Africa launched its first mobile phone network.[67] In the last two decades, Kenya has undergone a transformation in information communications and technology (ICT), which has also had an important impact on Kenya's social and economic structures.[68] As mobile phones were quickly being adapted and increasing in their sophistication in much of the developed world, Africa still had very limited access to basic mobile phones due to their cost and a lack of mobile networks.[69] However, there are now close to 500 million[70] mobile phone users, approximately half of Africa's total population.[71] The mobile penetration rate has grown, with four out of five new mobile connections in the world being made in the developing world.[72] In Kenya, the Kenya Posts and Telecommunications Corporation (KPTC) provided all telecommunication services up until 1998.[73] The KPTC was established after the East African Community (EAC) was dissolved in 1977.[74] Consequently,

Kenya's Parliament enacted the Kenya Communications Act (KCA)[75] to regulate the communications sector[76] and to liberalise telecommunications. Founded on the KCA, five companies were created.[77]

Established under the Postal Corporation Act of Kenya 1998,[78] the Postal Corporation of Kenya (PCK) emerged. Similarly, Telkom Kenya Ltd (Telkom)[79] was incorporated in April 1999 under the Companies Act[80] with its original intention to liberalise telecommunications in Kenya. Although the KCA did not allow a monopoly or even a duopoly in telecommunication operations, Telkom was granted a special licence spanning five years up to June 2004,[81] to permit Telkom to adjust to a competitive telecoms environment.[82] Telkom was the authority for all local access, national telephone services, internet mainstay networks, and very small aperture terminals (VSATs); additionally, they were responsible for the international gateway services. To this day, it is still the only nationally fixed telecommunications services operator.[83]

Mobile phone adoption has seen tremendous growth: 'from 17,000 mobile subscribers in 1999 to 11.3 million by December 2007'.[84] Mobile phone services in Kenya had been operated as a duopoly, with Safaricom and Celtel[85] taking the lead since 2000 but now rebranded as Airtel. France Telecom acquired 50 per cent of Telkom Kenya in December 2007 and proceeded to launch its Orange[86] brand in Kenya in September 2008. Since then, it is referred to as Telkom Orange, having issued out and fervently marketed its mobile services, which run on Global System for Mobile Communication (GSM) technology. In November 2008, Econet[87] was launched, bringing the total number of operators to four.[88]

Furthermore, mobile subscription almost tripled from 7.34 million subscribers in June 2006 to 24.96 million subscribers in December 2010, whilst the penetration rate more than doubled from 21.6 per cent of inhabitants to 55.9 per cent over the same period.[89] The number of minutes of local calls (mobile traffic) made on mobile networks increased by about 34 per cent, from 4.96 billion to 6.63 billion over the same period.[90] The reduced cost of mobile phones, innovation in the use of handsets (money transfer, internet access or payment services) and, in particular, the reduced tariff plans resulting from increased competition, have contributed to an increase in subscriptions, especially the escalation witnessed in the most recent period.[91] It can be argued that the state monopoly of the KPTC has shifted from the government to a private sector oligopoly.[92]

The government of Kenya, in the Kenya Information and Communications Amendment Act of 2013[93]vests the Communications Authority of Kenya (CA) (formerly the Communications Commission of Kenya, CCK) with, 'adjudicative powers in the discharge of its statutory mandate of licensing and regulating telecommunications, broadcasting and postal services within the country'.[94] Under Section n 23 of the Act, the CA exercises its mandate to ensure provision of 'quality communication services to consumers and to promoting effective competition in the provision of such services'.[95]

The more detailed strategic plan of the regulator aims to provide access to communication services for all by 2030.[96] The previous policy, from 2001, aimed to improve network access.[97] It also reduced Kenyan ownership in any operator or service provider to a minimum of 30 per cent.[98]

## 2.3 Introduction of mobile payments in Kenya

### 2.3.1 Definition of mobile payments

The definition of mobile payments as a payment instrument has been problematic. Mobile payments can be described as a payment instrument where each payment transaction requires a mobile device to execute the transaction. Each payment instrument should meet physical, legal and regulatory standards.[99] This payment instrument requires the use of one or more banks to complete a transaction. These payments are not accomplished simply by exchanging the payment instrument between a payer and a payee, but by transferring money between the payer's bank and the payee's bank.[100] The term 'mobile financial services' refers to several financial services accessible through mobile phones. As yet, there is no unanimity globally, let alone at national levels, on the characterization of mobile financial services and the term 'electronic payments through mobile devices' is often used in place of mobile payments, thus adding to confusion over what actually transpires in the payment.

However, according to Boyd and Jacob, the term 'mobile financial services' is widely accepted and used to suggest 'a comprehensive array of financial activities that consumers partake in or access using their mobile devices'.[101] These services can be classified into three groups: mobile banking, mobile money transfer and mobile payments.[102] Mobile banking suggests web-based banking services accessible through a mobile phone, such as balance enquiries, interbank transfers, and payments,[103] which has allowed for seamless transactions for consumers remotely.[104]

### 2.3.2 Introduction of M-Pesa to Kenya

M-Pesa, the first mobile payments product, has its origins in Vodafone's efforts to 'understand its role in addressing international development issues' such as the Millennium Development Goals.[105] The inception of M-Pesa focused on enabling micro- loan receipt and repayment in partnership with a microfinance institution called Faulu Deposit Taking Micro-Finance Ltd (Faulu).[106] Moreover, Faulu customers realised that the service use had an unintended benefit of transferring payments from person to person rather than simply the repayment of their loans. This precipitated the need for the company to focus solely on launching the product on just three essential services: 'deposits' at the agents and 'withdrawals', money transfers and prepaid airtime purchase.[107] Through the facilitation of financial services through mobile phones, this provided an entrepreneurial avenue and the creation of jobs and trade. Therefore, through this investment, Faulu's borrowers were able to pay a small amount each week instead of meeting with their treasurers. This was seen as a viable solution, as it reduced the risk of experimentation with new business models. Sending the treasurer with an appropriate contingent of group members for protection in order to deposit their funds in a local bank[108] was ultimately seen by Vodafone as an expensive process for borrowers, as it necessitated their removal from their business activities to deal with bank matters, which was deemed unproductive.[109]

This also highlighted the costly process involved in traditional bank methods when used as payment instruments. Consequently, M-Pesa illustrated a more useful system at the time for its customers than the microfinance institution Faulu. This was because Faulu's operating procedures and systems were not as integrative for users as they would have hoped. Hence, M-Pesa, mobile money, was debuted in 2007 by Safaricom, Kenya's largest mobile network operator, with the aim of providing basic financial services. The product facilitates a variety of financial transactions through mobile phones.[110] These functions include the checking of account balances, the ability to make 'deposits' and 'withdraw' funds, making bill and merchant payments, being able to purchase airtime and, most importantly the ability to transfer money through person-to-person payments.[111] The growth of the application was impressive. M-Pesa was able to scale to 50 per cent of Kenyan adults in less than two years.[112]

This resulted in a unique adoption rate through having 10,000 new users registering for the service daily.[113] By July 2007, there were just over 268,000 registered users. Two years later, the number had increased to 7.5 million, or 34 per cent of the adult population. Seven years[114] on, mobile money is widespread in Kenya but has yet to achieve the scale seen in other countries. M-Pesa was introduced as part of a medium-term business strategy with the aim of building brand loyalty rather than short-term financial reward. More than one in two mobile money transactions worldwide are carried out in Kenya.[115] M-Pesa has emerged as a powerful and innovative tool in financial inclusion and the economic development of the country.[116]

The value of transactions increased by 4600 per cent initially and 3700 per cent later.[117] A value of over US $535 million has been transferred through the system since its launch. These figures, compared to commercial bank deposits and gross domestic product (GDP) figures, show how significant mobile payments have become. The value of the M-Pesa transactions continued to increase to 0.2 per cent against bank deposits, and in two years it further increased to 4.4 per cent. By the following year, 2008, Kenya's GDP was estimated at US $30 billion and eventually increased to US $535 million, or 2 per cent of the year's GDP.[118]

Mobile technology has thus enabled residents of remote villages and towns to secure access to financial services previously unavailable to them.[119] Unlike other mobile transaction schemes[120] which add a new channel to existing banking services, M-Pesa offered an alternative solution and was therefore described and understood by the Kenyan regulators as a mobile payments system. This thesis will henceforth use the term 'mobile payments system' to describe all mobile financial services and products and will refer to M-Pesa interchangeably.

At the centre of M-Pesa is a float within which customers have a unique account to hold their balances that is entirely separate from the pre-pay airtime credit.[121]

The whole M-Pesa float is then banked with a commercial bank. In the case of M-Pesa, the Commercial Bank of Africa (CBA) has a banking contract for the M-Pesa float which creates a new entity, a trust company, formed by Vodafone.[122] It is through the trust company and service level agreements[123] with Safaricom that the account relationships are managed, bypassing banks and going directly to the individual M-Pesa customers. To open an M-Pesa account, a subscriber must have a Kenyan national identity card.[124] The mobile operator, Safaricom, provides the new account holder with a subscriber identity module (SIM) card that enables transactions using an application running in the SIM tool kit (STK) environment. Through specific M-Pesa agents,[125] the customers can carry out mobile payments, add cash into their accounts and make cash withdrawals.

At present,[126] M-Pesa's services are available only to M-Pesa account holders and certified agents, and they are not linked to the clearing system.[127] The mobile phone in use in the M-Pesa service acts as a 'virtual' bankcard.[128] A bankcard is fundamentally a memory or storage device in the customer's possession that serves two uses: the first is in the identification of the user and the other in the institution or account in which the user's funds are held.[129]

This was beneficial, as all this information could be stored within the mobile device, thus alleviating costly ventures that include the distribution of cards to the entire banked population which worked in the same way a smartcard would.[130] Additionally, the SIM card is able to store the user's PIN and account details, so it, in essence, acts as a virtual card.[131] While Safaricom may not have had a fully articulated marketing plan, it nonetheless took a series of decisions which helped it to overcome these daunting challenges when it first introduced M-Pesa to the market. Possibly their most important achievement was that the management recognised the potential impact of M-Pesa and committed the company to heavy investments in marketing before the proposition could be proven. Safaricom managed to develop a strong service brand for M-Pesa, which some market research has shown is even stronger than Safaricom's corporate brand – itself already a powerful brand in Kenya with a dominant share of the mobile phone market.[132]

M-Pesa easily surpassed its first-year forecasts. This quickly turned the network effects in their favour, thus changing M-Pesa into a lucrative business for many agents and retail outlets. It was then decided that for the maximum chance of acceptability in an unprepared market, Safaricom should go for a widespread national launch and be deliberate in its messaging and marketing mix.[133] Safaricom was able to leverage public goodwill which existed for the corporate brand and treated M-Pesa stores as valuable brand outposts. All this was supported by a service that was designed to be simple and easy to use. The growth in mobile financial services was fundamentally a result of the enabling regulatory environment that the KCA created in 1998.[134] An argument put forward by Gary Collins is that M-Pesa came into existence in a 'regulatory vacuum',[135] and that the service started operations without the need for a banking licence. This allowed Safaricom to diligently spread its services through its existing network of agents for airtime services,[136] making banks unable to compete.[137] However, KCA only regulates communications services, leaving electronic commerce and mobile financial services without a regulatory framework.[138]

Despite the fact that, in 2006, the Kenya ICT Policy was made available to promote electronic commerce, it was the first of many fragmented regulatory tools that encompassed the regulation of mobile financial services at that initial stage.[139] At the time, Kenya lacked a framework for electronic transactions, something it needed in order to participate effectively in the new internet economy, hence, the digital divide in the progression of e- commerce. The Electronic Transactions Bill of 2007 was drafted to oversee electronic commerce issues, such as recognition of electronic transactions and electronic signatures.[140] However, Kenya needed appropriate and comprehensive information legislation to address the specific details of electronic transactions, including the critical laws that should govern this particular fast growing sector; the Kenya Information and Communications Bill of 2007 had not been enacted and was still at its draft stage.

There are many stakeholders, mobile operators, merchants, banks, entrepreneurs and consumers that want to see an accurate and inclusive ICT Act enacted soon, which would enhance trust in electronic transactions and, more specifically, mobile payments. There is willingness to deal with change in partnership with commercial banks and microfinance, which have different cultures, operating environments and incentives. The CBK did not have a pre-existing regulatory framework for mobile payments; however, the national payments system regulations were under review. Therefore, the implementation of mobile payments and their regulation became increasingly important after the introduction of M-Pesa.

### 2.3.3 *The system design of M-Pesa*

The mobile payments system in Kenya uses a mobile network operator-led (MNO-led) model, which requires that the MNO converts its wireless network messaging functionality into a SIM-based[141] platform in order to provide mobile payments as value added services (VAS) under its telecommunications licence.[142] This SIM card enables subscribers of Safaricom to either transfer their funds or make payments from person to person, with the transactions settled via MNO's established agent network.[143]

The transactions, both transfers and payments, are affected completely within MNO's network using its platform, thus not requiring the subscriber to have a bank account.[144] Safaricom and other MNOs[145] have adopted this model as a means of bypassing the regulatory requirements for banking under the Banking Act of 1969,[146] the CBK Prudential Guidelines and other regulations.[147] The funds paid in by the payer, which are also said to be in transit[148] but which have not been withdrawn by the recipient, are referred to, in principle, as being in deposit in a separate 'trust account' with several banks and are hence not deposits in the context of banking business as defined in the Central Bank Act Cap 491 1966.[149]

MNOs make use of banking privileges, by way of trust accounts. This requirement is part of the authorisation and licensing conditions spelt out by the

CBK.[150] Through short messaging services (SMS) technology, M-Pesa lets users make four basic types of transactions: person-to-person transfers; person to bank transfers; cash deposits and withdrawals from agents who act as the designated outlets;[151] and they also can perform loan receipts or repayments. Customers have to register using an official form of identification.[152] Cash deposits are converted into a commodity called e-float[153] that is denominated in the same units as the domestic currency.

The MNO only effects the subscriber's payment instructions through its platform, but it does not perform the credit assessment that banks usually do.[154] This consequently highlights the contrasts to bank-led models where cash exchanged for electronic value is not repaid but rather remains with the customer. Agents must always have a float in a bank account so that they may offer the equivalent through M-Pesa services, and the lack of such float may precipitate liquidity risk as opposed to a credit risk to either the customer or the MNO.[155] It is unclear as to whether the customer funds in the trust account attract interest.[156] Although this pooled trust account cannot be accessed by the MNO, practice suggests that all interest earned on the pooled funds are used by the MNOs for charitable causes. This shows that there is no intermediation, a key part of the 'deposit taking' definition.[157] It is also unclear as to whether the customer deposits received by the MNO earn interest.

This uncertainty does not clarify whether the e-value created is or is not in fact a deposit.[158] Whether mobile payments constitute 'banking business' as defined in Section 2 of the Banking Act 2009,[159] which consequently suggests that they do not require or enjoy the scope of regulatory oversight expected for deposits that are used in banking.[160] While the bank in which the pooled funds are held does not have prudential oversight or responsibility or involvement in the payments through the MNO system, this is set against to the convenience of mobile payments, where there are no minimum balances or services charges. This has heralded the arrival of mobile payments in the financial inclusion agenda and the shift from informal financial systems to formally include cash in the formal financial system in this mostly cash dominant society.[161]

MNOs increased the competition for banks in Kenya through the introduction of mobile payments, especially by MNOs.[162] This has resulted in the innovative integration of banking and transfers through mobile payments services, which has greatly increased the access and services offered by banks to their customers as well as MNOs to their subscribers. This integration, led by the MNO model, where payments are via Safaricom, also led to the development of other products, such as M-Kopa and M-Shwari[163] and insurance.[164]

These hybrid models were, in conjunction with regulated financial institutions,[165] pooling strengths from both industries – the financial platform of the banks on one hand and the technological platform of the telecoms industry on the other – and hence M-Pesa thrived within the MNO-led model as opposed to other bank-led models.[166]

These hybrid models have resulted in increased transactions where data from the CBK shows that Kshs. 1.117 trillion was transacted through mobile payments as a result of the integration with commercial banks; by 2013, the increase was positively seen as a result of consumers transferring their funds through their mobile phones.[167] The MNO-led models and mobile financial services that have since launched following the successful premier of M-Pesa include M-Kesho, Mobicash, Yu-cash Orange Telkom's Orange money, Pesa-Pap Essar Telecom's, Elma and Pesa-Connect.[168]

## 2.4 The enabling environment for mobile payments

This part of the chapter will discuss the enabling environment for mobile payments in Kenya. An enabling environment is defined as the set of conditions which promote a sustainable curve of market development for mobile payments.[169] Of particular interest are the settings in which prevalent access is likely, or in essence, conditions in which mobile payments are more likely to succeed.[170] New markets require enablement in the form of a combination of legal and regulatory openness,[171] which creates the opportunity to start up and experiment with sufficient legal and regulatory certainty,[172] promising that there will not be indiscriminate or negative changes to the regulatory framework.[173] This gives providers the confidence to invest the necessary resources. Countries that lack the regulatory capacity may prove to have no certainty, primarily since their regulatory discretion may lead to arbitrary action.[174] Equally, countries with greater certainty such as those with better regulatory capacity may not have the adequate flexibility that would allow for an enabling environment and may be far more restrictive. This is especially the case in a new market sector like mobile payments where business models are not yet stabilised. An enabling environment ensures a gradient towards better certainty and openness.[175]

This part will first discuss the infrastructure of the financial services in Kenya as a precursor to the payment options gaps that mobile payments eventually filled. It will then move on to highlight the quality of the alternative financial services that impeded financial access to the large unbanked and under-banked population. A discussion will follow on the dominance and market share of the leading MNO, Safaricom. The conclusion will highlight other country specific attributes that led to the adoption of mobile payments and, as a consequence, financial inclusion.

### 2.4.1 Infrastructure and the quality of the pre-existing financial services

The penetration rate of financial services has been established as a key influence on the rate of adoption for mobile payments. On the one hand, the poor quality of existing traditional financial services, such as banks, promoted the adoption of mobile money services which, in comparison, offered efficiency, greater accessibility and more convenience. On the other hand, very poor financial services infrastructure could also slow the adoption of mobile payments and services by making it more challenging for service providers and agents to adequately manage their liquidity.[176] Kenya was being served by 400 bank branches and slightly over 600 ATMs, resulting in one bank branch per 100,000 inhabitants, a ratio of 1.38.[177] About 17 per cent of the population used formal financial services and 38 per cent of people were excluded.[178] It can be noted that in other jurisdictions, such as Tanzania, the inadequate number of bank branches inadvertently affected the ability of Vodacom[179] to effectively manage agent liquidity (cash) to meet user demand, thus resulting in the slower uptake of M-Pesa.[180]

Inadequate liquidity has a two-fold effect on the adoption rate of mobile payments. Firstly, it limits the provider's ability to effectively roll out mobile money schemes and services because the geographic coverage of the agents is limited by the access to the banks that aid liquidity.[181]Secondly, inadequate liquidity affects the quality of service provided by the agents. Due to unreliable liquidity, the agents may not be able to offer cash withdrawal services, forcing a customer to move from one agent to another in order to find one that can offer the service. This affects the quality of service provision which reduces the user's perception of the value, trust and credibility of the service provider and the services offered.[182] Kenya, on the other hand, had a relatively more developed financial system, and this was essential to Safaricom's ability to manage the agent network liquidity needs. The level of bank branches' penetration rate was just right for the uptake of M-Pesa: neither too high to impede the demand for the mobile payments services nor too low to hinder the ability of the agents to meet their liquidity needs. Hence, agents need to convert cash deposits to e-float for customers, and the rapidity and capability to rebalance their liquidity is of importance. This may be hampered if the bank branch network is very low, which creates cash in transit risks as agents transport their cash to deposit to banks.[183]

Prior to M-Pesa, alternative remittance channels, such as payment cards and bank branches, were not as popular.[184] The common ways of sending money in Kenya were through the post office, bus companies, sending relatives or friends or personally travelling to make the delivery.[185]

The post office money remittance services were perceived by many Kenyans as expensive and inconvenient due to their limited locations and high user fees.[186] Moreover, the other methods of transporting cash were unsafe as one could easily be mugged. These methods were also unreliable because there was no guarantee that the money would reach the intended destination or be received within the intended timeframe. In addition, it was time consuming as it was necessary to make plans and take time off work in order to travel to rural areas to deliver the money. These conditions facilitated the quick uptake of mobile payments in Kenya, as it offered a superior service to the alternative methods.[187]

Providing financial services to those in rural areas was not appealing to banks, mainly due to the fact that they were only interested in providing additional banking services to their existing client base, and mobile payments are simply an additional and more convenient access channel. Until now, transformational mobile money services – the use of ICTs and non-bank retail channels to extend financial services to clients who cannot be reached profitably with traditional branch-based financial services – have not given banks the right incentives to invest in these customers long term.[188] In fact, potential business at the bottom of the pyramid requires the traditional banking business model to be radically reworked, while the burgeoning middle classes in developing countries are presenting a tremendous business opportunity which is both easier and fits within the current business model. Moreover, banks have traditionally obtained very little benefit commercially from selling their most profitable products to low-income markets. This is because customer acquisition, channel development and compliance are all costly for banks, yet projected returns are not encouraging.[189]

As discussed, traditional categorisations whereby companies could be resolutely classified into compartments that broadly represented their core financial business[190] are becoming blurred. It may be noted that the nimbleness of MNOs in transforming into entities that provide transactional equivalents of bank services is such that 'branchless banking' in Africa is currently dominated by MNO-based models, using retail agents for their so-called cash-in and cash-out activities.[191] Mas states that this reflects the low levels of banking dispersion and the poor state of fixed communications infrastructures, and further explains the rate of acceptance of MNO-led financial services over banking services.

### 2.4.2 Mobile phone rate penetration

The degree of mobile phone penetration in Kenya provided an enabling environment for mobile payments. This penetration rate indicated the level of familiarity of the customers with the use of a mobile phone and the potential market reach of the service.[192] Individuals with prior experience using mobile phones were more likely to adopt mobile payments because they believed that they had the ability to use the service, compared to individuals without prior knowledge of using it.[193] Twenty-seven per cent of the Kenyan adult population owned a mobile phone, and a further 28 per cent had access to someone else's phone.[194] This provided a key platform for making the service available.

Safaricom was able to reach a wider population and, as of June 2012, the mobile phone penetration in Kenya stood at 75 per cent.[195] This growth of mobile phones, particularly in Kenya, according to Mbiti and Weil,[196] is where a tectonic and unexpected change in communications has occurred.[197] From being virtually unconnected in the 1990s, over 60 per cent of Africa now has mobile phone coverage and there are now over ten times as many mobiles as landline phones in use. In 1999, only 11 per cent of the African population had mobile phone coverage, primarily in Northern (Egypt, Algeria, Libya, Morocco, and Tunisia) and Southern (Kenya and South Africa) Africa. By 2008, 60 per cent of the population (477 million) could get a signal and an area of 11.2 million square kilometres had mobile phone coverage – equivalent to the United States and Argentina combined.[198] By the end of 2012, it was projected that most villages in Africa would have coverage with only a handful of countries relatively unconnected. Kenya has therefore undergone a remarkable ICT revolution.

The above information illustrates the potential of mobile phone technology to support the extension of access to financial services in developing countries. Developing regions in Africa mobile subscription levels have doubled every two years.[199] There were 3.3 billion mobile phone subscriptions in the world in 2007.[200] About one billion people in developing countries did not have a bank account but had a mobile phone,[201] and that number grew to 1.7 billion in 2012. This suggests that there is still a significant opportunity to expand financial access via mobile phones.

### 2.4.3 Market share and dominance of Safaricom

The popularity of a product influences its adoption. This is done by promoting awareness about the usefulness of the service to potential users. Safaricom was and continues to be the dominant MNO in Kenya and at the time of M-Pesa's launch.[202] Safaricom had a market share of 80 per cent.[203] This dominance enabled it to advantageously position itself against its competitors when it launched M-Pesa, mainly due to its existing subscribed users, which provided a ready market for the company to quickly reach and capture a wider market base for its service.[204]

Safaricom holds the largest market share, which in the voice sector of the telecoms market and based on its subscriber base and 81 per cent[205] by revenue, was above the threshold for presumption of dominance.[206] Safaricom had at the outset, and continues to have, an enduring significant market power in both mobile voice and SMS services, which has enabled it to behave, to a significant extent, independently of its competitors, customers and ultimately consumers. Safaricom's hegemony and associated competitiveness, superior tangible and intangible assets and managerial competencies,[207] first mover advantage and provision of cross-network effects for commercial users, all contributed to its dominance.[208]

Sutherland argues that this monopoly and dominance in Kenya is a result of corruption in the telecommunications industry.[209] Although problems of corruption in telecommunications are an established global phenomenon,[210] concerns have been expressed over the unprecedented success of Safaricom as the various other telecommunications companies have lagged behind in their entry and market penetration. Part of its success is because Safaricom was formed to boost mobile telephony by bringing in foreign expertise and capital.[211] Telkom Kenya[212] acquired a 60 per cent interest in Safaricom by contributing its Electronic Technical Assistance Centre (ETAC), its GSM network and its subscriber base, which was valued at US $30 million. It then lent Safaricom US $33 million as its portion of the US $55 million fee that Safaricom paid for its Kenyan cellular licence. Vodafone Kenya Limited acquired a 40 per cent interest in Safaricom by contributing US $20 million in cash.

It later lent Safaricom US $22 million as its portion of the fee paid by the company for its initial licence.[213] Other operators did not experience such a smooth entry into the Kenyan market. This means that Safaricom is not likely to be dislodged from its dominant position for many years.

Efforts to reduce its market share have been unsuccessful due to there being no suggestion of creating a competitive market. The complexities of issuing operating licences[214] to other players and the sagas behind the privatisations and their related investments, which ought to have eroded the position of Safaricom, have not yet done so.[215] Safaricom dominates the market share amongst the other four operators in Kenya's telecommunications industry.[216] Investigations into claims of unfair advantages and its dealings in the issuing of licences to its rivals appear to have been sidestepped as a result of the culture of impunity and lack of accountability.[217]

Safaricom's competitors in the banking sector had offered, at the beginning in 2007, their services only in the country's major centre. However, compared to M-Pesa, the services were not as efficient. Safaricom invested heavily in its mobile service provision and proved itself to be reliable in its service delivery; therefore, customers had to adjust to and adopt the three elements that their mobile services offered.[218] As the telecommunications industry is a public utility, public ownership requires strong government controls, which form a component of the industry's operations. After the liberalisation of the telecommunications sector in Kenya, the state monopoly of the KPTC shifted from the government to a private sector oligopoly. This shows that there was a shift from structuralism to neo-liberalism.[219]

Despite privatisation and the introduction of competition policies and laws, Safaricom, the incumbent, is still able to dominate the telecommunications markets while enjoying significant advantages through skewed competition and unfair business practices.[220] This highlights the fact that after a seven-year oligopoly, market liberalisation, market distortions and the competitive environment continue to be skewed in favour of Safaricom compared to other entrants.[221] This fact goes beyond the scope of the thesis but is pertinent to mention.

### 2.4.4 The regulatory environment

A regulatory environment guarantees the laws, rules and regulations instituted by states or governments and civil organisations in favour of business activities.[222] The regulatory structure for telecoms, and thereby MNOs, is regulated by the CCK. This falls under the Ministry of Information and Communications of the Government of Kenya and is headed by the cabinet secretary for Information and Communication.

International bodies also regulate telecommunications at a regional and global level. These bodies include the International Telecommunication Union (ITU); the African Telecommunications Union (ATU), which is a branch of the ITU that specifically deals with Africa; the Groupe Speciale Mobile Association (GSMA), which is an association of mobile operators and affiliate companies committed to supporting the standardisation, deployment and promotion of the GSM mobile telephone system; and the Commonwealth Telecommunications Organization (CTO).[223]

When M-Pesa was launched, there were no specific laws governing electronic or mobile payments. The applicable banking laws were antiquated or transplanted.[224] However, the banking sector paid no heed to that legislative vacuum. Instead, the CBK provided tremendous support to the operation of mobile payments.

Safaricom was allowed to operate independently of the existing financial services regulatory environment, thereby enabling MNOs to provide financial services alongside the traditional banking sector.[225] Furthermore, the CBK quickly recognised the broad economic benefits associated with M-Pesa's introduction and played a supporting role from the beginning.[226] This effectively lowered the legal hurdles. The approach of the CBK was that regulation set out to govern mobile payments operation had the ability to either promote or constrain the deployment of a mobile money service in two key ways. First, the regulations may have influenced the structure of the business model, and this determines the ability of a mobile money provider to quickly reach a wider base of clients or to scale up and increase the number of agents.[227] For instance, in Nigeria the mobile money service regulators mandated three mobile money business models that excluded MNOs, which had expertise with agent network management, from being lead providers of mobile money services.[228] This has greatly hampered the speed of mobile money roll-out in the country because non-MNOs have to form alliances with MNOs or build up an agent network – a process that can be complex and time consuming.[229]

Secondly, the regulations set out may encourage or undermine the nature of the user experience in, for instance, opening a mobile money account and transacting with retail agents.[230] This is best illustrated by the regulatory environment in Tanzania, where the requirement to comply with the know your customer (KYC) protocol has made the M-Pesa user experience more cumbersome.[231] The protocol mandates that agents must identify their clients with a picture ID during the registration process and in subsequent transactions. However, Tanzania does not have a national ID system and this has forced people to look for other documents that can fulfil this requirement.[232] However, Kenya has a long established national ID system which most people hold. This system was instituted by the colonial government whose aim was to radically restrict the mobility of Africans. The main intention of the policy was supposedly to keep track of the labour pool efficiently.[233] This is not the case in other developing countries that have attempted to adopt mobile payments as users are subject to a more cumbersome registration process.

This affects the ease of opening an account and transacting with clients, thus derailing the adoption rate of the service. The regulators also set various conditions. The value of an individual transaction was limited in order to prevent money laundering, and Safaricom was also required to integrate a system to prevent money laundering, including the monitoring of suspicious transactions. Regular audits in association with the Treasury Department;[234] inquiries relating to fraud and system downtimes[235] of the use of the technology or the robustness of the system; end-to-end inspection of encryption; SIM card function business processes; hardware security, organisational security backup control; and monitoring of all processes were met with a positive response by the Kenyan population.

Banks were initially apprehensive about the proliferation of mobile payments and the competition it posed for them.[236] It was not long before the banks grew nervous, and a year later, the CBK was lobbied to investigate M-Pesa.[237] Kenyan

banks were apprehensive about the ability of M-Pesa to meet the risk management requirements, due to the large payment system network.[238] This raised concerns over the ability for such an institution to operate outside of the regulatory
scope.

The CBK was seen by banks to have had a light touch approach to the way it
handled the entry of MNOs in providing mobile payments. This was in contrast
to the regulatory burden that is imposed on the banking industry. Initially the
regulatory environment did not allow for the discharging of financial services by
agents, whilst MNOs extended their services through agents, both through the
withdrawal of cash and depositing of cash for the e-float value.

Mobile payment agents[239] have to obtain their float from a bank, which increased
the need for providing liquidity in remote branches to facilitate agents.[240] This
increased the perception that mobile payments where in direct competition with
retail banks in the remittance market. Ironically, the CBK contributed to further
trust within the mobile financial services and uptake of mobile payments through
its initial response that secured trust. This response further solidified the regulatory approach which was deemed as enabling.[241] Since, M-Pesa was launched
without industry regulation, it provided a regulatory vacuum, as its structure did
not put it under the purview of the CBK, albeit submitting itself for voluntary
audit and 'slight' supervision.[242]

The market regulatory environment held challenges to new entrants and small
MNOs who were frustrated by the dominance of Safaricom. This further highlights the lack of analysis across sub-Saharan Africa and the rest of the developing
world on the social, political and institutional debates on ICT regulation. The
focus has largely been on the inclusivity of mobile payments without looking at
the social, political, institutional and legal issues that it has brought.

### 2.4.5 Urbanisation

The market size for domestic remittances is facilitated when rural–urban migration results in relatively high migration flows to urban areas without compromis-
ing the economic development in rural areas.[243] Therefore, urbanisation ratios
affect the demand for potential domestic remittances and these depend on rural–
urban migration patterns. About 41 per cent of Kenyans live in urban areas.[244]
This pattern of urbanisation was inherited from the British colonial institutions
following independence.[245] The term 'dual system' describes the persistent connection that urban migrants or citizens maintain with their rural dwellings where
their relatives still reside, nevertheless spending a significant amount of time living and working in urban towns.[246]

There are several reasons for these sustained connections which aid the ability to 'ease the transition to urban life'.[247] Nevertheless, the clarification for
these strong urban – rural links that most concerns this study is the financial
one. Due to the stark disparity between urban and rural wages, many labourers
and household breadwinners migrate from rural centres to urban areas, leaving
behind their families in search of more profitable employment opportunities. As

a consequence, many rural households rely on remittances from their relatives in urban centres for survival; the two societies thus become linked as a matter of economic necessity.[248] Kenya provides a particularly convincing case for this 'dual system'.[249]

In Kenya, '30% of households depend on remittances for their survival',[250] and over 78 per cent of Kenya's population lives in rural households. As such, Kenya's consumer market had articulated a significant demand for urban-to-rural remittance services prior to the implementation of M-Pesa. In fact, the urban-to-rural population ratio in Kenya struck an imbalance in the residency of those in the rural areas and those in urban areas. This imbalance generated a large demand for the domestic remittance services offered by M-Pesa.[251] This shows that the potential market size for domestic remittances is directly related to urbanisation ratios. Furthermore, these market segments that hold domestic remittances where large rural–urban migration is adequately embedded to provide large migration flows, are not however so advanced that rural communities are left out.[252] This demonstrates that both the history and culture coupled with public policy have worked together to establish and maintain this demand-producing urban-to-rural population ratio.[253]

During Kenya's colonial period,[254] policies[255] were implemented in the hope of preventing the establishment of permanent urban centres. For example, in urban areas, labour was only recruited for temporary periods, wages were kept low and only small accommodations, not suitable for family living, were available. As a result, 'migrant workers would oscillate between . . . urban and rural areas throughout their working life'.[256] Kenya's post-colonial government reversed these policies and sought to jumpstart economic development through a nationwide programme of urbanisation. Subsequently, urban wages and the number of permanent residents in urban areas significantly increased. However, the impact of these policies was muted due to the significant and sustaining links maintained by urban workers to their rural homes and rural communities.

This was enhanced by Kenya's migrants' ties with their rural homes, which are especially strong due to an ethnic conception of citizenship.[257]

Such ties are often expressed through burial, inheritance, cross-generational dependencies and social insurance, even in cases where migrants reside more or less permanently in cities.[258] Despite government policies seeking to increase urbanisation, there has not been an unsustainable drain of workers from rural areas to urban centres in Kenya. Naturally, those workers who migrated to urban centres in search of work continue to send remittances to their rural homes in order to support their relatives who still continue to dwell in the villages. This singularity is not only apparent in Kenya, as strong ties to rural homes is commonplace in many African cultures. However, what Kenya shows is that there still exists a strong demand for domestic remittance services in Kenya due to its history, culture and pattern of population growth. Additionally, this fact contributes to the financial inclusion of the Kenyan population. This is evident as a result of mobile payments due to the demographic character of Kenya's consumer population, especially now due to the mobile phone revolution and penetration rates as discussed.[259] Consequently, the poverty levels in Kenya remain relatively high, and as a result, for any financial service to be successful, it should take into consideration the need for any service not to be prohibitively expensive.[260]

The high urbanisation rate in Kenya promoted stronger urban–rural ties which favoured higher remittances.[261] This higher rate of urbanisation is attributed to Kenya's capitalism development ideology, and policies that encouraged urbanisation through modernising the urban areas and leaving the rural areas are largely under-developed.[262] This influenced people in rural areas, especially the males who were predominantly the heads of households, to move to urban areas to seek work opportunities. However, the existing cultural practices, such as ancestral land inheritance, created the need for urban migrants to maintain ties with their rural homes, and these were reinforced and maintained by sending remittances.[263] This resulted in the development of a dominant urban–rural remittance corridor that influenced the greater adoption of mobile payments in Kenya.

### 2.4.6 Other country specific factors

Developing countries have been plagued by political instability, and this has often impeded the ability of foreign investors to invest in Kenya.[264] Kenya's political and investment climate has been very important for the success of Safaricom's M-Pesa. Usually, poor political and economic certainty discourages investment in additional services; and as aforementioned, mobile payments do particularly well in extreme environments, where the quality of alternatives is low.[265] However, M-Pesa experienced a big surge in usage during Kenya's post-election violence[266] in January 2008, partly because it remained available and partly because customers believed that M-Pesa was less susceptible than banks to political manipulation.[267]

Countries experiencing high levels of conflict tend to have sizable diaspora creating strong remittance opportunities.[268] The use of financial services increases with the level of education in a country.[269] Generally, literacy is important in the provision of mobile money services, because the product delivery platform, a mobile device, requires an individual to have the basic knowledge of how to read the mobile device screen. However, the need for financial literacy is even more important, because it improves access to and utilisation of financial services. As a result, users are equipped with the capacity to gauge the value of a service and to demand other value added mobile money services. Regulation should facilitate innovation by removing barriers and ensuring a level playing field, which holds that legal standards should be equal, especially for diverse stakeholders who are involved in the same activity. Through the continued introduction of innovative products, an enabling environment would turn to mitigating various risks such as operational risk and improving consumer protection. This would in turn precipitate appropriate regulation as other risks become apparent.[270] It is evident that the proliferation of mobile payments hinges greatly on the effective association between a strategic business model, especially the one that Safaricom had, and an enabling environment that takes into account specific factors in the country in which it will be launched.[271]

## 2.5  Success of mobile payments: financial inclusion

In this part of the chapter, the discussion will focus on financial inclusion. This has been the main success of mobile payments in Kenya, although it is also recognised that there have been several other benefits that the nexus of telecommunications and financial services (mobile financial services) has brought, such as mobile agriculture,[272] mobile health[273] and mobile education programmes,[274] which have expanded socio- economic development. A definition of financial inclusion in the Kenyan context will be given, and the benefits of financial inclusion and the challenges it presents will be considered. This will be done because much of the discussions on mobile payments have tended to focus on the overall benefits of financial inclusion. Although this cannot be denied, there has been no focus on post-inclusion issues. This part will then show how mobile payments have been instrumental in including the financially excluded and will do so by explaining the shift from a microfinance perspective that focused on pro-poor financial service provision to a broader agenda of financial inclusion that reaches not only those who are on low incomes but also those who are unbanked.[275] It will discuss why financial inclusion is important in the context of access to finance through the expansion of a mobile payments network as an instrument for financial inclusion.

It will then conclude by showing that policy emphasis on financial sector development has indeed shifted away from microfinance and towards the development of inclusive financial markets through the proliferation of mobile payments systems. As such, regulatory frameworks must now be adjusted to accommodate this new function that mobile payments have presented both for regulators and for consumers. Most importantly, this part discusses the overall success of mobile payments as an instrument for financial inclusion, which in turn makes it systemically important to Kenya's financial system.

### 2.5.1  Definition of financial inclusion

The definition of financial inclusion at its broadest is the ability of an individual, household or group to access apposite financial services or products.[276] Without this ability, people are often referred to as financially excluded.[277] The proper definition of the financially excluded includes households that are denied credit in spite of their demand for it. Credit is usually a key need for those excluded; however, the scope of financial inclusion covers various other financial services, such as savings, insurance payments and remittance facilities by the formal financial system to those who tend to be excluded.[278] It also refers to access to, availability and usage of the formal financial system for all members of an economy.[279] Financial inclusion today is about financial markets that serve more people with more products at lower costs.[280] Few people would dispute that mobile money can be an engine of financial inclusion and that it has the potential to reach millions of customers, including those at the bottom of the socio-economic pyramid.[281] Other international development organisations, as well as policy-makers in developing countries, have increasingly emphasised the need to build more inclusive financial systems as an essential part of their development agendas.[282]

Therefore, this part discusses the prevalence and the over-emphasis on the importance of financial inclusion. As access to finance is fundamental to the sustainable development of any economy, the limited penetration and usage of the formal banking sector might therefore help in the understanding of the limited economic development of sub-Saharan Africa.[283] This thesis argues that any debate centred on the importance of financial inclusion cannot exclude innovation in the industry and the examination of financial stability and integrity, coupled with the need for consumer protection, as it is with these tenets that the full realisation of financial inclusion can be sustainable. Even so, there is a lot of debate about its definition, which has had a varied meaning depending on the national context and the stakeholders involved.[284] With regard to Kenya, especially most recently, financial inclusion has come to mean 'banking the unbanked' or 'branchless banking'.[285] Financial inclusion brings those from an informal economy to a more formal economy.

Low-income inequality countries tend to have relatively high levels of financial inclusion.[286] This isolation of poor people from formal banking means that they do not have the opportunity to understand how banks operate.[287]

### 2.5.2 Mobile payments as an instrument for financial inclusion

Financial exclusion provides that formal financial services are not accessible to a population, particularly in developing countries. For example, Bilodeaeau estimates that more than 2.5 billion people do not have access to formal financial services.[288] They attribute this to a 'lack of infrastructure, information and inadequate customer service' associated with traditional banking models.[289] This is particularly seen in developing countries such as Kenya, where the majority of the population resides in rural areas.[290]

A well-functioning financial sector and its economic development have clear linkages.[291] Financial services that function well are essential for economic development, and the access dimension of financial development has often been overlooked.[292] Prior to M-Pesa's launch, the average amount required to open a current bank account was US $105, while the average cost for operating the same was US $19 per month. This suggests that by the end of a year, the minimum one would owe a bank in fee charges would be US $123. This can be compared with the M-Pesa service where there are no fees charged for deposits or withdrawals or monthly ledger fees.[293] M-Pesa has helped to expand local economies, enhance security, help people to accumulate capital and make transactions easier.[294] Mobile payments have reduced the dependency on cash because its use has indirect costs and policy ramifications such as expending a large amount of energy and resources managing it, keeping it safe and transporting it.[295]

Thirdly, existing financial institutions required a minimum amount of money to remain in the account at all times, and also charged exorbitantly high monthly fees for going below the minimum requirement.[296] Closure of the accounts for non-performance was also a common practice by Kenyan banks. These issues made the idea of operating and maintaining banking accounts unattractive and expensive for most people.[297]

Mobile payments through M-Pesa have proven to be a viable business, and the government and civil society have been able to influence the market rate of adoption by changing how they conduct transactions and pay salaries.[298] In addition, non- governmental organisations (NGOs), development banks and bilateral development partners have been instrumental in introducing mobile payments as part of their relief initiatives.[299] The systemic coordination with private sector participants has also been instrumental in developing a receptive market, which has obscured the usual barriers to financial inclusion, such as market disruptions caused by armed conflict, extreme poverty and natural disasters.[300]

Policy-makers in this context have begun to pay closer attention to financial inclusion, as well as practitioners and academics who increasingly emphasise financial inclusion as a policy objective.[301] The perception of building inclusive financial systems recognises not only the goal of incorporating as many poor and previously excluded[302] people as possible into the formal financial system but also assigns to mainstream financial institutions the role of reaching out to the unbanked.[303]

It cannot be disputed that mobile payments are financially inclusive and offer the potential for financial integration by reaching millions more customers, including those at the bottom of the socio-economic pyramid.[304] Mobile payments have resulted in the increased need for accounts and this data has been instrumental in record keeping, which dispels the anonymity often associated with integrity concerns. Fraudulent and criminal activities have been difficult to ascertain if they are in cash, 'which is anonymous, fungible and largely invisible'.[305] This provides an adequate monitoring system as the volume of cash-based transactions are shifted into electronic-based transactions equipping those charged with monitoring.

M-Pesa has seemingly allowed for a safer cash-in-transit mechanism and storage for money, especially for Kenyans in rural areas. M-Pesa has minimised the long trips to banks for the payments of their utility bills.[306] This has considerably reduced the time taken out of productive activities and consequently the costs associated with this movement.[307] Mobile payments potentially increase net household savings through the facilitation of person-to-person transactions, which improve the distribution of savings within households and businesses by improving not only the person-to-person credit market but also by increasing the average return to capital in the market producing a feedback to the level of saving.[308]

Some mobile payments users use their mobile phones as a savings device, despite it not being the safest method to store money.[309] In 2009, the average savings balance of an M-Pesa account was around US $3.[310] Moreover, M-Pesa enables rural households to effectively spread risk. If a 'risk-related effect arises', M-Pesa facilitates a quick transfer of funds.[311] Instead of waiting for conditions to worsen to levels that cause long-term damage, mobile payments have enabled support networks to keep negative shocks such as medical emergencies and political instabilities manageable.[312]

Through financial inclusion, mobile payments have increased the bargaining power of weaker family members, in many cases women.[313] This further enables remittance receivers or family members to gain financial independence previously unavailable to them.[314] Customers of mobile payments are able to confirm their statements through the application in their mobile devices, and they are able to deposit or withdraw cash at any agent. This has created trust through consistency; this design is paramount in the successful implementation of mobile payments, as it hinges on a well distributed agent network.[315]

Studies from the World Bank have demonstrated that once money, production and investment are evaluated in an integrated manner, banks and non-financial intermediaries can be seen as performing complementary functions essential to the economy.[316] This could be why non-financial institutions become more important, if not equivalent, to banks in providing retail payment services as the systems develop. The issue of the 'blurring' distinction between banks and non-banks, and the importance of non- banks has long been recognised.[317] The participation of non-financial institutions in providing payment services can be a threat to financial institutions. Mobile payments have fundamentally transformed the way financial services are delivered in Kenya. As a consequence, MNOs have increased their products by diversifying their services and not only providing voice and data but now financial services.[318] For example, Safaricom's M-Pesa has become integral to the network operator's entire business model given that the revenue from its mobile payments services accounts for up to 13 per cent of its annual revenue.[319] The increasing profitability of mobile payments to the entire enterprise has prompted MNOs to increase their resources in efforts to develop their market share and dominance.[320] This fundamental service has become so integral in the Kenyan payment system that MNOs have now become systemically important.

## 2.6 Conclusion

The success of M-Pesa has become a key driver in lifting people out of poverty, and therefore, it has become an important feature in Kenya's financial system. This potential has been recognised by governments, experts and donor organisations.[321] Central banks in emerging economies[322] have recognised the potential economic benefit of financial inclusion and have included it in their developmental agendas.[323] However, after integration and inclusion the challenge is how to harness this success while ensuring that the stability of the financial system is not affected.[324]

In addition, now that the large unbanked population has been included, regulation should consider who safeguards their interests. Therefore, this thesis will determine how regulation should be applied to newly- emerging financial services, such as mobile payments, that include the financially excluded. It will also attempt to determine the trade-off between financial innovation and regulation.

While the academic literature has adequately discussed the relationship between financial development and economic growth,[325] there has been little discussion on whether financial development implies financial inclusion.

The success of mobile payments has evidenced that through technological innovation in financial services, it has been possible to expect growth in the financial sector. Mobile payments have also changed the links between the telecoms industry and financial regulation, particularly in developing countries such as Kenya, where both industries are developing. The examination of Kenya in this study is consequently important, as it offers the best example of how regulators and policy-makers alike can or have the opportunity to reach a consensus on the appropriate regulatory approach that would enable further development of this new innovative payment service. The regulatory challenges shall therefore be discussed in light of financial inclusion which presents unique challenges.[326]

# Notes

1  A Newsweek Interview on July 1994 published in The American Banker, 9 January 1995: The American Banker (9 January 1995) <www.highbeam.com/publica tions/american-banker-p392958/january-1995/3> accessed 3 September 2014.

2  David Marston, 'Financial System Standards and Financial Stability: The Case of Basel Core Principles' (2001) IMF Working Papers 1/62 <http://papers.ssrn. com/sol3/papers.cfm?abstract_id=1446185> accessed 3 September 2014.

3  Central Bank of Kenya, 'Kenya Payments System (Framework and Strategy)' (September 2004) <www.centralbank.go.ke/index.php/2012-09-21-11-44-41> accessed 3 September 2014.

4  Ibid.

5  Central Bank of Kenya, 'Payment System in Kenya' (September 2003) 1 <www. centralbank.go.ke/index.php/kepss> accessed 3 September 2014.

6  The Kenya Bankers Association (KBA) was registered as an industry association on 16 July 1962 by the Registrar of Trade Unions. In its formative years, the main aim of the Association was to cater for the interests of the member banks in negotiating terms and conditions of service of its union, its employees and, as far as possible, standardise management practices so as to ensure harmony in the industry. Kenya Bankers Association, <www.kba.co.ke/> accessed 3 September 2014.

7  Di Castri (n 46) Chapter 1. See also Sheri M. Markose and Yiing Jia Loke, 'Changing Trends in Payment Systems for Selected G10 and EU Countries 1990–1998' (2000) *Economic Discussion Papers* 508; Michelle Baddeley, 'Using E-Cash in the New Economy: An Economic Analysis of Micro-payment Systems' (2004) 5 *Journal of Electronic Commerce Research* 239.

8  Ibid. See also Mobile for Development, 'MMU Policy and Regulation', <www. gsma.com/mobilefordevelopment/programmes/mobile-money-for-the-unbanked/regulation> accessed 18 September 2014.

9  Financial inclusion is defined as the ability of an individual, household, or group to access appropriate financial services or products. Without this ability, people are often referred to as financially excluded. Various financial services and products have brought about financial inclusion. This thesis proposes mobile payments as one of the main drivers of financial inclusivity in Kenya. See, Peter Dittus and Michael U. Klein, 'On harnessing the potential of financial inclusion' (BIS Working Paper 247, 2011) <http://papers.ssrn.com/sol3/papers.cfm?abstract_id=1859412> accessed 3 September 2014.

10 Mwangi Kimenyi and Njuguna Ndung'u, 'Expanding the Financial Services Frontier: Lessons from Mobile Phone Banking in Kenya' (October 2009) Brookings Paper.

11 FDS Kenya, 'FinAccess 2009: Mapping the financial sector in Kenya' [2009]; Richard Duncombe and Richard Boateng, 'Mobile Phones and Financial Services in Developing Countries: a Review of Concepts, Methods, Issues, Evidence and Future Research Directions' (2009) 30(7) *Third World Quarterly* 1237.

12 Aleke Dondo, 'The Status of Microfinance in Kenya' (K-Rep Occasional Paper 34); Susan Johnson, Markku Malkamaki and Kuria Wanjau, 'Tackling the "Frontiers" of Microfinance in Kenya: the Role for Decentralized Services' (2006) 17(3) *Small Enterprise Development* 41. See also Dean Karlan, Jonathan Morduch and Sendhil Mullainathan, 'Take-Up: Why Microfinance Take-Up Rates Are Low & Why It Matters' (Financial Access Initiative Research Framing Note, June 2010) <www.financialaccess.org/sites/default/files/blog/RFN11_Why_microfinance_takeup_rates_are_low(6-17-10).pdf> accessed 3 September 2014.

13 Outreach for financial inclusion in Kenya was not considered seriously. The unbanked were not considered a viable segment of the population.

14 Franklin Allen and others, 'Improving Access to Banking: Evidence from Kenya' [2014] CEPR Discussion Paper No. DP9840. See also, Alberto Chaia and others, 'Half the World is Unbanked' (Financial Access Initiative Research Brief, November 2010). See also, Patrick Honohan, 'Cross-country Variation in Household Access to Financial Services' (2008) 32(11) *Journal of Banking & Finance* 2493

15 Ibid [Franklin].

16 'Financial Inclusion Agenda' will be used to describe the push to include the financially excluded through government directives and policies. Thorsten Beck and Asli Demirgüç-Kunt, 'Access to Finance: An Unfinished Agenda' (2008) 22(3) *The World Bank Economic Review* 383.

17 Massimo Russo and Piero Ugolini, 'Financial Sector Challenges in Africa's Emerging Markets' (2008) EMF Paper Series.

18 Isaac Mbiti and David N. Weil, 'Mobile Banking: The Impact of M-Pesa in Kenya' (2011) NBER Working Paper No 17129 <www.econstor.eu/bitstream/10419/62662/1/668481188.pdf> accessed 3 September 2014.

19 Regulatory capacity in this context is defined as the combination of individual competence, organisational capabilities, assets and relationships that enable a political entity to formulate, monitor and enforce regulation. Investment Climate Advisory Services (World Bank Group), 'Regulatory Capacity Review of Kenya' (2010) <www.wbginvestmentclimate.org/uploads/Kenya.pdf> accessed 3 September 2013. Regulatory capacity will be discussed in Chapter 5: The Regulatory Approach to Mobile Payments.

20 Safaricom, the leading MNO which first deployed M-Pesa.

21 As described in the first chapter, M-Pesa was the first mobile payment system deployed in Kenya.

22 Sebastiana Etzo and Guy Collender, 'The Mobile Phone Revolution in Africa: Rhetoric or Reality?' (2010) 109(437) *African Affairs* 659. See also, Gabriel Demombynes and Aaron Thegeya, 'Kenya's Mobile Revolution and the Promise of Mobile Savings' (2012) World Bank Policy Research Working Paper 5988 <https://openknowledge.worldbank.com/bitstream/handle/10986/3275/WPS5988.txt?sequence=2> accessed 3 September 2014

23 Christian Johnson and Robert Steigerwald, 'The Central Bank's Role in the Payment System: Legal and Policy Aspects' in Current Developments in Monetary and Financial Law, vol 5 (International Monetary Fund, 2008) 445.

24 William Jack and Tavneet Suri, 'Mobile Money: the Economics of M-PESA' (2011) NBER Working Paper No 16721 <http://www9.georgetown.edu/faculty/wgj/papers/Jack_Suri-Economics-of-M- PESA.pdf> accessed 3 September 2014.

25  Jan Ondrus, Kalle Lyytinen and Yves Pigneur, 'Why Mobile Payments Fail? Towards a Dynamic and Multi-Perspective Explanation' (42nd Hawaii International Conference on IEEE 2009) System Sciences 1. See also, World Economic Forum, 'The Mobile Financial Services Development Report' (2011) 4 <http://www3.weforum.org/docs/WEF_MFSD_Report_2011.pdf> accessed 3 September 2014. Afghanistan Argentina Bangladesh and others Mobile Financial Services Development Report'.

26  Ubiquitous success is used to imply the fact that Kenya leads the world in mobile payments deployment and this success has not been replicated elsewhere in Africa

27  David B. Humphrey, *Payment Systems: Principles, Practice, and Improvements*, vol 23 (World Bank Publications 1995).

28  Randall W. Sifers, 'Regulating Electronic Money in Small-Value Payment Systems: Telecommunications Law as a Regulatory Model' (1996) 49 *Fed Comm LJ* 701.

29  Whether that is electronic value or stored value.

30  Humphrey (n 27).

31  Electronic payments are instructions passed between banks without reliance on paper processing. This also includes card payments such as automated teller machine (ATM), credit and debit.

32  Ibid.

33  Clearing or clearance is the process of transmitting, reconciling and, in some cases, confirming payment orders or security transfer instructions prior to settlement, possibly including the netting of instruction and the establishment of final positions for settlement. See, Committee on Payment and Settlement Systems Secretariat, 'A Glossary of Terms Used in Payments and Settlement Systems' (2000) <www.bis.org/cpmi/publ/d00b.pdf> accessed 3 September 2014.

34  Ibid., at 33. Settlement is an act of discharging obligations in respect of funds or securities transfers between two or more parties.

35  A credit transaction, such as a direct deposit transaction, is an example of an immediate payment settlement. This is where the payment instrument flows from the paying corporation to the paying bank to the payee's bank and to the payee. The flow of funds follows the same path. See David B. Humphreys and Setsuya Sato, *Modernizing Payment Systems in Emerging Economies* (The International Bank for Reconstruction and Development 1995).

36  Ibid,. at 35. A debit transaction, such as a payment by cheque, is an example of settlement at a delayed period. Cheques flow through the banking system from the payee to the payee's bank to the payer. The flow of funds moves in the opposite direction from the transaction.

37  David B. Humphrey, *Transforming Payment Systems: Meeting the Needs of Emerging Market Economies*, vol 291 (The Internastional Bank for Reconstruction and Development 1995).

38  Ibid.

39  Sergio G. Garcia, 'The Contribution of Payment Systems to Financial Stability' (2000) <www.bis.org/publ/cpss41.pdf> accessed 3 September 2014.

40  Ibid. See also Chapter 3, where issues of risk are extensively discussed.

41  David B. Humphrey, *Transforming Payment Systems: Meeting the Needs of Emerging Market Economies*, vol 291 (The Internastional Bank for Reconstruction and Development 1995).

42  Ibid.

43  Anton Allahar, *Ethnicity, Class, and Nationalism* (1st edn, Lexington Books 2005).

44  Specific reports on retail payment systems, which include retail payment instruments such as electronic money, have been published. All reports on electronic money are under the Committee on Payment and Settlement Systems (CPSS) Publications section. The latest report by BIS on electronic money has also included electronic money.

45 Carlo Tresoldi, 'Report on the Activity of the CPSS Working Group on Retail Payment Systems' in 'The Contribution of Payment Systems to Financial Stability' (CEMELA Mexico City May 2000) <www.bis.org/publ/cpss41.pdf> accessed 3 September 2014.

46 Massimo Cirasino, 'The Role of the Central Banks in Supervising the Financial System: The Case of the Oversight of Payment Systems' (2003) <http://info. worldbank.org/etools/docs/library/155862/paymentsystems2003/pdf/Cira sino_Oversight_Coop.doc> accessed 3 September 2014

47 'The Canadian Payment System: Public Policy Objectives and Approaches' May 1997. 14 September 2014

48 See Humphrey (1995) n 41.

49 Ibid.

50 Ibid.

51 Paul W. Bauer and Gary D. Ferrier, 'Scale Economies, Cost Efficiencies, and Technological Change in Federal Reserve Payments Processing' (1996) 28(4) *Journal of Money, Credit and Banking* 1004.

52 Tanai Khiaonarong and Jonathan Liebena, 'The Analysis of Payment Systems Efficiency' in *Banking on Innovation* (Springer 2009)

53 Benjamin J. Cohen, *The Geography of Money* (Cornell University Press 1998).

54 Randall W. Sifers, 'Regulating Electronic Money in Small-Value. Payment Systems: Telecommunications Law as a. Regulatory Model' (1996) 49 *Fed. Comm. LJ* 701; Alan Greenspan, 'Remarks on Evolving Payment System Issues' (1996) 28(4) *Journal of Money, Credit and Banking* 689.

55 Ibid., at 54.

56 Maxwell J. Fry, *Payment Systems in Global perspective* (Routledge 2012).

57 Ibid.

58 Ibid.

59 David Cronin, 'Large-Value Payment System Design and Risk Management' [2011] Quarterly Bulletin 01/January 11

60 Role of National Payment Systems – Central Bank of Kenya (www.centralbank. go.ke/index.ph/2012-09-21-11-44-41/overview> accessed 23 September 2014.

61 Central Bank of Kenya, 'NPS Modernization' <www.centralbank.go.ke/index. php/upcoming-events/29-payment systems?start=6> accessed 3 September 2014.

62 Ibid.

63 GPay stands for government pay: the Kenyan government pays suppliers electronically instead of by cheque.

64 Risks shall be discussed in Chapter 3 in Section 3.4.1. Taxonomy of Risks, pg. 80.

65 Sebastiana Etzo and Guy Collender, 'The Mobile Phone "revolution" (2010) *Africa: Rhetoric or Reality?* 659–668. See also Ken Banks, 'Mobile Telephony and the Entrepreneur: an African Perspective' (2008) 8 *Microfinance Insights* <www. oecd.org/dataoecd/27/51/41789311.pdf> accessed 3 September 2014.

66 The term revolution, see also Banks (n 125); Vodafone, 'Africa: the Impact of Mobile Phones' Vodafone Policy Paper Series, 2 March 2005 <www.vodafone. com/content/dam/vodafone/about/public_policy/policy_papers/public_pol icy_series_2.pdf> accessed 3 September 2014 3; Thomas Kalil, 'Harnessing the Mobile Revolution' (Winter 2009) Innovations 4, 1 <http://econpapers.repec. org/scripts/redir.pf?u=http%3A%2F%2Fwww.mitpressjournals.org%2Fdoi2Fpdf plus%2F10.1162%2Fitgg.2009.4.1.9;h=repec:tpr:inntgg:v:4:y:2009:i:1:p:9–23> accessed 3 September 2014.

67 Ibid.

68 Poverty Reduction and Economic Management Unit Africa Region (World Bank), 'Kenya at the Tipping Point? With a special focus on the ICT Revolution and Mobile Money' (3rd edn, Kenya Economic Update, December 2010).

69  Kas Kalba, 'The Adoption of Mobile Phones in Emerging Markets: Global Diffusion and the Rural Challenge' (2008) 2 *International Journal of Communication* 31.

70  James Goodman, 'Linking Mobile Phone Ownership and Use to Social Capital in Rural South Africa and Tanzania' in Vodafone, 'Africa: the Impact of Mobile Phones' Vodafone Policy Paper Series, 2 March 2005 <www.vodafone.com/content/dam/vodafone/about/public_policy/policy_papers/public_policy_series_2.pdf> 3 accessed 3 September 2014

71  Jenny C. Aker and Isaac M. Mbiti, 'Mobile Phones and Economic Development in Africa' (2010) 24 (3) *Journal of Economic Perspectives* 207–232 <www.jstor.org/stable20799163> accessed 3 September 2014.

72  GSM Association Development Fund website <www.gsma.com/developmentfund/> accessed 3 September 2014.

73  In 1999, the KPTC was divided into three separate entities: Telekoms Kenya, Kenya Postal Corporation and the Communication Commission of Kenya (CCK), the licensing and regulatory authority of the government. 'Kenya Telecom Corporation Winds Up' *Africa News Service* (29 June 1999).

74  East African Community, 'History of the EAC' <www.eac.int/index.php?option=com_content&id=44&Itemid=54> accessed 3 September 2014.

75  The Kenya Communications Act (2009) found at <www.ca.go.ke/>. The Communications Commission of Kenya (CCK) is an independent regulator of all communications services in the country; the National Communications Secretariat (NCS) is a communications policy advisory think-tank within the Ministry of Information and Communications responsible for communications services. In September 2007, Telkom was also granted a mobile licence and began offering those services using code division multiple access (CDMA) 2000 technology.

76  Tonny Omwansa, 'M-PESA: Progress and Prospects' (2009) <www.strathmore.edu/pdf/innov-gsma-omwansa.pdf> accessed 3 September 2014.

77  Ibid.

78  Postal Corporation of Kenya Act 1998 (Cap 411).

79  Telkom Kenya is the sole provider of landline phone services in Kenya. It was previously a part of the Kenya Posts and Telecommunications Corporation (KPTC) which was the sole provider of both postal and telecommunication services.

80  The Companies Act 1978 (Cap 486).

81  Omwansa (n 76). See also, Elizabeth Martha Bakibinga, 'Regulating Market Entry in the Telecommunications Sector in an Integrated East Africa: Towards a Common Licensing Framework' (Master's Thesis, University of Oslo 2004).

82  Ibid.

83  Omwansa (n 76).

84  Omwansa (n 76).

85  At the time of inception, Celtel was a telecommunications company that operated in several African countries. Originally known as 'MSI Cellular Investments', the company began operating in 1998. In January 2004, the company name was changed to 'Celtel International'. In April 2005, the company was acquired by and became a subsidiary of Zain (formerly the Mobile Telecommunications Company). At the time it was purchased by Zain in April 2005, Celtel had about 24 million subscribers in 14 African countries. On 8 June 2010, the company was purchased by Bharti Airtel. On 22 November 2010, it was rebranded as 'Airtel'.

86  Orange is a mobile network operator and internet service provider in the United Kingdom which launched in 1993.

87  Cellular News, 'Econet Finally Launches its Network in Kenya Published' (25 November 2008) <www.cellular-news.com/story/34832.php> accessed 3 September 2014.

88 Omwansa (n 76).
89 Ibid., 85.
90 Alexander Shih, 'The Contribution of Mobile Telecommunication Technology To Sustainable Development in Selected Countries in Africa' (PhD Thesis, Massachusetts Institute of Technology 2011).
91 Ibid.
92 Monica Kerretts, 'ICT Regulation and Policy at a Crossroads: A Case Study of the Licensing Process in Kenya' (2005) 5 *Southern African Journal of Information and Technology*
93 Kenya Information and Communications Amendment Act 2009 (Cap 411A), s 5.
94 Ibid.
95 Simphiwe Nojiyez and Jocelyn Muthoka, 'Barriers to Entry of Kenya's Telecommunication Industry: Is there a Market Slice for New Entrants?' <http://reference.sabinet.co.za/webx/access/electronic_journals/jomad/jomad_v11_n1_a7.pdf> accessed 3 September 2014.
96 Communications Commission of Kenya, 'Strategic Plan: 2008–2013' (2008) <www.marsgroupkenya.org/documents/documents/11806/> accessed 3 September 2014.
97 Government of Kenya, 'Telecommunications and Postal Sector Statement' (2001) (77) *The Kenya Gazette CIII* 2675.
98 Ibid.
99 Robert Listfield and Fernando Montes-Negret, 'Modernizing Payment Systems in Emerging Economies' (1994) Policy Research Working Paper.
100 Robert Listfield and Fernando Montes-Negret, 'Modernizing Payment Systems in Emerging Economies' (1994) Policy Research Working Paper 1336 <http://books.google.co.uk/books?hl=en&lr=B5b7vjuymYcC&oi=fnd&pg=PA1&dq=Listfield,+Rober t%3B+Montes-Negret,+Fernando,+%E2%98Modernizing+Payment+Systems+In+Emerging+Economies%E2%80%99&ots=BQZESNBMYS&sig=MxNMWPVWyWLFXR3dGDHzq DXNso> accessed 3 September 2014
101 Caroline Boyd and Katy Jacob, 'Mobile Financial Services and the Underbanked: Opportunities and Challenges for M-banking and M-payments' (The Centre for Financial Services Innovation, 2007).
102 Erwin Alampay, 'Mobile Banking, Mobile Money and Telecommunication Regulations' (2010) *eBusiness & eCommerce Journal* 5.
103 Timothy Waema, '2007 Kenya Telecommunications Sector Performance Review: a Supply Side Analysis of Policy Outcomes' (2007) Research ICT Africa. See also, CCK, 'Annual Report Financial Year 2010/11' (2012) <www.cck.go.ke/resc/publications/annual_reports/CCK_Annual_Report_2011.pdf> accessed 3 September 2014. According to the CCK, the transport and communications sector recorded a 5.9 per cent growth, with the total output value for the sector growing by 9.5 per cent to KES 594.6 billion in 2010. The telecommunications industry continued to post considerable growth, spearheaded mainly by the mobile telephony segment of the ICT sector.
104 United States Agency for International Development (USAID) and Kenya School of Monetary Studies, 'Mobile Financial Services Risk Matrix' (United States Agency for International Development, 2010).
105 Nick Hughes and Susie Lonie, 'M-PESA: Mobile Money for the "Unbanked" Turning Cellphones into 24-Hour Tellers in Kenya' (2007) 2 *Innovations* 63.
106 Ibid. Faulu Deposit Taking Micro-Finance Limited is a deposit taking microfinance institution in Kenya. It is a limited liability company duly incorporated in Kenya under the Companies Act. The company changed its name to Faulu Kenya Deposit Taking Microfinance (DTM) Limited in 2008 as part of the requirements to obtain the deposit taking licence from the Central Bank of

Kenya. In May 2009, Faulu became the first registered DTM in Kenya under the Micro-Finance Act and is regulated by the CBK

107 William J. Kramer, Beth Jenkins and Robert S. Katz, 'The Role of the Information and Communications Technology Sector in Expanding Economic Opportunity' (Harvard University 2007) <www.hks.harvard.edu/m-rcbg/CSRI/publications/report_22_EO%20ICT%20Final.pdf> accessed 3 September 2014.

108 Ibid.

109 Ibid.

110 Ibid.

111 Hughes and Lonie (n 105).

112 Ibid

113 Pauline Vaughan, Wolfgang Fengler and Michael Joseph, 'Scaling Up through Disruptive Business Models: The Inside Story of Mobile Money in Kenya' in Laurence Chandy and others (eds), *Getting to Scale: How to Bring Development Solutions to Millions of Poor People* (Brookings Institution 2013) 189.

114 The period examined in this thesis is between 2007 and 2014; see, Capital Markets Authority, 'Kenya's Financial Sector Stability Report 2011' (Issue No 3, December 2011) 38.

115 Ibid.

116 Ibid.

117 Ibid., 39.

118 Mwangi S. Kimenyi and Njuguna S. Ndung'u, 'Expanding the Financial Services Frontier: Lessons from Mobile Phone Banking in Kenya' (Brookings, 16 October 2009) <www.brookings.edu/~/media/research/files/articles/2009/10/16%20mobile%20phone%20kimenyi/1016_mobile_phone_kenya_kimenyi.pdf> accessed 3 September 2014

119 Darian Dorsey and Katy Jacobs, 'Financial Services Trends and Innovations Trends in South Africa: Lessons for the United States' The Centre for Financial Service Innovations.

120 'Mobile banking' is an example of a mobile transaction scheme.

121 The use of advance payment options for mobile phone voice and data products.

122 Vodafone Group plc is a British multinational telecommunications company headquartered in London, United Kingdom.

123 A service level agreement (SLA) is part of a service contract where a service is formally defined. For instance, internet service providers and telecommunications companies will commonly include SLAs within the terms of their contracts with customers to define the level(s) of service being sold in plain language terms. Ron Sprenkels and Aiko Pras, 'Service Level Agreements' 2 *Internet NG D* 7. Jahyun Goo and others, 'The Role of Service Level Agreements in Relational Management of Information Technology Outsourcing: An Empirical Study' (2009) 33(1) *Management Information Systems Quarterly* 8.

124 Vodafone, 'The Transformational Potential of M-transactions' in *Moving the Debate Forward* (Policy Paper Series No 6, July 2007).

125 Stephen Devereux and Katharine Vincent, 'Using Technology to Deliver Social Protection: Exploring Opportunities and Risks' (2010) 20 *Development in Practice* 367; Vodafone, 'The Transformational Potential of M-transactions'

126 As early as 2014.

127 Globe Telecom, 'Globe G-Cash – a Breakthrough in Mobile Commerce being a Truly Mobile Solution – Cashless and Cardless' (Presentation at the CGAP Annual Meeting 2005) <www.microfinancegateway.org/files/30783_file_Gcash_presentation.pdf?PH> accessed 3 September 2014.

128 Ignacio Mas and Kabir Kumar, 'Banking on Mobiles: Why, How, for Whom?' (CGAP Focus Note 48, June 2008).

129 Ibid.

130 A card with a chip, similar to more modern bankcards.

131 Vodafone (n 124).

132 A survey commissioned by Super brands Kenya and conducted by TNS Research International in 2009 rated M-Pesa number 14 in brand strength in the Kenyan market, whereas Safaricom fell below at 17 (the lowest reported in the survey)

133 Paul Leishman, 'Is There really any Money in Mobile Money' (2010) <www.gsmworld.com/mobilefordevelopment/wp-content/uploads/2012/03/moneyinmobilemoneyfinal63.pdf> accessed 3 September 2014.

134 See Section 2.2.2. The Modernisation of the Payments System Prior To Mobile Payments at page 22.

135 Gary Collins, 'How Over-regulation Has Stifled the Pace of Mobile Money Adoption in Africa' (Memeburn 2011) <http://memeburn.com/2011/09/how-over-regulation-has-stifled-thepace-of-mobile-money-adoption-in-africa/> accessed 3 September 2014.

136 Bronwen A. Kausch, 'Regulating Mobile Money to Create an Enabling Business Environment' (Master's Thesis, Witwatersrand, October 2012).'

137 Erik Hersman, 'Do Banks Block Mobile Money Innovation in Africa?' (Memeburn, August 2010) <http://memeburn.com/2010/08/do-banks-block-mobile-money-innovation-inafrica/> accessed 3 September 2014.

138 Tonny Omwansa, 'M-PESA: Progress and Prospects' Innovations (Special Edition for GSMA Mobile World Congress 2009) 107–123.

139 Ibid.

140 Ibid.

141 Subscriber Identity Module.

142 Section 2 of the Kenya Communications Regulations 2001 defines VAS as such services as may be available over a telecommunications system in addition to voice telephony service under the Unified Licensing Framework provision VAS fall under the telecommunications licence.

143 Electronic money is an innovation of Safaricom, and it is not regulated by either the CBK or the CCK. Parliament is yet to enact a substantive electronic transactions law. Section 83(c) of the Kenya Information and Communications Act, however, gives the CCK the regulatory jurisdiction over electronic transactions.

144 USAID and Kenya School of Monetary Studies (n 104).

145 Such as Telkom Kenya and Essar Telecom.

146 This regulatory gap shall be explored in Chapter 4.

147 Consultative Group to Assist the Poor, 'Notes on Regulation of Branchless Banking in Kenya' (2007) <www.cgap.org/p/site/c/template.rc/1.26.1480/> accessed 3 September 2014.

148 Jeremy Okonjo, Nature and Impact of Mobile Financial Services on the Telecoms Sector in Kenya' (2014) <www.slideshare.net/JeremmyOkonjo/1-chapter-one-nature-and-impact-of-mobile-financial-services-on-thetelecoms-sector-in-kenya> accessed 3 September 2014

149 Ibid. As part of its risk management regulations, the CBK has required mobile network operators to hold their trust accounts in more than one bank. This came hot on the heels of the Kenyan banking sector expressing reservations that M-Pesa 'could not meet the risk management requirements associated with a large payment system network; and that it was dangerous for any institution to operate on that scale outside of regulation.'

150 Ibid.

151 These outlets are discussed in Chapter 4 as being the point of sale for agents.

152 This has proven to be an efficient way of obtaining customer details and enhancing KYC requirements. It has also contributed to M-Pesa's success in Kenya, and no other country requires its citizens to have national identity cards.

153 See, William Jack, Tavneet Suri and Mit Sloan, 'The Economics of M-PESA' (unpublished paper 2010). On the definition of e-float, where it has been defined as stored value measured in the same unit as money.

154 This causes concerns about integrity risks which shall be discussed in Chapter 3. 3.4.1.2. Integrity Risk pg. 81.

155 Alliance for Financial Inclusion (n 5).

156 This presents a regulatory challenge as this clarification provides one of the keys to identifying whether deposit-taking by the MNOs occurs.

157 Ibid., at 153.

158 Ibid.

159 Under Section 2 of the Banking Act 2010 (Cap 488), banking business means accepting from the public money on deposit, or a current account, or employing this money by lending, investment or in any other manner for the account and at the risk of the person so employing the money. Hence, banks are from the outset licensed to provide various financial deposits and transfer services, under different technologies. See *United Dominions Trust v Kirkwood* (1966) 1 *All ER* 968.

160 See generally, the CBK Prudential Guidelines on capital adequacy, liquidity management, proceeds of crime and money laundering, consumer protection issued under Section 33(4) of the Banking Act 2010.

161 James Bilodeaeau, William Hoffman and Sjoerd Nikkelen, 'Findings from the Mobile Financial Services Development Report' in the Mobile Financial Services Development Report (World Economic Forum, 2011).

162 Institute of Economic Affairs, 'The State of Competition Report: Mobile Money Transfer, Agricultural Bulk Storage and Milling, and the Media Sectors in Kenya' (IEA Research Paper Series No 1/2011) <www.ieakenya.or.ke/publications/doc_download/227-the-state-of-competition-report-mobile-money-transfer-agricultural-bulk-storage-and-milling-and-the-media-sectors-in-kenya> accessed 3 September 2014. Both MNOs and banks have their limitations. While MNOs cannot undertake banking business, banks in contrast do not have any outreach costs to rural areas, compelling MNOs and banks to cooperate to form MNO–bank models.

163 M-Shwari, on the other hand, allows customers to save and borrow money through their mobile phones while at the same time earning interest on the money saved. Safaricom partnered with M-KOPA Kenya Ltd in October 2012 to launch a credit sale, pay-as-you-go solar lighting solution.

164 Christine Zhenwei and others, 'Mobile Applications for Agriculture and Rural Development' (World Bank, ICT Sector Unit 2011). Since Kenya is largely dependent on agro finance, mobile applications for agriculture and rural development have increased access to finance and insurance products in rural areas

165 USAID (n 104).

166 Bank-led payments markets have middle levels of activity and a significant bank presence. These are in South Africa and Botswana, where 50 per cent and 47 per cent of senders, respectively, used banks, and to a lesser extent, Nigeria, where just over 50 per cent of cash-based, but also 44 per cent, used bank transfers. Mobile-led payments markets with mid- to higher levels of activity are dominated by mobile transfers, including Kenya Limited markets. Those dominated by cash and characterised by low levels of activity include DRC, Mali and Rwanda.

167 David Mugwe and Mark Okuttah, 'Mobile Money Transfers Reach Sh1trn as banks, telcos link up' *Business Daily* (Nairobi, 31 March 2013).

168 Central Bank of Kenya 'Bank Supervision Annual Report 2010' (2010) <Https://Centralbank.Go.Ke/Images/Docs/Bank%20Supervision%20Reports/Annual%20Reports/Bs d2010(2).Pdf> accessed 3 September 2014.

169 David Porteous 'Enabling Environment for Cell Phone Banking in Africa' <http://liberationtechnologydcourse.pbworks.com/f/the+enabling+environm ent+for+mobile+banking+in+kenya.pdf> accessed 18 September 2014.

170 David Porteous, 'Mobilizing Money Through Enabling Regulation' (2009) 4(1) *Innovations* 75.

171 Openness refers to whether the policy, legal and regulatory environment allows for, or better still encourages, the entry of new providers and approaches. If not, there is little room for innovation to enter the market. Keith Adams, 'The Emergence of M-Commerce Promises Great Benefits but also Poses Significant Regulatory Concern' www.slideshare.net/keith60/the-emergence-of-m-commerce- promises-great-benefits-but-also-poses-significant-regulatory-concern>accessed 24 September 2014.

172 Certainty refers to whether the policy, legal and regulatory environment provides sufficient certainty that there will not be arbitrary changes in the future which may prejudice the prospects of entrants If not, entrants, at least those with a longer term horizon, will be discouraged from incurring the cost and risk of entry.

173 'Mobile Payment and the Changing Payment Landscape in Nigeria' <www. eppan.org/eppan_library/Creating%20an%20Enabling%20Environment%20 for%20Mobi le%20Payment.pdf> accessed 18 September 2014.

174 Ibid. Also see, Kamoyo Elias Maore, Lecturer, Gretsa University, 'Critical Literature Review on Mobile Banking Regulatory Overlap and Gap in Kenya' School of Business, Department of Accounting & Finance & Management Science. <http://erepository.uonbi.ac.ke/bitstream/handle/11295/65039/ ORSEA%20PROCEEDINGS.pdf?sequence=1> accessed 3 September 2014.

175 David Porteous 'Enabling Environment for Cell Phone Banking in Africa' <http://liberationtechnologydcourse.pbworks.com/f/the+enabling+environm ent+for+mobile+banking+in+kenya.pdf> accessed 18 September 2014

176 Gunnar Camner and Emil Sjöblom, 'Can the Success of M-PESA be Repeated? A Review of the Implementations in Kenya and Tanzania' (Valuable bits Note, July 2009).

177 Thorsten Beck et al, 'Banking Sector Stability, Efficiency, and Outreach in Kenya' World Bank Policy Research Working Papers October 2010 <http://www-wds. worldbank.org/external/default/WDSContentServer/WDSP/IB/2010/10/ 06/000158349_20101006154729/Rendered/PDF/WPS5442.pdf> accessed 3 September 2014.

178 Where they did not use any form of formal, semi-formal or informal financial services. FSD Kenya, 'Financial Access in Kenya, Results of the 2006 National Survey' <www.fsdkenya.org/finaccess/documents/FinaccessReportFINAL Main.pdf> accessed 3 September 2014.

179 The leading MNO in Tanzania.

180 FSD Tanzania, 'Finscope National Survey on Access to and Demand for Financial Services in Tanzania' <www.fsdt.or.tz/images/uploads/english-finscope2006. pdf> accessed 3 September 2014.

181 International Finance Corporation, 'M-Money Channel Distribution Case – Tanzania's (IFC Report, 2010) <http://www1.ifc.org/wps/wcm/connect/ 3aa8588049586050a27ab719583b6d16/Tool%2B6.8.%2BCase%2BStudy%2B- %2BM-PESA%252C%2BTanzania.pdf?MOD=AJPERES> accessed 3 September 2014.

182 Ignacio Mas and Dan Radcliffe, 'Scaling Mobile Money' (2011) 5(3) *Journal of Payments Strategy & Systems* 298. (2010).

183 Ibid.

184 Although Western Union was prevalent, as a remittance method it was both expensive and inconvenient.

185  Camner and Sjöblom (n 176); Morawczynski (n 27).
186  Ignacio Mas and Anne Ng'weno, 'Three Keys to M-PESA's Success: Branding, Channel Management and Pricing' (2010) 4(4) *Journal of Payments Strategy & Systems* 352.
187  Morawczynski (n 6, Chapter 1).
188  Olga Morawczynski and Mark Pickens, 'Poor People Using Mobile Financial Services: Observations on Customer Usage and Impact from M-PESA' (CGAP Brief, August 2009).
189  Simone Di Castri and Brian Muthiora, 'Mobile Money: The Opportunity for India' (13 November 2013) MMAI/GSMA Position Paper <www.gsma.com/mobilefordevelopment/wp-content/uploads/2013/12/MMAI-GSMA-on-Mobile-Money-in-India-for-RBI-Financial-Inclusion-Committee_Dec13.pdf> accessed 3 September 2014.
190  For example, commercial banking, insurance, securities trading and investment banking. Claudio E. Borio and Renato Filosa, 'The Changing Borders of Banking: Trends and Implications' (October 1994) BIS Working Paper No 23 <http://papers.ssrn.com/sol3/papers.cfm?abstract_id=868431> accessed 3 September 2014.
191  See Ignacio Mas, 'The Economics of Branchless Banking' (2009) 4(2) *Innovations* 57, 59.
192  Simplice A. Asongu, 'How has Mobile Phone Penetration Stimulated Financial Development in Africa?' (2013) 14(1) *Journal of African Business* 7 <www.cck.go.ke/resc/downloads/SECTOR_STATISTICS_REPORT_Q1_12-13.pdf> accessed 3 September 2014.
193  Paul Gerhardt Schierz, Oliver Schilke and Bernd W. Wirtz, 'Understanding Consumer Acceptance of Mobile Payment Services: An Empirical Analysis' (2010) 9(3) *Electronic Commerce Research and Applications* 209.
194  FSD Kenya, 'FinAccess National Survey 2009: Dynamics of Kenya's Changing Financial Landscape' <www.fsdkenya.org/finaccess/documents/09-06-10_FinAccess_FA09_Report.pdf> accessed 3 September 2014
195  CCK 'Quarterly Sector Statistics Report' (2012)<www.cck.go.ke/resc/downloads/SECTOR_STATISTICS_REPORT_Q3_JUNE_2012.pdf> accessed 3 September 2014.
196  Isaac Mbiti and David Weil, 'Mobile Banking: the Impact of M-Pesa in Kenya' (June 2011) NBER Working Paper No 17129 <www.econ.brown.edu/faculty/David_Weil/Mbiti%20Weil%20NBER%20working%20paper%2017129.pdf> accessed 3 September 2014.
197  Ibid., 170.
198  Jenny C. Aker and Isaac M. Mbiti, 'Mobile Phones and Economic Development in Africa' 24(3) [2010] Journal of Economic Perspectives 207.
199  G20 Financial Inclusion Experts Group – Australian Government <http://aid.dfat.gov.au/Publications/Documents/G20financialinclusion.doc> accessed 18 September 2014.
200  Estimate by the ITU, 'The World in 2014: ICT Facts and Figures' <www.itu.int/en/ITU-D/Statistics/Documents/facts/ICTFactsFigures2014-e.pdf> accessed 3 September
201  CGAP-GSMA Mobile Money Market Sizing Quoted CGAP (2009) [www.gsma.com/mobilefordevelopment/wpcontent/uploads/2012/06/mmu_quarterly_update.p df]
202  William Jack and Tavneet Suri, 'The Economics of M-Pesa' (2011) MIT NBER Working Paper 16721 <www.mit.edu/~tavneet/M-PESA_Update.pdf> accessed 3 September 2014.
203  Safaricom, 'M-Pesa Statistics' <www.safaricom.co.ke/images/Downloads/Personal/M-PESA/m-pesa_statistics_-_2.pdf> accessed 3 September 2014.

204 Kevin Donovan, 'Mobile Money in the Developing World: The Impact of M-PESA on Development, Freedom, and Domination' (Master's Thesis, Georgetown University 2011).
205 Nojiyeza Simphiwe, and Jocelyn Muthoka, 'Barriers to Entry of Kenya's Telecommunication Industry: is there a Market Slice for New Entrants?' (2013) 11(1) *Journal of Management & Administration* 136–196.
206 Mark Okuttah, 'Safaricom: Telkom Targeted in New Power Rules' *Business Daily*, (17 August 2011) <http://mobile.businessdailyafrica.com/Corporate+News/Safaricom++Telkom+targeted+in+new+market+power+rules/-/1144450/1220104/-/format/xhtml/item/2/-/56d3a5z/-> accessed 3 September 2014
207 Nojiyeza Simphiwe and Jocelyn Muthoka, 'Barriers to Entry of Kenya's Telecommunication Industry: is there a Market Slice for New Entrants?'(2013) 11(1) *Journal of Management & Administration* 136–196.
208 Ibid.
209 Ewan Sutherland, 'A Short Note on Corruption in Telecommunications in Kenya' (January 2012) <http://papers.ssrn.com/sol3/papers.cfm?abstract_id=1996429> accessed 3 September 2014.
210 Ewan Sutherland, 'Corruption in Telecommunications: Problems and Remedies' (2012) 14(1) *info* 4. <http://papers.ssrn.com/sol3/papers.cfm?abstract_id=1937556> accessed 3 September 2014.
211 Ibid.
212 At that time, Kenya Post and Telecommunication Corporation.
213 Safaricom, 'Prospectus' (14 March 2008, revised 28 March 2008) <www.scribd.com/doc/7088318/Safaricom-Prospectus> accessed 3 September 2014.
214 Concern has been expressed by the Kenyan Parliament and the Kenyan Chapter of Transparency International (TI) over a mysterious 'investor' in Safaricom, while the Africa Centre for Open Governance (AfriCOG) has raised similar issues over an investor in Kenya Telkom which avoided the framework of the Privatisation Act.
215 Sutherland E, 'A Short Note on Corruption in Telecommunications in Kenya' [2012] Available at SSRN 1996429
216 Nojiyeza Simphiwe and Jocelyn Muthoka, 'Barriers to Entry of Kenya's Telecommunication Industry: is there a Market Slice for New Entrants?' (2013) 11(1) *Journal of Management & Administration* 136–196.
217 Including Airtel, Kenya Telkom (France Telecom Group) and Yu (Essar Telecom).
218 Ignacio Mas and Amolo Ng'weno, 'Three Keys to M-PESA's Success: Branding, Channel Management and Pricing' (2014) 4(4) *Journal of Payments Strategy & Systems* 352.
219 The active role of the state in driving economic development (freeing market forces from government control, reducing taxes, divesting state-owned enterprises, deregulation of telecommunication and weakening of the state's redistributive functions). Sonny Nwankwo, 'Assessing the Marketing Environment in Sub- Saharan Africa: Opportunities and Threats Analysis' (2000) 18 *Marketing Intelligence & Planning* 144
220 Charles Wachira, 'Airtel Challenges Safaricom Supremacy in Money-Transfer Industry' *Business Daily* (4 June 2014)<www.businessdailyafrica.com/Corporate-News/Airtel-Challenges-Safaricom-Supremacy-inMoney-Transfer-Industry/-/539550/2336696/-/12nqmmwz/-/index.html> accessed 20 January 2014.
221 Luca Manica and Michele Vescovi, 'Mobile Telephony in Kenya Is It "Making the life better"?' (2011) 23 <www.it46.se/projects/UNITN_ict4sd/assignments/ICT4SD_manica_vescovi.pdf> accessed 2 September 2014

222  Nojiyeza Simphiwe and Jocelyn Muthoka, 'Barriers to Entry of Kenya's Telecommunication Industry: is there a Market Slice for New Entrants?' (2013) 11(1) *Journal of Management & Administration* 136–196

223  Muriuki Mureithi, 'Evolution of Telecommunications Policy Reforms in East Africa: Setting New Policy Strategies to Anchor Benefits of Policy Reforms' (2011) 2 *Southern African Journal of Information and Communication.*

224  Ibid., at 218. This is elaborated in the chapter detailing Kenya's regulatory capability to adopt mobile payments law.

225  Nick Hughes and Susie Lonie, 'M-PESA: Mobile Money for the "Unbanked" Turning Cell phones into 24-Hour Tellers in Kenya' (2007) 2(1–2) *Innovations* 63.

226  Alliance for Financial Inclusion (n 5 Chapter 1).

227  Amrik Heyer and Ignacio Mas, 'Fertile Grounds for Mobile Money: Towards a Framework for Analysing Enabling Environments' (2011) 22(1) *Enterprise Development and Microfinance* 30.

228  Central Bank of Nigeria (CBN), 'Regulatory Framework for Mobile Payments Services in Nigeria' <www.cenbank.org/out/circulars/bod/2009/regulatory%20 framework%20%20for%20mobile%20payments%20services%20in%20nigeria. pdf> accessed 3 September 2014

229  Ibid.

230  Amrik Heyer, 'Factors Affecting Uptake of Mobile Money Services: M-Pesa in Kenya and Tanzania' (2011) <http://www.gsma.com/mobilefordevelop ment/wp-content/uploads/2012/03/fertile_grounds_mobile_money55.pdf> accessed 3 September 2014.

231  Simone Di Castri and Lara Gidvani, 'Enabling Mobile Money Policies in Tanzania' (February 2014) <http://www.gsma.com/mobilefordevelopment/wp-content/uploads/2014/03/Tanzania-Enabling-  Mobile-Money-Policies.pdf> accessed 3 September 2014.

232  Gunnar Camner and Emil Sjöblom, 'Can the Success of M-Pesa be repeated? A Review of Implementations in Kenya and Tanzania' (2009) <http://emil. sjoblom.com/pdf/M- Pesa_implementations_Ke_Tz.pdf> accessed 3 September 2014.

233  David M. Anderson, 'Master and Servant in Colonial Kenya' (2000) 41 *Journal of African History* 459.

234  Within the CBK.

235  These are part of the operational risks that will be examined in Chapter 3, pg. 71.

236  Jenny C. Aker and Isaac M. Mbiti, 'Mobile Phones and Economic Development in Africa' (2010) 24(3) *The Journal of Economic Perspectives* 207–232 <www. jstor.org/stable/20799163> accessed 3 September 2014; Isaac Mbiti and David N. Weil, 'Mobile banking: The Impact of M-Pesa in Kenya' (June 2011) NBER Working Paper No 17129 <www.econ.brown.edu/faculty/David_Weil/ Mbiti%20Weil%20NBER%20working%20paper%2017129.pdf> accessed 3 September 2014.

237  Alliance for Financial Inclusion

238  Mobile for Development, 'Enabling Mobile Money Transfer' (2013) <www. gsma.com/mobilefordevelopment/wpcontent/uploads/2013/09/enabling mobilemoneytransfer92.pdf> accessed 3 September 2014

239  Ibid.

240  Ibid.

241  Which is discussed in Section 2.4, The Enabling Environment for Mobile Payments on p 29.

242  The regulatory vacuum and its complexities will be examined in Chapter 4: The Legal and Regulatory Challenges of Mobile Payments.

243 Aishwarya Ratan, 'Using Technology to Deliver Financial Services to Low-income Households: a Preliminary Study of Equity Bank and M-PESA customers in Kenya' (TechReport, Microsoft Research, June 2008)

244 Gunnar Camner and Emil Sjöblom, 'Can the Success of M-Pesa be repeated? A Review of Implementations in Kenya and Tanzania' (2009) <http://emil. sjoblom.com/pdf/M-Pesa_implementations_Ke_Tz.pdf> accessed 3 September 2014.

245 William T. Morgan, 'Urbanization in Kenya: Origins and Trends' (1969) 46 *Transactions of the Institute of British Geographers* 167.

246 Olga Morawczynski, 'Surviving in the "Dual System": How M-PESA is Fostering Urban-to-Rural Remittances in a Kenyan Slum' (University of Edinburgh, Social Studies Unit Working Paper, 2008) 2 <www.mobileactive.org/files/file_uploads/Olga_Morawczynski-M-PESA-2008.pdf> accessed 3 September 2014.

247 Mercy Buku and Michael W. Meredith, 'Safaricom and M-Pesa in Kenya: Financial Inclusion and Financial Integrity' (2013) 8 *WASH. J.L. TECH. & ARTS* 375 <http://digital.law.washington.edu/dspace-law/handle/1773.1/1204> accessed 3 September 2014.

248 Ibid.

249 Mercy W. Buku and Michael W. Meredith, 'Mobile money in developing countries: financial inclusion and financial integrity. Safaricom and M-Pesa in Kenya (2013) 8(3) *Wash JL Tech & Arts* 375.

250 Ibid

251 Ibid.

252 Ibid.

253 Buku and Meredith 2013 (n 247).

254 Kenya's colonial period was between 1895 and 1963 when it gained independence from the British. Kenya was known as the British East African Protectorate.

255 These policies restricted movement by Kenyans from rural areas to urban centres by introducing a restrictive pass called a *Kipande*. *Kipandes* were used to identify the region of origin and had to be presented whenever called upon.

256 Amrik Heyer and Ignacio Mas, 'Seeking Fertile Grounds for Mobile Money' Bill & Melinda Gates Foundation (3 September 2009) Working Paper 5–6 <http://mmublog.org/wpcontent/files_mf/fertile_grounds_mobile_money. pdf.> accessed 3 September 2014

257 Mercy W. Buku and Michael W. Meredith, 'Mobile money in developing countries: financial inclusion and financial integrity. Safaricom and M-Pesa in Kenya (2013) 8(3) *Wash JL Tech & Arts* 375. Also during the colonial period, the colonial government created boundaries that fostered ethnic settlements and urban areas which represented a more cosmopolitan representation of the Kenyan people.

258 Morawczynski, (n 162).

259 See, Section 2.4.2, Mobile Phone Rate Penetration on pg. 31.

260 Ibid.

261 Amrik Heyer and Ignacio Mas, 'Seeking Fertile Grounds for Mobile Money' (3 September 2009) <www.gsma.com/mobilefordevelopment/wp-content/uploads/2012/03/fertile_grounds_mobile_money55.pdf> accessed 3 September 2014

262 Marc H. Ross and Thomas S. Weisner, 'The Rural-urban Migrant Network in Kenya: Some General Implications' (1977) 4 *American Ethnologist* 359.

263 Morawczynski (n 162).

264 Elizabeth Asiedu, 'Foreign Direct Investment in Africa: The Role of Natural Resources, Market Size, Government Policy, Institutions and Political Instability' (2006) 29(1) *The World Economy* 63

265 Heyer and Mas 2010 (n 261).

266   The 2007–2008 Kenyan crisis was a political, economic and humanitarian crisis that erupted in Kenya after incumbent President Mwai Kibaki was declared the winner of the presidential election held on 27 December 2007. Supporters of Kibaki's opponent, Raila Odinga of the Orange Democratic Movement, alleged electoral manipulation. Wangui Kanina, 'Kenya's Election Seen as Badly Flawed' *Reuters* (Nairobi, 18 September 2008) 18 September 2008 <www.reuters.com/article/2008/09/18/us-kenya-election-idUSLI38786120080918> accessed 3 September 2014

267   Olga Morawczynski and Mark Pickens, 'Poor People Using Mobile Financial Services' (2009) C-Gap Brief <www.cgap.org/p/site/c/template.rc/1.9.36723/> accessed 3 September 2014.

268   Supriya Singh, 'Sending Money Home: Money and Family in the Indian Diaspora' in Ajaya K. Sahoo and Brij Maharaj (eds), *Sociology of Diaspora: A Reader* (Rawat 2007).

269   Shawn Cole, Thomas Sampson and Bilal Zia, 'Prices or Knowledge? What Drives Demand for Financial Services in Emerging Markets?' (2011) 66(6) *Journal of Finance* 1933.

270   Irene Philippi, 'An Enabling Legal Environment for Mobile Payments and Peer-To-Peer Networks' UNCITRAL International Colloquium on Microfinance, creating an enabling legal environment for microbusiness, Vienna 16–18 January 2013, accessed 18 September 2014.

271   Jan Ondrus, Kalle Lyytinen and Yves Pigneur, 'Why Mobile Payments Fail? Towards a Dynamic and Multi-Perspective Explanation' Mobile Business (ICMB), 2011 Tenth International Conference on. IEEE, 2011.Jan Ondrus and Yves Pigneur, 'Towards a Holistic Analysis of Mobile Payments: A Multiple Perspectives Approach' (2006) 5(3) *Electronic Commerce Research and Applications* 246.

272   Christine Z. Qiang, Masatake Yamamichi, Vicky Hausman and Daniel Altman, Mobile Applications for the Health Sector (ICT Sector Unit, The World Bank 2011).

273   Sam Wambugu 'Mobile Phones to Offer Health Sector the Kiss of Life' *Daily Nation* (Nairobi, 9 April 2011) <http://technews.tmcnet.com/fixed-mobile-convergence/news/2011/04/11/5436940.htm>accessed 3 September 2014

274   Ibid.

275   Financial exclusion in Kenya is not only limited to the poor; it includes the elderly, the unemployed, the disabled, etc.; see, Subir Gokarn, 'Financial Inclusion – a Consumer Centric View' (VIth Narayanan Memorial Lecture, Kumbakonam, 21 March 2011

276   'Learn More About Financial Inclusion – Breckland' www.breckland.gov.uk/content/learn-more-about-financial-inclusion accessed 18 September 2014.

277   Ernest Aryeetey and Machiko Nissanke, *Financial Integration and Development: Liberalization and Reform in Sub-Saharan Africa* (Routledge 2005). On aspects of financial exclusion and efforts generally to increase financial inclusion around the world, see Amitabh Saxena, 'Accelerating Financial Inclusion through Innovative Channels: 10 Obstacles for MFIs Launching Alternative Channels – and What Can Be Done About Them' (2009) 27 *Insight*; KPMG ' "Underserved" Market Represents Opportunity for Banks' (2011) <www.kpmg.com/us/en/issuesandinsights/articlespublications/press-releases/pages/underserved-market-represents-opportunity-for-banks.aspx> accessed 3 September 2014.

278   S. Mahendra Dev, 'Financial Inclusion: Issues and Challenges' (2006) *Economic and Political Weekly* 4310; H. T. Parekh, Finance Forum Economic and Political Weekly 14 October 2006.

279   Mandira Sarma and Jesim Pais, 'Financial Inclusion and Development: a Cross Country Analysis' (ICRIER 2008) <www.icrier.org/pdf/Mandira%20Sarma-Paper.pdf> accessed 3 September 2014.

280 Tilman Ehrbeck, Mark Pickens and Michael Tarazi, 'Financially Inclusive Eco-systems: The Roles of Government Today' (2012) 76 *Focus*
281 Claire Alexandre and Lynn Chang Eisenhart, 'Mobile Money as an Engine of Financial Inclusion and Lynchpin of Financial Integrity' (2013) 8 *Wash JL Tech & Arts* 285.
282 Ibid.
283 Alliance for Financial Inclusion, 'The AFI Survey on Financial Inclusion Policy in Developing Countries: Preliminary Findings' (2010) <www.afi-global.org/sites/default/files/AFISurveyPresentation_2204_0.pdf> accessed 3 September 2014.
284 There is a wide-ranging discourse of financial inclusion from an economic per-spective; however, this thesis will not delve into those perspectives.
285 This part of the thesis does not wish to delve into broad macroeconomic approaches either interventionist, laissez faire or pro market activists. It is recog-nised that there will be a variety of government approaches. See Thorsten Beck, Asli Demirgüç-Kunt and Patrick Honohan, 'Access to Financial Services: Meas-urement, Impact, and Policies' (2009) 24 *World Bank Research Observer* 119.
286 Elaine Kempson, Adele Atkinson and Odile Pilley, 'Policy Level Response to Financial Exclusion in Developed Economies: Lessons for Developing Coun-tries' (2008) University of Bristol, Personal Finance Research Centre <www.pfrc.bris.ac.uk/Reports/dfid_report.pdf> accessed 3 September 2014.
287 Alice Allan, Maude Massu and Christine Svarer, 'Banking on Change: Break-ing the Barriers to Financial Inclusion' (January 2013) <www.barclays.com/content/dam/barclayspublic/docs/Citizenship/banking-on-change.pdf> accessed 3 September 2014.
288 James Bilodeaeau, William Hoffman and Sjoerd Nikkelen 'The Seven Pillars of Mobile Financial Services Development' in *The Mobile Financial Services Devel-opment Report* (World Economic Forum 2011) 3–14.
289 Ibid.
290 Jeremy Okonjo, Nature and Impact of Mobile Financial Services on the Telecoms Sector in Kenya' (2014) <www.slideshare.net/JeremmyOkonjo/1-chapter-one-nature-and-impact-of-mobile-financial-services-on-the-telecoms-sector-in-kenya> accessed 3 September 2014; T. S. Jayne and Milu Muyanga, 'Land Constraints in Kenya's Densely Populated Rural Areas: Implications for Food Policy and Institutional Reform' (Paper presented at 86th Annual Conference of the Agricultural Economics Society, University of Warwick, 16–18 April 2012).
291 OECD, 'Policy Framework for Effective and Efficient Financial Regulation' (2010) <www.oecd.org/finance/financial-markets/44362818.pdf> accessed 3 September 2014.
292 Asli Demirgüèc, Thorsten Beck and Patrick Honohan, *Finance for All? Policies and Pitfalls in Expanding Access* (World Bank 2008).
293 Finmark Trust, 'Understanding the Challenges and Opportunities in Promoting Savings Among Low Income Individuals in Lesotho, Malawi and South Africa' (November 2013) <www.finmark.org.za/wp-content/uploads/pubs/Rep_Savings_SA_Les_Mal_2013.pdf> accessed 3 September 2014.
294 Megan Plyer, Sherri Haas and Geetha Nagarajan, 'Community-Level Economic Effects of M-PESA in Kenya: Initial Findings' (IRIS Center Report, University of Maryland, 2010) <www.fsassessment.umd.edu/publications/pdfs/Community-EffectsMPESA-Kenya.pdf> accessed 3 September 2014.
295 Ibid.
296 Asli Demirgüèc, Thorsten Beck and Patrick Honohan, *Finance for All? Policies and Pitfalls in Expanding Access* (World Bank 2008).
297 Tarlok Singh, 'Does Domestic Saving Cause Economic Growth? A Time-series Evidence from India' (2010) 32 *Journal of Policy Modeling* 231. See also Carlos Pallordet, 'Brazil's Dearth of Domestic Savings, a Limit to Growth'

(March 2012) <http://byline.timetric.com/2012/03/23/brazils-dearth-of-domestic-savings-a-limit-to-growth/> accessed 3 September 2014.

298  See Pallordet, ibid.

299  Ibid.

300  Eduardo Cavallo, Andrew Powell and Oscar Becerra, 'Estimating the Direct Economic Damages of the Earthquake in Haiti' (August 2010) 120(546) The Economic Journal F298.

301  Alfred Hannig and Stefan Jansen, 'Financial Inclusion and Financial Stability: Current Policy Issues' (2010) ADBIWorking Paper Series No 259 <www.adbi.org/working-paper/2010/12/21/4272.financial.inclusion.stability.policy.issues/> accessed 3 September 2014.

302  Masahiro Kawai, Eswar Prasad, *Financial Market Regulation and Reforms in Emerging Markets* Brookings Institution Press 2011) 287; Coimbator K. Pralahad, *The Fortune at the Bottom of the Pyramid* (Pearson Education Inc 2006).

303  Ibid., 302; see UN Capital Development Fund (2006)

304  Coimbatore K. Prahalad, *The Fortune at the Bottom of the Pyramid, Revised and Updated 5th Anniversary Edition: Eradicating Poverty Through Profits* (FT Press 2009).

305  Claire Alexandre and Lynn Chang Eisenhart, 'Mobile Money as an Engine of Financial Inclusion and Lynchpin of Financial Integrity' (2013) 8 *WASH. J.L. TECH. & ARTS* 285 <http://digital.law.washington.edu/dspace-law/handle/1773.1/1200> accessed 3 September 2014.

306  Ibid.

307  On average US $3 per transaction.

308  Mercy W. Buku and Michael W. Meredith (n 247). Caroline Pulver, William Jack and Tavneet Suri, 'The Performance and Impact of M-Pesa: Preliminary Evidence from a Household Survey' (2009) FSD Kenya (unpublished).

309  Mas & Radcliffe (n 5) 180.

310  Ibid.

311  Ibid.

312  During the post-election violence in 2008, Kenyans were left stranded as a result of the closure of all financial institutions, and money transfer was hampered due to the lack of liquidity.

313  See generally, the dynamics of gender and the use of mobile payments, Yaobin Lu, Shuiqing Yang, Patrick Y. K. Chau, and Yuzhi Cao, 'Dynamics Between the Trust Transfer Process and Intention to Use Mobile Payment Services: A Cross-environment Perspective' (2011) 48(8) *Information & Management* 393–403.

314  Mercy W. Buku, and Michael W. Meredith, 'Safaricom and M-PESA in Kenya: Financial Inclusion and Financial Integrity' (2013) 8 *WASH. J.L. TECH. & ARTS* 375 (2013)<http://digital.law.washington.edu/dspace-law/handle/1773.1/1204>

315  Frederik Eijkman, Jake Kendall and Ignacio Mas, 'Bridges to Cash: the Retail End of M-PESA' (2010) 34 *Savings & Development* 219, 225.

316  Biagio Bossone, 'What Makes Banks Special? A Study on Banking, Finance and Economic Development' (2000) World Bank Policy Research Working Paper 2408 <http://papers.ssrn.com/sol3/papers.cfm?abstract_id=630780> accessed 3 September 2014.

317  P. A. Frazer, Plastic and Electronic Money – New Payment Systems and Their Implications (Woodhead-Faulkner 1985) 188.

318  David Cracknell, 'Policy Innovations to Improve Access to Financial Services in Developing Countries' [2013] Center for Global Development.

319  Safaricom Limited, 'Annual Report and Group Accounts for the Year Ended March 2012' (2012) <www.safaricom.co.ke/safaricom_annual_report/pdfs/

Safaricom_Annual_Report.pdf> accessed 3 September 2014. The size of M-Pesa's revenue is significant when Safaricom's business model, as a market leader, is put into the perspective of prohibited market practices under the Competition Act 2010.

320 Jeremy Okonjo, Nature and Impact of Mobile Financial Services on the Telecoms Sector in Kenya' (2014) <www.slideshare.net/JeremmyOkonjo/1-chapter-one-nature-and-impact-of-mobile-financial-services-on-the-telecoms-sector-in-kenya> accessed 3 September 2014

321 BIS Working Papers – Bank for International Settlements, <www.bis.org/publ/work347.pdf> (accessed 18 September 2014). It has even received special attention from the G20. In Seoul, in late 2010, the G20 launched the Global Partnership for Financial Inclusion, which among others things, has been tasked to implement the action plan for Financial Inclusion Principles (Access through Innovation Sub- Group of the G20 Financial Inclusion Experts Group (2010).

322 Subir Gokarn, 'Dr Subir Gokarn takes over as RBI Deputy Governor' (April 2011) <www.rbi.org.in/Scripts/BS_PressReleaseDisplay.aspx?prid=21700> accessed 3 September 2014.

323 Penelope Hawkins, 'Financial Access and Financial Stability' (2006) (BIS 2006) <www.bis.org/press/p060619.htm> 3 September 2014.

324 Ibid., n 316, See also, Alfred Hannig and Stefan Jansen, 'Financial Inclusion and Financial Stability: Current Policy Issues' (2010) ADBI Working Paper 259 (Tokyo: Asian Development Bank Institute) <www.adbi.org/working paper/2010/12/21/4272.financial.inclusion.stability.policy.issues/> accessed 3 September 2014.

325 Mark Gertler, 'Financial Structure and Aggregate Economic Activity: An Overview' (1988) NBER Working Paper No 2559 <www.nber.org/papers/w2559.pdf> accessed 3 September 2014.

326 See Alliance for Financial Inclusion (n 5 Chapter 1). At the inception of M-Pesa in Kenya in 2007, Safaricom lobbied the CBK and the CCK for authorisation to provide mobile money transfer services without a regulatory framework. The CCK's reluctance to step in as a primary regulator was probably due to its unfamiliarity with the new converged product. The CBK has used its macroprudential regulatory mandate under Section 3 of the Central Bank of Kenya Act to issue negative authorisation to the provision of mobile financial services by mobile network operators. This is by way of issuance of letters of No Objection. These issues shall be discussed in Chapters 3 and 4.

# Bibliography

'Accelerating Financial Inclusion through Innovative Channels: 10 Obstacles for MFIs Launching Alternative Channels – and What Can Be Done About Them' (2009) 27 *Insight*.

Aker, Jenny C. and Isaac M. Mbiti, 'Mobile Phones and Economic Development in Africa' (2010) 24(3) *Journal of Economic Perspectives* 207.

Aker, Jenny C. and Isaac M. Mbiti, 'Mobile Phones and Economic Development in Africa' (2010) 24(3) *The Journal of Economic Perspectives* 207–232 <www.jstor.org/stable/20799163> accessed 3 September 2014.

Aker, Jenny C. and Isaac M. Mbiti, 'Mobile Phones and Economic Development in Africa' (2010) 24 (3) *Journal of Economic Perspectives* 207–232 <www.jstor.org/stable20799163> accessed 3 September 2014.

Alampay, Erwin, 'Mobile Banking, Mobile Money and Telecommunication Regulations' (2010) *eBusiness & eCommerce Journal* 5.

Alexandre, Claire and Lynn Chang Eisenhart, 'Mobile Money as an Engine of Financial Inclusion and Lynchpin of Financial Integrity' (2013) 8 *WASH. J.L. TECH. & ARTS* 285 <http://digital.law.washington.edu/dspace-law/handle/1773.1/1200> accessed 3 September 2014.

Allahar, Anton, *Ethnicity, Class, and Nationalism* (1st edn, Lexington Books 2005).

Allan, Alice, Maude Massu and Christine Svarer, 'Banking on Change: Breaking the Barriers to Financial Inclusion'(January 2013) <www.barclays.com/content/dam/barclayspublic/docs/Citizenship/banking-on-change.pdf> accessed 3 September 2014.

Allen, Franklin and others, 'Improving Access to Banking: Evidence from Kenya' (2014) CEPR Discussion Paper No. DP9840.

Alliance for Financial Inclusion

Alliance for Financial Inclusion, 'The AFI Survey on Financial Inclusion Policy in Developing Countries: Preliminary Findings' (2010) <www.afi-global.org/sites/default/files/AFISurveyPresentation_2204_0.pdf> accessed 3 September 2014.

Anderson, David M., 'Master and Servant in Colonial Kenya' (2000) 41 *Journal of African History* 459.

Aryeetey, Ernest and Machiko Nissanke, *Financial Integration and Development: Liberalization and Reform in Sub-Saharan Africa* (Routledge 2005).

Asiedu, Elizabeth, 'Foreign Direct Investment in Africa: The Role of Natural Resources, Market Size, Government Policy, Institutions and Political Instability' (2006) 29(1) *The World Economy* 63.

Asongu, Simplice A., 'How Has Mobile Phone Penetration Stimulated Financial Development in Africa?' (2013) 14(1) *Journal of African Business* 7<www.cck.go.ke/resc/downloads/SECTOR_STATISTICS_REPORT_Q1_12-13.pdf> accessed 3 September 2014.

Baddeley, Michelle, 'Using E-Cash in the New Economy: An Economic Analysis of Micro-Payment Systems' (2004) 5 *Journal of Electronic Commerce Research* 239.

Banks, Ken, 'Mobile Telephony and the Entrepreneur: an African Perspective' (2008) 8 *Microfinance Insights* <www.oecd.org/dataoecd/27/51/41789311.pdf> accessed 3 September 2014.

Beck, Thorsten and Asli Demirgüç-Kunt, 'Access to Finance: An Unfinished Agenda' (2008) 22(3) *The World Bank Economic Review* 383.

Beck, Thorsten, Asli Demirgüç-Kunt and Patrick Honohan, 'Access to Financial Services: Measurement, Impact, and Policies' (2009) 24 *World Bank Research Observer* 119.

Bilodeaeau, James, William Hoffman and Sjoerd Nikkelen, 'Findings from the Mobile Financial Services Development Report' in the Mobile Financial Services Development Report (World Economic Forum, 2011).

Bilodeaeau, James, William Hoffman and Sjoerd Nikkelen, 'The Seven Pillars of Mobile Financial Services Development' in *The Mobile Financial Services Development Report* (World Economic Forum 2011) 3–14.

BIS Working Papers – Bank for International Settlements, <www.bis.org/publ/work347.pdf> (accessed 18 September 2014).

Borio, Claudio E. and Renato Filosa, 'The Changing Borders of Banking: Trends and Implications' (October 1994) BIS Working Paper No. 23 <http://papers.ssrn.com/sol3/papers.cfm?abstract_id=868431> accessed 3 September 2014.

Bossone, Biagio, 'What Makes Banks Special? A Study on Banking, Finance and Economic Development' (2000) World Bank Policy Research Working Paper 2408

<http://papers.ssrn.com/sol3/papers.cfm?abstract_id=630780> accessed 3 September 2014.

Boyd, Caroline and Katy Jacob, *Mobile Financial Services and the Under-banked: Opportunities and Challenges for M-Banking and M-Payments* (The Centre for Financial Services Innovation, 2007).

Buku, Mercy and Michael W. Meredith, 'Safaricom and M-Pesa in Kenya: Financial Inclusion and Financial Integrity' (2013) 8 *WASH. J.L. TECH. & ARTS* 375 <http://digital.law.washington.edu/dspace-law/handle/1773.1/1204> accessed 3 September 2014.

Buku, Mercy W. and Michael W. Meredith, 'Mobile Money in Developing Countries: Financial Inclusion and Financial Integrity. Safaricom and M-Pesa in Kenya' (2013) 8(3) *Wash JL Tech & Arts* 375.

Buku, Mercy and Michael W. Meredith, 'Safaricom and M-Pesa in Kenya: Financial Inclusion and Financial Integrity' (2013) 8 *WASH. J.L. TECH. & ARTS* 375 <http://digital.law.washington.edu/dspace-law/handle/1773.1/1204> accessed 3 September 2014.

Buku, Mercy W. and Michael W. Meredith, 'Mobile Money in Developing Countries: Financial Inclusion and Financial Integrity. Safaricom and M-Pesa in Kenya' (2013) 8(3) *Wash JL Tech & Arts* 375.

Buku, Mercy W., and Michael W. Meredith, 'Safaricom and M-PESA in Kenya: Financial Inclusion and Financial Integrity' (2013) 8 *WASH. J.L. TECH. & ARTS* 375 (2013) <http://digital.law.washington.edu/dspace-law/handle/1773.1/1204>

Camner, Gunnar and Emil Sjöblom, 'Can the Success of M-Pesa Be Repeated? A Review of Implementations in Kenya and Tanzania' (2009) <http://emil.sjoblom.com/pdf/M-Pesa_implementations_Ke_Tz.pdf> accessed 3 September 2014.

Camner, Gunnar and Emil Sjöblom, 'Can the Success of M-Pesa Be Repeated? A Review of Implementations in Kenya and Tanzania' (2009) <http://emil.sjoblom.com/pdf/M-Pesa_implementations_Ke_Tz.pdf> accessed 3 September 2014.

Castri, Simone Di, 'Mobile Money: Enabling Regulatory Solutions' (GSMA, Mobile Money for the Unbanked)

Castri, Simone Di and Brian Muthiora, 'Mobile Money: The Opportunity for India' (13 November 2013) MMAI/GSMA Position Paper <www.gsma.com/mobilefordevelopment/wp-content/uploads/2013/12/MMAI-GSMA-on-Mobile-Money-in-India-for-RBI-Financial-Inclusion- Committee_Dec13.pdf> accessed 3 September 2014.

Castri, Simone Di and Lara Gidvani, 'Enabling Mobile Money Policies in Tanzania' (February 2014) <www.gsma.com/mobilefordevelopment/wp-content/uploads/2014/03/Tanzania-Enabling- Mobile-Money-Policies.pdf> accessed 3 September 2014.

Cavallo, Eduardo, Andrew Powell and Oscar Becerra, 'Estimating the Direct Economic Damages of the Earthquake in Haiti' (August 2010) 120(546) *The Economic Journal* F298.

CCK, 'Annual Report Financial Year 2010/11' (2012) <www.cck.go.ke/resc/publications/annual_reports/CCK_Annual_Report_2011.pdf> accessed 3 September 2014.

CCK 'Quarterly Sector Statistics Report' (2012)<www.cck.go.ke/resc/downloads/SECTOR_STATISTICS_REPORT_Q3_JUNE_2012.pdf> accessed 3 September 2014.

Central Bank of Kenya, 'Bank Supervision Annual Report 2010' (2010) <Https:// Centralbank.Go.Ke/Images/Docs/Bank%20Supervision%20Reports/Annual%20 Reports/Bs d2010(2).Pdf> accessed 3 September 2014.

Central Bank of Kenya, 'Kenya Payments System (Framework and Strategy)' (September 2004) <www.centralbank.go.ke/index.php/2012-09-21-11-44-41> accessed 3 September 2014.

Central Bank of Kenya, 'Payment System in Kenya' (September 2003) 1 <www.cen tralbank.go.ke/index.php/kepss> accessed 3 September 2014.

Central Bank of Nigeria (CBN), 'Regulatory Framework for Mobile Payments Services in Nigeria' <www.cenbank.org/out/circulars/bod/2009/regulatory%20 framework%20%20for%20mobile% 20payments%20services%20in%20nigeria.pdf> accessed 3 September 2014.

CGAP-GSMA Mobile Money Market Sizing Quoted CGAP (2009b) <www.gsma. com/mobilefordevelopment/wpcontent/uploads/2012/06/mmu_quarterly_ update.pdf>

Chaia, Alberto and others, 'Half the World Is Unbanked' Financial Access Initiative Research Brief, November 2010.

Cirasino, Massimo, 'The Role of the Central Banks in Supervising the Financial System: The Case of the Oversight of Payment Systems' (2003) <http://info. worldbank.org/etools/docs/library/155862/paymentsystems2003/pdf/Cira sino_Oversight_Coop.doc> accessed 3 September 2014.

Cohen, Benjamin J., *The Geography of Money* (Cornell University Press 1998).

Cole, Shawn, Thomas Sampson and Bilal Zia, 'Prices or Knowledge? What Drives Demand for Financial Services in Emerging Markets?' (2011) 66(6) *Journal of Finance* 1933.

Collins, Gary, 'How Over-Regulation Has Stifled the Pace of Mobile Money Adoption in Africa' (Memeburn 2011) <http://memeburn.com/2011/09/how-over-regulation-has-stifled-thepace-of-mobile-money-adoption-in-africa/> accessed 3 September 2014.

Committee on Payment and Settlement Systems Secretariat, 'A Glossary of Terms Used in Payments and Settlement Systems' (2000) <www.bis.org/cpmi/publ/ d00b.pdf> accessed 3 September 2014.

Communications Commission of Kenya, 'Strategic Plan: 2008–2013' (2008) <www. marsgroupkenya.org/documents/documents/11806/> accessed 3 September 2014.

Consultative Group to Assist the Poor, 'Notes on Regulation of Branchless Banking in Kenya' (2007) <www.cgap.org/p/site/c/template.rc/1.26.1480/> accessed 3 September 2014.

Cracknell, David, 'Policy Innovations to Improve Access to Financial Services in Developing Countries' (2013) Center for Global Development.

Cronin, David, 'Large-Value Payment System Design and Risk Management' (2011) *Quarterly Bulletin* 01/January 11.

Demirguèc, Asli, Thorsten Beck and Patrick Honohan, *Finance for all? Policies and Pitfalls in Expanding Access* (World Bank 2008).

Demirguèc, Asli, Thorsten Beck and Patrick Honohan, *Finance for All? Policies and Pitfalls in Expanding Access* (World Bank 2008).

Demombynes, Gabriel and Aaron Thegeya, 'Kenya's Mobile Revolution and the Promise of Mobile Savings' (2012) World Bank Policy Research Working Paper 5988

<https://openknowledge.worldbank.com/bitstream/handle/10986/3275/WPS5988.txt?sequence=2> accessed 3 September 2014.

Dev, S. Mahendra, 'Financial Inclusion: Issues and Challenges' (2006) *Economic and Political Weekly* 4310

Devereux, Stephen and Katharine Vincent, 'Using Technology to Deliver Social Protection: Exploring Opportunities and Risks' (2010) 20 *Development in Practice* 367

Dittus, Peter and Michael U. Klein, 'On Harnessing the Potential of Financial Inclusion' (2011) BIS Working Paper 247 <http://papers.ssrn.com/sol3/papers.cfm?abstract_id=1859412> accessed 3 September 2014.

Dondo, Aleke, 'The Status of Microfinance in Kenya' K-Rep Occasional Paper 34.

Donovan, Kevin, 'Mobile Money in the Developing World: The Impact of M-PESA on Development, Freedom, and Domination' (Master's Thesis, Georgetown University 2011).

Dorsey, Darian and Katy Jacobs, 'Financial Services Trends and Innovations Trends in South Africa: Lessons for the United States' The Centre for Financial Service Innovations.

Duncombe, Richard and Richard Boateng, 'Mobile Phones and Financial Services in Developing Countries: A Review of Concepts, Methods, Issues, Evidence and Future Research Directions' (2009) 30(7) *Third World Quarterly* 1237.

East African Community, 'History of the EAC' <www.eac.int/index.php?option=com_content&id=44&Itemid=54> accessed 3 September 2014.

Eijkman, Frederik, Jake Kendall and Ignacio Mas, 'Bridges to Cash: The Retail End of M-PESA' (2010) 34 *Savings & Development* 219, 225.

Estimate by the ITU, 'The World in 2014: ICT Facts and Figures' <www.itu.int/en/ITU-

Etzo, Sebastiana and Guy Collender, 'The Mobile Phone "revolution"' (2010) *Africa: Rhetoric or Reality?* 659–668.

Etzo, Sebastiana and Guy Collender, 'The Mobile Phone Revolution in Africa: Rhetoric or Reality? (2010) 109(437) *African Affairs* 659.

FDS Kenya, 'FinAccess 2009: Mapping the Financial Sector in Kenya' (2009)

Financial Access in Kenya, 'Results of the 2006 National Survey' <www.fsdkenya.org/finaccess/documents/FinaccessReportFINALMain.pdf> accessed 3 September 2014.

'Finscope National Survey on Access to and Demand for Financial Services in Tanzania' <www.fsdt.or.tz/images/uploads/english-finscope2006.pdf> accessed 3 September 2014.

Frazer, P. A., *Plastic and Electronic Money – New Payment Systems and Their Implications* (Woodhead–Faulkner 1985) 188.

Fry, Maxwell J., *Payment Systems in Global perspective* (Routledge 2012).

FSD Kenya, 'FinAccess National Survey 2009: Dynamics of Kenya's Changing Financial Landscape' <www.fsdkenya.org/finaccess/documents/09-06-10_FinAccess_FA09_Report.pdf> accessed 3 September 2014.

G20 Financial Inclusion Experts Group – Australian Government <http://aid.dfat.gov.au/Publications/Documents/G20financialinclusion.doc> accessed 18 September 2014.

Garcia, Sergio G., 'The Contribution of Payment Systems to Financial Stability' (2000) <www.bis.org/publ/cpss41.pdf> accessed 3 September 2014.

Gertler, Mark, 'Financial Structure and Aggregate Economic Activity: An Overview' (1988) NBER Working Paper No 2559 <www.nber.org/papers/w2559.pdf> accessed 3 September 2014.

Globe Telecom, 'Globe G-Cash – a Breakthrough in Mobile Commerce Being a Truly Mobile Solution Cashless and Cardless' (Presentation at the CGAP Annual Meeting 2005) <www.microfinancegateway.org/files/30783_file_Gcash_presenta tion.pdf?PH> accessed 3 September 2014.

Gokarn, Subir, 'Dr Subir Gokarn takes over as RBI Deputy Governor' (April 2011) <www.rbi.org.in/Scripts/BS_PressReleaseDisplay.aspx?prid=21700> accessed 3 September 2014.

Goo, Jahyun and others, 'The Role of Service Level Agreements in Relational Management of Information Technology Outsourcing: An Empirical Study' (2009) 33(1) *Management Information Systems Quarterly* 8.

Goodman, James, 'Linking Mobile Phone Ownership and Use to Social Capital in Rural South Africa and Tanzania' in Vodafone, 'Africa: The Impact of Mobile Phones' Vodafone Policy Paper Series, 2 March 2005 <www.vodafone.com/con tent/dam/vodafone/about/public_policy/policy_papers/public_policy_series_2. pdf> 3 accessed 3 September 2014.

Government of Kenya, 'Telecommunications and Postal Sector Statement' (2001) (77) *The Kenya Gazette CIII* 2675.

Greenspan, Alan, 'Remarks on Evolving Payment System Issues' (1996) 28(4) *Journal of Money, Credit and Banking* 689.

GSM Association Development Fund website <www.gsma.com/developmentfund/> accessed 3 September 2014.

Hannig, Alfred and Stefan Jansen, 'Financial Inclusion and Financial Stability: Current Policy Issues' (2010) ADBI Working Paper Series No 259 <www.adbi.org/ working-paper/2010/12/21/4272.financial.inclusion.stability.policy.issues/> accessed 3 September 2014.

Hannig, Alfred and Stefan Jansen, 'Financial Inclusion and Financial Stability: Current Policy Issues' (2010) ADBI Working Paper 259 (Tokyo: Asian Development Bank Institute) <www.adbi.org/workingpaper/2010/12/21/4272.financial. inclusion.stability.policy.issues/> accessed 3 September 2014.

Hawkins, Penelope, 'Financial Access and Financial Stability' (2006) (BIS 2006) <www.bis.org/press/p060619.htm> 3 September 2014.

Hersman, Erik, 'Do Banks Block Mobile Money Innovation in Africa?' (Memeburn, August 2010) <http://memeburn.com/2010/08/do-banks-block-mobilemoney-innovation-inafrica/> accessed 3 September 2014.

Heyer, Amrik, 'Factors Affecting Uptake of Mobile Money Services: M-Pesa in Kenya and Tanzania' (2011) <www.gsma.com/mobilefordevelopment/wp-content/ uploads/2012/03/fertile_grounds_mobile_money55.pdf> accessed 3 September 2014.

Heyer, Amrik and Ignacio Mas, 'Fertile Grounds for Mobile Money: Towards a Framework for Analysing Enabling Environments' (2011) 22(1) *Enterprise Development and Microfinance* 30.

Heyer, Amrik and Ignacio Mas, 'Seeking Fertile Grounds for Mobile Money' (3 September 2009) Bill & Melinda Gates Foundation, Working Paper <www.gsma.com/ mobilefordevelopment/wp-content/uploads/2012/03/fertile_grounds_mobile_ money55.pdf> accessed 3 September 2014.

Honohan, Patrick, 'Cross-Country Variation in Household Access to Financial Services' (2008) 32(11) *Journal of Banking & Finance* 2493.

Hughes, Nick and Susie Lonie, 'M-PESA: Mobile Money for the "Unbanked" Turning Cell phones into 24-Hour Tellers in Kenya' (2007) 2(1–2) *Innovations* 63.

Humphrey, David B., *Payment Systems: Principles, Practice, and Improvements*, vol 23 (World Bank Publications 1995).

Humphrey, David B., *Transforming Payment Systems: Meeting the Needs of Emerging Market Economies*, vol 291 (The Internastional Bank for Reconstruction and Development 1995).

Humphrey, David B., *Transforming Payment Systems: Meeting the Needs of Emerging Market Economies*, vol 291 (The Internastional Bank for Reconstruction and Development 1995).

Humphreys, David B., and Setsuya Sato, *Modernizing Payment Systems in Emerging Economies* (The International Bank for Reconstruction and Development 1995).

Institute of Economic Affairs, 'The State of Competition Report: Mobile Money Transfer, Agricultural Bulk Storage and Milling, and the Media Sectors in Kenya' IEA Research Paper Series No 1/2011

International Finance Corporation, 'M-Money Channel Distribution Case – Tanzania's (IFC Report, 2010) <http://www1.ifc.org/wps/wcm/connect/3aa8588049586 050a27ab719583b6d16/Tool%2B6.8.%2BCas e%2BStudy%2B-%2BM-PESA %252C%2BTanzania.pdf?MOD=AJPERES> accessed 3 September 2014.

Investment Climate Advisory Services (World Bank Group), 'Regulatory Capacity Review of Kenya' (2010) <www.wbginvestmentclimate.org/uploads/Kenya.pdf> accessed 3 September 2013.

Jack, Christian and Tavneet Suri, 'Mobile Money: The Economics of M-PESA' (2011) NBER Working Paper No 16721 <http://www9.georgetown.edu/faculty/wgj/ papers/Jack_Suri-Economics-of-M-PESA.pdf> accessed 3 September 2014.

Jack, William and Tavneet Suri, 'The Economics of M-Pesa' (2011) MIT NBER Working Paper 16721 <www.mit.edu/~tavneet/M-PESA_Update.pdf> accessed 3 September 2014.

Jack, William, Tavneet Suri and Mit Sloan, 'The Economics of M-PESA' (unpublished paper 2010).

Jayne, T. S. and Milu Muyanga, 'Land Constraints in Kenya's Densely Populated Rural Areas: Implications for Food Policy and Institutional Reform' (Paper presented at 86th Annual Conference of the Agricultural Economics Society, University of Warwick, 16–18 April 2012).

Johnson, Christian and Robert Steigerwald, 'The Central Bank's Role in the Payment System: Legal and Policy Aspects' in *Current Developments in Monetary and Financial Law*, vol 5 (International Monetary Fund, 2008) 445.

Johnson, Susan, Markku Malkamaki and Kuria Wanjau, 'Tackling the "Frontiers" of Microfinance in Kenya: The Role for Decentralized Services' (2006) 17(3) *Small Enterprise Development* 41.

Kalba, Kas, 'The Adoption of Mobile Phones in Emerging Markets: Global Diffusion and the Rural Challenge' (2008) 2 *International Journal of Communication* 31.

Kalil, Thomas, 'Harnessing the Mobile Revolution' (Winter 2009) *Innovations* 4, 1 <http://econpapers.repec.org/scripts/redir.pf?u=http%3A%2F%2Fwww.mitpress journals.org%2Fdoi2Fpdfplus%2F10.1162%2Fitgg.2009.4.1.9;h=repec:tpr:inntgg: v:4:y:2009:i:1:p:9–23> accessed 3 September 2014.

Kanina, Wangui, 'Kenya's Election Seen as Badly Flawed' *Reuters* (Nairobi, 18 September 2008) < www.reuters.com/article/2008/09/18/us-kenya-election-*id*USLI38786120080918> accessed 3 September 2014.

Karlan, Dean, Jonathan Morduch and Sendhil Mullainathan, 'Take-Up: Why Microfinance Take-Up Rates Are Low & Why It Matters' (Financial Access Initiative Research Framing Note, June 2010)

Kausch, Bronwen A., 'Regulating Mobile Money to Create an Enabling Business Environment' (Master's Thesis, Witwatersrand, October 2012).'

Kawai, Masahiro and Eswar Prasad, *Financial Market Regulation and Reforms in Emerging Markets* (Brookings Institution Press 2011), 287

Kempson, Elaine, Adele Atkinson and Odile Pilley, 'Policy Level Response to Financial Exclusion in Developed Economies: Lessons for Developing Countries' (2008) University of Bristol, Personal Finance Research Centre <www.pfrc.bris.ac.uk/Reports/dfid_report.pdf> accessed 3 September 2014.

Kenya Bankers Association, <www.kba.co.ke/> accessed 3 September 2014.

Kimenyi, Mwangi and Njuguna Ndung'u, 'Expanding the Financial Services Frontier: Lessons from Mobile Phone Banking in Kenya' (October 2009) Brookings Paper.

Kimenyi, Mwangi S. and Njuguna S. Ndung'u, 'Expanding the Financial Services Frontier: Lessons from Mobile Phone Banking in Kenya' (Brookings, 16 October 2009) <www.brookings.edu/~/media/research/files/articles/2009/10/16%20 mobile%20phone%20ki menyi/1016_mobile_phone_kenya_kimenyi.pdf> accessed 3 September 2014.

KPMG '"Underserved" Market Represents Opportunity for Banks' (2011) <www.kpmg. com/us/en/issuesandinsights/articlespublications/press-releases/pages/under-served-market-represents-opportunity-for-banks.aspx> accessed 3 September 2014.

Kramer, William J., Beth Jenkins and Robert S. Katz, 'The Role of the Information and Communications Technology Sector in Expanding Economic Opportunity' (Harvard University 2007) <www.hks.harvard.edu/m-rcbg/CSRI/publications/report_22_EO%20ICT%20Final.pdf> accessed 3 September 2014.

'Learn More About Financial Inclusion – Breckland' www.breckland.gov.uk/con tent/learn-more-about-financial-inclusion> accessed 18 September 2014.

Leishman, Paul, 'Is There Really Any Money in Mobile Money' (2010) <www.gsm world.com/mobilefordevelopment/wp-content/uploads/2012/03/moneyin mobilemoneyfinal63.pdf> accessed 3 September 2014.

Listfield, Robert and Fernando Montes-Negret, 'Modernizing Payment Systems In Emerging Economies' (1994) Policy Research Working Paper 1336

Lu, Yaobin, Shuiqing Yang, Patrick Y. K. Chau, and Yuzhi Cao, 'Dynamics Between the Trust Transfer Process and Intention to Use Mobile Payment Services: A Cross-environment Perspective' (2011) 48(8) *Information & Management* 393–403.

Manica, Luca and Michele Vescovi, 'Mobile Telephony in Kenya Is It "Making the life better"?' (2011) 23 <www.it46.se/projects/UNITN_ict4sd/assignments/ICT4SD_manica_vescovi.pdf> accessed 2September 2014.

Markose, Sheri M. and Yiing Jia Loke, 'Changing Trends in Payment Systems for Selected G10 and EU Countries 1990–1998' (2000) *Economic Discussion Papers* 508.

Marston, David, 'Financial System Standards and Financial Stability: The Case of Basel Core Principles' (2001) IMF Working Papers 1/62 <http://papers.ssrn. com/sol3/papers.cfm?abstract_id=1446185> accessed 3 September 2014.

Mas, Ignacio and Amolo Ng'weno, 'Three Keys to M-PESA's Success: Branding, Channel Management and Pricing' (2014) 4(4) *Journal of Payments Strategy & Systems* 352.

Mas, Ignacio and Dan Radcliffe, 'Scaling Mobile Money' (2011) 5(3) *Journal of Payments Strategy & Systems* 298.

Mas, Ignacio and Kabir Kumar, 'Banking on Mobiles: Why, How, for Whom?' (CGAP Focus Note 48, June 2008).

Mas, Ignacio, 'The Economics of Branchless Banking' (2009) 4(2) *Innovations* 57, 59.

Mbiti, Isaac and David N Weil, 'Mobile Banking: The Impact of M-Pesa in Kenya' (2011) NBER Working Paper No 17129 <www.econstor.eu/bitstream/10419/62662/1/668481188.pdf> accessed 3 September 2014

Mobile for Development, 'Enabling Mobile Money Transfer' (2013) <www.gsma.com/mobilefordevelopment/wpcontent/uploads/2013/09/enablingmobile moneytr ansfer92.pdf> accessed 3 September 2014.

Morawczynski, Olga, 'Surviving in the "Dual System": How M-PESA Is Fostering Urban-to-Rural Remittances in a Kenyan Slum' (University of Edinburgh, Social Studies Unit Working Paper, 2008) 2 <www.mobileactive.org/files/file_uploads/Olga_Morawczynski-M-PESA-2008.pdf> accessed 3 September 2014.

Mobile for Development, 'MMU Policy and Regulation', <www.gsma.com/mobile fordevelopment/programmes/mobile-money-for-the-unbanked/regulation> accessed 18 September 2014.

Morawczynski, Olga and Mark Pickens, 'Poor People Using Mobile Financial Services: Observations on Customer Usage and Impact from M-PESA' (CGAP Brief, August 2009) <www.cgap.org/p/site/c/template.rc/1.9.36723/> accessed 3 September 2014.

Morgan, William T., 'Urbanization in Kenya: Origins and Trends' (1969) 46 *Transactions of the Institute of British Geographers* 167.

Mugwe, David and Mark Okuttah, 'Mobile Money Transfers Reach Sh1trn as Banks, Telcos Link Up' *Business Daily* (Nairobi, 31 March 2013).

Mureithi, Muriuki, 'Evolution of Telecommunications Policy Reforms in East Africa: Setting New Policy Strategies to Anchor Benefits of Policy Reforms' (2011) 2 *Southern African Journal of Information and Communication*.

'A Newsweek Interview on July 1994' *The American Banker* (9 January 1995) <www.highbeam.com/publications/american-banker-p392958/january-1995/3> accessed 3 September 2014.

Nojiyez, Simphiwe and Jocelyn Muthoka, 'Barriers to Entry of Kenya's Telecommunication Industry: Is There a Market Slice for New Entrants ?'<http://reference.sabinet.co.za/webx/access/electronic_journals/jomad/jomad_v11_n1_a7.pdf> accessed 3 September 2014.

OECD, 'Policy Framework for Effective and Efficient Financial Regulation' (2010) <www.oecd.org/finance/financial-markets/44362818.pdf> accessed 3 September 2014.

Okonjo, Jeremy, 'Nature and Impact of Mobile Financial Services on the Telecoms Sector in Kenya' (2014) <www.slideshare.net/JeremmyOkonjo/1-chapter-one-nature-and-impact-of-mobile-financial-services-on-the-telecoms-sector-in-kenya> accessed 3 September 2014

Okonjo, Jeremy, 'Nature and Impact of Mobile Financial Services on the Telecoms Sector in Kenya' (2014) <www.slideshare.net/JeremmyOkonjo/1-chapter-one-nature-and-impact-of-mobile-financial-services-on-the-telecoms-sector-in-kenya> accessed 3 September 2014

Okuttah, Mark, 'Safaricom: Telkom Targeted in New Power Rules' *Business Daily* (17 August2011)<http://mobile.businessdailyafrica.com/Corporate+News/Safaricom++Telkom+targeted+in+new+market+power+rules/-/1144450/1220104/-/format/xhtml/item/2/-/56d3a5z/-> accessed 3 September 2014.

Omwansa, Tonny, 'M-PESA: Progress and Prospects' (2009) <www.strathmore.edu/pdf/innov-gsma-omwansa.pdf> accessed 3 September 2014.

Omwansa, Tonny, 'M-PESA: Progress and Prospects' Innovations (Special Edition for GSMA Mobile World Congress 2009) 107–123.

Ondrus, Jan and Yves Pigneur, 'Towards a Holistic Analysis of Mobile Payments: A Multiple Perspectives Approach' (2006) 5(3) *Electronic Commerce Research and Applications* 246.

Ondrus, Jan, Kalle Lyytinen and Yves Pigneur, 'Why Mobile Payments Fail? Towards a Dynamic and Multi-Perspective Explanation' (42nd Hawaii International Conference on IEEE 2009) System Sciences 1. See also, World Economic Forum, 'The Mobile Financial Services Development Report'.

Parekh, H. T. *Finance Forum Economic and Political Weekly* 14 October 2006.

Philippi, Irene, 'An Enabling Legal Environment For Mobile Payments And Peer-To-Peer Networks' UNCITRAL International Colloquium on Microfinance, creating an enabling legal environment for microbusiness, Vienna 16–18 January 2013, accessed 18 September 2014.

Plyer, Megan, Sherri Haas and Geetha Nagarajan, 'Community-Level Economic Effects of M-PESA in Kenya: Initial Findings' (IRIS Center Report, University of Maryland, 2010) <www.fsassessment.umd.edu/publications/pdfs/Community-EffectsMPESA-Kenya.pdf> accessed 3 September 2014.

Porteous David, 'Enabling Environment for Cell Phone Banking in Africa' <http://liberationtechnologydcourse.pbworks.com/f/the+enabling+environment+for+mobile+banking+in+kenya.pdf> accessed 18 September 2014.

Porteous, David, 'Mobilizing Money Through Enabling Regulation' (2009) 4(1) *Innovations* 75. Camner, Gunnar and Emil Sjöblom, 'Can the Success of M-PESA Be Repeated? A Review of the Implementations in Kenya and Tanzania' (Valuable bits Note, July 2009).

Poverty Reduction and Economic Management Unit Africa Region (World Bank), 'Kenya at the Tipping Point? With a Special Focus on the ICT Revolution and Mobile Money' (3rd edn, Kenya Economic Update, December 2010).

Prahalad, Coimbatore K., *The Fortune at the Bottom of the Pyramid, Revised and Updated 5th Anniversary Edition: Eradicating Poverty Through Profits* (FT Press 2009).

Pulver, Caroline, William Jack and Tavneet Suri, 'The Performance and Impact of M-Pesa: Preliminary Evidence from a Household Survey' (2009) FSD Kenya (unpublished).

Qiang, Christine Z., Masatake Yamamichi, Vicky Hausman and Daniel Altman, *Mobile Applications for the Health Sector* (ICT Sector Unit, The World Bank 2011).

Ratan, Aishwarya, 'Using Technology to Deliver Financial Services to Low-income Households: A Preliminary Study of Equity Bank and M-PESA customers in Kenya' (TechReport, Microsoft Research, June 2008).

Ross, Marc H. and Thomas S. Weisner, 'The Rural-Urban Migrant Network in Kenya: Some General Implications' (1977) 4 *American Ethnologist* 359.

Russo, Massimo and Piero Ugolini, 'Financial Sector Challenges in Africa's Emerging Markets' (2008) EMF Paper Series.

Safaricom Limited, 'Annual Report and Group Accounts for the Year Ended March 2012' (2012) <www.safaricom.co.ke/safaricom_annual_report/pdfs/Safaricom_Annual_Report.pdf> accessed 3 September 2014.

Safaricom, 'M-Pesa Statistics' <www.safaricom.co.ke/images/Downloads/Personal/M-PESA/m-pesa_statistics_-_2.pdf> accessed 3 September 2014.

Safaricom, 'Prospectus' (14 March 2008, revised 28 March 2008) <www.scribd. com/doc/7088318/Safaricom-Prospectus> accessed 3 September 2014.

Sarma, Mandira and Jesim Pais, 'Financial Inclusion and Development: a Cross Country Analysis' (ICRIER 2008) <www.icrier.org/pdf/Mandira%20Sarma-Paper.pdf> accessed 3 September 2014.

Schierz, Paul Gerhardt, Oliver Schilke and Bernd W. Wirtz, 'Understanding Consumer Acceptance of Mobile Payment Services: An Empirical Analysis' (2010) 9(3) *Electronic Commerce Research and Applications* 209.

Banks, Ken, 'Mobile Telephony and the Entrepreneur: An African Perspective' (2008) 8 *Microfinance Insights* <www.oecd.org/dataoecd/27/51/41789311. pdf> accessed 3 September 2014.

Sifers, Randall W., 'Regulating Electronic Money in Small-Value Payment Systems: Telecommunications Law as a Regulatory Model' (1996) 49 *Fed Comm LJ* 701.

Simphiwe, Nojiyeza and Jocelyn Muthoka, 'Barriers to Entry of Kenya's Telecommunication Industry: Is There a Market Slice for New Entrants?' (2013) 11(1) *Journal of Management & Administration* 136–196.

Singh, Supriya, 'Sending Money Home: Money and Family in the Indian Diaspora' in Ajaya K Sahoo and Brij Maharaj (eds), *Sociology of Diaspora: A Reader* (Rawat 2007).

Singh, Tarlok, 'Does Domestic Saving Cause Economic Growth? A Time-series Evidence from India' (2010) 32 *Journal of Policy Modeling*

Sprenkels, Ron and Aiko Pras, 'Service Level Agreements' 2 *Internet NG D* 7.

Sutherland, Ewan, 'Corruption in Telecommunications: Problems and Remedies' (2012) 14(1) *info* 4 <http://papers.ssrn.com/sol3/papers.cfm?abstract_id=1937556> accessed 3 September 2014.

Sutherland, Ewan, 'A Short Note on Corruption in Telecommunications in Kenya' (January 2012) <http://papers.ssrn.com/sol3/papers.cfm?abstract_id=1996429> accessed 3 September 2014.

Thorsten Beck et al., 'Banking Sector Stability, Efficiency, and Outreach in Kenya' (October 2010) World Bank Policy Research Working Papers <http://www-wds.worldbank.org/external/default/WDSContentServer/WDSP/IB/2010/10/06/000158349_2010100  6154729/Rendered/PDF/WPS5442. pdf> accessed 3 September 2014.

Tresoldi, Carlo, 'Report on the Activity of the CPSS Working Group on Retail Payment Systems' in 'The Contribution of Payment Systems to Financial Stability' (CEMELA Mexico City May 2000)<www.bis.org/publ/cpss41.pdf> accessed 3 September 2014.

Trust, Finmark, 'Understanding the Challenges and Opportunities in Promoting Savings Among Low Income Individuals in Lesotho, Malawi and South Africa' (November 2013) <www.finmark.org.za/wp-content/uploads/pubs/Rep_Savings_SA_Les_Mal_2013.pdf> accessed 3 September 2014.

*United Dominions Trust v Kirkwood* (1966) 1 All ER 968.

United States Agency for International Development (USAID) and Kenya School of Monetary Studies, 'Mobile Financial Services Risk Matrix' (United States Agency for International Development, 2010).

Vaughan, Pauline, Wolfgang Fengler and Michael Joseph, 'Scaling Up Through Disruptive Business Models: The Inside Story of Mobile Money in Kenya' in Laurence Chandy and others (eds), *Getting to Scale: How to Bring Development Solutions to Millions of Poor People* (Brookings Institution 2013) 189.

Vodafone, 'Africa: The Impact of Mobile Phones' (2 March 2005) Vodafone Policy Paper Series <www.vodafone.com/content/dam/vodafone/about/public_pol icy/policy_papers/public_policy_series_2.pdf> accessed 3 September 2014.

Vodafone, 'The Transformational Potential of M-Transactions' in *Moving the Debate Forward* (July 2007) Policy Paper Series No 6.

Wachira, Charles, 'Airtel Challenges Safaricom Supremacy in Money-Transfer Industry' *Business Daily* (4 June 2014) <www.businessdailyafrica.com/Corpo rate-News/Airtel-Challenges-Safaricom-Supremacy-in-Money-Transfer-Industry/-/539550/2336696/-/12nqmmwz/-/index.html> accessed 20 January 2014.

Waema, Timothy, '2007 Kenya Telecommunications Sector Performance Review: A Supply Side Analysis of Policy Outcomes' (2007) Research ICT Africa.

Wambugu, Sam, 'Mobile Phones to Offer Health Sector the Kiss of Life' *Daily Nation* (Nairobi, 9 April 2011) <http://technews.tmcnet.com/fixed-mobile-con vergence/news/2011/04/11/5436940.htm> accessed 3 September 2014.

World Economic Forum, 'The Mobile Financial Services Development Report' (2011) 4 http://www3.weforum.org/docs/WEF_MFSD_Report_2011.pdf> accessed 3 September 2014. Afghanistan Argentina Bangladesh and others Mobile Financial Services Development Report'.

<www.financialaccess.org/sites/default/files/blog/RFN11_Why_microfinance_ takeup_rates_are_low(6-17-10).pdf> accessed 3 September 2014.

<www.ieakenya.or.ke/publications/doc_download/227-the-state-of-competition-report-mobile-money-transfer-agricultural-bulk-storage-and-milling-and-the-media-sectors-in-kenya>accessed 3 September 2014.

Zhenwei, Christine and others, 'Mobile Applications for Agriculture and Rural Development' (World Bank, ICT Sector Unit 2011).

# 3 Financial stability and integrity after financial inclusion through mobile payments

## 3.1 Introduction

Chapter 2 set out the broader context of the introduction of mobile payments into Kenya's national payments system, emphasising the enabling environment and the inclusive nature that mobile payments has accorded to Kenya. This chapter considers the ramifications of financial inclusion through mobile payments by highlighting not only the inherent risks in payments systems but also the unique risks that mobile payments now introduce.

The manner in which the payment system works has importance for the financial sector as a whole, for it influences the speed, financial risk, efficiency and reliability of domestic and international transactions.[1] It also acts as a conduit through which financial and non-financial firms, as well as other agents, affect the overall stability of financial systems.[2] Moreover, it influences the effectiveness of monetary policy, because of its impact on 'the transmission process in monetary management, the pace of financial deepening, and the efficiency of financial intermediation'.[3]

Banking is one of the most regulated and supervised economic sectors,[4] and the strength of the global financial system is such that most, if not all, financial institutions are connected, and systemic events in other countries or other sectors of the financial world buffet virtually all such institutions.[5] States have therefore imposed elaborate sets of interconnected regulations on many components of the financial system, including payments systems, in recognition of the fact that the ability to pay efficiently, reliably and securely is one of the guarantees of the development of modern economies.[6]

Payments and settlement systems therefore play an important role in improving the overall economic efficiency of developed and developing nations.[7] Kenya continues to rely heavily on cash payments in most transactions,[8] as the country's high percentage of cash holdings as a proportion of the money supply reflects,[9] in spite of the risk and expense of cash.[10] However, the introduction of mobile payments has changed the landscape for payments systems considerably, because a shift from cash to mobile payments, while reducing the risks inherent in cash, brings new risks. Using ubiquitous electronic channels, instead of currency or paper, the payment system on monetary policy; rather it will highlight its effects and the need for a stable payment system for a stable financial system in general. instruments brings Kenya's payments system significant efficiency.[11]

The lack of access to financial services can exaggerate inequalities around the world, because a large proportion of poorer customers in developing nations[12] lack the ability to take advantage of some crucial financial instruments,[13] but mobile financial services, particularly mobile payments, are financially inclusive.[14] The success[15] of the integration of mobile payments into Kenya's national payment systems' infrastructure reflects this.[16] This case suggests that addressing the link between financially inclusive payment systems and stable, integrated markets through an appropriate regulatory framework has strong potential to support financial inclusion.

Financial inclusion[17] aims at drawing the 'unbanked' and 'under banked'[18] population into the formal[19] financial system, thereby giving them[20] the opportunity to access financial services ranging from savings,[21] payments,[22] and transfers to credit and insurance. The 2011 white paper prepared on behalf of the GPFI 'Global Standard-Setting Bodies and Financial Inclusion for the Poor: Toward Proportionate Standards and Guidance' defines financial inclusion as 'a state in which all working age adults have effective access to credit savings, payments and insurance from formal service providers'. Effective access involves convenient and responsible service delivery, at a cost affordable to the customer and sustainable for the provider, with the result that financially excluded customers use formal financial services rather than existing informal options.[23]

Financial inclusion does not require that everybody should make use of the supply. The supply of financial services, in this case either financial institutions or banks or any other financial intermediaries available may be financially included in an informal financial system (although financial exclusion suggests that those who are excluded are typically excluded from the formal financial system), for instance, in the case of subsistence farmers in villages who do not trust banks and therefore 'bank' underneath their mattresses.

Neither does it require that providers should disregard risks[24] or other costs[25] when deciding to offer inclusive services.[26] Therefore, regulation and policy initiatives, through an appropriate regulatory framework, should intervene to correct market failures[27] by ensuring financial stability[28] and financial integrity through such measures as consumer protection, and regulation for mobile payments should reflect these objectives.[29]

Financial integrity, financial stability and financial inclusion have varying definitions depending on their context.[30] Financial stability has a multidimensional latitude that depends on the relationship of key elements of the 'financial system and requires that the key institutions and markets in the financial system remain stable'.[31]

Financial inclusion through mobile payments, the focus of this thesis, changes the transactions that take place,[32] the consumers that use the various services,[33] the risks they encounter, and the institutions in which they operate.[34] While financial inclusion is a lynchpin for financial integrity[35] because mobile money reduces the dependency on cash,[36] it creates integrity risks[37] through the generation of data that is useful in tracing transactions.[38] The question then arises, how do regulators promote financial inclusion while protecting the financial integrity and stability of the financial system, and how do these measures manifest in other regulatory domains relating to telecommunications, consumer protection and anti-money laundering regulation? At the same time, who safeguards the payment system?

This chapter highlights some of these issues in relation to the introduction and regulation of mobile payments in Kenya and presents them as a post-financial inclusion issue. It argues that regulators need to reform their regulatory approach in developing countries, as stakeholders should not have to sacrifice financial stability and integrity to access financial services. While inclusion creates better record-keeping mechanisms that enable states to enforce know your customer (KYC) rules, it also exposes mobile payments agents, banks and consumers to money laundering and other financial crimes.[39] The continued use and adoption of changing business models within the mobile financial services framework calls for a reconceptualization[40] of the borders within which mobile payments exist and the importance of a safe and sound payments system.[41]

Although mobile payments constitute low value payments,[42] the exposure of financial institutions to risk from low-income markets depends on the share of the revenues that they present, rather than the size of each payment,[43] and in Kenya, the share of mobile payments is quite significant for many businesses.[44] Many Kenyans, who previously paid for everything in cash, have adopted mobile payments as a safer way to transact.[45] Specialised microfinance institutions and large public banks with a significant impression in low-income segments in Kenya have particularly high-risk exposure.[46] I challenge the view that large numbers of consumers 'that frequently transact small amounts put substantial strain on supervisory resources but pose limited systemic risk'.

The proliferation of mobile payments not only imposes supervisory and oversight challenges,[47] due to the large population now entering the formal financial system, but also issues such as consumer protection that arise due to the lack of sophistication among low-income consumers, whose perception of risk is low combined with the lack of a system wide financial consumer protection safety net.[48]

The lessons of the Global Financial Crisis (2007–2009) apply here.[49] The crisis brought to light the changes and reforms any financial system requires for stability[50] in the face of rapid financial innovation[51] or technological advancements. Prolonged macroeconomic stability had resulted in highly complex and interconnected systems that regulators inadequately understood. Therefore, as payments systems expose the financial systems to risks, they warrant an appropriate regulatory approach such that they are able to reduce vulnerabilities in the banking and financial systems.[52] The existing regulatory framework cannot characterise the abrupt non-linear adjustments and systemic effects that may exist at the payments systems level,[53] as the research on new macroprudential frameworks that screens instruments,[54] markets, and institutions,[55] reflects.

It should recognise the potential for instability arising from the financial system, whether from what Claudio (2009) calls 'excessiveness in cycles'[56] or from spillovers through interconnectedness. Additionally, in accordance with a study from the Bank for International Settlements (BIS), two types of externalities drive systemic risk: joint failures of institutions and the fact that the undercurrents of the financial system and of the real economy are mutually reinforcing. The former reflects institutions' common exposures at a single point in time, either through, for example, mobile payments agents or through procyclicality.[57] The latter increases the amplitude of booms and busts and undermines stability in both the financial sector and the real economy. The research also shows that each financial institution's marginal contribution to systemic risk correlates with its size in a nonlinear way. Therefore, smaller institutions contribute disproportionately less risk than larger institutions.[58] Since no regulatory body oversees or supervises small institutions' activities, especially in Kenya as a result of a fragmented regulatory authority, the effects are offset, causing small institutions to pose certain unique risks that make consumers vulnerable.

To illuminate these points, I will first construct a contextual framework for the placement of payments systems in the overall financial infrastructure in Kenya and then examine the inherent risks[59] that they present to the financial system, which the regulatory approach and framework that Kenya has adopted since the inception of mobile payments does not adequately address. I will discuss the preconditions of a safe and sound payment system, which a financial regulator should safeguard, exploring the unique risks that mobile payments systems present through a multi-layered analysis of the risk exposures at every level of the mobile payment from the MNOs to the banks to the agents to the consumers, where these risks impinge on the financial stability and integrity[60] of Kenya's financial system. An appropriate regulatory framework for mobile payments will involve balancing different objectives such as stability and financial integrity and the protection of consumers.

## 3.2 Kenya's payment system structure: an overview

Kenya has a large wholesale and retail value payment system, where value is transferred via the real-time gross settlement system (hereafter, RTGS). The Kenya Electronic Payment and Settlement System (hereafter, KEPSS) was launched in July 2005, and the Government Domestic Debt Central Securities Depository is where the operation of other securities settlement systems occurs.[61] All these are under the greater ambit of the Automated Clearing House (ACH), which handles retail-based payments.

Under the RTGS system, both the processing and final settlement of funds transfers' instructions take place continuously (i.e., in real time) from one bank to another, on a transaction-by-transaction basis, assuming the sending participant has sufficient covering balance or credit (settlement limit). The payment is taken as final and irrevocable. This mitigates systemic settlement risk inherent in large net value settlements,[62] but a bank's obligations can accumulate during the day if it does not have the funds or credit capacity to make its payments instantly.

Therefore, if a large number and value of transfers are delayed, the initial impact could resemble that of a settlement failure.

No statutory power regulates mobile payments,[63] but the Central Bank Act (CBK Act),[64] as amended in 1996, gave the National Payment System Division (NSPD) of the CBK certain implicit powers to oversee and regulate the payments systems to safeguard the integrity, effectiveness, efficiency and security of the payments system. NPSD conducts periodic examinations of system integrity and the technical and risk management infrastructure (including back-up facilities) of payment systems.[65] This covers both large-value (wholesale) and retail-value payment systems including the bank's own internal systems[66] It, therefore, subscribes to the BIS' Core Principles for Systemically Important Payment Systems (hereafter CPSIPS) and deals with system registrations; system assessments; regulations and incentives; policy dialogue; monitoring; analysis and surveys; and contact with market players.

## 3.3 The need for an appropriate regulatory approach through the examination of the pre-conditions to a safe and sound payment system

A sound payment system requires sound and effective regulation and supervision. As it protects and maintains the confidence of the stakeholders – the MNOs, the agents and the consumers – it therefore plays an effective role in the overall economic development. The safeguarding and stability of the financial system should be the focus of Kenya's regulatory authorities. This includes the market infrastructure, which would strengthen the resilience of individual financial institutions. This would sustain the ability of central banks to regulate and supervise financial institutions in a periodic manner through the promotion of responsible fair dealings in the interest of consumers all in regard to financial stability.[67]

This requires taking key trends affecting the financial landscape into consideration, including the inherent risks in the payments system and the particular risks of a mobile payments system. The increasing size and complexity of the institutions involved in the mobile payment systems in Kenya, particularly MNOs, where there are higher levels of financial services innovation, complicates the task.

As mobile financial services in general continue to evolve and develop towards even more convergence, the legal standing and accountability of MNOs must be enshrined in law. Kenya must establish a competitive and vibrant operating environment that protects the interests of consumers, who are the most vulnerable stakeholders, through reconceptualising the greater role of development financial institutions (DFIs) in financial inclusion.[68] Furthermore, addressing potential risks to financial stability and market integrity through timely and appropriate regulatory measures will protect the entire system. Whether this calls for raising the standards of corporate governance, risk management and control functions or through imposing certain requirements on MNOs, a safe and sound payment system will eventually lead to a safe and sound financial system.

## 3.4  Relevance to stability and development: a nexus of financial inclusion, stability and integrity

Financial inclusion aims at drawing the unbanked population into the formal financial system, giving those who are excluded the opportunity to access financial services ranging from savings, payments and transfers to credit and insurance.[69] While finance contributes to economic development and poverty reduction,[70] financial sector policies in developing countries have now evolved over the past decades to encourage the offering of financial services to the poor, and microfinance institutions, credit unions and savings cooperatives have made considerable progress in the last two decades.[71] This has caused the absolute number of savings accounts worldwide to exceed the global population. However, half of the world's adult population – 2.5 billion people – has no access to savings accounts or other formal financial services.[72] Both voluntary exclusion and unfavourable risk-return characteristics may preclude a household or a small firm, despite unrestrained access, from using one or more of the services.[73]

This exclusion does not necessarily warrant policy intervention, but policy initiatives should aim to correct market failures and eliminate non-market barriers that smaller actors encounter.[74]

As a policy objective, financial services to the unbanked has piqued the interests of academics, governments, practitioners and policy-makers alike. Building inclusive financial systems identifies the need to integrate the unbanked and financially excluded into formal financial systems, but it also requires that financial institutions should reach out to those who are excluded.[75] As a result, countries like Kenya have embraced financial inclusion 'as an important policy goal that complements the traditional pillars of monetary and financial stability, as well as other regulatory objectives such as consumer protection and financial integrity'.[76]

Not all policy reflects scholars' changing views on household behaviour with respect to financial services. Low-income households rely on various financial instruments in their daily management of cash flows and risks and in their efforts to build assets through saving.[77] Studies that ask poor households to keep financial diaries[78] show that a key challenge faced by low-income household is the irregularity of their cash flows.[79]

The international poverty line of $2 a day, which is an average, demonstrates a highly variable flow that requires dynamic management to smooth consumption and reduce vulnerability to various shocks, such as health crises, political instability and the ability to cope with major life cycle events.[80] Due to the influence of asymmetric information between financial institutions and consumers, shocks to the system that dramatically worsen information problems cause financial instability, because financial intermediation between savings and productive investment opportunities breaks down.[81] A deteriorating financial sector or non-financial balance sheets, in particular, threaten financial inclusion.[82] Consequently, specialised microfinance institutions are most prone to these risks, as are large public banks that have developed a significant footprint in the low-income segments.[83]

Regulators have paid more attention to issues of consumer protection, especially with respect to low-income clients and to reputational risks, as a result of the large number of customers who are involved if a particular institution fails, rather than the overall macroeconomic effects that this proliferation of mobile payments have on the whole financial system. In Kenya's context, the mobile payments system increases the risk because large numbers of clients that frequently transact small amounts represent an under managed source of risk. While others point out that these groups represent a nominal share of overall financial sector resources, in Kenya, as information technology proliferates, the supervisory challenges of large numbers of transactions become unmanageable. These challenges strain governments' resources; in addition, the share of the revenue of the mobile payments market has increased over time.

The BIS, for example, emphasises the importance of joint failures of institutions and the reinforcing nature of the financial system and the real economy. They also argue that small financial institutions contribute a disproportionately small risk to the overall system, and that since mobile payments only involve small institutions, the system cannot pose a large risk to Kenya's economy. However, Safaricom, Kenya's largest MNO, cannot be regarded as a small institution, given its dominance of the mobile payments market,[84] as its importance to the mobile payments system makes it 'too important to fail'.[85] This chapter uses the term 'too important to fail' instead of 'too big to fail' to emphasise that the size of a bank, typically measured by the value of its assets, does not capture other important reasons why its failure might create havoc. Those reasons include its connections with other financial institutions (interconnectedness), the difficulty of its resolution (complexity), and a lack of substitutes for the services it provides. Like a large bank, it poses systemic risk exposure.

Values that are transferred through mobile payments, which may be in transit on deposit[86] through trustee accounts,[87] have shifted the dynamics of distributed risk. This is through conversion of consumer risk into a concentrated systemic risk.[88] This has caused regulators globally to react in disparate ways to this risk, leading to inconsistent operating environments for MNOs. This is not to say that a global standard should be applied, since the success of mobile payments varies from country to country as has been evidenced. However, a lack of standardisation means that inconsistencies in the operating environment place limits on the range of services that can be provided, which are not predicated on underlying risks.[89] The increasing number of customers who use mobile payments and transact small values creates risks at institutional levels; though small, their volumes are ever increasing, which requires action by the CBK to implement consumer protection issues.

Although as mentioned, financial inclusion is a lynchpin for financial integrity,[90] financial inclusion also raises concerns about market integrity. The implementation of the Financial Action Task Force (FATF) standards in relation to Kenya's mobile payments system requires a risk-based approach, similar to that employed by regulators of institutions serving low-income clients, because of the direct correlation between financial inclusion and financial integrity. However, these strict requirements, such as customer due diligence through restrictive KYC rules, may limit the outreach potential. National regulations could either exclude people who cannot provide certain proofs of identity or impose restrictive costs of compliance on financial institutions.[91] In Kenya, KYC rules have not presented any real challenge, at least at the adoption level,[92] but mobile payments have created an accessible avenue for money laundering and other financial crimes. They provide a convenient and swift means to transfer illicit funds that law enforcement cannot contain and regulators cannot mitigate.

Financial inclusion through mobile payments is an ideal goal for developing countries. The imposition of unique risks threatens the development of a more inclusive financial service, as this indicates one of the post-financial inclusion issues. Furthermore, stability and integrity as a broad concept encompasses different aspects of finance and the financial system infrastructure, institutions and markets, where all actors, private and public, contribute optimal components of the financial system, which includes the legal frameworks for financial regulation, supervision and surveillance.[93] Ensuring stability, integrity and a safe and sound payment system requires an understanding of these inherent payment system risks.

## 3.5 Inherent payments system risks: a taxonomy of risks

Payments systems are coming under increased regulation,[94] reflecting governments' increasing recognition of the stability risks[95] inherent in payment systems,[96] through the acknowledgement that markets fail to protect consumer participants in the payment system[97] and the need to facilitate access to payments in the interests of increased competition, particularly in retail payments.[98] All payments systems raise a similar set of risks, and regulatory agencies tend to address them in particular ways.[99] The payments system is one of the first places where financial stress is manifested, when firms in financial difficulty fail to meet their payment obligations.[100] Similarly, disruptions in the payments system result in disruptions in aggregate economic activity. Instability in the payments system is more threatening than instability in deposits, because the large volume of mobile payments occurring daily, speedy movement of the funds and unfamiliarity with the clearing process cause concern.[101]

Payment systems, due to their nature, involve limited possible legal and regulatory approaches.[102] Any form of payment involves some risk to one or more participants in the payment.[103] Risks occur primarily because many payments involve implicit or explicit extension of credit, where a lag occurs between the occurrence of a transaction and the time that settlement occurs,[104] and because multiple parties[105] handle the payment instruments,[106] any of whom could fail to perform their function and execute funds delivery.[107] In other words, the risks in the payment system arise from institutional inter-dependency in the payment process that creates different risks among parties in the payments system and from timing delays between the transaction and the final settlement of the associated payment.

The central bank has consequently assumed these roles for the relevant currency, which transfers funds between accounts held within it by the commercial banks, known as 'settlement in central bank money', which guarantees unconditional and irrevocable settlement. Therefore, the payment lag and involvement of multiple parties distinguishes between the risks borne in the payment process itself and other underlying risks in the financial system. A payment system will provide unsatisfactory risk protection if it is deficient in security, reliability, timeliness, certainty of value or accuracy. Increasing the values and volumes of payment transactions tests these measures of the robustness of a payment system, as do long payment lags.[108]

Inappropriate design may be exacerbating risk in the system. The volume of transactions per period, the average transaction value, the length of the payment cycles, and the payment system design constitute the main factors influencing the gravity of risks in payments and settlement transactions.[109] Financial institutions in Kenya have increasingly argued that the payment system presents risk in one or more of these dimensions.[110] The governor proudly reported that on 23 November 2011, Parliament had 'finally' passed the National Payments System Bill 2011. The bill is designed to regulate and supervise the payment systems and payment service providers in Kenya.

In efforts to address the challenges, debates have centred on how financial institutions can ensure that risks are mitigated.[111] They have also tended to focus on the role of the CBK as the sole regulator. Therefore, regulations have not adequately addressed the new mobile payments system as a creator of risk; in this system, there is often a lag between the time of a transaction and the settlement.[112] Kenyans who have come to rely on this new payment system for their basic financial needs and business purposes are at risk that they will be handled securely and efficiently.

M-Pesa is a telecom-led[113] model that offers full liquidity and security outside of the banking system, which demonstrates that a payments system can operate independently of a banking system[114] and offer liquidity and maturity transformation, which makes banks less critical for the financial system as a whole.[115] Splitting off this public good aspect of banking – the payments and safe custody functions[116] – strengthens the system. However, M-Pesa still places its trust account in a bank. This highlights the interconnections between MNOs and banks. It further clarifies the nature of financial regulation in developing countries and sheds important light on the real sources of market failure and regulatory requirements in developed countries as well. Most economic transactions in market economies involve an exchange of goods, services or securities for money where money largely consists of bank liabilities and, hence, the role of payments systems is to effect the transfer of bank liabilities among those who transact.[117]

Economies depend on the systemic stability of the payments system,[118] which in turn fuels the whole economy. As Kenya has modernised its payments systems,[119] economic activity and trade have increased in response to increased industry competition,[120] and the convergence of the telecommunications industry with the financial system has spurred innovation to create inclusive retail payments systems, such as mobile payments. The sheer size of the average daily values of the transactions of mobile payments[121] has induced policy-makers, central banks and researchers to give more attention to mobile payments system risks, as well as to look at the ways in which their costs can be reduced and efficiency increased. The advent of new non-financial industry stakeholders,[122] like MNOs and mobile payment agents, through other mobile financial services,[123] has produced new threats and new opportunities for banking and monetary systems.

Mobile payments systems have positioned developing countries to compete globally through their now inclusive nature; as a result, the need for their analysis has increased. This is particularly because overall economic performance hinges on the completion of transferred funds.[124] This effectiveness establishes trust in the financial systems, particularly banking systems in developing countries, where a lack of trust impedes access to financial services. These efforts face a potential trade-off between the safety and efficiency of a payment system,[125] as well as a trade-off between risk on the one hand and speed and cost on the other. Therefore, risk is defined by the BIS as 'the possibility of something bad happening at some time in the future; a situation that could be dangerous or have a bad result'. For payment systems, it identifies 'credit risk, liquidity risk, operational risk and systemic risk'.[126] The failure of one participant in a financial market to settle its required obligation could potentially cause a chain reaction of settlement failures, which could have serious ramifications for the financial system.

### 3.5.1 Taxonomy of risks

#### 3.5.1.1 Systemic risk

Monetary authorities consider the prevention of systemic risk as their raison d'etre, since systemic crises impose real costs.[127] Payment systems do not use legal tender;[128] rather they use a complex fabric of claims on private organisations which usually distribute in the same manner as legal tender. Regulators emphasise the safety and soundness of participants in the payment system due to the large number of payments made, especially on the reliance of the creditworthiness of third parties. Contagion would occur through the failure at one point in the payment system, which would cause disruption throughout the economy, causing unforeseen losses for those parties who were not prepared. If liquidity is affected, a contraction in the level of economic activity would occur.[129]

Consequently, regulators should evaluate not just the degree to which participants in the payment system observe the system rules, but also the likelihood that a party will fail to meet its obligations to other parties. Further, regulators should require systems to have the ability to withstand the failure of a major participant; in this case, if an MNO, the platform and services provider winds up, or fails as an institution, the real costs would be to the economy through the ripple effects within the payment system itself.[130] Payments systems within banking systems, such as cheque clearing systems and fund transfers systems, have been subject to higher level of government oversight than payments systems outside the banking systems; as reliance on mobile payments systems increases, this poses a threat to the safety and soundness of a financial system.[131] The pace of financial innovation has intensified with banks, such as Equity Bank, developing their own mobile payment system, the first bank-led mobile payment system of its kind in Kenya. This increases the interconnectedness of the payments system and therefore creates the risk of contagion in case of financial instability.[132]

Central banks, therefore, have a particular interest in limiting systemic risk in large-value funds transfer systems (LVTS), with a significantly higher aggregate value of transactions and exposures than those in retail funds transfer systems.[133] However, various stakeholders in Kenya and institutions increasingly rely on retail funds transfers, increasing their systemic risk. The debate about regulation of and intervention in banking and payment systems has typically disregarded the presence of non-financial institutions such as MNOs in the system.[134]

Similarly, strategic interaction between members of the payments system presents systemic risk. Agents operating within the system make strategic decisions in an environment of uncertainty. For instance, facing concerns over the solvency of another participant, a bank may withhold payments to that participant. This may, in turn, affect the participant's bank's capacity to settle its own obligations. The overall flow of liquidity within the system breaks down, imposing settlement delays and liquidity costs on other participants. If the whole payment system or a substantial part of it ceases to function, it poses a threat to the whole payment system, in which case the operability of the entire financial system and real economy could be at risk.

Technology, a bank or the market may cause systemic risk in a payment system – a major participant bank might experience an information systems insolvency, or the settlement of transactions might cause a crash in a market. As system volumes and degrees of integration increase, payment transactions become more centralised and international linkages increase, and systemic risks pose an increasing threat. The failure of the settlement institution itself also poses a systemic risk.[135] The cost of a systemic disruption can be high. The domino effect can expand into an overall systemic crisis and endanger the operation of the entire financial system. Central banks have sought to limit systemic risk in Finland, Denmark, and Canada through such measures as the Core Principles for Systemically Important Payment Systems,[136] and these measures have made the possibility of contagion caused by exposures in these systems relatively low.[137] A study of Sweden also finds these regulations effective but points out that foreign exchange exposures nonetheless present systemic risk.[138]

### 3.5.1.2 Integrity risk

The contemporary convergence of mobile technology and financial services setting gives safeguarding the integrity of the payment system particular significance;[139] market participants and relevant regulatory authorities (such as central banks) should increase risk management procedures. Moreover, the spectacular growth of mobile payment transactions, which bring large numbers of unbanked consumers into the financial system, has highlighted the importance of regulation. Payments systems pose integrity risks; these channels permit money laundering, the financing of terrorism, and other financial risks and risks grow as payments grow. Therefore regulation should promote accessible, efficient and secure payment flows

The FATF has set international anti-money laundering (AML) and counter-terrorist financing (CTF) standards to address financial crime, and an increasing number of countries have adopted them. Conversely, interpretations of these standards were negating initiatives to provide practical and appropriate financial services to consumers;[140] for instance, due diligence requirements and the application of KYC rules did not include the unbanked.[141] This therefore became an important developmental issue, as the impact of stringent AML/CTF requirements on financial inclusion strategies in developing countries became increasingly clear.[142] The FATF responded with published reports on applying its risk-based approach to new payment methods, including mobile money,[143] and issued guidance on financial inclusion policies generally.[144] Equally, the challenges posed by AML/CFT requirements for financial inclusion compelled the FATF Guidance to suggest that there exists a need to 'take account of the nexus between financial integrity and financial inclusion and the cross-reinforcement between these two objectives'.[145]

### 3.5.1.3 *Liquidity risk*

Liquidity is the ease with which an asset can be bought or sold for money. The ease of making a payment at a given time determines a payment system's liquidity. Liquidity risk is the risk of a settlement not being realised at the desired time but at an unspecified time in the future and the risk that such a failure will adversely affect the liquidity of the intended recipient. The providers of payment services absorb liquidity pressures by committing themselves to effect payments through particular channels,[146] thereby concentrating liquidity risk. In the process they normally take on credit risks their customers would otherwise have absorbed – the risk that participants will not be paid in full for an outstanding claim. The difference between a credit and liquidity risk is that credit risk refers directly to the possibility of a loss, while liquidity risk refers to a cash-flow shortfall.[147] While the payer enters into a transaction with the intention of paying, insolvency or liquidity problems prevent the payment. Concentrating this risk, payment systems incur sizable intra-sectoral exposures, which raise the potential for chain defaults among payment intermediaries.

A well-designed large-value payment system (LVPS) usually allows users to access their funds when necessary and upon demand through intraday credit.[148] Rapidity hinges on liquidity of the system. This is evident in liquid payment systems where payments can be made at any time, at the convenience of the payee, despite the payee's current balance and central bank.[149] Unlimited intraday borrowing at little to no cost would eventually create a completely liquid system; it would also increase risk of credit default,[150] as users at one point may not be able to meet their obligations from the credit issuing institution causing a liquidity risk. This shows that the risk is highly dependent on how likely users are to default on their obligations. Hence, a compromise exists between liquidity and settlement risk, where default would not occur if there were no risks in the system.[151] This would only occur if only risk-free transactions were enabled, which is entirely impractical.

Liquidity is hence linked to the costs of payment delays and the cost of liquidity.[152] These delays could be due to various reasons, such as banks delaying payments until adequate funds to settle have been received.[153] Liquidity ensures that other users are able to receive their payments early, issue them late in order to save liquidity, while increasing costs to other users due to the delay.[154] Where there are delays due to liquidity shortfalls, users would have to seek substitute and expensive payment options. Virtually every payments system involves liquidity risk, whether as a precipitating risk or the outcome of one of the other risks. Consequently, lack of liquidity always appears to be one of the principal precursors to and consequences of the inability of a participant to settle. However, settlement risk includes both credit and liquidity risks. One of the best ways to mitigating settlement risk is a safe and efficient payments system, based on internationally accepted law, standards and practices combined with the financial health (i.e., assets) of participating financial institutions.

### 3.5.1.4 *Operational risk*

Operational risk is the 'risk of direct or indirect loss resulting from inadequate or failed internal processes', peoples or systems and from external events.[155] This refers to the possibility of costly errors in the information system, administration or organisation of a payment transfer system or when outsiders misuse or access such a system without authorisation. Operational risk arises from the potential loss due to significant deficiencies in the payment system's reliability or integrity. According to the BIS, operational risks relate to computers and telecommunications systems breakdowns;[156] they may arise from attacks on the system or the payment instrument and from consumers' misuse. Inadequate design or inadequate implementation can also be the reason for this risk,[157] as can deficiencies in the information system, from internal control or human error.[158] Even the most modern system incurs risk from human error.[159] Failing to manage operational risk may create loss to the consumer, damages confidence in the financial system, or make the system susceptible to financial crime.[160] Operational risk can increase with new technology designed for faster payment services that is increasingly complex and using open networks such as the internet, which makes security and system design less stable.[161]

Operational risk such as security risk, access risk and authentication problems are potentially tremendous. The security of a payment system can be compromised externally or internally. An outsider, such as a hacker,[162] operating through the internet to gain access, might retrieve and use the information on the system. Employees might also abuse the system to commit fraud. The system's design, implementation and maintenance also have a great impact on users as technology develops. As complexity and sophistication increase, users' expectations increase. When interruptions and breakdowns occur in the system, they can erode public confidence. With the rapid development in technology, retail payment service providers, be they financial institutions or non-financial institutions, may rely on external parties to implement, operate or support their systems. While outsourcing can be beneficial in terms of expertise and cost, it can also increase operational risk.[163] There are also concerns of inadequacy of due diligence, poor documentation of rights and responsibilities and weak ongoing management practices employed in conjunction with outsourcing activities. Some banks or industries have underestimated the cost savings from outsourcing and have unrealistic timetables, and potential disruption of operations can be associated with outsourcing system breakdowns.[164] Because outsourcing depends on drafting quality contracts for work, it can also lead to impaired quality of performance of outsourced activities.[165]

Prior to the 'Basel II'[166] reforms to banking supervision, operational risk was principally an enduring category for risks and uncertainties. These were seen as challenging to quantify, insure and manage in orthodox ways.[167] ICT systems and their manual support operations, as well as manual payment transfer processes, incur information system risks. As the use of cash declines in Kenya, information transfers come to dominate payment transfers. The heavy dependence on ICT systems in Kenya underlines the importance of these risks.

Awareness of operational risk has increased sharply in recent years, partly due to the sizable losses a number of large financial institutions have suffered over the past decade as a result of weaknesses in internal controls. The financial consequences of these rare events are extremely damaging. Further, a severe operational problem within a single financial institution can create problems for important parts of the financial system architecture. When the Bank of New York (BONY) suffered a 28-hour computer malfunction that prevented it from carrying out its securities-related activities, BONY had to borrow more than $20 billion from the Federal Reserve's discount window. Due to BONY's key role in clearing US dollar securities, other financial institutions were left with a corresponding excess of cash. Their efforts to dispose of this surplus temporarily drove the federal funds rate down by about 300 basis points.[168] A similar situation arose following 11 September 2001, as problems contributed to liquidity disruptions and problems in securities markets in the United States. In another example, a fire in New York left the Federal Reserve BONY without power for six days in 1990, which placed severe demands on operations and backup facilities.[169]

Operational risk in the financial infrastructure can also spill over into international markets. In April 2000, a software problem caused trading on the London Stock Exchange (LSE) to stop for almost eight hours. The London International Futures Exchange, which uses spot prices obtained from the LSE to value futures contracts, was also affected. A number of investors sold European shares, and prices on European exchanges fell, in response.[170]

Nor were the events of 11 September 2001 restricted to US securities markets. The terrorist attacks ultimately affected the entire financial infrastructure in the United States and parts of the infrastructure in Canada and other countries. LVPS around the world remained open during that period, and the financial architecture functioned remarkably well under the circumstances, but the settlement of bond transactions in the United States was severely disrupted and dislocations in US payment systems contributed to severe liquidity problems at some institutions. Major stock exchanges in the United States and Canada closed. The two largest electronic interbank trading systems for foreign exchange transactions, Reuters and EBS, also closed for a short time due to an overload of backup systems. In Canada, domestic financial institutions' concern that disruptions in US payment systems would prevent timely payments altered the flow of payments in the LVPS. On a smaller scale, operational problems of these types occur in Kenya when the payment system becomes unavailable. Customers lose access to their funds and payments cease. Network outage is very common in Kenya, either through the system breaking down or sabotage of the platform through which MNOs provide their services.

As well as a problem that damages the ability of a stakeholder to operate its business or a direct or indirect loss from failed internal processes, persons, systems or external events, operational risk can also result from human error, natural disasters or system design flaws, which are not impossible.[171] Therefore, operational risk refers to the reliability and integrity of the payment system with respect to the processing of payments. Any system malfunction because of information technology or mechanical failure, including unreliable electricity supply, or failures in the national communications infrastructure, presents operational risk. Mobile payments for instance, have the possibility of developing failures for various reasons, such as malware, privacy violations and malicious applications, all of which present operational risks.[172]

Any system reliant on technology may experience technology failure. Reliable and safe payment systems depend on a legal framework and basic social infrastructure to ease these operational risks, and regulators and consumers alike should be concerned about operational risk.

On 28 October 2012, Safaricom's servers collapsed. This led to the suspension of M-PESA services. Coinciding with the end of the month, this crash caused disruption to the millions of Kenyans who operate outside of the normal banking system who depended on the service to pay bills at the end of the month. This crucial role in the lives of those at the bottom of the sector pyramid of Kenya's financial services market calls for internal procedures or governmental intervention to mitigate operational risks.[173] This risk is not limited to the unbanked. Retail stores such as supermarkets have seen a significant increase in transaction volumes because they allow customers to use Safaricom. Equity Bank[174] is the second largest M-Pesa agent after Uchumi Supermarket, which was the first Kenyan supermarket to include mobile payments in its point of sale solution. The growth significantly since it became the leading M-Pesa agent in Kenya in terms of transaction volumes. Additionally, suspension of the service hit both entities. These impacts call for better protection of Safaricom's servers, or a more robust back-up server for the firm's money transfer business.

Regulators should also address operational risk related to human error, or problems with hardware, software or communications systems that are crucial to settlement. A cash position manager's mismanagement can cause a bank to face a shortage of funds. A bank's computer system can break down, preventing a bank from sending receiving payment orders to and from the payment system, and financial crimes, illicit activities, natural disasters and terrorist attacks can all cause operational risk.

Managing operational risk is intimately linked to security and business continuity. Reducing risk in these areas demands the implementation of coordinated and harmonised end-to-end procedures. Security and availability must therefore extend to all components, staff procedures, information technology (IT) hardware and software, telecommunications, power and cooling supply at the central system, subcontractors and each participant in the system. Most systems insist on technical and process qualification tests before a participant can operate live.[175]

The increased data collection associated with this transparency also poses a different species of operational risk. Mobile money users in Kenya are vulnerable to governmental or corporate abuse of the data generated by mobile transactions, as well as to cyber security attacks from outside. Privacy breaches and malware could completely erode users' trust in the payment system, reversing adoption trends and eliminating potential gains.[176]

Here again outsourcing poses a threat as unregulated third parties without clear lines of accountability and oversight undermine operational risk management. For instance, Safaricom's servers, are located abroad with a the UK-based company, Vodafone, which operates the servers that support the MNO's platform, and they are not subject to regulation in Kenya.[177]

Stakeholders, processes and technologies would have to be cautiously developed to make security an intrinsic element of all mobile payment systems.[178] New laws will have to protect the system from financial crime by authorised users. Regulation should require each organisation involved in the chain of the transaction data to protect the data while in its custody. Two-factor authentication is one measure to provide effective identity protection for the consumer and higher identity assurance to the agent. Similarly, the merchant side should offer the same type of assurance to the consumer.

These issues characterise a larger set of issues regarding reliability of identities and credentials for mobile payments. This shared transaction system is conducive to abuse by fraudsters using both technological and criminal attacks if regulators fail to establish the appropriate protection mechanisms and accountability controls throughout the mobile payment system.

However, few mobile financial services are reaching scale as internal and external factors, which range from the level of ventures, business strategies and organisational structures and the level of mobile phone penetration and competition and other regulatory architecture, usually impinge the uptake of mobile payments.[179]

These factors, though, are determinate of a successful mobile payment system; regulation appears to impose the biggest challenge.[180]

Operational risks, as I use the term, also include technology risk, security risk and legal risk. Technology risk occurs when technological investments do not produce the expected cost savings in economies of scale and scope.[181] Measures to increase payment system design and efficiency incur this risk. Security risk refers to illegal access to payment information or funds by a third party.[182] Breaches can create financial loss, risks to privacy, fraud or negligence. Legal risk exists when uncertainties or gaps in the legal framework for payments or payment systems impose liquidity or credit risk on participants.[183] These uncertainties or misinterpretations have implications for legal enforceability of parties' rights and obligations with regard to the payments.[184]

### 3.5.1.5 Reputational risk

Public opinion is critical in ensuring that trust is maintained in any payment system. Reputational risk is the risk of significant negative public opinion.[185] These opinions are a result of lasting negative public image or the loss of confidence in the overall operations of a financial institution or a non-bank that provides retail payments. Although difficult to quantify, the loss of confidence in a system may exceed the direct associated financial loss. Reputational risk can arise for instance through unwanted publicity from a cyber-attack on a financial institution's online banking network, thus affecting the confidence of users of the financial institution's payment system.[186] Institutions have become progressively more aware of the significance of reputational risk. For instance, PriceWaterhouseCoopers (PWC) ranked reputational risk as the largest risk they face, preceding both credit and operational risk. However, almost two-thirds of those institutions surveyed failed to appreciate the existence of an appropriately resourced compliance function as a key mitigator of operational risk.[187]

### 3.5.2 Summary of risks

Payments systems present inherent risks, and the specific design of mobile payments has particular risks due to the use of mobile devices to access bank accounts, access stored value or prepaid products and to buy products. This complex design presents new dimensions to the landscape of non-cash payments, where the MNO's position in the payment arena has now shifted from being simply third-party service providers to the lead, in direct contract with their users. As such, they increasingly seek to provide payment services on their own.

This complex design introduced an array of regulatory and legal issues, especially risks, as a result of the unorthodox roles played by the parties and the complexity of the legal relations in the market place. This would first require a proper understanding of the issues before a resolution is reached: the mobile payment mechanism and the actual role of each participant. Mobile payments do not represent a single system;[188] rather multiple players and providers operate to make mobile payments possible.[189] These players include MNOs, banks (which effect the payment on behalf of the debtor and remit the funds to the creditor), and a settlement agent that discharges the obligation. There are also various designs to the execution of mobile payments. For instance, a payment failure using a messaging-based approach may not necessarily cast doubt upon a proximity provider.[190] However, this separation of mobile payment failure from the larger financial system of the country presents distinctive risks. Therefore, while other governments provide some level of insurance on bank deposits, in Kenya, no standard exists requiring insurance for 'deposits' in mobile payment systems.[191]

## 3.6  Unique risks in mobile payment systems: a multi-layered analysis

This part of the chapter aims to identify the areas in which risks may arise in the mobile payments system. It aims to show the risks at the most basic, yet fundamental parts of the mobile money system, which, if left ignored, could lead to systemic, liquidity and integrity risks.[192] These risks affect all participants in the mobile payment system – the MNOs, the banks, the agents and the consumers. Examining AML issues and fraud reveals integrity risk, while examining technological standards that would be applicable to the MNOs either through standardisation or industry self-regulation reveals operational risk;[193] examining trust in the lower segment users of mobile payments, as a result of either operational risk or integrity risk, reveals reputational risk. Legal risk and integrity risks may be the most important risk categories for mobile payments.[194]

The impact of each type of risk differs, especially in the context of new financial services. The actors in a given mobile payment transaction alter the degree of a particular risk; the type of electronic retail payment instrument used and the payment scheme also affects the degree of risk.[195] This section will use a multi-layered approach to analyse the risk exposure at the different levels of the mobile payment system. It will critically assess these risks as presented by the Mobile Financial Services Risk Matrix,[196] a study carried out by the Kenya School of Monetary Studies that contributed to the clarity of the systemic and consumer risks involved in mobile payments and the choices most usually obtainable for addressing those risks. The interconnection between the participants[197] in mobile payments and their inherent risk exposures[198] and obligations to each other is an important area to be examined. I highlight the risks at every level to reveal a cumulative effect of a precipitous loss of value of aggregate mobile wallet holdings, which is due not only to the complexity of mobile payments within the financial system but also to the cross-border context and the speed of these transactions.

The study, (Mobile Financial Services Risk Matrix)[199] identifies several transaction stages, any one of which, if compromised, could halt a transaction.[200] This multi-layered analysis of the mobile payments system's risks identifies how regulators can establish an appropriate regulatory framework while protecting the financial system as a whole and, more importantly, protect consumers. I identify these levels as the MNO level, bank level, agent level and consumer level.

### 3.6.1 *Risks at the mobile network operator level*

An MNO is a telecommunications company that provides and extends the wireless network messaging functionality to provide payment services that enable customers to remit funds that are settled through its own established agent network.[201] Individual payment transactions occur entirely within the MNO and do not require the service user to have a bank account.[202] The funds in transit – paid in by the remitter but not yet withdrawn by the recipient – are in principle on 'deposit'[203] in a segregated account with one or more banks (Trust Account in Kenya) and so are within the formal financial system.[204] Since the service provider is only executing client payment instructions and not performing the credit evaluation and risk management function of a bank, these services do not, according to the Banking Act CAP 488,[205] constitute 'banking'. The Act describes 'banking' as accepting money from members of the public on deposit repayable on demand or at the expiry of a fixed period or after notice. It also describes it as accepting money from members of the public on current account and payment on and acceptance of cheques and the employing of money held on deposit or on current account, or any part of the money, by lending, investment, or in any other manner for the account and at the risk of the person so employing the money. Therefore, the MNOs, in principle, seem to have avoided the level of regulatory oversight needed for the 'deposits' held in banks. The depository bank, then, has no involvement in or responsibility for payments through the MNO's system. The MNOs provide the infrastructure and communications service, while providing agent oversight and quality control. However, this thesis questions whether this oversight and control is sufficient for mobile payments.

Kenya's best known MNO is Safaricom which, although it provides telecommunication services, is also a de facto mobile money issuer. No law or regulation in Kenya establishes[206] MNO as a distinct type of institution that provides financial services, although the National Payment System Act 2011 describes non-financial institutions that provide payment services as 'payment providers', it still does not offer clarification as to their functions and the CBK's mandate in their oversight.

Safaricom could begin operating pursuant to a 'No Objection' letter agreement with the Central Bank of Kenya;[207] it enjoys freedoms other financial services providers do not.[208] Through M-Pesa, Safaricom operates under an MNO-led[209] payment model, with the MNOs offering mobile payment services as a means to add value to their core communications services.[210] This presents legal challenges that this study highlights in Chapter 4 and imposes risks to stakeholders. The MNO incurs both operational risk and technological risks through its own system as a private institution and through the introduction of funds that are not properly screened.

For instance, the MNO or a subsidiary holds customer funds in a prepaid account. In some jurisdictions, even if the MNO assumes the bulk of the financial risk and operational responsibility of offering the service, a partner bank formally holds the licence. If the funds are post-paid, the MNO has effectively provided short-term credit or payment service to its customers, in the same way as some third-party payment card schemes.[211]

Agents are generally not employees of the MNO and thus are related only through contractual arrangements.[212] If an MNO fails to adequately train and supervise agents and super agents who act on its behalf, these agents may damage the MNO's business reputation with both the public and regulators. For instance, if agents fail to meet the required regulatory AML responsibilities, depending on the division of responsibilities where AML procedures may be carried out by agents, and if roles are not clearly stipulated and enforced, the CBK will impose capacity challenges.[213] MNO-led models concentrate transaction activities in the hands of one or only a few large telecommunications institutions, which is not only a function of the 'first mover' establishing market dominance, but also of the telecom industry players' already well-established and expansive mobile phone user networks; this concentration introduces systemic risk. Moreover, MNOs tend to concentrate trust accounts in one, or a few, large commercial banks, leading to a concentration risk of the account.[214]

Safaricom, the dominant MNO, for instance, holds its customer funds in Commercial Bank of Africa.[215] Furthermore, Safaricom's dominant position in Kenya means that it creates a large institution in itself by virtue of the nature of the transactions, being low value, high volume transactions, and those undertaking the transactions, who are a large population of previously unbanked and under banked, which increases the inherent risks of the transactions themselves.[216] MNOs should train and supervise through policies and procedures that are acceptable to regulators, which should be standardised to avoid the flagrancy of their misconduct, but this has not yet occurred.

Moreover, high concentration of risk leads to systemic risk within the broader economic context in which the mobile financial services take place. Figures reported by Safaricom as of January 2014 include US $320 million per month in person-to-person transfers.[217] On an annualised basis, this is equivalent to roughly 10 per cent of Kenyan gross domestic product (GDP).[218] Furthermore, 27[219] companies are using M-Pesa for bulk distribution of payments. Since the launch of the 'bill pay' function in 2009, hundreds of companies are using M-Pesa to collect payments from their customers. Utility companies such as the electric and water companies have more than 20 per cent of their millions of customers pay through M-Pesa.[220] These figures point to the systemic importance of payment institutions,[221] which have served as the transactional channel through which a significant portion of Kenya's GDP-associated financial and economic funding flows.[222] I estimate M-Pesa's role related to Kenya's overall GDP will only increase.[223]

However, the unravelling or forced unwinding of large numbers of illegitimate mobile payment transactions could have the opposite effect on economic growth and financial stability.[224] To the extent that M-Pesa has captured the global imagination as a successful MNO-led model, its hypothetical fall could lead to a negative effect for many MNO-led models, causing a domino effect if several MNOs' business strategies and operations are intertwined.[225] In summary,

MNOs should pose no greater risk than banks. MNOs do not necessarily face inherently higher money laundering/finance of terrorism (ML/FT) risks than banks through mobile payments, nor do they pose inherently higher ML/FT threats than banks. The risks and threats are largely influenced by the risk mitigation measures, namely effective risk-based regulations and supervision. So if MNOs are not appropriately regulated, the risk of illicit flows through these MNOs increases, independent of the risk that is inherent to payments. The lack of appropriate regulation has highlighted that risks are not related to the types of transactions but to the weakness in the supervisory regimes and supervision applicable to MNOs. Those wishing to hide illicit financial flows are likely to seek unsupervised entities to reduce their chance of detection.[226]

### 3.6.2 Risk exposure at the bank level

In the mobile payment context, banks offer banking services via the mobile device.[227] They hold the e-float[228] on behalf of the MNOs and handle cross-border transactions while managing foreign exchange risk.[229] Foreign exchange risk is that which exists when a financial transaction is denominated in a currency other than that of the base currency of the company. Foreign exchange risk also exists when the foreign subsidiary of a firm maintains financial statements in a currency other than the reporting currency of the consolidated entity. The risk is that there may be an adverse movement in the exchange rate of the denomination currency in relation to the base currency before the date when the transaction is completed. In Kenya, banks whose primary function is to take deposits for distribution in loans and other permitted investments dominate retail payments.[230] These banks are well positioned to employ risk management programmes that ensure regulatory compliance, and they have an important role as the mobile payment system deposits funds in bank accounts held by the mobile network operator in exchange for e-float.

To diversify their risk, MNOs hold such deposits in different banks. These accounts impose no restrictions of access on MNOs, and the banks face no special reserve requirements with regard to the MNOs' deposits. Similarly, no regulation compels the MNO to give notice of their purpose to withdraw large quantities of cash at whatever time, since the Central Bank treats these trusts like current account deposit in terms of regulatory policy. This absence of particular regulation makes the framework within which mobile payments currently operate vulnerable, as the MNOs and the banks have no legal obligation to fulfil expectations.[231]

The bank imposes the most identifiable risks that mobile payments systems incur, since the bank holds all deposits from the mobile money chain, including consumer funds. This forms a concentration of risk as the trust account expands; this may have a material impact on the trustee bank's balance sheet, particularly for those trust funds on deposit with the trustee bank.[232] Most MNOs use a single bank to hold the trust fund, for instance, Safaricom uses one bank, Commercial Bank of Africa.[233] Therefore a successful MNO's trust fund could become significant to the point of representing a funding concentration risk for the trustee bank, which would therefore be vulnerable to systemic risk. The trust account would also be vulnerable to liquidity risk, should the volume of items in transit through the MNO's system suddenly reduce, for example, because of losing market share to other MNOs, changes in regulations, an MNO's decision to diversify its own risks, or through civil disturbances that cause a flight to cash.[234]

The Central Bank of Kenya typically limits risk concentrations as a normal part of its supervisory activities, but it is presently unclear in the regulation whether this process includes funds held in trust.[235] Regulators typically impose this key prudential requirement to ensure that a customer's funds are available on demand. This means that funds held in trust would require the MNO, according to Brian Muthiora, 'to maintain liquid assets equal in value to the amount of money issued electronically'.[236] One common approach is to require entities to ring-fence assets[237] and hold them in a bank account in several prudentially regulated banks. All funds are then backed in the pooled accounts. These requirements would be more stringent than those imposed on deposit-taking financial institutions, which typically mandate only small amounts to be deposited to guarantee potential depositor claims.[238]

The trust account in a prudential bank imposes legal uncertainty and risks, especially in the event of bank insolvency. The stored value in the funds is usually matched to the float in the bank account.[239] The money on deposit is the float held against customers' mobile money accounts.[240] The MNO should ring-fence this money from the custodial bank's other assets to protect it from bankruptcy and shareholder claims. However, only minimal legal guidance dictates how capital reserves and/or deposit insurance should and can protect the trust account contents, how banks in distress would handle insolvency or how such proceedings would evolve.[241] This lack of legal clarity leaves many stakeholders within the mobile money transfer ecosystem exposed.

Concerns with managing risk concentrations may restrict bank's interests in providing trust services. The financial institution which holds the trust account for the MNO takes on reputational risk in the event of the MNO's mismanagement of the trust account or mismanagement of its payment system.[242] Although the MNOs claim that the funds held in trust are not invested, if this claim is false and the trust funds are invested in instruments that do not conserve their value, the liability coverage provided by the trust assets may become inadequate, potentially leading to a crisis in confidence in the service.

### 3.6.3 Risks at the agent level

Mobile payment agents[243] introduce risks at various levels. Their use can trigger integrity, operational, reputational and legal risks. Agents are engaged in a large variety of activities including, in particular, cash-in and cash-out services. Their principal role is to accept and distribute cash,[244] in principle providing cash-in and cash-out services from the customer's mobile device. In this role, the agents serve as branches[245] for the MNOs and act as the point of sale for the customer relationship.[246] As the conduit between the MNO and the consumer, the agent holds responsibility for account opening, customer due diligence and KYC compliance.[247]

Mobile payment agents are non-bank entities such as retailers (either the MNO's own retail centre or a retailer such as a small store) that manage customer registration and liquidity requirements for the mobile money users on behalf of the MNOs.[248] They offer services such as disbursements of loans or micro-loans approved by banks or by a microfinance institution. Agents also facilitate bill payments and transfers; take deposits and loan payments; allow inquiries on account balances or recent movements of funds; and open savings accounts, loans, and debit cards (all with approvals from the bank). MNOs may also contract them for additional outsourcing functions. In all, the agent may offer frontline customer service; facilitate bank transactions through its balance sheet; transform cash in-the-till into money-in-the-bank and vice versa; and need to go to the bank from time to time to rebalance its cash in the till versus its money[249] in a collateral or trust bank account.[250]

In many areas, agents' primary business is separate from their agent functions: pharmacies, mobile airtime sale kiosks, lottery kiosks, post offices or grocery stores. Stores providing services to illiterate customers who require assistance are likely to benefit from repeat business. However, the agent may not always act in the best interests of the consumer, for example, insisting that a moderate sum of money be sent in one or two tranches, each of which costs the same set commission. Agents already selling prepaid airtime vouchers may be ideally suited, in terms of technical proficiency and financial literacy, to transition to providing more comprehensive mobile financial services using the same basic infrastructure. Although agents conduct customer due diligence, this action is limited to requiring a postal address and is insufficient to protect the system. All agents go through a vetting process for AML purposes. Agents also bear responsibility for reporting suspicious transactions in accordance with AML and combating the financing of terrorist on behalf of the MNO they represent;[251] the agent is the MNOs' interface between the cash flow and the consumer.[252] To facilitate purchases and sales of e-float, mobile network operators maintain and operate an extensive network of over 96,000 agents across Kenya.[253] Registered mobile payment users are able to make deposits and withdrawals of cash (i.e., make purchases and sales of e-float) at an agent outlet, which receives a commission on a sliding scale for both deposits and withdrawals.[254]

This network of local agents enlarges the MNOs' reach to rural areas in order to achieve a higher level of penetration in those markets[255] that lack a physical bank or branch network. This financially inclusive element of the mobile payment system is one of its main advantages; it essentially enables a branchless payment system which is outside the traditional bank-led business model.

The number of mobile payments agents in Kenya has grown in response to demand. While Safaricom store revenues depend on the number of transactions they facilitate,[256] and they have been careful to control the number of M-Pesa retail agents, as of 30 December 2013, 96,000 M-Pesa agents operated in such diverse sectors as supermarkets, fuel stations and Safaricom dealers.[257] As a report from the Bill and Melinda Gates Foundation describes, there are 'over five times the number of M-Pesa outlets in Kenya than the total number of bank branches, post offices, and automated teller machines (ATMs)'.[258]

The agents hold e-float balances on their own mobile phones, purchased either from the MNOs or obtained from customers, and they maintain cash on their premises. Agents consequently face an inventory management challenge, as they have to forecast customer needs through various assessments, particularly for their net e-float needs, all of which usually require the maintenance of security for their operations.[259] Their function is to provide cash-in and cash-out transactions which hinge on the sufficient liquidity of the float at the agent outlets.[260] Mobile money liquidity and cash liquidity therefore pose key risks in mobile money deployment and in their examination of risks.[261] Various models exist through which agent networks operate. MNOs have evolved into two-tier structures with master agents who manage liquidity as the liaison between themselves and the individual stores, or sub-agents under their management framework. The master agent buys and sells cash from the MNO, makes it available to the sub-agents and distributes agent commissions.[262] 'Super Agents' who now characterise a new model, perform the functions of the aggregator of the second model which allows for the integration of the MNO with banks without it being a bank-led model. Other developments in this vein include users with accounts at certain commercial banks being able to transfer funds between those accounts and their mobile payment accounts. The agent network positioning exposes the payment system's agents to some risks; they occupy a sensitive position in the payment cycle of mobile services: the loading of cash payments, the point of redemption or pay-out, and also the sellers of the handsets themselves, which can be used to make payments.[263]

Agents are therefore in a position to falsify records or ignore suspicions of financial crime; they may also be a point of weakness if they do not perform their roles in a diligent manner.[264] In particular, agents present systemic, integrity, liquidity and operational risks if not properly supervised, as their use often triggers various risks. Among them include operational, technological, legal and reputational risks. Agents engaged in limited activities, such as those registering users, present fewer risks in comparison to those who are engaged in a larger variety of activities, such as the disbursement of funds.[265]

Agents earn money on customer registration, and their agreements with the MNO or bank usually give them additional bonuses for securing customers who regularly use the service. They may also receive a payment for each transaction. In spite of the range and complexity of services agents provide, regulators have not typically given agents significant attention.[266] Rather, they require MNOs to oversee agents by assigning to MNOs ultimate liability for the actions of their agents.[267] As both MNOs and banks continue to extend the reach of their services through the use of these agents to expand branchless banking, this may represent a significant vulnerability.[268]

Liquidity for mobile payments transactions are provided by the agents[269] who typically provide liquidity with revenues from other business activities, which include selling airtime. They receive commissions for transactions from withdrawals, much like ATMs,[270] and hold balances on their own mobile phones. The agent's liquidity management system contains airtime balances and cash on premises.[271]

The system allows agents to take cash that will prove to be counterfeit from customers. Customers may use the agent network to pass counterfeit notes into the money supply, and agents may use this money for payments. With no oversight by any regulatory authority to provide a mechanism for reporting, retrieval and criminal investigation of suspected counterfeit notes obtained from a mobile payment agent, agents represent a risk to the system. Mobile payment agents currently cannot guarantee the same integrity assurance that bank branches have in assessing the authenticity and integrity of the currency they receive.

Given that agent networks are meant to act as bank branches, regulation should set parameters for training material for use by both MNOs and their agents.[272] The training should also be modelled on bank teller training and provided commensurate to the perceived risk.[273] However currently, MNOs do not offer this training for their subscribed agents.[274] Additionally, MNOs such as Safaricom claim to provide AML/CFT/Fraud training programmes to institute and monitor agent compliance commensurate with perceived risk. Although these programmes may lead to reporting, no verification mechanism exists. Since these counterfeit currencies would be rejected if deposited in the agent's bank account, reporting would lead to a financial loss to the agent. Passing counterfeit currency, whether as cash outs to e-payments or as change on trade purchases, is a criminal issue for the police, not a regulatory issue.[275] However, MNOs should provide agent training to facilitate identification of issues, investigation and apprehension of counterfeiters.[276] Agents have not been offered any form of assistance to mitigate counterfeiting risks.

The risk of passing counterfeit currency represents an agent using access to a financial system to manipulate balances for their own financial gain. Although MNOs are responsible for their own internal security as a cost of doing business, which may threaten the financial viability of the service, agents' malfeasance may pose a systemic impact which could affect customers. Requiring MNOs to obtain fraud insurance to protect against insider threats and maintain 1:1 e-money reserve requirement in their trust account would significant mitigate the risk.[277] In addition, regulators should have the authority to arrest and prosecute agents who have committed fraud. Any required fraud insurance may not be available or may price MNOs out of entrance into the market.

Risks at the agent level occur at various levels; first, the agent is vulnerable to theft, due to the nature of dealing with cash;[278] most agents in Kenya hold their cash at their business premises and have no safety measures, such as safes or strong rooms, to store their cash, which leaves them vulnerable to thefts. If an agent is robbed, as they hold large sums of cash within their point of sale, they do not have the same security protocols that bank branches have, yet they perform financial services in much the same way as cashiers. This risk may be heightened if the volume of cash/e-money required follows a predictable remittance cycle, requiring a higher than normal cash-in-hand position.[279]

The agent may be forced to transfer all or part of its e-money inventory to the robber or other party.[280] While agents who are also merchants may find that accepting e-money as payment for goods and services reduces the need for cash in hand and, therefore, the risk of robbery, agents' contracts with MNOs do not clearly outline the responsibility for cash security,[281] and where the agent is collecting 'deposits', the cash in the till may belong to the customers, which imposes the need for greater security measures. No regulatory requirement calls for agents to have insurance or for MNOs to insure them against theft. While an insurance requirement may constitute a barrier to entry for agents, this failure poses risks to the system. Regulation might also require MNOs to provide or reimburse agents if sufficient evidence is given for robberies. This liability for the safety of their cash also poses a barrier to entry for agents, while at the same time creates a moral hazard for thieves.

Agents also pose slight but significant liquidity risks if they become unable to perform cash-out transactions and individuals or larger groups protest. KYC/CDD policies, insufficient cash in hand to meet occasional heightened demand or system or network outages,[282] which can prevent KYC/CDD and transaction verification, all might result in such barriers.[283] This verification only requires that customers show their national identification to the agent, which may not be a sufficient form of identification.

Such events pose a reputation risk to MNOs. In 2007 during Kenya's post-election violence, when agents were unable to receive the necessary float from banks and many agents in Kenya became unable to make cash-out payments, customers could not retrieve their funds in remote areas; this created a widespread panic, supporting the need for regulation. Failure of receipt of funds from an agent (if, e.g., an agent has a credit line to help manage its liquidity) due to robbery of the agent or agent theft poses a credit risk. All agents have an account with a contracting bank, but if cash in the till does not allow the agent to provide the cash customers require, panic can ensue.

In sum, MNOs do not have guidelines for the operations of their agents. Kenya's 2010 agent regulations[284] take a different approach, specifying that the bank is responsible for determining, based on an assessment of risk, the services that any particular agent should provide. However, MNOs have not made the necessary clarifications. The situation calls for an account agreement or regulatory requirement that stipulates access requirements and service level agreements for agents, similar to having capital requirements for banks; however, this creates an added barrier to entry for agents, considering the nature and characteristics of those who become agents.[285]

The M-Pesa system, for example, has complex contractual relationships across the entire system. These include the agent agreement between Safaricom and the agent, which contains a declaration of trust that favours all M-Pesa account holders. It also includes a management agreement; commercial bank agreement; customer terms and conditions agreement; and agent network manager agreement.[286] Again, depending on the regulatory regime, users would obtain these services directly from an MNO without any direct contractual relationship with a prudentially licensed and supervised financial institution.[287] Their contractual relationship would be with the MNO who, in turn, may have contractual relationships with the cash-in and cash-out agents who accept and pay out cash on the MNO's behalf.

The reputational risks described above may precipitate negative perceptions if and when there are system failures. This would reverse all trust previously fostered amongst consumers.[288] Agent-related AML/CFT lapses that result in either the banks or the agents themselves being used for financial crimes may result in the public associating the bank with criminals.[289] Although the Kenyan public has undoubtedly become accustomed to such system failures,[290] regulators should address Safaricom's accountability and whether insulation of dominant MNOs such as Safaricom from reputational risk would be worthwhile, although this may create a moral hazard within MNOs, as they are systemically important payment providers.

### 3.6.4 Risks at the consumer level

The 'consumer' is the mobile payment user. Mobile payment users have generated robust demand in Kenya, and the system's success reflects their adoption of and trust in the system, whereas payment instruments that were introduced to the market without an expressed demand from the consumers in the past have failed to grow the way mobile payment systems have, and the market environment in Africa and other developing countries is generally not consumer oriented.[291] Research on consumer protection and dissatisfaction for less sophisticated consumer segments in developing countries is sparse.[292] It is even sparser in mobile payments and retail banking service issues.[293] This part of the chapter discusses the risks identified at the consumer level; Chapter 4 will further expound on the complexities these risks impose on consumers due to a fragmented regulatory framework.

Consumers bear more risks in mobile payments systems than in other payments systems, which typically place more risk on the financial institution.[294] Kenyans access mobile payments by presenting their national identification[295] cards, which all adult citizens in Kenya receive. This offers universality[296] but in turn exposes consumers to account fraud, if for instance their national identity card is stolen and used to open a mobile payment account.[297] This creates further challenges as this risk has multiple implications: their identity could be used to access other services, and the account could also be used for fraudulent transactions made in their name. Consumers may be unable to access mobile services because an account using their identity has already been established fraudulently.

These risks are 'actual' because Kenyan national identification records do not provide verifiable details of an individual that can be used to trace or track them in the event of a fraudulent event.[298] They do not contain a physical address or biometric documentation that could be used to dispel any fraudulent activity; they only contain fingerprints and the name of the holder.[299]

This creates a challenge in ensuring KYC/CDD are maintained to an international standard,[300] as different biometric options have varying associated costs, (e.g., voice recognition tends to be inexpensive as it can occur over the phone, whereas fingerprinting and retinal scans are expensive in both technical capacity and infrastructure). This remains the remit of the Kenyan state, rather than the MNOs or the CBK; consumers who cannot prove their identity will have difficulty accessing mobile payment services.[301] This risk became prominent in May 2012, when it emerged that employees of Telco MTN Uganda had stolen around US $3.5 million from an account used to store cash which had been incorrectly sent through its e-money service.[302]

Consumers incur liquidity risks because, for instance, an agent who owes funds is unable to meet its payment obligation on time, which potentially adversely affects the liquidity position of the recipient of funds at the time the funds are due and when their agents have insufficient e-float.[303] High cash-out requests due to special events, including public events and disturbances such as the 2008 post-election violence in Kenya,[304] or loss of public confidence precipitate these events.[305] Consumers seeking to avoid this risk may decide to use super agents,[306] usually banks or larger institutions or companies, such as supermarkets, with the capacity to have large reserves of e-float, as opposed to individual agents. This further highlights the importance of account providers, in this case, agents who are responsible to customers for providing cash-out services in a timely manner and having contingency plans to deal with liquidity crises, which may be subject to regulatory review.

Loss of funds due to bank or MNO failure remains a critical risk for consumers. Because regulation does not require MNOs or banks to legally segregate[307] trust accounts from the general pool of bank assets available to satisfy creditors, the bankruptcy process may raid these accounts.[308] Even if an institution technically segregates the trust account,[309] there may not be a rapid procedure for transferring funds held in trust to another trustee, preventing access to the funds.[310] This creates by far the greatest risk to consumers as these funds receive no legal protection. Trust funds holding the value of items in transit are legally segregated from the trustee's own assets in bankruptcy, but no legislation enforces this segregation. The trust accounts should be divisible so that the risks are spread and transferable in case of a failure or insolvency.

Furthermore, pooled deposits within a trust account can create a funding concentration risk which would not protect individual customers if trust is impaired,[311] which Chapter 4 discusses in further detail. This concentration of risk suggests that if the deposits are not fully protected under bank closing, insolvency or deposit guarantee rules, consumers, who are often unaware of their risks, are particularly vulnerable. For example, the only deposit insurance available in Kenya is at the account level, and if the trust account is viewed as a single account, rather than many, the cap would be insignificant compared to the size of the trust account.[312] Since no law clarifies the status of the funds held in the bank, the value of trust funds invested may be reduced by a decline in market value of the investments, as significant and unusual outflows could present the trust with liquidity difficulties if investments cannot be unwound.[313]

Consumers are at risk of not being able to seek redress, especially when they are unable to dispute a transaction or account charge efficiently. Consumers are not able to resolve disputes with an MNO or to seek recourse to the regulatory authority to arbitrate a dispute because of the weak and/or non-existent measures available,[314] if they initiate a transaction on their own phones, or if an agent makes a transaction on behalf of a customer.[315] A lack of financial literacy by the unbanked and the under banked means that users are able to ask others to use this service.[316] While MNOs can provide an efficient dispute resolution process and clearly publish their service standards to minimise the cause of disputes, the regulator has not been able to define consumer protection for error resolution, in terms of responsibilities, time frames and liabilities, all of which leaves consumers vulnerable.

A lack of consumer protection raises the cost for consumers, which would in turn create a barrier to adoption; however, this would only be the case for those consumers who are aware of the problem; many payment users are not.[317] Additionally, the CBK may not have the capacity to handle complaints or disputes, which puts additional burden on the regulator. The only incentive for resolving customer disputes will be customer retention and reputation, which will be stronger in competitive environments.

Another, more minimal, risk that consumers face is government taxation. The Kenyan government may decide to tax transactions to raise funds and meet its financial obligations, which would increase the marginal cost of each transaction. The high volume of transactions in the mobile payment system presents an opportunity for government. If governments decide to institute a transaction tax on mobile payment system transactions, they will raise the marginal cost of each transaction to consumers (as MNOs would pass this cost along), thus pricing out many of the consumers that the system most benefits.[318] Low cost largely drives the high adoption rate of mobile payments in most communities, and the benefits of expanding access to financial services. Any transaction tax will reduce the system's volume, and consumers that leave the system will be the poorest, as they are the most price-sensitive.[319]

Lastly, the lack of network interoperability[320] prevents consumers from transacting with desired parties. Although this hindrance is beyond the scope of this thesis, it is worthwhile to mention that dominant players have closed loop networks with no capability to transfer funds between account holders with different MNOs' payment networks due to lack of interoperability. Since the first MNO to enter, Safaricom, has limited competition amongst other providers, this creates a pricing issue for those less able to afford other means of payments.[321]

## 3.7 Conclusion

In this chapter, I have shown that disturbances that disrupt the payment system can have profound ramifications across the economy. Payments systems represent the connective tissue of all financial and real economic activity, as the ability to settle transactions and the confidence that the counterparties will do likewise, underpins it. Therefore, payments systems can be a key channel for the transmission of shocks across institutions and markets, even when they are not the original source. From this perspective, payment systems, and particularly mobile payment systems, deserve particular attention, given that they lie at the heart of the settlement process.[322] Furthermore, this lack of clarity in the legal framework can be a source of risk in its own right, to the extent that it creates uncertainty about or leads to incorrect perceptions of exposures to potential losses.[323] Therefore regulators, particularly the central banks, must take an active interest in payment systems to safeguard the soundness and smooth functioning of the financial system.[324]

Regulators need to examine the risks in mobile payment systems in order to ensure an effective financial system, protect consumers and establish an appropriate regulatory framework for mobile payments. The extensive growth[325] of mobile payments in Kenya makes this imperative. Given the unintended[326] benefit of increasing public involvement[327] in the formal financial system – including expansion of savings accounts in the banks extending systemic exposure[328] – by converting widely distributed consumer risk into a concentrated systemic risk, the system presents an important vulnerability[329] to the Kenyan economy, given the value of the 'float'[330] in transit on 'deposit',[331] through 'trustee accounts'.[332] The Central Bank does not exclusively provide these payments, but as a prudential regulator it should do so, as a means of mitigating risk. The purpose of this chapter is to contribute to these debates and to promote well-balanced regulatory approaches, as scholars do not always clearly understand international standards. Ill-designed and overly rigid (AML/CFT) regulatory frameworks create conditions that favour informal financial channels, which undermine the very objectives of AML/CFT efforts and hamper the progress of financial inclusion.

The most vulnerable stakeholders are exposed to risks they may not recognise, either through perceived risks or risks to retail payments. Risks that affect consumers are not readily addressed, even in the form of guidelines that spell out the nature and types of risks involved.[333]

In conclusion, while mobile financial services in general, and mobile payments in particular, have been very inclusive, consumers who are the most vulnerable segment of the mobile payment system need to be protected through the examination of the gaps in the legal and regulatory framework that have left consumers vulnerable. Chapter 4 will discuss the legal and regulatory challenges in regulating mobile payments. The reliance of a financial system for its stability on the soundness of institutions, the stability of markets, the absence of shocks[334] and minimal volatility has been pointed out, along with the difficulty of achieving these through individual private actions and unfettered market forces alone. In addition, the chapter has pointed to the public sector's role in fostering financial stability as opposed to private collective action, making way for the private sector to achieve an optimum result on its own to take a proactive role necessary to achieve the full private and social benefits of finance.

To create the required regulatory framework requires a discussion of the preconditions to a safe and sound payment system. This should occur either through the examination of macroprudential or microprudential requirements. A further examination of who safeguards the payment system should be enhanced, which this thesis will attempt to highlight in Chapter 4 through the analysis of the role of the financial regulator. Despite the fact that the improvements in payment methods and payment innovations have contributed to more efficient trade and economic specialisation, both at national and international levels, bringing about financial inclusion, I have argued that regulators need to have complementary policy objectives that strike a balance between strict KYC controls and lax regulation. Given the lack of compromise between financial inclusion and financial integrity, payment systems such as mobile payments have a significant role in enhancing systemic risk, as they have become a significant component of the national payment system of Kenya and, therefore, have the potential to generate and transmit systemic disturbances to the financial sector.[335]

## Notes

1 Roger Ferguson, 'Should Financial Stability Be an Explicit Central Bank Objective?' (Presentation at the policy panel of BIS Conference on 'Monetary Stability, Financial Stability and the Business Cycle', (2003) 18 *BIS Papers* 7–15.
2 Wilhelmina C. Mañalac, Agnes M. Yap and Magno Torreja, Jr., 'Real Time Gross Settlement (RTGS) System and Its Implications'(2003) <www.bsp.gov.ph/downloads/publications/2003/BSR2003_03.pdf> accessed 3 September 2014. See generally, Andrew Crockett, 'The Theory and Practice of Financial Stability' (1997) 144 *De Economist* 531; Garry J. Schinasi, 'Defining Financial Stability' (EPub) (International Monetary Fund 2004) which states that there is no analytical framework for defining financial stability, but that financial stability can be assessed through the safety and soundness of a financial system.
3 Ibid., Wilhelmina Mañalac, at 25; See also, *Omotunde EG Johnson, Payment Systems, Monetary Policy and the Role of the Central Bank* (International Monetary fund 1998). However, this study does not discuss the impact of monetary policy.
4 Many states review banking balance sheets as often as daily, which is internationally recognised by banking principles such as those put forward by the Bank of International Settlement.
5 Daniel C. Hardy, 'Regulatory Capture in Banking' (2006) 34 *International Monetary Fund*
6 Leon Perlman, 'Mobile Money and Financial Inclusion' (2012) <www.cellular.co.za/042012-mmoney-inclusion.htm> accessed 3 September 2014.
7 Although neither the United Nations nor any other authority provides an established convention for the designation of 'developed' and 'developing' countries or areas. 'Composition of Macro Geographical (Continental) Region' <http://unstats.un.org/unsd/methods/m49/m49regin.htm#ftnc> accessed 3 September 2014. I also use the words 'developed' and 'developing' for statistical convenience, although they do not necessarily express a judgment about the stage reached by a particular country or area in the development process. Also see, 'United Nations Statistics Division – Standard Country and Area Codes Classifications (M49)'. <Unstats.un.org> accessed 15 January 2014.' However, the examination of gross domestic product offers a universally accepted requirement for this definition.
8 Cash dominance refers to the preference of people to use cash as the main instrument of payment rather than other non-cash forms of payments such as cheques

or bank cards. See generally, Simone Di Castri, 'Mobile Money: Enabling Regulatory Solutions' GSMA, London, United Kingdom available at <www.gsma.com/mobilefordevelopment/wp-content/uploads/2013/02/MMU-Enabling-Regulatory-Solutions-di-Castri-2013.pdf> accessed 14 August 2014.

9  Central Bank of Kenya Publication, 'Kenya Payments System (Framework and Strategy)' (2004) <www.docin.com/p-433903551.html> accessed 3 September 2014.

10 Cash in transit concerns where money may be stolen at the points of sale, or in transit to the bank.

11 Leon Perlman, 'Mobile Money and Financial Inclusion' (2012) <http://cellular.co.za/042012-mmoney-inclusion.htm> accessed 3 September 2014.

12 Ibid.

13 These can include seamless and efficient savings facilities and payments networks that are some of the hallmarks of developed nations. Ibid. See also, Ferguson, The Ascent of Money: A Financial History of the World (2008) 16

14 See Chapter 2 on Financial Inclusion A Resultant Success of Mobile Payments.

15 See Section 3.3.1. Relevance to Stability and Development.

16 'Mobile financial services' is the collective term for financial services provided through mobile phones or mobile phone networks as a platform for delivery. Mobile payments are now part of the varied payments instruments first mentioned in 2007. <www.centralbank.go.ke/index.php/retail-payment-statistics/mobile-payments?yr=2014> accessed 3 September 2014.

17 Chapter 2, 2.5.1 Definition of Financial Inclusion. 38.

18 The 'unbanked' and the 'under banked' will be used in this study to refer to persons who do not have a bank account or those who rely on alternative financial services. See Federal Deposit Insurance Corporation (FDIC),'Tapping the Unbanked Market Symposium' <www.fdic.gov/news/conferences/TUM_bio.html> accessed 3 September 2013.

19 Though I use formal financial system in this case, there are informal financial systems that exist in developing countries which unbanked and under banked persons in these countries use and trust over the formal financial systems. See generally, Meghana Ayyagari and Asli Demirgüç-Kunt, 'Formal Versus Informal Finance:Evidence from China'(2007) <http://siteresources.worldbank.org/INTFR/Resources/Formal_verus_Informal_Finance_Evidence_from_China.pdf> accessed 3 September 2014; Mukwanason Hyuha, Mo Ndanshau and Jonas Paul Kipokola, *Scope, Structure and Policy Implications of Informal Financial Markets in Tanzania* (African Economic Research Consortium 1993).

20 Alfred Hannig, Stefan Jansen, 'Financial Inclusion and Financial Stability' (2010) ADBI Working Paper Series No 259 <www.adbi.org/files/2010.12.21.wp259.financial.inclusion.stability.policy.issues.pdf> accessed 3 September 2014. The financially excluded, which this thesis will not delve into include, are those who cannot access formal financial services. As elaborated in: Amitabh Saxena, 'Accelerating Financial Inclusion through Innovative Channels: 10 Obstacles for MFIs Launching Alternative Channels – and What Can Be Done About Them' (2009) 27 <http://goo.gl/BwmHj>; Ahmed Dermish and others, 'Branchless and Mobile Banking Solutions for the Poor: A Survey of the Literature' (2011) 6 *Innovations* 81; KPMG Study, 'Underserved" Market Represents Opportunity for Banks,' <http://goo.gl/FHzAj> accessed 3 September 2014; Oya P. Ardic, Maximilien Heimann and Nataliya Mylenko, 'Access to Financial Services and the Financial Inclusion Agenda around the World: A Cross-Country Analysis with a New Data Set' (2011) (The World Bank, Financial and Private Sector Development, Financial Access Team of the Consultative Group to Assist the Poor) Policy Research Working Paper No 5537, 1–55 <http://goo.gl/8EZS3>

accessed 3 September 2014; Thorsten Beck, Asli Demirgüç-Kunt and Ross Levine, 'Finance, Inequality, and the Poor' (2007) 12(1) *Journal of Economic Growth* 27–49 <http://goo.gl/0Pkyi;> accessed 3 September 2014; Thorsten Beck, Asli Demirgüç-Kunt and Maria M. Peria, 'Reaching Out: Access to and Use of Banking Services Across Countries' (2007) 85(1) *Journal of Financial Economics* 234–266, available at <www.yearofmicrocredit.org/docs/Reaching_Out_Sept9.pdf> accessed 3 September 2014.

21 For instance, through M-Kesho which is a bank account enabling the user to send money/transfer funds between the bank account (M-KESHO) and M-PESA system (Deposit & Withdrawal) <www.equitybank.co.ke/index.php/self-service/mobile-banking/m-kesho> accessed 3 September 2014.

22 For instance, through M-Pesa.

23 Global Partnership for Financial Inclusion. See also, Alfred Hannig and Stefan Jansen, 'Financial Inclusion and Financial Stability: Current Policy Issues' <www.econstor.eu/bitstream/10419/53699/1/654899762.pdf> accessed 3 September 2014.

24 The inherent payment systems risks, which Section 3.3. Pre-Conditions to a Safe and Sound Payment System: The Need for an Appropriate Regulatory Approach will discuss. The likelihood of the dispersion of problems derived from system participants to the financial system as a whole via payment systems has increased the importance of payment systems risks. Risks emerging from payment systems can be mainly classified as credit risk, liquidity risk, and operational risk. Federal Reserve Policy on Payment System Risk <www.federalreserve.gov/paymentsystems/psr_policy.htm?> accessed 3 September 2014.

25 Costs any financial provider incurs in order to scale up their services such as the cost of setting up branches or a branch network in remote areas.

26 Financially inclusive services, see, Mark Pickens, David Porteous and Sarah Rotman, 'Banking the Poor via G2P payments' 58 Focus Note and also Tilman Ehrbeck, Mark Pickens and Michael Tarazi, 'Financially Inclusive Ecosystems: The Roles of Government Today' (2012) 76 *Focus Note*

27 The causes of market failure occur due to inefficiency in the allocation of goods and services. Although markets are imperfect, government intervention through regulation may seek to correct distortions from mobile financial services markets to improve efficiency. See *Tyler Cowen: The Theory of Market Failure: A Critical Examination* (George Mason University Press 1988).

28 Garry Schinasi, *Safeguarding Financial Stability: Theory and Practice* (International Monetary Fund 2005)

29 Mwangi Kimenyi and Njuguna Ndung'u, 'Expanding the Financial Services Frontier: Lessons from Mobile Phone Banking in Kenya' (Brookings Institution, October. R. W. Ferguson, 'Should Financial Stability be an Explicit Central Bank Objective' Challenges to Central Banking from Globalized Financial Systems, International Monetary Fund, Washington DC 2008.

30 Chatain and others have documented that this exposure typically had not existed before. Financial inclusion, financial stability, financial integrity and financial consumer protection can have varying definitions depending on the context. The 2011 white paper prepared on behalf of the Global Standard-Setting Bodies and Financial Inclusion for the Poor: 'Toward Proportionate Standards and Guidance', defines financial inclusion as 'a state in which all working age adults have effective access to credit, savings, payments, and insurance from formal service providers. Effective access involves convenient and responsible service delivery, at a cost affordable to the customer and sustainable for the provider, with the result that financially excluded customers use formal financial services rather than existing informal options.'

31  Alfred Hannig and Stefan Jansen, 'Financial Inclusion and Financial Stability: Current Policy Issues' (2010) ADBI Working Paper Series No 259 <www.adbi.org/files/2010.12.21.wp259.financial.inclusion.stability.policy.issues.pdf> accessed 3 September 2014; Andrew Crockett, 'Market Discipline and Financial Stability' (2002) 26 *Journal of Banking & Finance* 977

32  Where the transactions have been steadily increasing since the inception of M-Pesa in 2007. In 2007 the transactions totalled 1.5 billion Kenya shillings; in 2014, the figure was 351 billion Kenya shillings, <www.centralbank.go.ke/index.php/retail-payment-statistics/mobile-payments?yr=2014> accessed 3 September 2014.

33  Ibid., pg. 3.

34  Both financial institutions and non-financial institutions, stakeholders, MNOS, and mobile payments agents, through the convergence of the telecoms and the financial industries.

35  Claire Alexandre and Lynn Chang Eisenhart, 'Mobile Money in Developing Countries: Financial Inclusion and Financial Integrity: Mobile Money As an Engine of Financial Inclusion and Lynchpin of Financial Integrity' (2013) 8 *Wash JL Tech & Arts* 285.

36  Roger Ballard, 'Coalitions of Reciprocity and the Maintenance of Financial Integrity within Informal Value Transmission Systems: The Operational Dynamics of Contemporary Hawala Networks' (2005) 6 *Journal of Banking Regulation* 4; also, Global Financial Integrity, 'Illicit Financial Flows from Africa: Hidden Resource for Development' <www.gfintegrity.org/storage/gfip/documents/reports/gfi_africareport_web.pdf> accessed 3 September 2014.

37  Valerie Dias, 'Evaluating the Integrity of Consumer Payment Systems' <www.visaeurope.com/idoc.ashx?docid=ee00fe8c-ca32-4d75-bf90-de1ff5e7d5ae&version=-1> accessed 3 September 2014; Pierre-Laurent Chatain et al, *Protecting Mobile Money Against Financial Crimes: Global Policy Challenges and Solutions* (World Bank Publications 2011); Dev Kar and Devon Cartwright-Smith, 'Illicit Financial Flows from Developing Countries: 2002–2006' (GFI 2006) <www.gfintegrity.org/storage/gfip/executive%20-%20final%20version%201-5-09.pdf> accessed 3 September 2014.

38  Simone Di Castri, 'Mobile Money: Enabling Regulatory Solutions' (2013) <www.gsma.com/mobilefordevelopment/wp-content/uploads/2013/02/MMU-Enabling-Regulatory-Solutions-di-Castri-2013.pdf> accessed 3 September 2014.

39  See, James Gobert and Maurice Punch, *Rethinking Corporate Crime* (Cambridge University Press 2003).

40  This term refers to the redefining of conventional or traditional views or approaches to how financial services, especially innovative financial services, have been defined.

41  Claudio E. Borio and Renato Filosa, 'The Changing Borders of Banking: Trends and Implications' (1994) BIS Working Paper No 23 <http://papers.ssrn.com/sol3/Delivery.cfm/SSRN_ID868431_code543654.pdf?abstractid=868431&mirid=1> accessed 3 September 2014. This paper explores the analytical questions concerned with the case for and against closer integration between different financial activities and the implications for prudential regulation and supervision. Their intention was to provide a general framework and cross-country background against which the interrelations between the various policy issues can be highlighted. This is juxtaposed against the interrelationship between the various regulatory authorities and the complexities in prudential regulation.

42  Michael Klein and Ignacio Mas, 'A Note on Macro-financial Implications of Mobile Money Schemes' (2012) Frankfurt School Working Paper No 188 <http://papers.ssrn.com/sol3/Delivery.cfm/SSRN_ID2033816_code829576.

pdf?abstractid=2033816&mirid=1> accessed 3 September 2014. See also Amir Herzberg, 'Payments and Banking with Mobile Personal Devices' (2003) 46 *Communications of the ACM* 53.

43 Dale F. Gray, Robert C. Merton and Zvi Bodie, A New Framework for Analyzing and Managing Macrofinancial Risks of an Economy (2006) Working Paper No 07–026 <www.hbs.edu/faculty/Pages/download.aspx?name=07-026.pdf> accessed 3 September 2014.

44 Ibid., pg. 39. Thirty-one per cent of Kenya's GDP is spent through mobile phones; MNOs are clearly 'too important to fail'.

45 Financial Stability Report, 'Kenya 2012' (2012) 47 <www.centralbank.go.ke/images/docs/kfs/financial%20stability%20report%202012.pdf> accessed 3 September 2014.

46 Equity Bank is one such bank that has developed this impression on the low-income segments of Kenya's population.

47 Chapter 4 discusses these challenges.

48 *Consumer Understanding of Financial Risk* (FSA Consumer Reach 2004) 33. Information asymmetries contribute to the justification for consumer protection. See Olga Morawczynski and Mark Pickens, 'Poor People using Mobile Financial Services: Observations on Customer Usage and Impact from M-PESA.' (2009) <http://www-wds.worldbank.org/external/default/WDSContentServer/WDSP/IB/2009/09/11/000333037_2009091 1001822/Rendered/PDF/503060BRI0Box31MPESA1Brief01PUBLIC1.pdf> accessed 3 September 2014.

49 This is the period between 2007 and 2009, as defined in John Raymond LaBrosse, Rodrigo Olivares- Caminal and Dalvinder Singh, *Financial Crisis Containment and government Guarantees* (Edward Elgar 2013). See also Anup Shah, 'Global Financial Crisis' (2013) 25 *Global Issues*; Kevin Rudd, 'The Global Financial Crisis' (2009) *The Monthly* <www.themonthly.com.au/issue/2009/february/1319602475/kevin-rudd/global-financial-crisis> accessed 3 September 2014.

50 Prassana Gai, *Systemic Risk: The Dynamics of Modern Financial Systems* (OUP 2013); also, Prasanna Gai and Sujit Kapadia, 'Contagion in Financial Networks' (2007) <http://www2.warwick.ac.uk/fac/soc/economics/staff/academic/miller/esrcproffellows/summer2007/programme2/prasanna_gai_-_contagion infinancialnetworks.pdf> accessed 3 September 2014.

51 Dan Awrey '*Complexity, Innovation and the Regulation of Modern Financial Markets*' (2012) 2(2) *Harvard Business Law Review* 235; Dan Awrey, 'Regulating Financial Innovation: A More Principles-based Alternative?' (2011) 5(2) *Brooklyn Journal of Corporate, Financial and Commercial Law* 273, although this term is open to interpretation, however; see William Silber, *Towards a Theory of Financial Innovation* (Lexington Books 1975).

52 Piet Clement, 'The Term "Macroprudential": Origins and Evolution' (2010) 6 *BIS Quarterly Review* 59; Claudio Borio and Christopher J. Green, 'Implementing the Macroprudential Approach to Financial Regulation and Supervision' Ben Bernanke, 'Implementing a Macroprudential Approach to Supervision and Regulation' (2011) <www.federalreserve.gov/newsevents/speech/bernanke20110505a.pdf> accessed 3 September 2014.

53 IMF, 'Singapore: Financial System Stability Assessment, including Reports on the Observance of Standards and Codes on the following topics: Banking Supervision, Insurance Regulation, Securities Regulation, Payment and Settlement Systems, Monetary and Financial Policy Transparency, and Anti- Money Laundering' (2004) <www.imf.org/external/pubs/ft/scr/2004/cr04104.pdf> accessed 3 September 2014; 'Trade-offs and Synergies between Financial Inclusion and Financial Stability' (7 Aug. 2014) <www.adbi.org/workingpaper/2010/12/21/4272.

financial.inclusion.stability.policy.issues/tradeoffs.and.synergies.between.finan
cial.inclusion stability/> accessed 3 September 2014.

54  Alfred Hannig and Stefan Jansen, 'Financial Inclusion and Financial Stability: Current Policy Issues' (2010) ADBI Working Paper Series No 259 <www.adbi.org/
files/2010.12.21.wp259.financial.inclusion.stability.policy.issues.pdf>     accessed
3 September 2014.

55  Stijn Claessens, Swati R. Ghosh and Roxana Mihet, 'Macro Prudential Policies
to Mitigate Financial Vulnerabilities in Emerging Markets' (2014) 155 <www.
worldbank.org/content/dam/Worldbank/document/Poverty%20documents/
EMERGING_WB_CH05_155–178.pdf> accessed 3 September 2014.

56  Claudio E. Borio and Mathias Drehmann, 'Towards an Operational Framework
for Financial Stability: "Fuzzy" Measurement and Its Consequences' (2009)
Working Paper No 284 <www.bis.org/publ/work284.htm> accessed 3 September 2014.

57  Procyclicality refers to the tendency of financial variables to fluctuate around a
trend during the economic cycle. Increased procyclicality, thus, simply means
fluctuations with broader amplitude such as the fluctuation of gross domestic
products. Jean-Pierre Landau, Procyclicality: What It Means and What Could Be
Done (2009) Also see, Claudio Borio, Craig Furfine and Philip Lowe, 'Procyclicality of the Financial System and Financial Stability: Issues and Policy Options'
BIS Papers No 1 <www.bis.org/publ/bppdf/bispap01a.pdf> accessed 3 September 2014. This explains that procyclicality refers to the tendency of financial variables to fluctuate around a trend during the economic cycle.

58  Alfred Hannig and Stefan Jansen, 'Financial Inclusion and Financial Stability: Current Policy Issues' (2010) ADBI Working Paper Series No 259 <www.adbi.org/
files/2010.12.21.wp259.financial.inclusion.stability.policy.issues.pdf> accessed
3 September 2014.

59  The probability of a loss arising out of circumstances or existing in an environment in the absence of any action to control or modify the circumstances.

60  This thesis uses market integrity narrowly, to encompass anti-money laundering
initiatives and efforts to counter the financing of terrorism where a broader concept would also cover transparency and government elements.

61  Central Bank of Kenya, 'Presentation to the Board of Directors of Domestic Regulators July 2009' (2009) <http://goo.gl/6cK6D> accessed 3 September 2014.

62  Kenya Electronic Payment and Settlement System (KEPSS) <www.centralbank.
go.ke/index.php/2012-09-21-11-44-41/kepss> accessed 3 September 2014.

63  The National Payments System Act was enacted in 2013, but the Act is not fully
operational as of this writing. Payment Systems in Kenya 2003 page 1 Central
Bank Publication, although the CBK published a framework and strategy document on the payment system in 2013 that mooted a drafted national payment
system bill. In the absence of any payment laws, the Payment Systems Division has
the authority to ask for information from non-bank payment service providers,
but it does not have the power to inspect them.

64  The CBK considers oversight of payment systems to be one of its core functions.
CBK (2009c) Section (4).

65  National Payments Systems Framework (August 2004) <www.docstoc.com/
docs/83536188/nps_framework> accessed 3 September 2014. This involves
requisitioning selected information from system participants or through regular
off-site data reporting by participants and system operators and onsite inspections
or online monitoring of real time payment and settlement flows and of risk levels
across the payment systems.

66  The Kenyan Payment System consists of electronic payment systems, ATM networks (maintained by large banks), KenSwitch (maintained by some small and
medium banks), PESA point (maintained by a private provider linked to one

commercial bank), remittances (commercial banks licensed to send/receive domestic/foreign remittances), the Post Office Savings Bank (receives foreign remittances), Western Union (uses agents) sends and receives.

67 'Safeguarding the Stability of the Financial System' <www.bnm.gov.my/files/publication/fsbp/en/06_Safeguarding_the_Stability_Financial_System.pdf> accessed 18 September 2014.

68 Ibid.

69 Alfred Hannig and Stefan Jansen, 'Financial Inclusion and Financial Stability: Current Policy Issues' (2010) ADBI Working Paper Series No 259 <www.adbi.org/files/2010.12.21.wp259.financial.inclusion.stability.policy.issues.pdf> accessed 3 September 2014; Thorsten Beck, Asli Demirgüç-Kunt and Maria S. Martinez Peria, 'Banking Services for Everyone? Barriers to Bank Access and Use Around the World' (2008) 22(3) *World Bank Economic Review* 397–430 <http://papers.ssrn.com/sol3/papers.cfm?abstract_id=1318112> accessed 3 September 2014; John Caskey, Clemente Duran and Tova M. Solo, 'The Urban Unbanked in Mexico and the United States' (2006) World Bank Policy Research Working Paper No 3835 <http://www-wds.worldbank.org/external/default/WDSContentServer/WDSP/IB/2006/01/26/000016406_20060126162730/Rendered/PDF/wps3835.pdf> accessed 3 September 2014.

70 Alberto Chaia et al., 'Half the World Is Unbanked' (2011) <http://financialaccess.org/sites/default/files/110109%20HalfUnbanked_0.pdf> accessed 3 September 2014; Also, Tushar K. Das, 'Financial Inclusion and Regulation in India' (2012) <http://eldis.org/vfile/upload/1/Document/1306/FIRI2.pdf> accessed 3 September 2014.

71 Stijn Claessens, 'Access to Financial Services: A Review of the Issues and Public Policy Objectives' (2006) 21(2) *World Bank Research Observer* 207–240 <http://www-wds.worldbank.org/servlet/WDSContentServer/WDSP/IB/2005/05/15/000090341_20050515132903/ Rendered/INDEX/wps3589.txt> accessed 3 September 2014 ; Asli Demirgüç-Kunt, Thorsten Beck and Patrick Honohan, *Finance for All? Policies and Pitfalls in Expanding Access* (World Book Publications 2008) <http://books.google.co.uk/books/about/Finance_for_All.html?id=GYMP9miaK5cC> accessed 3 September 2014; Gary Dymski and Pamela Friedman, 'Banking the Unbanked: Helping Low-Income Families Build Financial Assets' (2005) <http://text.123doc.vn/document/1148313-banking-the-unbanked-helping-low-income-families-build-financial-assets-pptx.htm> accessed 3 September 2014; Deon Glajchen, 'A Comparative Analysis of Mobile Phone-Based Payment Services in the United States and South Africa' (PhD Dissertation, Northcentral University, 2011).

72 Alberto Chaia et al., 'Half the World Is Unbanked' (2011) <http://financialaccess.org/sites/default/files/110109%20HalfUnbanked_0.pdf> accessed 3 September 2014.

73 Alfred Hannig, and Jansen Stefan (n 1 Chapter 1); Gary Dymski, 'Banking Strategy and Financial Exclusion: Tracing the Pathways of Globalization' (2005) 31 *Revista de Economia* 1–29, 107–143 <http://papers.ssrn.com/sol3/papers.cfm?abstract_id=901834> accessed 3 September 2014. FDIC, 'FDIC National Survey of Unbanked and Underbanked Households December 2009' (2009) <www.fdic.gov/householdsurvey/2009/executive_summary.pdf> accessed 3 September 2014; FDIC, 'FDIC Advisory Committee on Economic Inclusion: Strategic Plan' (2010) <www.fdic.gov/about/comein/finalPlan.pdf> accessed 3 September 2014.

74 Asli Demirgüç-Kunt, Thorsten Beck and Patrick Honohan, *Finance for All? Policies and Pitfalls in Expanding Access* (World Book Publications 2008) <http://books.google.co.uk/books/about/Finance_for_All.html?id=GYMP9miaK5cC> accessed 3 September 2014; Gary Dymski and Pamela Friedman, 'Banking

the Unbanked: Helping Low-Income Families Build Financial Assets' (2005) <http://text.123doc.vn/document/1148313-banking-the-unbanked-helping-low-income-families-build-financial-assets-pptx.htm> accessed 3 September 2014; Deon Glajchen, 'A Comparative Analysis of Mobile Phone-Based Payment Services in the United States and South Africa' (PhD Dissertation, Northcentral University, 2011); Alfred Hannig and Stefan Jansen, 'Financial Inclusion and Financial Stability: Current Policy Issues' (2010) ADBI Working Paper Series No 259 <www.adbi.org/files/2010.12.21.wp259.financial.inclusion.stability.policy.issues.pdf> accessed 3 September 2014.

75 Asli Demirgüç-Kunt, Thorsten Beck and Patrick Honohan, *Finance for All? Policies and Pitfalls in Expanding Access* (World Book Publications 2008.

76 What Is Financial Inclusion? – Asian Development Bank Institute, <www.adbi.org/working-paper/2010/12/21/4272.financial.inclusion.stability.policy.issues/what.is.financial.inclusion/> (accessed September 24, 2014.

77 Tushar K. Das, 'Financial Inclusion and Regulation in India' (2012) <http://eldis.org/vfile/upload/1/Document/1306/FIRI2.pdf> accessed 3 September 2014.

78 Ibid.

79 'The Financial Diaries' project is a year-long household survey that examines financial management in poor households in South Africa. Data are 'captured into a specially designed Access Database that produces customised diary questionnaires for each household, as well as a system of reports that allows for continuous data surveillance.' Asian Development Bank. The overall aim of the project, which is funded by the Fin Mark Trust, the Ford Foundation, and the Micro Finance Regulatory Council, is to improve understanding of how poor people manage their finances. See <www.financialdiaries.com>.

80 Tushar K. Das, 'Financial Inclusion and Regulation in India' (2012) <http://eldis.org/vfile/upload/1/Document/1306/FIRI2.pdf> accessed 3 September 2014.

81 Andrew Crockett, 'Market Discipline and Financial Stability' (2002) 26 *Journal of Banking & Finance* 977. General Manager of the Bank for International Settlements and Chairman of the Financial Stability Forum, at the Banks and Systemic Risk Conference, Bank of England, London, 23–25 May 2001<www.bis.org/speeches/sp010523.htm> accessed 3 September 2014.

82 Andrew Crockett, 'Market Discipline and Financial Stability' (2002) 26 *Journal of Banking & Finance* 977.

83 UN Capital Development Fund (2006).

84 See Chapter 2, Section Enabling Environment for Mobile Money adoption, pg 46.

85 See FSB (2010). <www.imf.org/external/pubs/ft/gfsr/2014/01/pdf/c3.pdf> accessed 3 September 2014. The size, interconnectedness, complexity, and lack of substitutability of SIBs are by themselves sources of externalities in the absence of any government protection, as the risks imposed by SIBs to the economy are not well reflected in the equity or bond prices of those institutions.

86 The characterization of deposits has been expounded in Chapter 4, 4.5.2 The definition of 'deposits'.

87 Trustee accounts have been explained in the context of mobile payments in Chapter 4.

88 Mobile-Financial.com, 'Mobile Financial Services Risk Matrix' (2010) <http://mobile-financial.com/blog/mobile-financial-services-risk-matrix> accessed 3 September 2014

89 Ibid.

90 Claire Alexandre and Lynn Chang Eisenhart, 'Mobile Money as an Engine of Financial Inclusion and Lynchpin of Financial Integrity' (2013) 8 *Wash. J.L. Tech. & Arts* 285 <http://digital.law.washington.edu/dspace-law/handle/1773.1/1200> accessed 3 September 2014.

91 Financial Action Task Force, Annual Report (2008) <www.fatf- gafi.org/media/ fatf/documents/reports/2008%202009%20ENG.pdf> accessed 10 September 2014.

92 Chapter 2 discusses the enabling environment for mobile payments where the national identification cards issued by the government encouraged the adoption of mobile payments and ensure KYC rules were observed.

93 IMF, 'Defining Financial Stability'(2004) <www.imf.org/external/pubs/ft/ wp/2004/wp04187.pdf> accessed 3 September 2014.

94 The Financial Conduct Authority calls for inputs on payments systems regu- lation <www.fca.org.uk/static/documents/psr-call-for-inputs.pdf> accessed 3 September 2014. Also see the FCA Thematic review 'Mobile Banking and Payments.' FCA, 'TR13/6 – Mobile Banking and Payments' (2013) <www. fca.org.uk/news/tr13-6-mobile-banking-and-payments> accessed 3 Septem- ber 2014.

95 Olivier De Bandt and Philipp Hartmann, 'Systemic Risk: A Survey' (2000) ECB Working Paper No 35 <http://papers.ssrn.com/sol3/papers.cfm?abstract_ id=258430> accessed 3 September 2014.

96 Dirk Schoenmaker, Peter M. Garber and David Folkerts-Landau, 'The Reform of Wholesale Payment Systems and its Impact on Financial Markets' (1996) IMF Working Papers 96/37 <http://papers.ssrn.com/sol3/papers.cfm?abstract_ id=882937> accessed 3 September 2014; David Folkerts-Landau, 'Systemic Financial Risk in Payment Systems' (1990) IMF Working Paper No 90/65 <http://papers.ssrn.com/sol3/papers.cfm?abstract_id=884911> accessed 3 September 2014.

97 Andrew Crockett, 'Market Discipline and Financial Stability' (2002) 26 *Journal of Banking & Finance* 977.

98 Ibid.

99 Benjamin Geva, Collections and Payment Transactions: Comparative Study of Legal Aspects (Oxford, Oxford University Press 2001).

100 Bruce J. Summers, *The Payment System: Design, Management, and Supervision* (International Monetary Fund 1994).

101 Darryl Biggar, 'An Increasing Role for Competition in the Regulation of Banks' (2005) <http://123doc.vn/document/1257133-an-increasing-role-for-com petition-in-the-regulation-of-banks-doc.htm> accessed 3 September 2014.

102 Rhys Bollen, 'Best Practice in the Regulation of Payment Services' (2010) <http://researchbank.rmit.edu.au/eserv/rmit:7919/RhysBollen.pdf> accessed 3 September 2014.

103 Ibid.

104 Allen N. Berger, Diana Hancock and Jeffrey C. Marquardt, 'A Framework for Analyzing Efficiency, Risks, Costs, and Innovations in the Payments System' (1996) 28(4) *Journal of Money, Credit and Banking* 696.

105 In this case, the various mobile payments system stakeholders and actors.

106 In this case, mobile phone devices are payment instruments.

107 Jeffrey C. Marquardt, 'Payment System Policy Issues and Analysis' The Payment System: Design, Management, and Supervision

108 Settlement periods or intraday delays.

109 Maxwell J. Fry, *Payment Systems in Global Perspective* (Routledge 2003) 13.

110 'The bill will enable Kenya's payment system to comply with the Bank for Inter- national Settlement core principles and give the central bank enhanced legal and regulatory powers over the payment systems', said Ndung'u. <www.nbt.tj/files/ Fin_mon/draft_01.pdf> accessed 3 September 2014.

111 'A Guide to Risk in Payment Systems Owned and Operated By the CPA' <www. cdnpay.ca/imis15/pdf/pdfs_publications/Risk_Guide.pdf>. Specificity to the particular payment instrument risks, such as electronic payment or mobile payments.

112  Allen N. Berger, Diana Hancock and Jeffrey C. Marquardt, 'A Framework for Analysing Efficiency, Risks, Costs, and Innovations in the Payments System' (1996) 28(4) *Journal of Money, Credit and Banking* 696–732.

113  Where the telecommunications operator owns the customer.

114  Michael Klein and Colin Mayer, 'Mobile Banking and Financial Inclusion – The Regulatory Lesson' (2011) World Bank Policy Research Working Paper No 5664 <http://papers.ssrn.com/sol3/papers.cfm?abstract_id=1846305> accessed 3 September 2014.

115  Douglas W. Diamond and Raghuram G. Rajan, 'Liquidity Risk, Liquidity Creation and Financial Fragility: A Theory of Banking' (1999) NBER Working Paper No w7430 <http://papers.ssrn.com/sol3/papers.cfm?abstract_id=227588> accessed 3 September 2014.

116  Klein and Mayer Supra, note 115.

117  The evolution of modern banking systems received strong impetus from the demand for an efficient mechanism to facilitate the payments flows needed to sustain a growing economy through the transfer of securities among buyers and sellers. Ian Kessler and John Purcell, 'Performance Related Pay: Objectives and Application' (1988) 2 *Human Resource Management Journal* 16.

118  Elisabeth Wentworth, 'Direct Debits, Consumer Protection and Payment System Regulation – Issues of Policy and Reform' (2002) 13 *JBFLP* 77 at 77; cf Jane Winn, 'Symposium: Clash of The Titans: Regulating the Competition Between Established and Emerging Electronic Payment Systems' (1999) 14 *Berkeley Technology Law Journal* 675 at 678 where the author breaks up the four risks into liquidity, finality, transaction risk and systemic risk.

119  As discussed in Chapter 2 Section 2.2.

120  Competition from other retail payments systems such as electronic payments, debit cards and cheques.

121  Central Bank of Kenya, 'Transactions valued at 341 Billion Kenya Shillings in February 2014' <www.centralbank.go.ke/index.php/rate-and-statistics/rtgs-2?yr=2014> accessed 3 September 2014.

122  The stakeholders are MNOs, banks, agents and consumers in general.

123  M-Kesho, M-KOPO, M-Shwari, all of which are mobile financial services and products introduced by Safaricom and Equity Bank.

124  Bangko Sentral Ng Pilipinas, 'Payment Systems' <www.bsp.gov.ph/financial/payment_payment.asp> accessed 3 September 2014.

125  Bangko Sentral Ng Pilipinas, 'The Payments Systems and the Financial Stability' (2014) <www.cnb.cz/miranda2/export/sites/www.cnb.cz/en/public/media_service/conferences/speeches/download/racocha_paym_syst_090704.pdf> accessed 3 September 2014.

126  Committee on Payment and Settlement Systems, 'A Glossary of Terms used in Payments and Settlement Systems' (2003) <www.bis.org/publ/cpss00b.pdf> accessed 3 September 2014.

127  Claudio E. V. Borio and Paul Van den Bergh, *The Nature and Management of Payment System Risks: An International Perspective* (Bank for International Settlements Basle 1993) 30.

128  Ibid.

129  Jane Kaufman Winn, 'Clash of the Titans: Regulating the Competition between established and emerging Electronic Payment Systems' (1999) 14 *Berkeley Technology Law Journal* 675

130  Ibid.

131  Ibid., pg. 131. Also, banks face similar risk in foreign currency markets; obligations denominated in different currencies will not be settled at the end of the trading day if there are significant differences between operating times of the payment systems.

132 Borio and Van den Bergh (n 130).
133 Yoris A. Au and Robert J. Kauffman, 'The Economics of Mobile Payments: Understanding Stakeholder Issues for an Emerging Financial Technology Application' (2008) 7 *Electronic Commerce Research and Applications* 141. 'An Overview Real Time Gross Settlement Systems' <www.sbp.org.pk/rtgs/Article RTGSGeneral.pdf> accessed 18 September 2014.
134 Ibid.
135 Ágnes Lublo, 'Topology of the Hungarian Large-value Transfer System' (2006) *MNB Occasional Papers* 57. For general studies on systemic risk stemming from netting systems, see BIS, 'Report on Netting Schemes' (1989) <www.bis.org/cpmi/publ/d02.pdf> accessed 3 September 2014; James McAndrews and George Wassillie, 'Simulations of Failure in a Payment System' (1995) Federal Reserve Bank of Philadelphia Working Paper 95–19 <http://econpapers.repec.org/paper/fipfedpwp/95-19.htm> accessed 3 September 2014; Paolo Angelini, G. Maresca and D. Russo, 'Systemic Risk in the Netting System' (1996) 20(6) *Journal of Banking & Finance* 863; C. Borio and P. Van den Bergh, 'The Nature and Management of Payment System Risks: An International Perspective' (1993) BIS Economic Paper No 36 <www.bis.org/publ/econ36.pdf> accessed 3 September 2014 1–86. For a comparison of gross and net settlement systems, see Xavier Freixas and Bruno Parigi, 'Systemic Risk, Interbank Relations and Liquidity Provision by the Central Bank' (1998) Economics Working Papers 440 <www.econ.upf.edu/docs/papers/downloads/440.pdf> accessed 3 September 2014.
136 See BIS (2001).
137 See Harri Kuussaari, 'Systemic Risk in the Finnish Payment Systems: An Empirical Investigation' (1996) Bank of Finland Discussion Paper; Morten Bech, Bo Madson and Lone Natorp, 'Systemic Risk in the Danish Interbank Netting System' (2002) Danmarks National Bank Working Paper No 8 <www.docin.com/p-92340430.html> accessed 3 September 2014; Paul Millar and Carol A. Northcott, 'The CLS Bank: Managing Risk in Foreign Exchange Settlement' (2002) Financial System Review <www.bankofcanada.ca/wp-content/uploads/2012/02/fsr-1202-miller.pdf> accessed 3 September 2014.
138 Martin. Blavarg and Patrick Nimander, 'Inter-Bank Exposures and Systemic Risk' (2002) *Sveriges Riksbank Economic Review* 2, 19–45.
139 C. Borio and P. Van den Bergh, 'The Nature and Management of Payment System Risks: An International Perspective' (1993) BIS Economic Paper No 36 <www.bis.org/publ/econ36.pdf> accessed 3 September 2014.
140 Hennie Bester et al., 'Implementing FATF Standards in Developing Countries and Financial Inclusion: Findings and Guidelines' (2008) World Bank First Initiative, Final Report <www.cenfri.org/documents/ AML/AML_CFT%20 and%20Financial%20Inclusion.pdf.d> accessed 3 September 2014.
141 Symposium: Mobile Money in Developing Countries: <https://litigationessentials.lexisnexis.com/webcd/app?action=DocumentDisplay&crawlid=1&doctype=c ite&docid=8+Wash.+J.L.+Tech.+%26+Arts+165&srctype=smi&srcid=3B15& key=ac1869da6efe0aa ef20a35e844ae39c1> accessed 22 September 2014.
142 Jennifer Isern, David Porteous, Raul Hernandez-Coss and Chinyere Egwuagu, 'AML/CTF Regulation: Implications for Financial Service Providers That Serve Low-Income People' (2005) <http://siteresources.worldbank.org/EXTAML/Resources/396511–1146581427871/AML_implications_complete.pdf> accessed 3 September 2014.
143 FATF, 'FATF Report on New Payment Methods' (2006) <www.fatf-gafi.org/media/fatf/documents/reports/Report%20on%20New%20Payment%20 Methods.pdf> accessed 3 September 2014; FATF, 'Money Laundering Using New Payment Methods' (2010) <www.fatf-gafi.org/media/fatf/documents/

reports/ML%20using%20New%20Payment%20Methods.pdf> accessed 3 September 2014.

144 FATF, 'FATF Guidance on Anti-Money Laundering and Terrorist Financing Measures and Financial Inclusion' (2011) <www.fatf-gafi.org/media/fatf/content/images/AML%20CFT%20measures%20and%20financial%20inclusion.pdf> accessed 3 September 2014.

145 Ibid.

146 Borio and Van den Bergh (1994) supra note 149 pg. 31. Although the central bank can eliminate liquidity risk from the system by standing ready to supply the settlement medium without limit. This, however, would shift credit risk to the Central Bank to a degree which would depend on the terms on which funds were granted. This grant would require the Central Bank to institute the terms through which 'trust' accounts are set up in conjunction with MNOs.

147 'A Guide to Risk in Payment Systems Owned and Operated by the CPA' <www.cdnpay.ca/imis15/pdf/pdfs_publications/Risk_Guide.pdf?bcsi_scan_B895EDBE82A479 62=PGBDY/ >accessed 18 September 2014.

148 Antoine Martin, 'Recent Evolution of Large-Value Payment Systems: Balancing Liquidity and Risk' (2005) <www.kansascityfed.org/PUBLICAT/ECON REV/Pdf/1Q05mart.pdf> accessed 3 September 2014.

149 Ibid.

150 Ibid.

151 Ibid.

152 Ibid.

153 Ibid.

154 Ibid.

155 This definition of operational risk (BIS 1997a) seems too narrowly focused. The operational risk can also relate to human error, natural disasters, or system design flaws (Bank of Canada 1997a). Therefore, it refers to the reliability and integrity of the payment system with respect to the processing of payments.

156 Basel Committee on Banking Supervision Consultative Document <www.bis.org/publ/bcbsca07.pdf> accessed 24 September 2014.

157 Ibid.

158 Bank of International Settlements, 'A Glossary of Terms Used in Payments and Settlement Systems' (2003) <www.bis.org/publ/cpss00b.pdf> accessed 3 September 2014.

159 The way a service provider manages its employees can be a major source of operational risk. A poorly serviced provider of a payment system may find that the availability of its employees or its ability to replace them can influence its ability to recover from interruptions to the continuity of its operations. See Financial Services Authority, 'Operational Risk Systems and Controls' (2002) Consultation Paper No 142 at 14 <www.bankofengland.co.uk/financialstability/fsc/Documents/FSAConsultationPaper142.pdf> 3 September 2014.

160 Ibid.

161 John Hawke Jr, 'Risk Management for Electronic Banking and Electronic Money Activities' (1998) International Monetary Seminar Paris 92.

162 A 'hacker' is a person who gains unauthorised access to computer systems and networks. See *The New Penguin Dictionary of Computing* (n 62) 217. See 'Operational Risk Systems and Controls' (n 149) 4 and 8

163 See Setsuya Sato and John Hawkin, 'Electronic Finance: An Overview of the Issues' (2001) BIS Paper No 7 <www.bis.org/publ/bppdf/bispap07.htm> accessed 3 September 2014.

164 See R. Harris, 'Does Outsourcing Reduce Operational Risk?' *Operational Risk Federal Reserve Bank of Chicago* (September 2001) 6. Available at <www.

chicaofded.orw/bankinginformation/files/operationalriskarchieve2001out
source.ndt> accessed July 2005.

165 See 'Operational Risk Systems and Controls (n 149) 16.
166 The Basel Accord, set of principles for effective banking supervision.
167 Michael Power, 'The Invention of Operational Risk' (2005) 12 *Review of International Political Economy* 577.
168 K. McPhail, 'Managing Operational Risk in Payment, Clearing, and Settlement Systems' (2005) Bank of Canada, Working Paper 2/2003 <www.bankofcanada.ca/wp-content/uploads/2012/02/fsr-0603-mcphail.pdf> accessed 3 September 2014.
169 Ibid.
170 Ibid.
171 Bank of Canada 1997(a).
172 Jake Akervik, 'Mobile-Payments-Emerging-Markets' (2013) <www.slideshare.net/jakervik/akervik-mobilepaymentsemergingmarket> accessed December 2013. Other vulnerabilities include, violations relative to application collection and distribution of data, wireless carrier infrastructure, payments infrastructure/ecosystem SMS vulnerabilities, hardware and operating system vulnerabilities.
173 'Safaricom Should Consider M-Pesa Fall Back Servers' *The Standard Newspaper* (Nairobi, 29 October 2012) at <www.standardmedia.co.ke/?articleID=200006 9486%3E> accessed 3 September 2014.
174 One of Kenya's largest banks with concentration within the low-income markets.
175 Dominique Rambure and Alec Nacamuli, Payment Systems: From the Salt Mines to the Board (Palgrave Macmillan 2008) 58.
176 Uganda Law Commission Cautions on Mobile Money Regulation, <www.africa-uganda-business-travel-guide.com/uganda-law-commission-cautions-on-mobile-money-regulation.html> accessed 3 September 2014.
177 Nikolaos Zacharopoulos, 'Money to go' (2012) Financial Director Feature <www.financialdirector.co.uk/financial-director/feature/2140175/money> accessed 3 September 2014.
178 Ibid.
179 Mobile Money – GSMA <www.gsma.com/mobilefordevelopment/wp-content/uploads/2013/02/MMU-Enabling-Regulatory-Solutions-di-Castri-2013.pdf> accessed 18 September 2014.
180 Claire Pénicaud, 'State of the Industry: results from the 2012 Global Mobile Money Adoption Survey' (2012) GSMA, London, United Kingdom <www.gsma.com/mobilefordevelopment/wp-content/uploads/2013/03/MMU_Results-from-the-2012-Global-Mobile-Money-Adoption-Survey.pdf> accessed 3 September 2014.
181 Anthony Saunders, 'Banking and Commerce: An Overview of the Public Policy Issues' (1994) 18 *Journal of Banking & Finance* 231.
182 Mobile Money GSMA, <www.gsma.com/mobilefordevelopment/wp- content/uploads/2013/02/MMU-Enabling-Regulatory-Solutions-di-Castri-2013.pdf> accessed 3 September 2014.
183 'Risk Management Framework for Microfinance Institutions' (2000) <www.ruralfinance.org/fileadmin/templates/rflc/documents/1126266387218_A_risk_management_framework_for_MFIs.pdf> accessed 3 September 2014.
184 Canadian Payments Association, 'A Guide to Risk in Payment Systems Owned and Operated by the CPA' (2005) <www.cdnpay.ca/imis15/pdf/pdfs_publications/Risk_Guide.pdf> accessed 3 September 2014.
185 BIS, 'Risk Management for Electronic Banking and Electronic Money Activities' (1998) 7 <www.bis.org/publ/bcbs35.pdf> accessed 3 September 2014.
186 Ibid.

187 PriceWaterhouseCoopers in conjunction with the Economist Intelligence Unit, 'Compliance: A Gap in the Heart of Risk Management' (2003) <www.sum2.us/images/PWCcompliancenadriskmgmt.pdf> 8.
188 Chapter 2 discusses the stakeholders in the mobile payment system in detail.
189 Multiple providers would come in if the Kenyan mobile payments scheme made interoperability possible. At present, interoperability has been stalled due to the competitive market for MNOs
190 Jarkko Vesa, Mobile Services in the Networked Economy (IGI Global 2005).
191 Paul Golding, *Next Generation Wireless Applications: Creating Mobile Applications in a Web 2.0 and Mobile 2.0 World* (John Wiley & Sons 2008); Stijn Claessens, Thomas Glaessner and Daniela Klingebiel, 'Electronic Finance: Reshaping the Financial Landscape Around the World' (2002) 22 *Journal of Financial Services Research* 29.
192 CGAP, 'Agent Networks' <www.cgap.org/topics/agent-networks> accessed 3 September 2014.
193 Chapter 5 examines the regulatory strategies.
194 These risks are identified as most important and even though these risks result from a single problem, several methods of remedy may be required to address each of the risks.
195 For example, even if the payment instrument is electronic money, different degrees of risk exist, depending on the type of scheme in which it operates.
196 This section is based on GSMA, 'Mobile Financial Services Risk Matrix' (2010) <http://mobile-financial.com/blog/mobile-financial-services-risk-matrix> accessed 3 September 2014.
197 Ibid.
198 Section page, Titled, the Nature of payment systems risks.
199 Mobile-Financial.com, 'Mobile Financial Services Risk Matrix' (2010) 71 <http://mobile-financial.com/blog/mobile-financial-services-risk-matrix> accessed 3 September 2014.
200 Maria C. Stephens, 'Promoting Responsible Financial Inclusion: A Risk-based Approach to Supporting Mobile Financial Services Expansion' (2010) <www.ftc.gov/sites/default/files/documents/public_comments/ftc-host-workshop-mobile-payments-and-their-impact-consumers-project-no.124808–561018–00012%C2%A0/561018–00012–82712.pdf> accessed 3 September 2014; Mobile-Financial.com, 'Mobile Financial Services Risk Matrix'(2010) 71 <http://mobile-financial.com/blog/mobile-financial-services-risk-matrix> accessed 3 September 2014.
201 Joy Malala, 'Consumer Protection for Mobile Payments in Kenya: An Examination of the Fragmented Legislation and the Complexities It Presents for Mobile Payments' (2014) Kenya Bankers Association, Centre for Research on Financial Markets and Policy Working Paper Series No 7 <www.kba.co.ke/workingpaper series/img/pdf/Working%20Paper%20WPS-07-13.pdf> accessed 3 September 2014.
202 Mobile-Financial.com, 'Mobile Financial Services Risk Matrix' (2010) 71 <http://mobile-financial.com/blog/mobile-financial-services-risk-matrix> accessed 3 September 2014. The M-Pesa can operate with the mobile device serving as a store of value. Chapter 4 Part II.
203 Joy Malala (2014) (n 208) 16.
204 Joy Malala (2014) (n 208) 20.
205 The Banking Act 1969 s 2 (a) (1).
206 Joy Malala (2014) (n 208) 23.
207 This refers to the letter issued to Safaricom by the Central Bank of Kenya authorising its operations after a risk assessment was conducted in February 2007.

Alliance for Financial Inclusion, 'Enabling Mobile Money Transfer: The Central Bank of Kenya's Treatment of M-Pesa' (2010) <www.gsma.com/mobileforde velopment/wp-content/uploads/2013/09/enablingmobilemoneytransfer92. pdf> accessed 3 September 2014. See also, Bankable Frontier Associates LLC, 'Enabling Mobile Money Transfer – The Central Bank of Kenya's Treatment of M-PESA' (2010) Alliance for Financial Inclusion.
208 See Chapter 2 on the introduction of mobile payment systems.
209 This model requires the MNO, rather than a financial institution, to provide the payment functions and technology.
210 This means that aside from providing data and voice functions in their capacity they provide mobile financial services.
211 Joy Malala (2014) (n 208) 25. Also in this model, the issuer (having a rela-tionship with the cardholder) and the acquirer (having a relationship with the merchant) is the same entity. This means that there is no need for any charges between the issuer and the acquirer. Since it is a franchise set-up, there is only one franchisee in each market, which is the incentive in this model. There is no competition within the brand; the competition is with other brands.
212 These contractual arrangements are likened to franchise agreements; however, they tend to favour the MNO rather than the agent.
213 Regulatory capacity is explored in Chapter 4.
214 Maria C. Stephens, 'Promoting Responsible Financial Inclusion: a Risk-based Approach to Supporting Mobile Financial Services Expansion' (2011) 27 *Bank-ing and Finance Law Review* 329 In this case the trust account which is dis-cussed in Chapter 4.
215 This is a commercial bank in Kenya.
216 Joy Malala, 'Consumer Protection for Mobile Payments in Kenya: An Examina-tion of the Fragmented Legislation and the Complexities It Presents for Mobile Payments' (2014) Kenya Bankers Association, Centre for Research on Financial Markets and Policy Working Paper Series No 7 <www.kba.co.ke/workingpaper series/img/pdf/Working%20Paper%20WPS-07-13.pdf> accessed 3 September 2014.
217 Ibid.
218 Ibid.
219 Although these figures are from 2009.
220 Ignacio Mas and Dan Radcliffe, 'Mobile Payments go Viral: M-PESA in Kenya' (2010) 353–369 <http://siteresources.worldbank.org/AFRICAEXT/ Resources/258643-1271798012256/M-PESA_Kenya.pdf> accessed 3 Sep-tember 2014.
221 Ibid.
222 Ibid.
223 See Chapter 2 on the enabling environment for mobile payments systems.
224 Joy Malala, (2014) (n 208) 26.
225 Maria C. Stephens, 'Promoting Responsible Financial Inclusion: A Risk-Based Approach to Supporting Mobile Financial Services Expansion' (2011) 27 *Bank-ing and Finance Law Review* 329.
226 Joy Malala (2014) (n 208) 28
227 See Chapter 2 System Design of Mobile Payments.
228 The stored value of the payment.
229 See generally Maurice D. Levi, International Finance: Contemporary Issues (4th edn, Routledge 2005).
230 See Generally, Cynthia Merritt, 'Mobile Money Transfer Services: The Next Phase in the Evolution of Person-to-Person Payments' (2011) 5 *Journal of Pay-ments Strategy & Systems*.

231 Ibid.
232 Mobile-Financial.com, 'Mobile Financial Services Risk Matrix' (2010) 71 <http://mobile-financial.com/blog/mobile-financial-services-risk-matrix> accessed 3 September 2014.
233 Ibid.
234 This civil disturbance reflects political instability in a state such as the post-election violence in Kenya after the disputed 2007 general elections.
235 Trust accounts are accounts in which a bank or trust company (acting as an authorised custodian) holds funds for specific purposes.
236 Brian Muthiora, 'Ring-fencing and Safeguard of Customer Money' (2014) <www.gsma.com/mobilefordevelopment/kenyas-new-regulatory-framework-for-e-money-issuers> accessed 3 September 2014.
237 Ring-fencing occurs when a portion of a company's assets or profits are financially separated without necessarily being operated as a separate entity. This might respond to regulation, protect assets from financing arrangements, or segregate funds into separate income streams for taxation purposes.
238 Joy Malala, (2014) (n 208) 29.
239 Maria C. Stephens, 'Promoting Responsible Financial Inclusion: A Risk-Based Approach to Supporting Mobile Money Transfer Services Expansion' (2011) 27(1) *Banking and Finance Law Review*.
240 Ibid.
241 Ibid.
242 Mobile-Financial.com, 'Mobile Financial Services Risk Matrix' (2010) 71 <http://mobile-financial.com/blog/mobile-financial-services-risk-matrix> accessed 3 September 2014.
243 See Chapter 4 for a discussion on the challenges of defining an agent in the mobile payments context.
244 Cynthia Merritt, 'Mobile Money Transfer Services: The Next Phase in the Evolution of Person-To- Person Payments' (2011) 5 *Journal of Payments Strategy & Systems*. Disbursement of cash poses a cash in transit risk where the vulnerability to theft is apparent.
245 While agents are not literally bank branches, for 'branchless banks' they function as such. CGAP and DFID define branchless banking as the delivery of financial services outside conventional bank branches using information and communications technologies and non-bank retail agents, for example, over card-based networks or with mobile phones. See, CGAP, 'Scenarios for Branchless Banking in 2020' (2009) <www.gsma.com/mobilefordevelopment/wp-content/uploads/2009/10/Scenarios-for-Branchless-Banking-in-2020.pdf> accessed 3 September 2014.
246 Joy Malala, (2014) (n 208) 30.
247 Cynthia Merritt, 'Mobile Money Transfer Services: The Next Phase in the Evolution of Person-To- Person Payments' (2011) 5 *Journal of Payments Strategy & Systems* 143.
248 Ibid.
249 This money forms the liquidity shortfall.
250 Usually the bank assigned to hold the telecommunications company funds.
251 Safaricom's website details agent requirements: Safaricom, 'M-Pesa Agents' <www.safaricom.co.ke/personal/m-pesa/m-pesa-agents> accessed 3 September 2014.
252 Malala Joy (2014) (n 208) 31.
253 According to 2013 figures from Safaricom <www.safaricom.co.ke> accessed 3 September 2014.
254 Cynthia Merritt, 'Mobile Money Transfer Services: The Next Phase in the Evolution of Person-To- Person Payments' (2011) 5 *Journal of Payments Strategy & Systems*

Registration and deposits are free, and most other transactions are priced based on a tiered structure to allow even the poorest users to be able to use the system at a reasonable cost. Transaction values are typically small, ranging from US $5 to US $30.); Mas & Radcliffe (2010) at 170 ('[Retail] stores are paid a fee by Safaricom each time they exchange [cash for M-PESA credit] on behalf of customers').

255 Joy Malala (2014) (n 208) 32.
256 Claire Alexandre, Ignacio Mas and Daniel Radcliffe, 'Regulating New Banking Models to Bring Financial Services to All' (2011) 54 Challenge 116.
257 Ignacio Mas and Dan Radcliffe, 'Mobile Payments go Viral: M-PESA in Kenya' (2010) 353–369 <http://siteresources.worldbank.org/AFRICAEXT/Resources/258643-1271798012256/M-PESA_Kenya.pdf> accessed 3 September 2014.
258 Ibid.
259 Ibid.
260 George Obera, 'Safaricom Marks 5 Years amidst Agent Liquidity Concerns' <www.mobilepaymentstoday.com/blogs/safaricom-marks-5-years-amidst-agent-liquidity- concerns/> accessed 22 September 2014.
261 Joy Malala (2014) (n 208) p33.
262 Ibid, also see, Lennart Bångens and Björn Söderberg, 'Mobile banking- Financial services for the unbanked?' (2008) <http://spidercenter.org/polopoly_fs/1.146036.1378747792!/menu/standard/file/Mobile%20banking%20-%20financial%20services%20for%20the%20unbanked.pdf> accessed 3 September 2014.
263 Marina Solin and Andrew Zerzan, 'A Mobile Money: Methodology for Assessing Money Laundering and Terrorist Financing Risks' (2010) GSMA Discussion Paper <www.gsma.com/mobilefordevelopment/wp-content/uploads/2012/03/amlfinal35.pdf> accessed 3 September 2014.
264 Business Daily, 'Banks lose Sh1.7 Billion to fraudsters in 3 Months' *Business Daily* (25 November 2010) <www.businessdailyafrica.com/Kenyan-banks-lose-Sh1-7bn-to-fraudsters-in-3-months/-/539552/1059808/-/4kmod8/-/index.html> accessed 3 September 2014.
265 Kate Lauer, Denise Dias and Michael Tarazi, 'Bank Agents: Risk Management, Mitigation, and Supervision' (2012) 75 *Focus Note.*
266 In this case the Central Bank of Kenya. See Chapter 4 on discussion on the regulatory authority of payments systems.
267 Chapter 4 explains this in detail; the legal and regulatory challenges in the legal definition of agents does not clarify to whom they are accountable. Recent amendments to the agent regulations of the Central Bank of Brazil reflects this principle, which now provides that agents dealing with credit and leasing be trained and certified on relevant technical matters, applicable regulations, the consumer protection code, ethics, and ombudsman duties.
268 Louis De Koker, 'Client Identification and Money Laundering Control: Perspectives on the Financial Intelligence Centre Act 38 of 2001' 4 Journal of South African Law 715–746.
269 Liquidity in the form of cash from the transferred funds.
270 Joy Malala (2014) (n 208).
271 Frederik Eijkman, Jake Kendall, and Ignacio Mas, 'Bridges to Cash: the Retail End of M-PESA The Challenge of Maintaining Liquidity for M-PESA Agent Networks' Page 51.
272 GSMA, 'Mobile Financial Services Risk Matrix' (2010) <http://mobile-financial.com/blog/mobile-financial-services-risk-matrix> accessed 3 September 2014.
273 The consumer's subjective expectation of suffering a loss in pursuit of a desired outcome. See, Yi-Shun Wang and others, 'Determinants of User Acceptance of Internet Banking: An Empirical Study' (2003) 14 *International Journal of Service Industry Management.*

274 The training is only limited to AML/CFT and given once during the registration period.

275 Louis De Koker, 'The Money Laundering Risk Posed By Low Risk Financial Products in South Africa: Findings and Guidelines' (2009) 12(4) *Journal of Money Laundering Control* 323–339.

276 Ibid.

277 Ibid.

278 Katharine Vincent and Tracy Cull, 'Cell Phones, Electronic Delivery Systems and Social Cash Transfers: Recent Evidence and Experiences From Africa' (2011) 64 *International Social Security Review* 37.

279 Ibid.

280 Ibid.

281 The agency agreement between the agents and the MNOs shall also be referred to as the 'contract' between the MNOs and the agents.

282 As a result of operational risks, as discussed in this chapter.

283 See Roger Clarke, 'Human Identification in Information Systems: Management Challenges and Public Policy Issues' (1994) 7(4) *Information Technology & People* 6–37; Louis De Koker, 'Client Identification and Money Laundering Control: Perspectives on the Financial Intelligence Centre Act 38 of 2001' (2004) 4 *Journal of South African Law* 715–746.

284 Central Bank of Kenya Agent Guidelines 2010.

285 Mobile-Financial.com, 'Mobile Financial Services Risk Matrix' (2010) <http://mobile-financial.com/blog/mobile-financial-services-risk-matrix> accessed 3 September 2014.

286 Tilman Ehrbeck and Michael Tarazi, 'Putting the Banking in Branchless Banking: Regulation and the Case for Interest-Bearing and Insured E-money Savings Accounts, Consultative Group to Assist the Poor' (2013) <www.gsma.com/mobilefordevelopment/wp-content/uploads/2013/09/puttingthe-bankingin90.pdf> accessed 3 September 2014; World Economic Forum, 'The Mobile Financial Services Development Report 2011' (2011) <http://www3.weforum.org/docs/WEF_MFSD_Report_2011.pdf> accessed 3 September 2014.

287 Timothy Lyman, Mark Pickens and David Porteous, 'Regulating Transformational Branchless Banking: Mobile Phones and Other Technology to Increase Access to Finance' (2008) <http://goo.gl/YboX0> accessed 3 September 2014.

288 Mobile-Financial.com, 'Mobile Financial Services Risk Matrix' (2010) <http://mobile-financial.com/blog/mobile-financial-services-risk-matrix> accessed 3 September 2014.

289 Ibid.

290 Anecdotal inferences from discussions with Kenyans about their use with mobile payment agents.

291 Joy Malala (2014) (n 208) 33. See also Timothy Lyman, Gautam Ivatury and Stefan Staschen, 'Use of Agents in Branchless Banking for the Poor: Rewards, Risks, and Regulation' (2006) 38 *Focus Note* <www.cgap.org/sites/default/files/CGAP-Focus-Notes-Use-of-Agents-in-Branchless-Banking-for-the-Poor-Rewards-Risks-and-Regulation-Oct-2006-Chinese.pdf> accessed 3 September 2014.

292 Ibid.

293 Denise Dias and Katharine McKee, 'Protecting Branchless Banking Consumers: Policy Objectives and Regulatory Options' (2010) <http://www-wds.worldbank.org/external/default/WDSContentServer/WDSP/IB/2014/05/01/000469252_2014050 1092816/Rendered/PDF/704750B

RI0CHIN00Box377351B00PUBLIC0.pdf> accessed 3 September 2014; Laura Brix and Katharine McKee, 'Consumer Protection Regulation in Low-access Environments: Opportunities to Promote Responsible Finance' (2010) 60 *Focus Note* <http://documents.worldbank.org/curated/en/2010/02/18607437/consumer-protection-regulation-low-access-environments-opportunities-promote-responsible-finance> accessed 3 September 2014; CGAP, 'Agent Management Toolkit' (2011) <www.cgap.org/publications/agent-management-toolkit> accessed 3 September 2014.

294 GSMA, 'Mobile Financial Services Risk Matrix' (2010) <http://mobile-financial.com/blog/mobile-financial-services-risk-matrix> accessed 3 September 2014.

295 Ibid.

296 Ibid.

297 Maria Stephens and Lisa Dawson, 'A Risk Based Approach to Regulatory Policy and Mobile Financial Services' (2011) Federal Reserve Bank of Atlanta America Centre <www.frbatlanta.org/documents/news/conferences/11consumer_banking_dawson_stephens_pres.pdf> accessed 3 September 2014.

298 GSMA, 'Mobile Financial Services Risk Matrix' (2010) <http://mobile-finan cial.com/blog/mobile-financial-services-risk-matrix> accessed 3 September 2014.

299 Ibid.

300 FATF, 'Guidance on the Risk-based Approach to Combating Money Laundering and Terrorist Financing: High Level Principles and Procedures' (2007) <www.fatf-gafi.org/media/fatf/documents/reports/High%20Level%20Princi ples%20and%20Procedures.pdf> accessed 3 September 2014.

301 Louis De Koker, 'Anonymous Clients, Identified Clients and the Shades in Between: Perspectives on the FATF AML/CFT Standards and Mobile Banking' (2009) 27th Cambridge International Symposium on Economic Crime 4; See also, Bill Maurer, 'Due Diligence and "Reasonable Man", Offshore' (2005) 20(4) *Cultural Anthropology* 474–505; FATF, 'Global Money Laundering and Terrorist Financing Threat Assessment: A View of How and Why Criminals and Terrorists Abuse Finances – the Effect of This Abuse and the Steps to Mitigate These Threats' (2010) <www.fatf-gafi.org/media/fatf/documents/reports/Global%20Threat%20assessment.pdf> accessed 3 September 2014.

302 Andrew James Lake, 'Risk Management in Mobile Money, Observed Risk and Proposed Mitigants for Mobile Money Operators' (2013) <www.ifc.org/wps/wcm/connect/37a086804236698d8220ae0dc33b630b/Tool+7.1.+Risk+Management.pdf?MOD=AJPERES> accessed 3 September 2014; Finextra, 'Ugandan Telco Says Employees Stole $3.5m in Mobile Money Fraud' *Finextra* (28 May 2012) <www.finextra.com/news/fullstory.aspx?newsitemid=23759> accessed 3 September 2014.

303 Reserve Bank of India, 'Report of the Technical Committee on Enabling Public Key Infrastructure (PKI) in Payment System Applications' (2014) <www.rbi.org.in/scripts/PublicationReportDetails.aspx?UrlPage=&ID=759> accessed 3 September 2014.

304 GSMA, 'Mobile Financial Services Risk Matrix' (2010) <http://mobile-finan cial.com/blog/mobile-financial-services-risk-matrix> accessed 3 September 2014.

305 Ibid.

306 Although super agents who provide physical cash distribution to individual agents are not necessarily able to manage cash stocks effectively, as that may not be their core business.

307 GSMA, 'Mobile Financial Services Risk Matrix' (2010) <http://mobile-financial.com/blog/mobile-financial-services-risk-matrix> accessed 3 September 2014; Also see Chapter 4, The Legal Definition of Deposits.

308 Ibid.
309 Funds segregation is common in the trading of futures industry, which helps protect customer capital in the event of a brokerage bankruptcy and, in this case, the bankruptcy of an MNO. Managed Futures Today, 'Safeguarding Customers Through Segregated Funds' (2011) <www.managedfuturestodaymag. com/safeguarding-customers-through-segregated-funds> accessed 3 September 2014.
310 Ibid.
311 GSMA, 'Mobile Financial Services Risk Matrix' (2010) <http://mobile-finan cial.com/blog/mobile-financial-services-risk-matrix> accessed 3 September 2014.
312 Ibid.
313 Similarly, the European Union Money Directive stipulates that all EMIs must safeguard funds received from customers so that, in the case of insolvency, the funds will be protected from other creditors' claims and can be repaid to customers.
314 GSMA, 'Mobile Financial Services Risk Matrix' (2010) <http://mobile-finan cial.com/blog/mobile-financial-services-risk-matrix> accessed 3 September 2014.
315 This is because in many rural areas in Kenya many consumers do not have their own phones.
316 John Tatom and David Godstead, 'Targeting the Unbanked-Financial Literacy's Magic Bullet?' (2006) University Library of Munich, MPRA Paper 4266 <http://mpra.ub.uni-muenchen.de/4266/1/MPRA_paper_4266.pdf> accessed 3 September 2014.
317 Ibid.
318 The East African, 'Safaricom Raises M-Pesa Tariffs as Kenya Slaps Telcos with New Tax' <www.theeastafrican.co.ke/news/Safaricom-raises-MPesa-tariffs/-/ 2558/1681810/-/view/printVers ion/-/gvug2l/-/index.html> accessed 3 September 2014.
319 Ibid.
320 See Chapter 4 for a further analysis of this challenge.
321 Ibid.
322 Borio and Van den Bergh (1994) supra. pg. 29.
323 Ibid.
324 Borio and Van den Bergh (1994) supra. pg. 22.
325 Chapter 2 described the proliferation and success of M-PESA in Kenya.
326 As in Chapter 2, 'unintended' here reflects the fact that mobile payments through M-PESA were introduced with a micro-financial aim and the shift from its originally intended use to a major payment system has become financially inclusive.
327 This public involvement refers to the large population of the unbanked as described in Chapter 2, into the financial realm.
328 The 'intermediaries' here are the commercial banks and financial institutions. Banks, building societies credit unions, financial advisers or brokers insurance companies' collective investment schemes, and pension funds.
329 GSMA, 'Mobile Financial Services Risk Matrix' (2010) <http://mobile-finan cial.com/blog/mobile-financial-services-risk-matrix> accessed 3 September 2014. Ibid.
330 The balance of e-money or physical cash or money in a bank account that an agent can immediately access to meet customer demands to purchase cash in or sell cash out electronic money.
331 Deposit in the context of mobile payment transactions is defined as cashing in at the mobile payments agents.

332 The trustee account is the bank that holds the mobile money and payments in trust. Rasheda Sultana, 'Mobile Banking: Overview of Regulatory Framework in Emerging Markets' (2009) <http://papers.ssrn.com/sol3/papers.cfm?abstract_id=1554160> accessed 3 September 2014

333 Maria C. Stephens, 'Promoting Responsible Financial Inclusion: A Risk-Based Approach To Supporting Mobile Financial Services Expansion' (2012) 27 *Banking and Finance Law Review* 329.

334 Garry J. Schinasi, 'Defining Financial Stability and Establishing a Framework to Safeguard It' (2011) 15 Central Banking, Analysis, and Economic Policies Book Series. International Monetary Fund <www.imf.org/external/pubs/ft/wp/2004/wp04187.pdf> accessed 22 September 2014)

335 Ryan Hahn, 'Payment Systems and Systemic Risk' (2008) *The World Bank* <http://blogs.worldbank.org/psd/payment-systems-and-systemic-risk> accessed 3 September.

## Bibliography

Akervik, Jake, 'Mobile-Payments- Emerging Market' (2013) <www.slideshare.net/jakervik/akervik-mobilepaymentsemergingmarket> accessed December 2013.

Alexandre, Claire and Lynn Chang Eisenhart, 'Mobile Money as an Engine of Financial Inclusion and Lynchpin of Financial Integrity' (2013) 8 *Wash. J.L. Tech. & Arts* 285 <http://digital.law.washington.edu/dspace-law/handle/1773.1/1200> accessed 3 September 2014.

Alexandre, Claire and Lynn Chang Eisenhart, 'Mobile Money in Developing Countries: Financial Inclusion and Financial Integrity: Mobile Money as an Engine of Financial Inclusion and Lynchpin of Financial Integrity' (2013) 8 *Wash JL Tech & Arts* 285.

Alexandre, Claire, Ignacio Mas and Daniel Radcliffe, 'Regulating New Banking Models to Bring Financial Services to All' (2011) 54 *Challenge* 116.

Angelini, Paolo, G. Maresca and D. Russo, 'Systemic Risk in the Netting System' (1996) 20(6) *Journal of Banking & Finance* 863.

Ardic, Oya P., Maximilien Heimann and Nataliya Mylenko, 'Access to Financial Services and the Financial Inclusion Agenda Around the World: A Cross-Country Analysis with a New Data Set' (2011) (The World Bank, Financial and Private Sector Development, Financial Access Team of the Consultative Group to Assist the Poor) Policy Research Working Paper No 5537, 1–55 <http://goo.gl/8EZS3> accessed 3 September 2014.

Au, Yoris A. and Robert J. Kauffman, 'The Economics of Mobile Payments: Understanding Stakeholder Issues for an Emerging Financial Technology Application' (2008) 7 *Electronic Commerce Research and Applications* 141. 'An Overview Real Time Gross Settlement Systems' <www.sbp.org.pk/rtgs/ArticleRTGSGeneral.pdf> accessed 18 September 2014.

Awrey, Dan 'Complexity, Innovation and the Regulation of Modern Financial Markets' (2012) 2(2) *Harvard Business Law Review* 235

Awrey, Dan, 'Regulating Financial Innovation: A More Principles-based Alternative?' (2011) 5(2) *Brooklyn Journal of Corporate, Financial and Commercial Law* 273

Ayyagari, Meghana and Asli Demirgüç-Kunt, 'Formal Versus Informal Finance: Evidence from China'(2007)<http://siteresources.worldbank.org/INTFR/Resources/Formal_verus_Informal_Finance_Evidence_from_China.pdf> accessed 3 September 2014.

Ballard, Roger, 'Coalitions of Reciprocity and the Maintenance of Financial Integrity Within Informal Value Transmission Systems: The Operational Dynamics of Contemporary Hawala Networks' (2005) 6 *Journal of Banking Regulation* 4.

Bandt, Olivier De and Philipp Hartmann, 'Systemic Risk: A Survey' (2000) ECB Working Paper No 35 <http://papers.ssrn.com/sol3/papers.cfm?abstract_id=258430> accessed 3 September 2014.

Bångens, Lennart and Björn Söderberg, 'Mobile Banking- Financial Services for the Unbanked?'(2008) <http://spidercenter.org/polopoly_fs/1.146036.1378 747792!/menu/standard/file/Mobile%20banking%20-%20financial%20services%20for%20the%20unbanked.pdf> accessed 3 September 2014.

Bangko Sentral Ng Pilipinas, 'Payment Systems' <www.bsp.gov.ph/financial/payment_payment.asp> accessed 3 September 2014.

Bangko Sentral Ng Pilipinas, 'The Payments Systems and the Financial Stability' (2014) <www.cnb.cz/miranda2/export/sites/www.cnb.cz/en/public/media_service/conferences/speec hes/download/racocha_paym_syst_090704.pdf> accessed 3 September 2014.

Bank of International Settlements, 'A Glossary of Terms Used in Payments and Settlement Systems' (2003) <www.bis.org/publ/cpss00b.pdf> accessed 3 September 2014.

Bankable Frontier Associates LLC, 'Enabling Mobile Money Transfer – the Central Bank of Kenya's Treatment of M-PESA' (2010) Alliance for Financial Inclusion.

Basel Committee on Banking Supervision Consultative Document <www.bis.org/publ/bcbsca07.pdf> accessed 24 September 2014.

Bech, Morten, Bo Madson and Lone Natorp, 'Systemic Risk in the Danish Interbank Netting System' (2002) Danmarks National Bank Working Paper No 8 <www.docin.com/p-92340430.html> accessed 3 September 2014.

Beck, Thorsten, Asli Demirgüç-Kunt and Maria M. Peria, 'Reaching Out: Access to and Use of Banking Services Across Countries' (2007) 85(1) *Journal of Financial Economics* 234–266, <www.yearofmicrocredit.org/docs/Reaching_Out_Sept9.pdf> accessed 3 September 2014.

Beck, Thorsten, Asli Demirgüç-Kunt and Maria M. Peria, 'Banking Services for Everyone? Barriers to Bank Access and Use Around the World' (2008) 22(3) *World Bank Economic Review* 397–430 <http://papers.ssrn.com/sol3/papers.cfm?abstract_id=1318112> accessed 3 September 2014.

Beck, Thorsten, Asli Demirgüç-Kunt and Ross Levine, 'Finance, Inequality, and the Poor' (2007) 12(1) *Journal of Economic Growth* 27–49 <http://goo.gl/0Pkyi> accessed 3 September 2014.

Berger, Allen N., Diana Hancock and Jeffrey C Marquardt, 'A Framework for Analyzing Efficiency, Risks, Costs, and Innovations in the Payments System' (1996) 28(4) *Journal of Money, Credit and Banking* 696.

Berger, Allen N., Diana Hancock and Jeffrey C. Marquardt, 'A Framework for Analysing Efficiency, Risks, Costs, and Innovations in the Payments System' (1996) 28(4) *Journal of Money, Credit and Banking* 696–732.

Bernanke, Ben, 'Implementing a Macroprudential Approach to Supervision and Regulation' (2011) <www.federalreserve.gov/newsevents/speech/bernanke20110505a.pdf> accessed 3 September 2014.

Biggar, Darryl, 'An Increasing Role for Competition in the Regulation of Banks' (2005) <http://123doc.vn/document/1257133-an-increasing-role-for-competition-in-the-regulation-of-banks- doc.htm> accessed 3 September 2014.

BIS, 'Report on Netting Schemes' (1989) <www.bis.org/cpmi/publ/d02.pdf> accessed 3 September 2014.

BIS, 'Risk Management for Electronic Banking and Electronic Money Activities' (1998) 7 <www.bis.org/publ/bcbs35.pdf> accessed 3 September 2014.

Blavarg, Martin and Patrick Nimander, 'Inter-Bank Exposures and Systemic Risk' (2002) *Sveriges Riksbank Economic Review* 2, 19–45.

Bollen, Rhys, 'Best Practice in the Regulation of Payment Services' (2010) <http://researchbank.rmit.edu.au/eserv/rmit:7919/RhysBollen.pdf> accessed 3 September 2014.

Borio, Claudio and P. Van den Bergh, 'The Nature and Management of Payment System Risks: An International Perspective' (1993) BIS Economic Paper No 36 <www.bis.org/publ/econ36.pdf> accessed 3 September 2014.

Borio, Claudio and Christopher J. Green, 'Implementing the Macroprudential Approach to Financial Regulation and Supervision' in Christopher J. Green, Eric J. Pentecost and Thomas G. Weyman-Jones (eds), *The Financial Crisis and the Regulation of Finance* (Edward Elgar 2009).

Borio, Claudio E. and Mathias Drehmann, 'Towards an Operational Framework for Financial Stability: "Fuzzy" Measurement and Its Consequences' (2009) Working Paper No 284 <www.bis.org/publ/work284.htm> accessed 3 September 2014.

Borio, Claudio E. and Renato Filosa, 'The Changing Borders of Banking: Trends and Implications' (1994) BIS Working Paper No 23 <http://papers.ssrn.com/sol3/Delivery.cfm/SSRN_ID868431_code543654.pdf?abstractid=868431&mir id=1> accessed 3 September 2014.

Borio, Claudio E. and P. Van den Bergh, *The Nature and Management of Payment System Risks: An International Perspective* (Bank for International Settlements Basle 1993) 30.

Borio, Claudio, Craig Furfine and Philip Lowe, 'Procyclicality of the Financial System and Financial Stability: Issues and Policy Options' BIS Papers No 1

Brix, Laura and Katharine McKee, 'Consumer Protection Regulation in Low-Access Environments: Opportunities to Promote Responsible Finance' (2010) 60 *Focus Note* <http://documents.worldbank.org/curated/en/2010/02/18607437/consumer-protection-regulation-low-access-environments-opportunities-promote-responsible-finance> accessed 3 September 2014.

Business Daily, 'Banks lose Sh1.7 Billion to Fraudsters in 3 Months' *Business Daily* (25 November 2010) <www.businessdailyafrica.com/Kenyan-banks-lose-Sh1-7bn-to-fraudsters-in-3-months/-/539552/1059808/-/4kmod8/-/index.html> accessed 3 September 2014.

Canadian Payments Association, 'A Guide to Risk in Payment Systems Owned and Operated by the CPA' (2005) <www.cdnpay.ca/imis15/pdf/pdfs_publications/Risk_Guide.pdf> accessed 3 September 2014.

Caskey, John, Clemente Duran and Tova M Solo, 'The Urban Unbanked in Mexico and the United States' (2006) World Bank Policy Research Working Paper No 3835 <http://www-wds.worldbank.org/external/default/WDSContentServer/WDSP/IB/2006/01/26/000016406_2006012 6162730/Rendered/PDF/wps3835.pdf> accessed 3 September 2014.

Castri, Simone Di, 'Mobile Money: Enabling Regulatory Solutions' GSMA, London, United Kingdom <www.gsma.com/mobilefordevelopment/wp-content/uploads/2013/02/MMU-Enabling-Regulatory-Solutions-di-Castri-2013.pdf> accessed 14 August 2014.

Castri, Simone Di, 'Mobile Money: Enabling Regulatory Solutions' (2013)<www.gsma.com/mobilefordevelopment/wp-content/uploads/2013/02/MMU-Enabling-Regulatory-Solutions-di-Castri-2013.pdf> accessed 3 September 2014.

Central Bank of Kenya Publication, 'Kenya Payments System (Framework and Strategy)' (2004) <www.docin.com/p-433903551.html> accessed 3 September 2014.

Central Bank of Kenya, 'Presentation to the Board of Directors of Domestic Regulators July 2009' (2009) <http://goo.gl/6cK6D> accessed 3 September 2014.

Central Bank of Kenya, 'Transactions Valued at 341 Billion Kenya Shillings in February 2014' <www.centralbank.go.ke/index.php/rate-and-statistics/rtgs-2?yr=2014> accessed 3 September 2014.

The Central Bank of Kenya's Treatment of M-Pesa. (2010) <www.gsma.com/mobilefordevelopment/wpcontent/uploads/2013/09/enablingmobilemoneytransfer92.pdf> accessed 3 September 2014.

15 Central Banking, Analysis, and Economic Policies Book Series. International Monetary Fund <www.imf.org/external/pubs/ft/wp/2004/wp04187.pdf> accessed 22 September 2014.

CGAP, 'Agent Management Toolkit' (2011) <www.cgap.org/publications/agent-management-toolkit> accessed 3 September 2014.

CGAP, 'Agent Networks' <www.cgap.org/topics/agent-networks> accessed 3 September 2014.

CGAP, 'Scenarios for Branchless Banking in 2020' (2009) <www.gsma.com/mobilefordevelopment/wp-content/uploads/2009/10/Scenarios-for-Branchless-Banking-in-2020.pdf> accessed 3 September 2014.

Chaia, Alberto et al., 'Half the World Is Unbanked' (2011) <http://financialaccess.org/sites/default/files/110109%20HalfUnbanked_0.pdf> accessed 3 September 2014.

Chaia, Alberto et al., 'Half the World is Unbanked' (2011) <http://financialaccess.org/sites/default/files/110109%20HalfUnbanked_0.pdf> accessed 3 September 2014.

Claessens, Stijn, 'Access to Financial Services: A Review of the Issues and Public Policy Objectives' (2006) 21(2) *World Bank Research Observer* 207–240 <http://www-wds.worldbank.org/servlet/WDSContentServer/WDSP/IB/2005/05/15/000090341_20050515132903/ Rendered/INDEX/wps3589.txt> accessed 3 September 2014.

Claessens, Stijn, Swati R. Ghosh and Roxana Mihet, 'Macro Prudential Policies to Mitigate Financial Vulnerabilities in Emerging Markets' (2014) 155 <www.worldbank.org/content/dam/Worldbank/document/Poverty%20documents/EMERGIN G_WB_CH05_155–178.pdf> accessed 3 September 2014.

Claessens, Stijn, Thomas Glaessner and Daniela Klingebiel, 'Electronic Finance: Reshaping the Financial Landscape Around the World' (2002) 22 *Journal of Financial Services Research* 29.

Clarke, Roger, 'Human Identification in Information Systems: Management Challenges and Public Policy Issues' (1994) 7(4) *Information Technology & People* 6–37.

Clement, Piet, 'The Term "Macroprudential": Origins and Evolution' (2010) 6 *BIS Quarterly Review* 59.

Committee on Payment and Settlement Systems, 'A Glossary of Terms used in Payments and Settlement Systems' (2003) <www.bis.org/publ/cpss00b.pdf> accessed 3 September 2014.

'Composition of Macro Geographical (Continental) Region' <http://unstats. un.org/unsd/methods/m49/m49regin.htm#ftnc> accessed 3 September 2014.

*Consumer Understanding of Financial Risk* (FSA Consumer Reach 2004) 33

Cowen, Tyler, *The Theory of Market Failure: A Critical Examination* (George Mason University Press 1988).

Crockett, Andrew, 'Market Discipline and Financial Stability' (2002) 26 *Journal of Banking & Finance* 977 <www.centralbank.go.ke/index.php/retail-payment-sta tistics/mobile-payments?yr=2014> accessed 3 September 2014.

Crockett, Andrew, 'Market Discipline and Financial Stability' (2002) 26 *Journal of Banking & Finance* 977.

Crockett, Andrew, 'Market Discipline and Financial Stability' (2002) 26 *Journal of Banking & Finance* 977.

Crockett, Andrew, 'Market Discipline and Financial Stability' (2002) 26 *Journal of Banking & Finance* 977.

Crockett, Andrew, 'The Theory and Practice of Financial Stability' (1997) 144 *De Economist* 531

Das, Tushar K., 'Financial Inclusion and Regulation in India' (2012) <http://eldis. org/vfile/upload/1/Document/1306/FIRI2.pdf> accessed 3 September 2014.

Demirgüç-Kunt, Asli, Thorsten Beck and Patrick Honohan, *Finance for All? Policies and Pitfalls in Expanding Access* (World Book Publications 2008) <http://books. google.co.uk/books/about/Finance_for_All.html?id=GYMP9miaK5cC> accessed 3 September 2014.

Diamond, Douglas W. and Raghuram G. Rajan, 'Liquidity Risk, Liquidity Creation and Financial Fragility: A Theory of Banking' (1999) NBER Working Paper No w7430 <http://papers.ssrn.com/sol3/papers.cfm?abstract_id=227588> accessed 3 September 2014.

Dias, Denise and Katharine McKee, 'Protecting Branchless Banking Consumers: Pol icy Objectives and Regulatory Options' (2010) <http://www-wds.worldbank.org/ external/default/WDSContentServer/WDSP/IB/2014/05/01/000469252_ 20140501092816/Rendered/PDF/704750BRI0CHIN00Box377351B00PUB LIC0.pdf> accessed 3 September 2014.

Dias, Valerie, 'Evaluating the Integrity of Consumer Payment Systems' <www.visaeurope. com/idoc.ashx?docid=ee00fe8c-ca32-4d75-bf90-de1ff5e7d5ae&version=-1> accessed 3 September 2014.

Dymski, Gary and Pamela Friedman, 'Banking the Unbanked: Helping Low-Income Families Build Financial Assets' (2005) <http://text.123doc.vn/docu ment/1148313-banking-the-unbanked-helping-low-income-families-build-finan cial-assets-pptx.htm> accessed 3 September 2014.

The East African, 'Safaricom Raises M-Pesa Tariffs as Kenya Slaps Telcos with New Tax' <www.theeastafrican.co.ke/news/Safaricom-raises-MPesa-tariffs/-/2558/1681 810/-/view/printVersion/-/gvug2l/-/index.html> accessed 3 September 2014.

Ehrbeck, Tilman, Mark Pickens and Michael Tarazi, 'Financially Inclusive Ecosys tems: The Roles of Government Today' (2012) 76 *Focus Note*

Ehrbeck, Tilman and Michael Tarazi, 'Putting the Banking in Branchless Bank ing: Regulation and the Case for Interest-Bearing and Insured E-Money Savings Accounts, Consultative Group to Assist the Poor' (2013) <www.gsma.com/mobile fordevelopment/wpcontent/uploads/2013/09/puttingthebankingin90.pdf> accessed 3 September 2014.

FATF, 'FATF Guidance on Anti-Money Laundering and Terrorist Financing Measures and Financial Inclusion' (2011) <www.fatf-gafi.org/media/fatf/content/images/AML%20CFT%20measures%20and%20financial%20inclusion.pdf> accessed 3 September 2014.

FATF, 'FATF Report on New Payment Methods' (2006) <www.fatf-gafi.org/media/fatf/documents/reports/Report%20on%20New%20Payment%20Methods.pdf> accessed 3 September 2014.

FATF, 'Global Money Laundering and Terrorist Financing Threat Assessment: A View of How and Why Criminals and Terrorists Abuse Finances – the Effect of This Abuse and the Steps to Mitigate These Threats' (2010) <www.fatfgafi.org/media/fatf/documents/reports/Global%20Threat%20assessment.pdf> accessed 3 September 2014.

FATF, 'Guidance on the Risk-Based Approach to Combating Money Laundering and Terrorist Financing: High Level Principles and Procedures' (2007) <www.fatf-gafi.org/media/fatf/documents/reports/High%20Level%20Principles%20and%20Procedures.pdf> accessed 3 September 2014.

FATF, 'Money Laundering Using New Payment Methods' (2010) <www.fatf-gafi.org/media/fatf/documents/reports/ML%20using%20New%20Payment%20Methods.pdf> accessed 3 September 2014.

FCA Thematic review 'Mobile Banking and Payments.' FCA, 'TR13/6 – Mobile Banking and Payments' (2013) <www.fca.org.uk/news/tr13-6-mobile-banking-and-payments> accessed 3 September 2014.

FDIC, 'FDIC Advisory Committee on Economic Inclusion: Strategic Plan' (2010) <www.fdic.gov/about/comein/finalPlan.pdf> accessed 3 September 2014.

FDIC, 'FDIC National Survey of Unbanked and Underbanked Households December 2009' (2009) <www.fdic.gov/householdsurvey/2009/executive_summary.pdf> accessed 3 September 2014.

Federal Deposit Insurance Corporation (FDIC), 'Tapping the Unbanked Market Symposium' <www.fdic.gov/news/conferences/TUM_bio.html> accessed 3 September 2013.

Federal Reserve Policy on Payment System Risk <www.federalreserve.gov/payment systems/psr_policy.htm?> accessed 3 September 2014.

Ferguson, Roger, *The Ascent of Money: A Financial History of the World* (Penguin Books 2008).

Ferguson, Roger, 'Should Financial Stability Be an Explicit Central Bank Objective?' (Presentation at the policy panel of BIS Conference on 'Monetary Stability, Financial Stability and the Business Cycle', (2003) 18 *BIS Papers* 7–15.

Ferguson, R. W., *Should Financial Stability Be an Explicit Central Bank Objective' Challenges to Central Banking from Globalized Financial Systems* (Washington, DC: International Monetary Fund 2008).

Financial Action Task Force, Annual Report (2008) <www.fatf-gafi.org/media/fatf/documents/reports/2008%202009%20ENG.pdf> accessed 10 September 2014.

The Financial Conduct Authority calls for inputs on payments systems regulation <www.fca.org.uk/static/documents/psr-call-for-inputs.pdf> accessed 3 September 2014.

Financial Services Authority, 'Operational Risk Systems and Controls' (2002) Consultation Paper No 142 <www.bankofengland.co.uk/financialstability/fsc/Documents/FSAConsultationPaper142.pdf> accessed 3 September 2014.

Financial Services Expansion, (2010) <www.ftc.gov/sites/default/files/documents/public_comments/ftc-host-workshop-mobile-payments-and-their-impact-con sumers-project-no.124808–561018–00012%C2%A0/561018–00012–82712. pdf> accessed 3 September 2014; Mobile-Financial.com.

Financial Stability Report, 'Kenya 2012' (2012) 47 <www.centralbank.go.ke/images/docs/kfs/financial%20stability%20report%202012.pdf> accessed 3 September 2014.

Finextra, 'Ugandan Telco Says Employees Stole $3.5m in Mobile Money Fraud' *Finextra* (28 May 2012) <www.finextra.com/news/fullstory.aspx?newsitemid=23759> accessed 3 September 2014.

Folkerts-Landau, David, 'Systemic Financial Risk in Payment Systems' (1990) IMF Working Paper No 90/65 <http://papers.ssrn.com/sol3/papers.cfm?abstract_id=884911> accessed 3 September 2014.

Freixas, Xavier and Bruno Parigi, 'Systemic Risk, Interbank Relations and Liquidity Provision by the Central Bank' (1998) Economics Working Papers 440 <www.econ.upf.edu/docs/papers/downloads/440.pdf> accessed 3 September 2014.

Fry, Maxwell J., *Payment Systems in Global Perspective* (Routledge 2003) 13.

FSB (2010). <www.imf.org/external/pubs/ft/gfsr/2014/01/pdf/c3.pdf> accessed 3 September 2014.

Gai, Prassana, *Systemic Risk the Dynamics of Modern Financial Systems* (OUP 2013); also, Gai, Prasanna and Sujit Kapadia, 'Contagion in Financial Networks' (2007) <http://www2.warwick.ac.uk/fac/soc/economics/staff/academic/miller/esrcproffellows/summer2007/programme2/prasanna_gai_-_contagioninfinancialnetworks.pdf> accessed 3 September 2014.

General Manager of the Bank for International Settlements and Chairman of the Financial Stability Forum, at the Banks and Systemic Risk Conference, Bank of England, London, 23–25 May 2001 <www.bis.org/speeches/sp010523.htm> accessed 3 September 2014.

Geva, Benjamin, *Collections and Payment Transactions: Comparative Study of Legal Aspects* (Oxford University Press 2001).

Glajchen, Deon, 'A Comparative Analysis of Mobile Phone-Based Payment Services in the United States and South Africa' (PhD Dissertation, Northcentral University, 2011).

Global Financial Integrity, 'Illicit Financial Flows from Africa: Hidden Resource for Development'<www.gfintegrity.org/storage/gfip/documents/reports/gfi_africareport_web.pdf> accessed 3 September 2014.

Gobert, James and Maurice Punch, *Rethinking Corporate Crime* (Cambridge University Press 2003).

Golding, Paul, *Next Generation Wireless Applications: Creating Mobile Applications In A Web 2.0 And Mobile 2.0 World* (John Wiley & Sons 2008)

Gray, Dale F., Robert C. Merton and Zvi Bodie, 'A New Framework for Analyzing and Managing Macrofinancial Risks of an Economy (2006) Working Paper No 07–026 <www.hbs.edu/faculty/Pages/download.aspx?name=07-026.pdf> accessed 3 September 2014.

GSMA, 'Mobile Financial Services Risk Matrix' (2010) <http://mobile-financial.com/blog/mobile-financial-services-risk-matrix> accessed 3 September 2014.

'A Guide to Risk in Payment Systems Owned and Operated by the CPA' <www.cdnpay.ca/imis15/pdf/pdfs_publications/Risk_Guide.pdf?bcsi_scan_B895ED BE82A479 62=PGBDY/ >accessed 18 September 2014.

Hahn, Ryan, 'Payment Systems and Systemic Risk' (2008) *The World Bank* <http://blogs.worldbank.org/psd/payment-systems-and-systemic-risk> accessed 3 September 2014.

Hannig, Alfred and Stefan Jansen, 'Financial Inclusion and Financial Stability: Current Policy Issues' (2010) ADBI Working Paper Series, No 259 <www.adbi.org/files/2010.12.21.wp259.financial.inclusion.stability.policy.issues.pdf> accessed 3 September 2014.

Hannig, Alfred, and Jansen Stefan (n 1 Chapter 1); Gary Dymski, 'Banking Strategy and Financial Exclusion: Tracing the Pathways of Globalization' (2005) 31 *Revista de Economia* 1–29, 107–143 <http://papers.ssrn.com/sol3/papers.cfm?abstract_id=901834> accessed 3 September 2014.

Hannig, Alfred, Stefan Jansen, 'Financial Inclusion and Financial Stability' (2010) ADBI Working Paper Series,No.259<www.adbi.org/files/2010.12.21.wp259.financial.inclusion.stability.policy.issues.pdf> accessed 3 September 2014.

Hardy, Daniel C., 'Regulatory Capture in Banking' (2006) 34 *International Monetary Fund.*

Harris, R., 'Does Outsourcing Reduce Operational Risk?' *Operational Risk Federal Reserve Bank of Chicago* (September 2001) <www.chicaofded.orw/bankinginformation/files/operationalriskarchieve2001outsource.ndt> accessed July 2005.

Hawke Jr, John, 'Risk Management for Electronic Banking and Electronic Money Activities' (1998) *International Monetary Seminar Paris* 92.

Hennie Bester et al., 'Implementing FATF Standards in Developing Countries and Financial Inclusion: Findings and Guidelines' (2008) World Bank First Initiative, Final Report <www.cenfri.org/documents/ AML/AML_CFT%20and%20Financial%20Inclusion.pdf.d> accessed 3 September 2014.

Herzberg, Amir, 'Payments and Banking with Mobile Personal Devices' (2003) 46 *Communications of the ACM* 53.

Hyuha, Mukwanason, Mo Ndanshau and Jonas Paul Kipokola, *Scope, Structure and Policy Implications of Informal Financial Markets in Tanzania* (African Economic Research Consortium 1993).

IMF, 'Defining Financial Stability' (2004) <www.imf.org/external/pubs/ft/wp/2004/wp04187.pdf> accessed 3 September 2014.

IMF, 'Singapore: Financial System Stability Assessment, including Reports on the Observance of Standards and Codes on the Following Topics: Banking Supervision, Insurance Regulation, Securities Regulation, Payment and Settlement Systems, Monetary and Financial Policy Transparency, and Anti- Money Laundering' (2004) <www.imf.org/external/pubs/ft/scr/2004/cr04104.pdf> accessed 3 September 2014.

Isern, Jennifer, David Porteous, Raul Hernandez-Coss and Chinyere Egwuagu, 'AML/CTF Regulation: Implications For Financial Service Providers That Serve Low-Income People' (2005) <http://siteresources.worldbank.org/EXTAML/Resources/396511–1146581427871/AML_implications_complete.pdf> accessed 3 September 2014.

Johnson, Omotunde E. G., *Payment Systems, Monetary Policy and the Role of the Central Bank* (International Monetary fund 1998).

Kar, Dev and Devon Cartwright-Smith, 'Illicit Financial Flows from Developing Countries: 2002–2006' (GFI 2006)<www.gfintegrity.org/storage/gfip/executive%20-%20final%20version%201-5-09.pdf> accessed 3 September 2014.

Kenya Electronic Payment and Settlement System (KEPSS) <www.centralbank.go.ke/index.php/2012-09-21-11-44-41/kepss> accessed 3 September 2014.

Kessler, Ian and John Purcell, 'Performance Related Pay: Objectives and Application' (1988) 2 *Human Resource Management Journal* 16.

Kimenyi, Mwangi and Njuguna Ndung'u, 'Expanding the Financial Services Frontier: Lessons from Mobile Phone Banking in Kenya' (Brookings Institution, October).

Klein, Allen N. and Colin Mayer, 'Mobile Banking and Financial Inclusion – The Regulatory Lesson' (2011) World Bank Policy Research Working Paper No. 5664 <http://papers.ssrn.com/sol3/papers.cfm?abstract_id=1846305> accessed 3 September 2014.

Klein, Michael and Ignacio Mas, 'A Note on Macro-Financial Implications of Mobile Money Schemes' (2012) Frankfurt School Working Paper No 188 <http://papers.ssrn.com/sol3/Delivery.cfm/SSRN_ID2033816_code829576.pdf?abstractid=2033816&mirid=1> accessed 3 September 2014.

Koker, Louis De, 'Anonymous Clients, Identified Clients and the Shades in Between: Perspectives on the FATF AML/CFT Standards and Mobile Banking' (2009) 27th Cambridge International Symposium on Economic Crime 4.

Koker, Louis De, 'Client Identification and Money Laundering Control: Perspectives on the Financial Intelligence Centre Act 38 of 2001' 4 *Journal of South African Law* 715–746.

Koker, Louis De, 'The Money Laundering Risk Posed by Low Risk Financial Products in South Africa: Findings and Guidelines' (2009) 12(4) *Journal of Money Laundering Control* 323–339.

KPMG Study, ' "Underserved" Market Represents Opportunity for Banks,' <http://goo.gl/FHzAj> accessed 3 September 2014.

Kuussaari, Harri, 'Systemic Risk in the Finnish Payment Systems: An Empirical Investigation' (1996) Bank of Finland Discussion Paper.

LaBrosse, John Raymond, Rodrigo Olivares-Caminal and Dalvinder Singh, *Financial Crisis Containment and government Guarantees* (Edward Elgar 2013).

Lake, Andrew James, 'Risk Management in Mobile Money, Observed Risk and Proposed Mitigants for Mobile Money Operators' (2013) <www.ifc.org/wps/wcm/connect/37a086804236698d8220ae0dc33b630b/Tool+7.1.+Risk+Management.pdf?MOD=AJPERES> accessed 3 September 2014.

Landau, Jean-Pierre, *Procyclicality: What It Means and What Could Be Done*. Bank of Spain's conference on Procyclicality and the Role of Financial Regulation, Madrid, 4 May 2009.

Lauer, Kate, Denise Dias and Michael Tarazi, 'Bank Agents: Risk Management, Mitigation, and Supervision' (2012) 75 *Focus Note*.

Levi, Maurice D., *International Finance: Contemporary Issues* (4th edn, Routledge 2005).

Lublo, Ágnes, 'Topology of the Hungarian Large-Value Transfer System' (2006) MNB Occasional Papers 57.

Lyman, Timothy, Gautam Ivatury and Stefan Staschen, 'Use of Agents in Branchless Banking for the Poor: Rewards, Risks, and Regulation' (2006) 38 *Focus Note* <www.cgap.org/sites/default/files/CGAP-Focus-Notes-Use-of-Agents-in-Branchless-Banking-for-the-Poor-Rewards-Risks-and-Regulation-Oct-2006-Chinese.pdf> accessed 3 September 2014.

Lyman, Timothy, Mark Pickens and David Porteous, 'Regulating Transformational Branchless Banking: Mobile Phones and Other Technology to Increase Access to Finance' (2008) <http://goo.gl/YboX0> accessed 3 September 2014.

Malala, Joy, 'Consumer Protection for Mobile Payments in Kenya: An Examination of the Fragmented Legislation and the Complexities It Presents for Mobile Payments'

(2014) Kenya Bankers Association, Centre for Research on Financial Markets and Policy Working Paper Series No 7 <www.kba.co.ke/workingpaperseries/img/pdf/Working%20Paper%20WPS-07-13.pdf> accessed 3 September 2014.

Managed Futures Today, 'Safeguarding Customers Through Segregated Funds' (2011) <www.managedfuturestodaymag.com/safeguarding-customers-through-segregated-funds> accessed 3 September 2014.

Mañalac, Wilhelmina C., Agnes M. Yap and Magno Torreja, Jr., 'Real Time Gross Settlement (RTGS) System and Its Implications' (2003) <www.bsp.gov.ph/down loads/publications/2003/BSR2003_03.pdf> accessed 3 September 2014.

Marquardt, Jeffrey C., 'Payment System Policy Issues and Analysis' *The Payment System: Design, Management, and Supervision.*

Martin, Antoine, 'Recent Evolution of Large-Value Payment Systems: Balancing Liquidity and Risk' (2005) <www.kansascityfed.org/PUBLICAT/ECONREV/Pdf/1Q05mart.pdf> accessed 3 September 2014.

Mas, Ignacio and Dan Radcliffe, 'Mobile Payments Go Viral: M-PESA in Kenya' (2010) 353–369 <http://siteresources.worldbank.org/AFRICAEXT/Resources/258643-1271798012256/M-PESA_Kenya.pdf> accessed 3 September 2014.

Maurer, Bill, 'Due Diligence and "Reasonable Man", Offshore' (2005) 20(4) *Cultural Anthropology* 474–505.

McAndrews, James and George Wassillie, 'Simulations of Failure in a Payment System' (1995) Federal Reserve Bank of Philadelphia Working Paper 95–19 <http://econpapers.repec.org/paper/fipfedpwp/95-19.htm> accessed 3 September 2014.

McPhail, K., 'Managing Operational Risk in Payment, Clearing, and Settlement Systems' (2005) Bank of Canada, Working Paper 2/2003 <www.bankofcanada.ca/wp-content/uploads/2012/02/fsr-0603-mcphail.pdf> accessed 3 September 2014.

Merritt, Cynthia, 'Mobile Money Transfer Services: The Next Phase in the Evolution of Person-to-Person Payments' (2011) 5 *Journal of Payments Strategy & Systems* 143.

Merritt, Cynthia, 'Mobile Money Transfer Services: The Next Phase in the Evolution of Person-to-Person Payments' (2011)

Millar, Paul and Carol A. Northcott, 'The CLS Bank: Managing Risk in Foreign Exchange Settlement' (2002) *Financial System Review* <www.bankofcanada.ca/wp-content/uploads/2012/02/fsr-1202-miller.pdf> accessed 3 September 2014.

'Mobile Banking Solutions for the Poor: A Survey of the Literature' (2011) 6 *Innovations* 81.

'Mobile Financial Services Risk Matrix' (2010) 71 <http://mobile-financial.com/blog/mobile-financial-services-risk-matrix> accessed 3 September 2014.

Mobile Money – GSMA, <www.gsma.com/mobilefordevelopment/wp- content/uploads/2013/02/MMU-Enabling-Regulatory-Solutions-di-Castri-2013.pdf> accessed 18 September 2014.

Mobile-Financial.com, 'Mobile Financial Services Risk Matrix' (2010) <http://mobile-financial.com/blog/mobile-financial-services-risk-matrix> accessed 3 September 2014.

Morawczynski, Olga and Mark Pickens, 'Poor People Using Mobile Financial Services: Observations on Customer Usage and Impact from M-PESA.' (2009) <http://www wds.worldbank.org/external/default/WDSContentServer/WDSP/IB/2009/09/11/000333037_20090911001822/Rendered/PDF/503060BRI0Box31MPESA1Brief01PUBLIC1.pdf> accessed 3 September 2014.

'M-Pesa Agents' <www.safaricom.co.ke/personal/m-pesa/m-pesa-agents> accessed 3 September 2014.

Muthiora, Brian, 'Ring-Fencing and Safeguard of Customer Money' (2014) <www.gsma.com/mobilefordevelopment/kenyas-new-regulatory-framework-for-e-money-issuers> accessed 3 September 2014.

National Payments Systems Framework (August 2004) <www.docstoc.com/docs/83536188/nps_framework> accessed 3 September 2014.

Ndung'u. <www.nbt.tj/files/Fin_mon/draft_01.pdf> accessed 3 September 2014.

*The New Penguin Dictionary of Computing*, 217.

Obera, Ignacio, 'Safaricom Marks 5 Years Amidst Agent Liquidity Concerns' <www.mobilepaymentstoday.com/blogs/safaricom-marks-5-years-amidst-agent-liquidity-concerns/> accessed 22 September 2014.

Pénicaud, Claire, 'State of the Industry: Results from the 2012 Global Mobile Money Adoption Survey' (2012) GSMA, London, United Kingdom <www.gsma.com/mobilefordevelopment/wp-content/uploads/2013/03/MMU_Results-from-the-2012-Global-Mobile-Money-Adoption-Survey.pdf> accessed 3 September 2014.

Perlman, Leon, 'Mobile Money and Financial Inclusion' (2012) <http://cellular.co.za/042012-mmoney-inclusion.htm> accessed 3 September 2014.

Pickens, Mark, David Porteous and Sarah Rotman, 'Banking the Poor via G2P Payments' 58 *Focus Note*

Pierre-Laurent Chatain et al., *Protecting Mobile Money Against Financial Crimes: Global Policy Challenges and Solutions* (World Bank Publications 2011).

Power, Michael, 'The Invention of Operational Risk' (2005) 12 *Review of International Political Economy* 577.

PriceWaterhouseCoopers in conjunction with the Economist Intelligence Unit, 'Compliance: A Gap in the Heart of Risk Management' (2003) <www.sum2.us/images/PWCcompliancenadriskmgmt.pdf> 8. Vesa, Jarkko, *Mobile Services in the Networked Economy* (IGI Global 2005).

Rambure, Dominique and Alec Nacamuli, *Payment Systems: From the Salt Mines to the Board* (Palgrave Macmillan 2008) 58.

Reserve Bank of India, 'Report of the Technical Committee on Enabling Public Key Infrastructure (PKI) in Payment System Applications' (2014) <www.rbi.org.in/scripts/PublicationReportDetails.aspx?UrlPage=&ID=759>

'Risk Management Framework for Microfinance Institutions' (2000) <www.ruralfinance.org/fileadmin/templates/rflc/documents/1126266387218_A_risk_managem ent_framework_for_MFIs.pdf> accessed 3 September 2014.

Rudd, Kevin, 'The Global Financial Crisis' (2009) *The Monthly* <www.themonthly.com.au/issue/2009/february/1319602475/kevin- rudd/global-financial-crisis> accessed 3 September 2014.

'Safaricom Should Consider M-Pesa Fall Back Servers' *The Standard Newspaper* (Nairobi, 29 October 2012) <www.standardmedia.co.ke/?articleID=2000069486%3E> accessed 3 September 2014.

'Safeguarding the Stability of the Financial System'<www.bnm.gov.my/files/publication/fsbp/en/06_Safeguarding_the_Stability_Financial_System. pdf> accessed 18 September 2014.

Sato, Setsuya and John Hawkin, 'Electronic Finance: An Overview of the Issues' (2001) BIS Paper No 7 <www.bis.org/publ/bppdf/bispap07.htm> accessed 3 September 2014.

Saunders, Anthony, 'Banking and Commerce: An Overview of the Public Policy Issues' (1994) 18 *Journal of Banking & Finance* 231.

Saxena, Amitabh, 'Accelerating Financial Inclusion Through Innovative Channels: 10 Obstacles for MFIs Launching Alternative Channels – and What Can Be Done About Them' (2009) 27 <http://goo.gl/BwmHj>.

Schinasi, Garry J., 'Defining Financial Stability and Establishing a Framework to Safeguard It' (2011)

Schinasi, Garry J., *Safeguarding Financial Stability: Theory and Practice* (International Monetary Fund 2005).

Schoenmaker, Dirk, Peter M. Garber and David Folkerts-Landau, 'The Reform of Wholesale Payment Systems and Its Impact on Financial Markets' (1996) IMF Working Papers 96/37 <http://papers.ssrn.com/sol3/papers.cfm?abstract_id= 882937> accessed 3 September 2014.

Shah, Anup, 'Global Financial Crisis' (2013) 25 *Global Issues*.

Silber, William, *Towards a Theory of Financial Innovation* (Lexington Books 1975).

Solin, Marina and Andrew Zerzan, 'A Mobile Money: Methodology for Assessing Money Laundering and Terrorist Financing Risks' (2010) GSMA Discussion Paper <www.gsma.com/mobilefordevelopment/wp-content/uploads/2012/03/aml final35.pdf> accessed 3 September 2014.

Stephens, Maria C., 'Promoting Responsible Financial Inclusion: A Risk-Based Approach to Supporting Mobile Money Transfer Services Expansion' (2011) 27(1) *Banking And Finance Law Review* 329.

Stephens, Maria C. and Lisa Dawson, 'A Risk Based Approach to Regulatory Policy and Mobile Financial Services' (2011) *Federal Reserve Bank of Atlanta America Centre* <www.frbatlanta.org/documents/news/conferences/11consumer_bank ing_dawson_stephens_pres.pdf> accessed 3 September 2014.

Sultana, Rasheda, 'Mobile Banking: Overview of Regulatory Framework in Emerging Markets' (2009) <http://papers.ssrn.com/sol3/papers.cfm?abstract_id=155 4160> accessed 3 September 2014.

Summers, Bruce J., *The Payment System: Design, Management, and Supervision* (International Monetary Fund 1994).

Symposium: Mobile Money in Developing Countries: <https://litigationessentials. lexisnexis.com/webcd/app?action=DocumentDisplay&crawlid=1&doctype=cite& docid=8+Wash.+J.L.+Tech.+%26+Arts+165&srctype=smi&srcid=3B15&key=ac18 69da6efe0aa ef20a35e844ae39c1> accessed 22 September 2014.

Tatom, John and David Godstead, 'Targeting the Unbanked-Financial Literacy's Magic Bullet?' (2006) University Library of Munich, MPRA Paper 4266 <http:// mpra.ub.uni-muenchen.de/4266/1/MPRA_paper_4266.pdf> accessed 3 September 2014.

'Trade-Offs and Synergies Between Financial Inclusion and Financial Stability' (7 August 2014) <www.adbi.org/workingpaper/2010/12/21/4272.financial. inclusion.stability.policy.issues/tradeof fs.and.synergies.between.financial.inclusion stability/> accessed 3 September 2014.

Uganda Law Commission Cautions on Mobile Money Regulation, <www.africa-uganda-business-travel-guide.com/uganda-law-commission-cautions-on-mobile-money-regulation.html> accessed 3 September 2014.

UN Capital Development Fund (2006).

'United Nations Statistics Division – Standard Country and Area Codes Classifications (M49)'. <Unstats.un.org> accessed 15 January 2014.'

Vincent, Katharine and Tracy Cull, 'Cell Phones, Electronic Delivery Systems And Social Cash Transfers: Recent Evidence and Experiences From Africa' (2011) 64 *International Social Security Review* 37.

Wentworth, Elisabeth, 'Direct Debits, Consumer Protection and Payment System Regulation – Issues of Policy and Reform' (2002) 13 *JBFLP* 77.

'What Is Financial Inclusion? – Asian Development Bank Institute', <www.adbi. org/working-paper/2010/12/21/4272.financial.inclusion.stability.policy.issues/ what.is.financial.inclusion/> accessed 24 September 2014.

Winn, Jane Kaufman, 'Clash of the Titans: Regulating the Competition Between Established and Emerging Electronic Payment Systems' (1999) 14 *Berkeley Technology Law Journal* 675.

Winn, Jane Kaufman, 'Symposium: Clash of the Titans: Regulating the Competition Between Established and Emerging Electronic Payment Systems' (1999) 14 *Berkeley Technology Law Journal* 675.

World Economic Forum, 'The Mobile Financial Services Development Report 2011' (2011) <http://www3.weforum.org/docs/WEF_MFSD_Report_2011.pdf> accessed 3 September 2014.

<www.bis.org/publ/bppdf/bispap01a.pdf> accessed 3 September 2014

<www.centralbank.go.ke/index.php/retail-payment-statistics/mobile-payments? yr=2014> accessed 3 September 2014.

<www.equitybank.co.ke/index.php/self-service/mobile-banking/m-kesho> accessed 3 September 2014.

<www.safaricom.co.ke> accessed 3 September 2014.

# 4 The legal and regulatory challenges in the current regulatory framework

## 4.1 Introduction

Regulation is a phenomenon that is, according to Karen Yeung, 'notoriously difficult to define with clarity and precision because its meaning and the scope of its inquiry are unsettled and contested'.[1] As a result, there has been a lot of discomfort amongst regulators[2] attached to mobile financial services and how best to regulate mobile payments.[3] Financial regulators have the mandate to preserve the stability of the financial system,[4] to ensure financial integrity[5] and resilience,[6] while encouraging innovation and financial inclusion.[7] These functions exist in tension with each other, as sustaining financial stability requires bearing down on risks,[8] which can limit innovation. As a result, there has been a lot of discomfort amongst regulators[9] attached to mobile financial services and how best to regulate mobile payments.[10] In Kenya, the convergence[11] of telecommunications and financial services has caused a convergence in policies amongst regulatory authorities[12] who have different objectives,[13] which has led to regulatory and legal challenges. Furthermore, there is a lack of specific payments systems law[14] that addresses mobile payments specifically, coupled with the fragmentation[15] of the consumer protection laws, where the Consumer Protection Act 2012 does not have specific provisions for financial service consumers and was enacted six years after the introduction of mobile payments. This further highlights the complexities of regulation and innovation and also highlights the fact that new products have been a catalyst for the adoption of new laws in Kenya. This has impeded the development of appropriate regulation that would address the needs of consumers in mobile financial services[16] (a problem that goes beyond mobile payments). Regulators have prioritised innovation over regulation. Further, regulatory overlap,[17] inertia[18] and arbitrage[19] have obstructed the efficiencies of these authorities and led to duplicative and conflicting regulation, which is inefficient and unduly burdensome for regulators.[20] This in turn inhibits more rational regulation and contributes to random selection of regulatory priorities as well as inconsistencies in regulatory authorities' approach.[21]

Still, these challenges have not overtly piqued the interests of prudential authorities in Kenya, who should be concerned with the potential of mobile financial services, in general, which have come to bypass central banks and governments in the issuing of money and the control of payments systems.[22] The very indication of funds, be it electronic or otherwise, being taken by an entity financial or otherwise, immediately raises 'deposit taking'.[23] The term deposit taking has always been the determining factor or identifier of what a bank thinks could prompt some prudential oversight or analogy with common law views of banks and deposits,[24] which Kenyan regulation, or at least its approach to mobile payments regulation, has at present not addressed.[25]

Clarification in statute for stored value payments[26] has been lacking. The term 'deposit', as well as the position of mobile network operators (MNOs) (although they provide payments through stored value[27]) in relation to the 'business of banking' as defined by the Banking Act, Cap 488,[28] are unclear in Kenyan law.[29] Allowing MNOs to bypass laws applying to banks allows them to operate without clear legal accountability, which puts the payment system and the stakeholders at legal risk.[30] Clarification would give the Central Bank of Kenya (CBK), the main financial regulator in Kenya, the clear mandate it requires in the new converged environment.

This chapter therefore advances discourse on the need for stability integrity and inclusion described in Chapter 3, arguing that Kenyan regulators should focus on clarifying the law and reconceptualising the changing nature of today's financial activities in Kenya. I envision a role for both the CBK and the industry regulator, Communications Commission of Kenya (CCK), and regulatory capabilities and capacities[31] for the effective regulation of mobile payments for each. The approaches to regulation prioritise the interests of consumers, the most vulnerable stakeholders.[32]

The arguments are structured in three parts. The first part will analyse the regulatory framework in place before the National Payments System Act of 2011 (NPSA), which is still in the process of implementation, examining the functions and roles of the regulatory authorities and the CBK as a regulator of all retail payments systems under the law.[33] The legal and regulatory challenges of applying the provisions of the Banking Act CAP (488)[34] to a MNO provide a rationale for special provisions under the NPSA for mobile payments. As I will show, the gaps between the theory and practice of financial regulation as regards mobile payments create a special regulatory arbitrage that affects its application and prescription to the mobile payment system.[35] Part two assesses how the current legal framework affects the regulatory authorities' roles and functions in the payments system. Part three discusses how these challenges impact consumers and the inadequacy of the current regulation in relation to their oversight and protection. Part four discusses the normative regulatory approach[36] that the CBK has taken in relation to mobile payments. It also assesses its adequacy and appropriateness to regulate mobile payments based on regulatory strategies it might apply and particularly its appropriateness to protect consumers.[37]

## PART I

### 4.2 An examination of the current regulatory framework for mobile payments systems

In Kenya, financial services regulation is characterised by fragmented or multiplicity of regulatory authorities that oversee different subsectors of the financial system,[38] with regulatory gaps, overlaps, inconsistency of regulations and differences in operational standards.[39] Since mobile payments exist in a converged regulatory space between the telecommunications industry, which provides the platform for the operation of the technology, and central banks, which regulate financial services functions, mobile financial services readily fall through regulatory gaps.[40]

Because the NPSA has only recently taken effect,[41] and before the Banking Act of 1989 (CAP 488)[42] and the Banking Act of 1969, banking in Kenya was regulated under a piece of legislation from the colonial era, namely, the Banking Ordinance. The 1969 Act allowed the Minister of Finance to license banks and non-bank financial institutions. It also gave the CBK the responsibility of inspecting all financial institutions. The Banking (Amendment) Act of 1985 changed the licensing regime, such that the CBK did so with the minister's approval. A series of bank failures in Kenya led to the Deposit Protection Fund (DPF) in 1986. For a comparative and historical perspective on banking in East Africa, the Bills of Exchange Act of 1882, the Companies Act (Cap 486) of 1978, the Building Society Act (Cap 489) of 1989 and the Cheques Act of 1957 provide a relevant legal framework.[43] Kenya has some 169 institutions in the formal banking sector. There are about 43 commercial banks,[44] about 123 foreign exchange (hereafter forex) bureaus,[45] several but few mortgage finance companies, and six licensed deposit taking microfinance institutions.[46] The Central Bank holds the primary financial system regulator's mandate, which includes the regulation of banking, payments and financial services, as prescribed under the Central Bank Act (Cap 481) 1966.[47] Section 4 of the Act states that the CBK's core mandate is to 'formulate and implement monetary policy directed at achieving and maintaining stability in the general level of prices, by fostering the liquidity, solvency and proper functioning of a stable market-based financial system, and will support the economic policy of the Government, including its objectives for growth and employment'.[48]

Before the drafting of the National Payment Systems Draft Bill, there were two divisions charged with the regulatory oversight of payments systems,[49] the National Payment System Division and the Banking Supervision Department (herein BSD) which oversaw banking activities until 2011. The BSD oversaw commercial banks as well as non-bank financial institutions, mortgage finance companies, building societies, foreign exchange bureaus, deposit-taking microfinance institutions and credit reference bureaus.[50] The BSD licensed financial institutions under the Banks Act and had a broad mandate in policy and surveillance.[51] Along with the National Payment System Division, it dealt with the development of legal and regulatory frameworks and effectively ensured the stability and efficiency of accessing financial services through supervision of their financial conditions, either through institutions or through examining their compliance. They regulated payments systems.[52] Mobile payments had no specific industry regulatory oversight;[53] however, mobile payment systems were generally regulated through ad hoc supervision by both the CCK and the CBK.

### 4.2.1 *The regulatory authorities*

As previously stated, there is very little analysis or attention paid to the role of the CCK in regulating mobile payments. While the CBK certainly has primary authority, the Kenya Information and Communications Act 1998 classifies mobile payment systems such as M-Pesa as value added services (VAS) in the context of telecommunications.[54] In addition, mobile financial services, including mobile payments systems, are modelled into essentially electronic transactions regulated by the CCK.[55]

### 4.2.1.1 *The Central Bank of Kenya*

Article 231 of the Constitution of Kenya 2010[56] and Section 3 of the Central Bank Act[57] establish the CBK. The CBK's mandate calls for formulating monetary policy, promoting price stability, issuing currency and formulating and employing policies to promote stability and the establishment, regulation and supervision of efficient and effective payment and settlement systems. The CBK licenses, regulates and supervises banking and microfinance businesses and regulates and supervises payment systems and payment service providers.[58] Therefore, the CBK has core regulatory oversight of mobile payments.

Kenya's Central Bank is typical in that it has three monetary policy imperatives,[59] and it has a natural monopoly over issuing legal tender. Some scholars, however, believe that monetary policy and the Central Bank monopoly is trite and artificial, that money is a commodity and that therefore 'no institution is required to regulate the supply of money on a free market'. The premise is based, however, more on the use of gold as the standard of determining a currency's unit of account. However, mobile money and electronic money generally deplete this monopoly. While some national or supra-national[60] governments give their central bank general monopoly rights too many fiscal systems, the CBK has monopoly rights to interest rates, the creation of policies for money supply, legal tender issuance, banknotes and the oversight of the integrity of national payments systems.[61] Several developing countries have recognised the importance of payment systems and have made amendments to their legislation to extend their central bank's powers to verse the systems, a model the CBK might follow.[62] The Bank of International Settlement (BIS) also concurs that payment systems are of great importance.[63] The Central Bank of Kenya also controls the national payments system (hereafter NPS) through the reduction of systemic risk as discussed in Chapter 3.[64] The CBK examines risks within Kenya's banks to ensure against panic among participants or within the banking and payments system by examining deposits.[65] The Central Bank also has oversight over payment mechanisms,[66] facilitating the interchange of payments in the settlement of debt between banks, and by extension, others engaged in payment services.[67] Thus national payment systems are at the core of the modern Central Bank's role, with the Central Bank acting to supply money for settlement of payments.[68]

### 4.2.1.2 *The Communications Commission of Kenya*

CCK[69] is the independent regulatory authority for Kenya's communications industry. It licenses and regulates telecommunications, including radio communication, postal and courier services. It also issues licenses to internet service providers and other industries; its purview extends beyond unlicensed frequencies. Its role extends to the development and coordination of policies and strategies for the development and operation of telecommunications services in Kenya. Its establishment in 1999 was welcomed after the Kenya Post and Telecommunication Corporation (KP&TC) was divided into CCK, the Postal Corporation of Kenya (PCK) and Telkom Kenya.[70]

The Kenya Communications Act No. 2 of 1998 established the CCK, which came into existence in 1999. The Act unbundled the KP&TC into five separate entities: the CCK, which is the regulator; the National Communications Secretariat (NCS), which serves as the policy advisory arm of the government on all matters pertaining to the information and communications sector; the fixed-line operator, Telkom; the Postal Corporation of Kenya (POSTA); and a Communications Appeals Tribunal.[71] In recognition of the rapid changes and developments in technology which have blurred the traditional distinctions between telecommunications, IT and broadcasting, the Kenya Communications (Amendment) Act 2009 improved the regulatory space and jurisdiction of CCK and successfully transformed it to a converged regulator.

The CCK regulates all MNOs, the oldest of which is Safaricom Limited, which was established in 1997 as a fully owned department of the KP&TC.[72] Forty per cent of Safaricom shares were transferred to Vodafone Kenya Limited, which sold 25 per cent of its own shareholding while 10 per cent of Safaricom's shares went to Mobitelea Ventures Limited, a company resident in Guernsey in the United Kingdom. The CCK took over the KP&TC's 60 per cent of shares.[73]

## 4.3 Functions, roles and powers of the Central Bank of Kenya in regulating mobile payments

The central bank has the responsibility of overseeing the payment systems in the country.[74] The CBK, as the financial regulator,[75] has taken the lead to shape and implement the regulatory framework for mobile payments systems.[76] Since mobile financial services have developed and evolved, and continue to do so,[77] the role of the central bank has to be re-examined in order to strike a balance between protecting the interests of the public[78] (the consumers) and over burdening the central bank to the exclusion of its main roles.[79] The CBK has recognised that it must regulate new mobile financial services[80] but has not provided specific regulation for stored value payments, on the logic that a rigorous regulatory framework would stifle innovation and impede the development of new technologies in the delivery of financial services and, therefore frustrate efforts to include the unbanked and under banked.[81] I argue that this failure leaves the mobile payment system vulnerable to risks.[82]

The mobile payment system has equipped non-financial institutions and non-banks to provide financial products and services that are not under the purview of the financial regulatory authority, the CBK. This has complicated the regulation of MNOs; I argue that this definition as a payment system provider has been problematic and the CBK needs to extend its reach in its regulatory roles and functions.[83] The need to protect the public from risk without over-regulating imposes a regulatory challenge.[84] Baldwin et al.[85] discuss the four-fold challenge central banks face in developing countries:[86] limited capacity, limited commitment, limited accountability and limited fiscal efficiency. Limited capacity refers to the state's structural and resource limitations in the face of well-resourced private interests; limited commitment refers to the frequent failure of governments of developing countries to fulfil their promises; limited accountability refers to the lack of expectation of transparency; and limited fiscal efficiency refers to the general poverty of such governments; therefore, their limited capacity to pay for infrastructure services.[87] Such governments are vulnerable to capture[88] as well as arbitrary or biased decision-making.

These challenges make reform all the more necessary, and further, the regulatory framework, which should be applicable to exclusive provision of mobile payments, should permeate different ministries[89] within the Kenyan government. The development of mobile payments has made it imperative that the CCK and the CBK have clearly defined roles.[90] Kenya at present does not have a single regulator for its non-financial institutions that perform financial functions.[91] This calls for a clear definition of the two entities' roles and functions under separate legislation as a necessary precursor to enforcement. Relevant regulatory authorities would have to ensure a workable relationship and prevent regulatory overlaps and conflicts and that the regulatory functions protect consumers.

Section 4 A (i)d of the Central Bank of Kenya Act requires the CBK to formulate and implement policies to promote the establishment, regulation and supervision of efficient, effective payment, clearing and settlement systems.[92] It also calls on the CBK to ensure smooth implementation and transmission of monetary policy objectives and public confidence in the domestic financial system.[93] The CBK already has the specific mandate to establish a clearinghouse in order to facilitate the clearing of cheques and other credit or payment instruments for banking institutions and other financial institutions,[94] and the NPSA strengthens the CBK's role with respect to mobile payment systems.[95] The CBK, however, has no wide powers that cover the regulation of non-financial institutions, as Kenya lacks a consolidated financial sector regulator.[96] This then calls for regulatory oversight of non-financial institutions in the payment systems arena by the CBK and not just the industry regulator the CCK.

The CBK must examine its resources, which would include adequate personnel to be responsible for various regulatory tasks or the overall microprudential oversight. Their involvement would not only include monitoring the provider of the retail payment services, but also in gathering and analysing the information on the payment instruments, including issues related to the market and development of mobile payments products and the concerns of a rigid regulatory framework for an evolving payment system to assess whether it can realistically take on this regulatory role.[97] The CBK would have to discern the various risks that might arise and assess how these risks can be properly managed.[98] This would include oversight over the acceptable degree of risks.[99] The systemic nature of the payments system has to be examined, as the failure of one participant may have systemic implications.[100] This would mean that various risks, such as integrity risks and reputational risk, would have to be considered in order to restore confidence amongst consumers and the financial stability of the payment system as whole.[101]

For the CBK to accommodate all these issues, it has to expand its ambit and reach into what it monitors. As mobile payments grow, they increasingly affect the stability of the financial system.[102] The Committee on Payment and Settlement Systems of the BIS has made a comprehensive review of retail payments. Previously concentration was placed on the payment instruments themselves and how they were settled, but recently focus has shifted to the implications of retail payments, especially innovative ones that have proven financially inclusive on central banks. Therefore, to fulfil its regulatory role, the CBK has to keep abreast of the development of new and innovative retail payments systems. New alternatives for payment will likely continue to develop, and the CBK's role in protecting consumers is crucial.[103]

To date, the CBK has allowed mobile payment systems to develop without its oversight; it particularly allows MNOs to act independently.[104] Consumers, ill equipped by scant knowledge and understanding of payment systems, do not understand the risks, and the CBK's neglect leaves them vulnerable.[105] The introduction of M-Pesa[106] has brought about an explosion in mobile payments; the CBK should give significant attention to the design and operation of and oversight of payment systems, acknowledging its contribution to the stability of the financial system.[107] The development of the financial system and its concurrent technological demands should recognise the ensuing regulatory challenges, as the monitoring and the operation of the payment system will affect the smooth implementation of monetary policy and stability of the financial system.[108]

The CBK would therefore have to examine all these schemes, but it may not have the appropriate resources.[109] These are identified as the regulatory capacities, since as a developing country Kenya may not have all the necessary expertise on issues related to mobile money, especially where the central bank is relied upon for the safety and soundness of its payment systems. The NPSA has not provided a comprehensive regulatory framework.[110] Further, externalities of a comprehensive regulatory framework may discourage innovation due to compliance costs and the rigidity of the regulation instituted.[111] Arguably, mobile payments should rely on market discipline[112] to shape their regulation. However, I argue the CBK should offer guidance to the industries for the complete development of mobile payments and mobile financial systems due to their significance in the Kenyan retail payment system.

The CBK has been very enabling and flexible to date. It has been lax in installing the regulatory framework and has adopted a 'test and learn'[113] approach to regulate mobile payments. Both market needs and consumer needs should drive the legal and regulatory framework on mobile payments; active participation by user groups to incorporate their specific requirements and circumstances, including consumer finance groups,[114] through public consultations should guide the CBK's actions. Public consultation should become a norm for legal and regulatory changes affecting mobile payment systems.

As discussed in Chapter 2,[115] the CBK has taken a piecemeal approach to regulating mobile payments. Various issues related to the implementation and the dichotomy and clarification of the status of MNOs and agents were left and continue to be unresolved. While the enactment of the NPSA does not necessarily indicate such deficiencies, currently, without better public consultations[116] and with the liberal framework of mobile money, the regulatory framework may become haphazard.[117]

The regulatory capacity of the CBK is an important aspect to assess. Developing[118] countries often embrace legal transplantation,[119] shaping their legislation by adapting the legal frameworks of developed[120] countries, either through the continuation of post-colonial legal frameworks or through transplantation from elsewhere.[121] However, such transplantation must reflect the CBK's regulatory capacity with respect to mobile payments.[122]

It is important to note that there is a hierarchy in the formation of laws in Kenya. The Constitution[123] is the supreme law, and any law or custom in conflict with it is null and void to the extent of its inconsistency.[124] The second tier of the hierarchy is statute law or Acts of Parliament, which are published in the Official Gazette. Laws transplanted from the UK or India make up the third tier. The fourth source is decree law,[125] and the fifth is case law, comprising judgments from the Court of Appeal and the High Court, which serve as precedents for lower courts. The sixth source of law is customary law.[126] The seventh source is Islamic customary law. Finally, international treaties and conventions are a source of domestic law, as long as they have been ratified by Parliament.[127]

The CBK does not grant MNOs operating licences that allow for the provision of mobile payments; the CCK has this power. So, regulation should begin by clarifying the distinction between the CCK and the CBK. A consensus has not yet been reached over the best way to address this interconnection and convergence of the telecommunication service and the financial services they offer,[128] and the varying institutional and capacity constraints will have to be reframed for Kenya.[129] The scope of formal financial systems is severely limited and poses an even greater set of conceptual and practical challenges, which shall be discussed.[130]

The regulatory measures currently adopted and under consideration form part of the CBK's regulatory capacity. While Kenya seeks to ensure financial regulators' political independence, it also avoids overregulation generally. Instituting effective regulatory structures in developing countries does not only include the technical design of the most appropriate regulatory instruments; it is also concerned with the quality of supporting regulatory institutions and their capacities.[131] Therefore, this part will briefly show how regulation has evolved over time, from simply adopting foreign or international models and legal transplantation, towards creating models unique to local circumstances to accommodate mobile payments and the challenges they bring.[132]

Regulatory capacity is an important aspect in a discussion of Kenya's legal development in efforts to reconcile innovation and regulation[133] to offer an enabling regulatory environment.[134] Examining Kenya's regulatory capacity requires considerable attention to be paid to regulatory design and operations regarding the creation of particular institutional devices or making resources available to allow strengthened regulatory capacity.[135] Therefore, regulatory reform in infrastructure industries such as telecommunications is at the heart of changing doctrines of development.[136]

The CBK's powers should prescribe and define the best practices and guidelines under which mobile payments should operate. For instance, I argue in favour of limiting the funds that are stored in mobile accounts and on the amount that can be spent per transaction and per day. The CBK should require KYC (know your customer) regulations to apply when subscribers register for the service.[137] It should also require MNOs to address security issues and possibly to pay interest on mobile accounts. Enforcement would require regular reports from the MNOs in order to assess and detect anomalies. The CBK should impose the management of float accounts through a guarantee of deposits which backs the float with real money in the bank.[138] This offers protection against the misuse of customer money and protection to customers in the event of an MNO bankruptcy. The CBK should conduct regular and unscheduled audits to ensure that MNOs follow the regulations.[139] The CBK should also be able to process the data collected from the various MNOs to perform studies on the local economy.

## 4.4 Functions, roles and powers of the communications commission of Kenya in mobile payments

The Kenya Communications Act, the Kenya Communications (Amendment) Act 1 of 2009,[140] and the Kenya Communications Regulations[141] govern telecommunications in Kenya. The Communications Commission of Kenya, telecommunications regulator alongside the National Communications Secretariat, is housed in the Ministry of Information Communication.[142] The Communications Act gives the CCK the right to issue regulations[143] guided by the provisions of the relevant statutes. Its regulatory mandate encompasses telecommunications, broadcasting, and information technology.[144] The terms and conditions allow for licensees to set up telecommunications systems and provide telecommunications services to third parties.[145] Their Unified Licensing Framework is technology and service neutral. It is structured as follows:

4.4.1 network facilities provider,
4.4.2 application service provider, and
4.4.3 content service provider.

An entity may be issued multiple commercial licences, provided that it maintains separate accounts for each licence. With respect to content, licensees under this category provide 'contents services material, information services and data processing services'.[146]

Licensing, a form of regulatory power, especially applied to the telecommunications sector, has legal, economic and social foundations. This power has the main objective of balancing public and private interests by controlling the benefits and disadvantages of a telecommunications market.[147] In Kenya, mobile telephony and related services are fundamental for social and financial inclusion.[148] The CCK selects applicants to provide telecommunications services, imposes conditions on licensees and has the power to withdraw licences.[149] Specific objectives of authorisation and licensing include revenue collection,[150] regulation of market liberalisation, market entry, public notification through transparency requirements, quality of service control and regulatory enforcement.[151] Other objectives include allocation of scarce resources[152] vesting of proprietary rights,[153] and licensing as a form of competition regulation that allows market entry.[154]

Through this liberalisation, MNOs have entered mobile payments with minimal oversight, expecting to recoup investment in a sub-optimal market.[155] The CCK initially restricted the telecommunications market to a duopoly; the two main MNOs, Safaricom and Airtel, invested their profits into infrastructure services such as M-Pesa,[156] developing mobile payments players.[157]

The CCK also regulates competition within telecommunications services, although the Competition Act 2012 covers this in part. Section 23(2) (b) of the Kenya Information and Communications Act[158] extends to mobile financial services, which have thoroughly integrated into the voice and data service provision. As James Bilodeaeau contends, however, competitiveness does not necessarily guarantee high adoption rates.[159] In fact, Kenya, Tanzania and Ghana, all of which have high mobile financial service adoption levels, lack highly competitive markets.[160] With the opening up of the market to two additional players, Telkom Kenya[161] and Essar,[162] the market dynamics have changed. This has driven Safaricom, the dominant MNO, to be more careful in its infrastructure investments, as its market shrinks.[163] Hence, the CCK must carefully wield its licensing powers to promote competition, while also guaranteeing the growth of the telecom sector.[164]

In summation, it is inevitable and imperative that in the mobile financial services environment, regulators should begin to rely on the market for self-discipline to an acceptable extent, since markets develop faster than the regulators can regulate. The correction of information asymmetry is a central role of regulators.[165] In adherence with systemically important payments systems (SIPS), the CBK has to issue regulations related to the management of credit and liquidity risks by MNOs. The failure of the CBK to issue regulations and to identify certain polices pertaining to various matters on mobile payments in conjunction with the enforcement of NPSA poses the question of whether the CBK is ready to formulate a comprehensive regulatory framework for the service, as at present, the NPSA is not being applied.

## 4.5 An examination of the legal and regulatory challenges in the current regulatory framework

Kenya's Financial Institutions Supervision Department is responsible for the prudential regulation of banks and deposit taking microfinance institutions. The department's primary concern is whether MNOs, such as Safaricom, are stretching or even breaking the rules of the business of banking.[166] However, the NPS division of the Central Bank and NPS Department, which emphasises the integrity, effectiveness, efficiency and security of the payment system, views the MNOs as payment service providers.[167]

While the NPS division appeared more willing than the Financial Institutions Supervision Department to permit experimentation with mobile payments,[168] due to the lack of a payment systems law at inception, the NPS division has lacked the necessary tools, such as the specific regulations, to supervise the payment system.[169] I offer some pertinent legal and regulatory aspects that present challenges in the effective regulation of mobile payments – specifically, challenges that exist in the statutes and the statutory instruments that defines the regulatory space[170] in which they have been operating.

### 4.5.1 The Banking Act (CAP 488)

The Banking Act of 1969[171] regulated banks in Kenya, until the passage of the 1989 Banking Act replaced it,[172] while the 2006 Microfinance Act regulates microfinance institutions. The Banking Act of 1989, like many laws around the world, requires banks to have a valid licence from the CBK[173] and defines banks as companies that carry on, or propose to carry on, banking business in Kenya, including taking deposits from the public.[174]

Section 2(1) defines a 'banking business' as:

'(a) the acceptance from members of the public of money on deposit repayable on demand or at the expiry of a fixed period or after notice;
(b) the acceptance from members of the public of money on current account[175] and payment on and acceptance of cheques; and
(c) the employment of money held on deposit or on current account, or any part of the money, by lending'.

Further, a 'financial business' is defined as:[176]

'(a) the acceptance from members of the public of money on deposit repayable on demand or at the expiry of a fixed period or after notice; and
(b) the employing of money held on deposit or any part of the money, by lending, investment or in any other manner for the account and at the risk of the person so employing the money'.

A 'financial institution' in turn is defined in Section 2 as:

'A company, other than a bank, which carries on, or proposes to carry on, financial business and includes any other company which the minister may, by notice in the Gazette, declare to be a financial institution for the purposes of the Act.'

Section 3 restricts the carrying on of 'banking business'[177] in that no one shall:

'(a) transact any banking business or financial business or the business of a mortgage finance company unless it is an institution which holds a valid licence;

(b) unless it is a bank and has obtained the consent of the Central Bank, use the word "bank" or any of its derivatives or any other word indicating the transaction of banking business, or the equivalent of the foregoing in any other language, in the name, description or title under which it transacts business in Kenya or make any representation whatsoever that it transacts banking business;

(c) unless it is a financial institution or mortgage finance company and has obtained the consent of the Central Bank, use the word "finance" or any of its derivatives or any other word indicating the transaction of financial business or the business of a mortgage finance company, or the equivalent of the foregoing in any other language, in the name, description or title under which it transacts business in Kenya or make any representation whatsoever that it transacts financial business'.

### 4.5.1.1 Challenges in the application of the current regulatory framework for mobile payments systems

The definitions in the Banking Act 1989 are problematic in relation to the specific regulatory needs of mobile payments, as they seem to create a gap in which MNOs can carry out 'banking business', without the preconditions and prerequisites that banks in Kenya need.[178] Although non-bank financial institutions may provide financial services – local currency and payment services – without carrying out banking business as defined,[179] the regulatory framework does not clarify what MNOs are in so far as they are defined as telecommunications companies that accept funds from the public. The only reference to such institutions is as 'payment service providers'.[180] There should be a compulsion to adequately define these institutions. To avoid MNOs taking advantage of these regulatory gaps, regulators' understanding of the scope and concept of banking business as the Act defines it has changed and may continue to change as a result of innovation in the financial services industry.

In fact, the concept of banking business has changed dramatically since the seventeenth century, when the precursor to the modern banking system appeared as money deposited with goldsmiths.[181] Historically, banking business has included the exchange of goods for economic advantage by providing a 'deposit',[182] as well as the provision of loans to third parties based on the depositors and the safekeeping of the goods.[183] What would be regarded as modern banking emerged from the activities of organisations that collected savings from the general public in Europe during the mid-1800s, when large limited liability commercial banks were established in many countries.[184]

Deposit taking activities have increased gradually into account transfer-based payments, slowly replacing currency and coin, since the mid-1800s.[185] Banks today encompass a wide range of financial institutions and activities that provide services beyond payments, deposit taking and loan activities,[186] primarily as intermediaries between depositors and borrowers. In that sense they manage assets and liabilities between customers. This channelling of funds between borrowers and savers is known as financial intermediation. In some contexts, intermediation may also be taken to mean the taking of loans from one party and loaning the values out fractionally to others at a higher interest rate. This may rather be described as bank intermediation. The process of creating a new asset (a loan) from liabilities (deposits) with different characteristics is called asset transformation. Financial intermediation could also be a synonym for payment intermediation, where the bank acts as a means to allow one person to pay another. Usually, though, this is simply known as 'payment' rather than intermediation, as the latter term has a lending and credit connotation. Although banks have always asserted responsibility over providing credit, and handling deposits as well as cash and cheques, through technology, banks have now entered into increasingly profitable, albeit risky territories.[187] These risky territories are now becoming increasingly complex, and the boundaries of their business are becoming unclear.

Furthermore, these territories may include niche markets and generalist banks that offer anything from bespoke payment, deposit and lending services, to real estate services, stock brokering, derivative trading, life insurance and even telecommunications and mobile products.[188] The definition of what activities constitute banking has been problematic, due to the different existing business models. These models encompassed merchant banks, clearing banks, cooperative banks, mutual banks and building societies as policy imperatives. In the context of the mobile payments systems it creates, as Leon Perlman states, a *lacuna* between banking law and banking practice.[189]

These variants beg the question of whether an entity whose main venture is not banking can be classed as a 'bank' engaged in the 'business of banking'. Despite the fact that common law definitions of what constitutes a bank usually fill any statutory gap, this definition remains elusive.[190] Still, as transformational technological advances such as mobile payments bring traditional banking services into the home, the local store, or the mobile handset, and previously held notions of a physical bank with branches dealing with customers physically to provide core retail banking services are out of date.[191] This should give rise to a reconceptualization of the traditional form of banking, vis-à-vis modern ways of advancing financial inclusion. Consumers who use mobile payments for functions other than person-to-person payments perceive their mobile payments as accounts, just as bank customers perceive banks.[192]

Nevertheless, this examination of the meaning of 'bank' and the activities that constitute banking is an important one. Adequate regulation of MNOs requires clarifying their activities and their status in law. The customer–bank relationship creates a fiduciary duty to ensure the safety of customer funds through deposit guarantees. Banks' important place in the financial system and unique privileges, which are both legal and practical,[193] especially at the prudential level, justify being the most regulated and supervised of economic sectors. Regulation ensures the safety and soundness of the financial system as a whole.

On the other hand, definitions embedded in statutory instruments may not always provide accurate answers. New financial models challenge the views of what constitutes a bank, as an institution, and what constitutes banking business, especially in the context of mobile payments. As MNOs engage in a plethora of pseudo banking activities, reconceptualization of what banks are necessary.

Around the world, the understanding of bank and bank activities continues to change.[194] At the same time, different countries define these terms differently[195] and an entity's reputation may influence its determination as a bank.[196] Common law views of banking as they stand provide some insight, but I emphasise that MNOs ingeniously escaped being classified as banks through the regulatory gap affixed to the statutory interpretation of the Banking Act. My inquiry will examine what and how institutions that provide financial services remain outside of the full application of the Banking Act in the Kenyan context.

The examination of banking as a construct of law has been fairly recent. Its evolution originates from English law which has been both transplanted[197] and incorporated into Kenyan law over time.[198] The tapestry of laws and precedent that comprises a common law view of banking includes municipal banking legislation, while secondary law – such as banking law and precedents in other, similar jurisdictions – is used by Kenyan jurists to elucidate Kenyan law where it may be unclear, underdeveloped or not developed at all on certain points.[199]

Legal transplantation from English law to Kenyan law has shown the overarching influence of English law in the development of commercial and private law aspects as a result of the post-colonial transition.[200] However, since English law has no all-encompassing definition of banking for financial intermediation[201] or clarification of what constitutes 'business of banking',[202] neither does Kenyan law. Therefore, as RST Chorley acknowledged 40 years ago, with respect to British law, 'to construct a definition which would embrace the whole of it is manifestly impossible'.[203] Therefore, Kenya has to take a practical approach to defining the core 'business of banking',[204] and it has done so by categorising characteristics that constitute banking business.[205]

While the law has generally held that 'deposits' are part of the 'business of banking', whether stored value payments are deposits remains unclear, a question that leaves the lines between traditional bank participants and non-banks such as MNOs blurred.[206] The fact that MNOs' activities involve services from a pool of user funds complicates the question. Primarily around transactional services sourced from a pool of user funds, which may be conducted by non-bank entities, even though some of their activities and relationships with customers may resemble those of licensed banks.

### 4.5.2 The definition of 'deposits'

Deposit taking by banks is subject to an interventionist and regulatory regime,[207] and jurisdictions around the world use deposit taking as a decisive indication of the 'business of banking', a definition that extends outside of banks – a deposit taking entity need not be a bank.[208] If MNOs are taking deposits, the law requires them to apply deposit protection regimes, which has consequences for customers and MNOs alike. Further, there is no *de minimus*[209] measure of deposits; even small amounts deposited or paid into an account of sorts may trigger deposit analogies, even if an entity's main business – based on aggregate transactions and profit – is not financial intermediation. MNOs' primary business is telecommunications services, but common law has not held that this disqualifies it from providing banking services or being regulated as such. In a general context, statute has determined the understanding of 'bank', 'banker' and the 'business of banking'. The common law and primary statutory definitions of banking in domestic law are 'complementary'; where the common law proclaims that a 'bank' is an entity engaged in the 'business of banking', a statute may provide the important detail by defining exactly what the 'business of banking' entails.[210]

Section 16(1) of the Banking Act of 1989 requires a valid licence to invite or accept deposits; Section 16(2) defines a 'deposit' as:

> '[A] sum of money paid on terms under which it will be repaid, with or without interest or a premium, and either on demand or at a time or in circumstances agreed by or on behalf of the person making the payment and the person receiving it; and which are not referable to the provision of property or services or the giving of security.'[211]

A business is a deposit taking business if:[212]

> '(a) in the course of the business money received by way of deposit is lent to others; or
> (b) any other activity of the business is financed, wholly or to any material extent, out of the capital of or the interest on money received by way of deposit.'[213]

The law further specifies that an entity that does not accept deposits on a day-to-day basis, but only accepts them on particular occasions, is not a deposit taking business, whether or not it sells debentures or other securities.[214] Additionally, to qualify as 'banking business', an entity must accept money on current accounts[215] and cheques from members of the public and employ the money or any part of the money held on deposit or on current account by lending. These criteria suggest that an entity must not only take deposits but must also lend funds in order to be captured by the statute. Another provision states that a deposit taking business must:

(a) receive money by way of deposit in that business which is lent to others via 'intermediation',[216] or
(b) finance activities of the business, to a material extent, out of the capital of or the interest on money received by way of deposit.[217]

Hence, if

(a) customer funds received are not loaned to others, and
(b) any interest received from those user deposits or the capital itself is somehow used to finance the business, the business may not qualify as a deposit taking entity.

The CBK's in-house counsel investigated[218] M-Pesa and concluded it was not engaging in banking business. M-Pesa accepts repayable funds from the public, but, CBK concluded, Safaricom structured its services in such a way that it effectively fell outside the definitions of 'banking business', 'financial business' and 'deposit'. As a 'transaction' and 'financial business', M-Pesa:

'(a) accepted from members of the public money on deposit repayable on demand or at the expiry of a fixed period or after notice; and also
(b) employed this money held on deposit or any part of the money, by lending, investment or in any other manner for the account and at the risk of the person so employing the money'.[219]

The CBK concluded that agents' practice of depositing their float into an M-Pesa account in a commercial bank mitigated any solvency risk, as required by Section (b). According to CBK's legal opinion, holding the (deposited) funds in a pooled trust account at a commercial bank that it could not access to fund its business via the capital and/or the interest meant that Safaricom avoided engaging in a 'banking business'.[220] MNOs often place consumer funds used to prefund the value in mobile money in pooled accounts (also called master or reservoir accounts) with prudentially supervised banks, where the trust is set up for safety and soundness to hold accounts. The commercial bank holds the value and remains distinct from the MNO, although both entities monitor the value increments or decrements.

Safaricom engaged the CBK from the pilot stage to avoid designation as a deposit taking entity; the then-acting governor of the CBK issued a letter of 'No Objection' to the commercial launch of the service in February 2007.[221] The letter indicated that if M-Pesa began to operate bank accounts[222] its status might change. It required Safaricom to, 'put appropriate measures in place to safeguard the integrity of the system and protect customers against fraud, loss of money and loss of privacy', to implement measures to protect the quality of service, 'to guard against money laundering, to keep proper records and supply them to regulatory authorities in formats as may be required from time to time, and to observe all existing laws governing its relationship with its agents and customers'.[223]

These requirements are related to operational risk, AML/KYC, systemic risk, consumer protection, agency risks[224] and avoiding insolvency.

At M-Pesa's inception, the funds paid in were in specie,[225] that is, at CBK's insistence[226] M-Pesa placed them in a special trust company, the not-for-profit M-Pesa Trust Company Limited.[227] The Commercial Bank of Africa held the pooled account, from which[228] any interest pooled accrues to the trust company, rather than to Safaricom or its users. Safaricom would cover any claims from fault by the trust company or by Safaricom,[229] and through a fractional reserve model, it would offer a justification for instituting a deposit protection scheme, while M-Pesa (and its agents) earn revenue on fees for withdrawals, deposits and transfers.[230] Over time, Safaricom has begun to use trust accounts[231] with two commercial banks that pool client funds;[232] it uses interest earned on these accounts as part of its corporate social responsibility programme and thereby avoids taxes on the interest.[233] There has always been a lack of clarity about where mobile money actually resides, who controls it and who can profit from the idle funds or float while they are sitting in the trust account.

As such, M-Pesa is not designed as a savings mechanism earning interest. Furthermore, since M-Pesa is not regulated as a bank, the NPSA has not yet come into effect,[234] M-Pesa acted as a payments system, with users able to make payments and money transfers from their balance. The CBK's decision to allow, enable[235] and support M-Pesa at the time precipitated furious lobbying by the licensed banks to the Kenyan Ministry of Finance on the basis that M-Pesa was an 'unlicensed bank' and should be shut down.[236] The CBK's January 2009 audit of M-Pesa declared it safe[237] on the basis that the average balance on M-Pesa accounts at around US $3 could not pose any systemic risk to the financial system; as stated in Chapter 3, this is a questionable finding.[238]

### 4.5.3 Challenges in its application to the current regulatory framework of mobile payments

From an economic point of view, a deposit is an entitlement to receive the credit standing to a customer's account.[239] In common law, *Foley v. Hill*[240] (hereafter *Foley*) established the legal view of a deposit, as it was found that an entity taking deposits is to be the debtor of the person making the deposit.[241] Central banks seek to assist banks and provide stability before they reach a crisis point by mandatory monitoring and mandatory periodic reporting requirements.[242] This ensuring of systemic soundness ultimately provides consumer protection.[243]

Therefore, deposits in a banking context usually imply intermediation, where the deposit taking entity will lend out the value received at a higher rate of interest than it pays to the depositor. However, Tyree asks the question of whether a business which accepts deposits but does not make any loans (or a business that provides loans but does not accept deposits) is carrying on 'banking business'?[244] He argues that taking funds and lending are not necessarily siren indications of deposit taking and intermediation leading to the 'business of banking', especially where it may relate to a closed, private entity of participants. As Safaricom only accepts funds from its subscribers, Tyree's view suggests it should not be subject to regulation as a bank, although Ellinger[245] takes a different view, indicating parallels between banks and mobile financial services systems. These scholars suggest the existence of room for the reconceptualising of the concept of a 'deposit', which would facilitate the rethinking of the nature of deposits and their role in Kenya's mobile payments system.

In a mobile payments context, the stored value payment, or float, is taken from the public and converted into a stored value account. The value received and exchanged for the 'store of value' could amount to a deposit and therefore trigger a prudential deposit regime or the alternative law precepts of deposit and banking.[246] Because Kenyan law refers obliquely only to customers and banks, what constitutes a bank and the 'business of a bank' are couched in functional descriptions of the activities of an entity.

For example, whether the entity takes in monies in a process that can amount to its being legally described as a deposit, and if the associated activity can be seen as the licence-requiring activity of 'deposit taking', remains unclear.

Given the multitude of prospective service providers involved in taking funds from the public as in mobile financial services, the bespoke legal and commercial categorisations of companies by their core financial business are becoming blurred.[247] Service providers in mobile financial services may take redeemable and non-redeemable funds and may ultimately be classified as 'banks'.

Further complicating MNOs' position, the 'usual characteristics of a bank are not its sole characteristics'.[248] A deposit is not a payment; a deposit of funds gives the depository the right to use the depositor's money until it is called for by the depositor or another authorised person, while a payment occurs when a debtor transfers funds to a creditor to extinguish an existing debt.

The focus of MNOs on taking user funds not for intermediation purposes, but primarily and narrowly for payments, speaks to the broader issue of defining, or in this context redefining, the traditional concepts of the 'business of banking' and the 'deposit'. Establishing appropriate regulation therefore remains complicated; the question arises, do mobile payments or any other mobile financial service schemes amount to deposit taking, and, if so, is this deposit taking carrying out the business of banking, and does it, therefore, give rise to the normal incidences of the bank–customer relationship? The fact that the primary business of the entity is to provide telecommunications becomes irrelevant.

As a 'deposit' becomes a transient source for the primary use of making payments, the 'business of banking' is becoming so stratified that continuing to consider the 'deposit' as we know it as a crucial signal of the 'business of banking' may become irrelevant. It is also unclear how mobile money is to be secured, should there be a run on the commercial bank that holds the trust account or should an MNO become insolvent.[249] Kenyan law should address these questions. Just as the CBK dictates the amount of capital reserves banks that hold other people's money must maintain if they use those funds to make profit and the legal terms of those accounts, it should address the legal question of whether giving value to someone else through a mobile device can be seen as a public good.[250] Ultimately, taking redeemable money from the public resembles public deposits very closely;[251] strict prudential requirements should protect such funds. Adequate supervision, systemic stability and deposit protection usually apply to electronic value issued by banks in exchange for deposited funds, and exempting MNOs from such prudential regulation raises concerns about the adequate protection of the prepaid money that is in essence customer funds.[252]

There is no global definition of mobile money and electronic money (e-money) suitable for use.[253] Kenya has not defined mobile money or stored value in relation to mobile payments, and this poses a legal challenge.[254] Mobile money provides a storage facility for electronic value in the form of an account that offers a mechanism for transactions to take place electronically; for many customers, this represents their first 'account'. While existing banking regulation in Kenya does not clearly define whether the issuing of mobile money constitutes retail deposit taking and whether this type of business can be undertaken by anyone except for a licensed and regulated financial institution, authorities have allowed the MNOs to exist in an ambiguous regulatory framework.[255]

The CBK should have consultations to remove legal uncertainty to avoid sudden market-jeopardizing changes in its regulatory treatment of MNOs.[256] Regulatory uncertainty deprives consumers of a public mechanism for redress or legal accountability for wrongdoing by Safaricom; consumers may not be fully aware of the private mechanisms for seeking redress when a crisis arises.[257] This highlights the lack of coordination between the CBK and MNOs in attaining appropriate regulation, as CBK is not a conduct-of-business regulator and would therefore not have the resources to deal with consumer complaints.

Ownership of the funds does not mean that the beneficiaries have a customer–banker relationship with the banks that hold the trust funds; therefore, they have no entitlement to a protected deposit by the bank.[258] Brian Muthiora claims that without intermediation or interest, and as the funds are ring fenced[259] and not available for operations,[260] customer funds protection is unnecessary. He further argues that 'pass-through' deposit insurance coverage for mobile money, which Kenya has borrowed in its newly enacted but not yet operationalised, Kenya Deposit Insurance Act 2012,[261] for omnibus custodial accounts holding pooled funds underlying stored value cards, represents sufficient protection.[262]

### 4.5.4 The definition and placement of agents

MNOs and banks have extended their reach and services through agents[263] as the point of sale.[264] The agents are commonly known as 'outlets',[265] 'correspondents' (particularly in Brazil), and 'retail partners 'or 'cash merchants'.[266] This chapter will use 'agents', the colloquial term MNOs[267] use, which highlights the fact that as a commercial term, agent may not necessarily be an accurate legal descriptor.[268]

Agents take cash funds from the public, often outside a 'bricks and mortar'[269] setting and convert them into an electronic store of value, mobile money.[270] Agents do not always transact business in person. In many areas agents may primarily be chemists, airtime sellers or grocers.[271] These are financial institutions that provide services to illiterate customers who require assistance and are likely to benefit from repeat business. However, the agent may not always act in the best interests of the consumer, for example, insisting that a moderate sum of money must be sent in one or two tranches, each of which costs the same set commission.

Section 8(1) of the Banking Act 1989 requires CBK[272] approval for opening or relocating bank branches – any premises, other than their head offices, at which an institution transacts business inside or outside.[273] No regulations explicitly govern outsourcing of functions by banks,[274] but this requirement would potentially change MNOs' business a good deal if the CBK deemed them a bank and considered agents and super agents to be bank branches.[275]

In April 2010, the CBK issued new agent banking guidelines[276] that allowed banks to engage a wide range of retail outlets for transaction handling (cash-in and cash-out) and product promotion (receiving account applications, though applications must be approved by a bank staff member).[277] These enabled banks to start utilising the M-Pesa platform and the associated network of M-Pesa outlets as a channel to access new customers. M-Pesa was encroaching on banking business,[278] and Safaricom's non-bank status and consequent free hand in creating an agent network, proved useful for banks. As of August 2011, M-Pesa had 23,000 agents[279] to facilitate customer registration and so-called cash-in/cash-out facilities;[280] by 2014, it had 43,000.[281] The CBK only approves outsourcing by banks to agents on a case-by-case basis;[282] permitting them to have agents that are not their physical branches, as required by Section 8(1) of the Banking Act 1989, has changed the landscape.[283] Provisions that relate inter alia to AML/KYC and consumer protection do not necessarily apply to these agents.[284]

The lack of registration of M-Pesa agents by the CBK highlights the gaps through which these guidelines are to be prescribed and applied to mobile payments, as such action requires approval by the CBK itself. Customers have discovered a legal workaround by using M-Kesho[285] accounts alongside M-Pesa accounts; customers cannot use M-Pesa agents to deposit funds directly into M-Kesho accounts, even though the interface is the same as that for M-Pesa, and, therefore, most deposit separate funds into their M-Kesho account. This offers a clear example of regulatory arbitrage as any customer with dual M-Pesa and M-Kesho accounts will deposit funds into their M-Pesa account via an M-Pesa agent and then transfer funds to the M-Kesho account following confirmation via SMS that the deposited funds are available.[286]

### 4.5.4.1 Challenges in applying the current regulatory framework to mobile payments

Financial service providers' liability for the acts of their agents is a fundamental principle of regulation.[287] The CBK has not held MNOs accountable for agents' actions, which complicates its task of protecting customers. Relying on the CBK to monitor agents directly imposes significant supervisory costs; leaving it to consumers will have social costs, and low-income customers will bear the brunt.[288] Avoiding this situation need not impose unreasonable burdens on MNOs by creating unlimited liability or require a new regulatory framework; appropriate regulation should require MNOs to apply effective risk management systems, and ensure redress for consumers when agents do them harm.

However, Safaricom, as a principal, claims to be liable for the acts of their agents and has claimed they have taken appropriate steps to ensure that they comply with the law at all times including due diligence and operational compliance. In this regard they carry out appropriate vetting of agents at the recruitment stage.[289] They are also engaged in ongoing training programmes that cover AML and operational compliance, which incorporate periodic checks and sanctions for non-compliance, which can entail termination.[290] While this may be possible for Safaricom due to its resources, the same cannot be guaranteed for all other MNOs.

While some policy-makers have proposed that the mobile payment system industry is too new to create market conduct rules, I argue that the CBK should set minimum business practice standards and establish providers' liability for agents' compliance with regulation that should cut across all MNOs as compliance requirements. Appropriate regulation should also account for mechanisms for consumer protection to include fostering a level playing field that enables competition and sound market development. Jurisdictions such as the Reserve Bank of India, Malaysia, Indonesia, and the Philippines have created rules for e-money issued by non-banks that have focused on specific regulation for agents who process mobile money and thereby addressed a regulatory vacuum; Kenya should follow suit.[291]

In Mexico, regulation gave express powers to the banking supervisor over agency schemes set up by banks, allowing the direct inspection of agents if necessary.[292] In contrast, Kenya has not established a legal authority that regulates mobile payments. Due to this, overlapping or unclear authority has created opportunities for undesirable business practices and reduced the effectiveness of supervision; agents can question the jurisdiction of either the CCK or the CBK in relation to one another,[293] a problem that coordination and cooperation might address.

Agents provide the network through which mobile payments are executed – the bridge to cash and channels for financial inclusion. Given the reliance on agents by customers, MNOs require regulation, but their legal status poses a challenge; without legal accountability[294] for agents, customers and agents themselves become vulnerable.[295] It also facilitates circumvention of conduct-of-business rules and laws governing finance. While agents and MNOs use service level agreements,[296] these agreements do not create an agent–principal relationship in the true legal sense. Regulation should require MNOs to address consumer claims in instances where agents have contravened the law, including fraudulent circumstances.[297]

MNOs and banks pay agents by the transaction. Agents offer front line customer services and intermediate bank transactions, through banks' balance sheets, by transforming the cash in the till into money in the bank, and vice versa. This requires them to go to a bank from time to time to rebalance their cash in the till versus money in collateral or a trust bank account.[298] Liquidity is a key factor for their functioning; agents must have enough cash in hand to provide consistent cash-out facilities, as failing to pay a customer at any one time can create a negative feeling in a community and threaten the adoption of mobile financial services, including mobile payments.[299]

Profiting by giving mobile payments thus suggests agents that should be accountable, but it also makes them vulnerable. Some models include a hierarchy of agents; for example, in the hybrid MNO-bank model, the MNO is the agent of a bank, and its airtime kiosks (that provide cash-in/-out services) may be sub-agents authorised to open accounts (although their contracts may not name them as such). This interconnectedness creates systemic risks and therefore offers a justification for a clear definition of the mobile payments agent in law and through an appropriate regulatory framework. Moreover, some super-agents provide (cash) liquidity to agents in the street, and these super-agents are primarily banks who outsource their services to reach a wider market.[300] The proliferation of agents puts cash in transit at risk and provides opportunity for fraud and theft, against which MNOs do not provide insurance to consumers as a bank would.[301]

Many agents enter the mobile payments system with experience selling prepaid airtime vouchers, which gives them the technical proficiency and financial literacy the position requires. Current regulations also impose a vetting process for AML purposes on them.[302] However, MNOs have designed this process, and it has lower standards than a prudential authority would provide. Although appropriate technology, supported by an agreement between the agent and its MNO that specifies how the technology is to be used,[303] ensures some trust, a contract based on the MNO's liability for agents' actions would provide greater protection. A series of interrelated contracts – MNO–agent, agent–super-agent, MNO–super-agent, MNO–bank, customer–MNO, customer–bank – would provide superior protection.[304] However, this would clearly create burdensome compliance costs, inconsistencies and further barriers to entry for new MNOs or agents.

Part I of this chapter has assessed the main arguments in statute for the clear definition and codification of the various terms used in the regulation of payments systems and the challenges they present in its application to mobile payments, especially in their practical application. Part II will assess the overall regulatory challenges authorities face in relation to mobile payments.

## PART II

## 4.6 Overall regulatory challenges for regulatory authorities in regulating mobile payments

The regulatory agencies' main objective in regulating MNOs should be to protect consumers from operators reducing output to increase prices on low quality services.[305] They should also protect the unbanked and under banked and ensure that the money pooled in the mobile money system does not introduce systemic risk. The convergence of industries involved in mobile payment systems complicates regulation, and regulatory agencies should prioritise their objectives to address challenges such as regulatory overlap, conflict, inertia and arbitrage.

### 4.6.1 The inconsistencies in regulation that result from multiple regulatory authorities

Kenya's government supported a telecommunications monopoly for years; the industry now has oligopolies.[306] As change continues, regulatory reform is necessary. Distinct markets now have coalesced across their old boundaries with investments from private sector participants,[307] resulting in nascent markets and stakeholders, and continued legal and regulatory challenges.

The liberalisation of the markets has changed telecommunications in Kenya a good deal, including the successful partial privatisation of Telkom Kenya Ltd,[308] the Kenyan government's 25 per cent stake in Safaricom Ltd through a public listing,[309] and the launch of fourth mobile operator Econet Wireless Kenya,[310] which also resulted in the introduction of international telecommunications companies such as Vodafone, France Telecoms and Essar Communications through their investments in Safaricom Limited, Telkom Kenya Limited and Econet Limited, respectively. MNOs such as Safaricom have focused on network expansion and nationwide coverage; Safaricom's reach and stability exceeds that of the Kenyan government. The Kenyan government has found little reason to regulate quality or prices in this highly competitive telecommunications sector.

Traditionally, the CBK regulates financial services and the CCK regulates telecommunications; these two industries have traditionally been separated, and therefore the two regulating authorities have had minimal overlapping functions. The risks to consumers, MNOs, and banks clearly require the need for a re-examination of the preconditions to safety and soundness for a payment system in this new converged space.[311] Industry players want predictable regulation; the diffuse or uncertain regulatory authority constitutes a risk to their business. But the interdependence of the agencies and operators who potentially have authority to regulate mobile payment systems complicates the picture, as does the perception that they are subject to political pressures.[312]

### 4.6.2 Regulatory overlaps

Regulatory overlap has two dimensions. On the one hand, two regulatory authorities can offer a check and balance on one another. If one fails to regulate an important area, the other may do so.[313] Regulatory overlap occurs where, for example, the CCK and the CBK exercise licensing regulatory jurisdiction over the mobile financial service aspect of MNOs. This overlap results in regulatory conflict, where, for example, each regulator provides conflicting licensing guidelines, one for the operation of financial services and the other for the telecommunications platform that facilitates financial services.[314] This is manifest in the existence of both the CCK and CBK, a result of the liberalisation of the telecoms industry.[315]

While the CBK has been more proactive in taking regulatory responsibility over mobile financial services, including authorisation of MNOs,[316] the CCK has taken a passive role in the face of possible regulatory overlap.[317] Regrettably, the financial sector and the telecommunication sector both lack provisions for dealing with regulatory overlap.[318] This calls for the coordination between the two regulators through a possible memorandum of understanding (MoU)[319] that would address regulatory overlaps. The Constitution of Kenya 2010, through Article 10, requires state structures such as regulators to refer to such documents, prior to applying their regulatory functions.[320] Regulatory overlap is not conducive to promoting innovation and investments, due to the costs of regulatory compliance and the fear of multiple penalties from multiple regulators.[321] A real risk of coordination failure arises due to the different regulators such as bank supervisor, payment regulator, telecommunications regulator and perhaps competition regulator.

### 4.6.3 Regulatory arbitrage

The traditional regulatory structure defines regulator jurisdiction by institutional groups. Thus for example, a banking regulator regulates banks, but not quasi-banking products provided by microfinance institutions, such as lines of credit and loans. This permits regulatory arbitrage, wherein a financial institution can choose among different regulators by altering its corporate form or its institutional label, to seek the regulator that imposes the smallest regulatory burden.[322] A new, unregulated institution that avoids or minimises regulation can put the stability of the whole financial system at risk.

When regulation does not yet exist for interconnected services or in conglomerates that could fall under the supervision of more than one regulator, regulatory arbitrage[323] raises problems.[324] Regulatory arbitrage is a challenge when regulation is not in place, particularly for services offered under the supervision of more than one regulator. Choosing the best regulator or the one that has the least regulation may not be the best option for the industry as a whole.[325] Market players have encouraged mobile payments to capitalise on regulatory loopholes by circumventing unfavourable regulations. While regulatory arbitrage is a form of market innovation,[326] it should only be encouraged to the extent that it helps industry respond appropriately to the inherent risk of unregulated markets, as discussed in Chapter 3. This gap in the regulatory framework allows particular business initiatives and allocates various rights and responsibilities in their operations, without attracting investments commensurate with the opportunities mobile payment schemes provide.[327]

Licensing the hybridised institutions and unregulated private sectors could close these loopholes. Innovation is a challenge for regulation as this fragmentation undermines consumer protection; it may also be characterised as a risk to the market. Then minister for finance, Hon. John Michuki, ordered a brisk audit of M-Pesa in 2009 in response to this risk,[328] stating that he 'did not think M-Pesa, . . . if left unregulated would end well'.[329] The contribution in regulation through the CCK and its licensing mandate over MNOs as service providers brings forth misunderstanding through the absence of regulatory coordination between the two regulatory authorities, which enhances the need for their coordination and further contributes to the arbitrage.

### 4.6.4 Regulatory inertia

In regulatory inertia, a regulator with inferior power, such as the CCK in relation to the CBK, is reluctant or unwilling to impose any regulation on a particular industry.[330] This inertia may in turn precipitate regulatory arbitrage, which did occur as M-Pesa sought regulation by the CCK to avoid the more intrusive CBK, although neither had much idea how to regulate M-Pesa,[331] though both rightly hesitated to impose barriers that impede innovation in financial services.[332] Further, the state's partial ownership of Safaricom encouraged flexibility.[333] This inertia has manifested itself in the development of measures to address competition issues in mobile payments such as interoperability in Kenya.[334]

### 4.6.5 The political interference with the collective will to regulate

Political considerations can compromise the promotion of public interest through beneficial regulation;[335] government incentives in the private sector in Kenya potentially make the government reluctant to intervene in the regulation of private companies. Mobile payments have faced intense scrutiny from other financial institutions, but the government had, in the beginning, little will to regulate the systems.[336] Although making MNO supervision immune to interference by government in order to foster faster uptake of mobile payments and increase and enable innovation for the purposes of financial inclusion has some advantages, the interests of the public require the involvement of governments in case MNOs run into difficulties.[337]

In summary, there exist regulatory inadequacies for a regulatory framework for mobile payments. This discussion has made it clear that an appropriate regulatory framework that focuses on consumer protection has a strong justification. The Kenya Information and Communications Act 2013 does not expressly provide for mobile payments. The CCK has surrendered the regulatory mandate of mobile payments to the CBK, as it is clear that Kenyan telecoms regulations have not addressed the regulatory issues adequately. However some telecoms aspects must remain under the purview of telecoms regulators. There needs to be a coordination of functions through a MoU between the CCK and the CBK. Part III analyses the impact of these challenges on consumers.

## PART III

## 4.7 The impact of the regulatory challenges on consumers

The Global Financial Crisis[338] revealed the importance of financial consumer protection.[339] Difficulties determining the amount of client monies an entity holds in a pooled account, and who should receive money from that pool, precipitated the Global Financial Crisis in relation to Lehman Brothers International Europe (LBIE).[340] While the cause of potential confusion certainly differs – Safaricom's size may not resemble LBIE's, which was one of the largest investment banks operating in the United States, prior to its collapse – but the case suggests the urgency of regulation to protect Kenya's financial stability, given that MNOs' trust accounts could be subject to the same confusion.

Low-income customers with low levels of financial literacy were particularly vulnerable to misconduct,[341] making consumer protection a key objective of all financial regulators,[342] requiring an effective and standardised regulatory frame-work. Low-income groups who gain access to financial services through mobile phones are the most vulnerable to financial shocks and an indication of a post-financial inclusion, as they are at a higher risk of losing their savings whenever a bank fails or if the MNO fails.[343] Consumer protection will increase consumer confidence in the financial system, which in turn mitigates risks to the financial system, and builds trust and confidence in the adoption of inclusive services, thereby broadening and diversifying banks' deposit reserve. I therefore argue that regulatory agencies must protect the post-financial inclusion of these groups.

The concept of a weaker party is usually used in legal literature to refer to consumers as a justification for their protection. Disparities in the consumer–supplier relationship in mobile payments systems leave consumers 'weaker' than their contracting partners, the professionals, and unable to protect their interests due to inferior bargaining power.[344] Legislation has already recognised the concept of vulnerability.

As Peter Cartwright asserts, we know that vulnerable consumers exist, even if we may disagree in terms of how to identify them and about how their interests might best be addressed.[345] Consumers have few options and this forms a theory for the protection of consumers, as they have few purchases and contract on terms set by increasingly large and powerful companies such as Safaricom Ltd.[346] Second, companies are able to exploit significant information and sophistication disparities in their favour.[347] However, economists no longer regard exploitation theory as valid,[348] because it fails to account for competition between companies, and the resulting limits on companies' bargaining power.[349] Rather, economists argue for consumer protection because consumers know less about products and contracts than professionals do,[350] an asymmetry that applies to mobile payments. While they contend that free markets protect consumers, they posit a restrictive role for regulation.[351] Law should ensure that the markets function as freely as possible. In imperfect markets, the law should intercede to address the imperfections or failures, although the distinction between market and social goals are not always clear.[352]

In the context of mobile payments, consumers are people who use communication services or products offered by a licensee including telecommunications and mobile financial services. Through improved efficiency, regulation offers transparency, competition and access to retail financial markets.[353] Consumer protection is of particular importance in Kenya, where financial education levels are generally low and information flows constrained.[354] Since mobile payments provide one of the largest mass-market service provisions – as of May 2013, there were 10.5 million active mobile payment users in Kenya[355] – regulations offer the most beneficial strategy for safeguarding financial consumer protection in Kenya. The CBK, the Insurance Regulatory Authority,[356] or the Ministry of Finance might lead regulatory reforms to the current regulations, by improving financial consumer protection.

The CBK has been watchful, but it has, however, seemingly offer a piecemeal approach in its oversight and guidance since the inception of mobile payments.[357] However, this oversight and guidance has not been as exhaustive and extensive as it ought to be. The CBK and Safaricom[358] have addressed emerging challenges in the introduction of mobile payments, but these consumer protection measures that exist are as yet not codified in law. MNOs[359] have the responsibility to inform their consumers, and in turn, consumers have a responsibility to inform themselves. This would be similar to the caveat emptor principle, where the purchaser assumes the risk that the product might be either defective or unsuitable to his or her needs. This rule is not designed to shield sellers who engage in fraud or bad faith dealing by making false or misleading representations about the quality or condition of a particular product. It merely summarises the concept that a purchaser must examine, judge and test a product considered for purchase themselves.

However, this can be difficult for low-income customers due to limited awareness, knowledge and skills to assess products' appropriateness, costs and risks. Policy-makers and regulators should therefore ensure that consumer protection measures meet the needs of the poor or inexperienced consumers.[360]

The most informed consumers are able to protect themselves from risks.[361] This increases the transparency of the credit risk assumed by the financial system and lowers monitoring costs for financial supervisors.[362] Consumer protection addresses the imbalance of power information and resources between consumers and their financial service providers, which highlights a typical market failure.[363] The information asymmetry may prove costly for customers who seek more information on financial products. Moreover, complex financial services or products may not always be easily understood, even when MNOs have disclosed and shared all the information necessary.[364] Thirdly, they promote efficiency and transparency of retail financial markets. This empowerment, a necessary source of market discipline, would eventually sway the MNOS to offer better products and services, rather than take advantage of poorly informed consumers.[365]

The current regulatory framework leaves Kenyan consumers to find out for themselves what protections apply to each competing new payments system.[366] The new integration of mobile telecommunications companies and the financial industry provides Kenya with an opportunity to harmonise[367] and extend consumer protections for mobile payments. However, two things should occur immediately; firstly, the CCK should publicly commit to including consumer protection in their mandate. Secondly, MNOs should include in their contracts with agents the consumer rights the law already guarantees for debit and credit cards. The CBK should ensure to the extent possible that existing consumer protections are applied to new payment methods by reforming its legislation to extend the Consumer Protection Act 2012 to financial services and products.[368]

Consumer protection can reduce information asymmetries to protect end-users' interests with respect to financial services.[369] It can contribute to improved efficiency, transparency, competition and access to retail financial markets.[370] Consumer financial protection can contribute to an increase in consumer education, ensuring that transparency is maintained.[371]

In addition to regulatory policy focusing on the structure of the market and its infrastructure, payment instruments require adequate protection of users. In particular, and in addition to transparency requirements, KYC guidelines and observance of AML regulation, the protection of users' funds and their traceability are a must, as well as protection from any risk arising from the use of electronic means and the intermediation of non-financial agents. Indeed, regulating service providers to level the playing field will guarantee competition and competitiveness and provide a general understanding of consumer protection and an adequate consideration of the role of agents.[372] Regulators in Kenya, however, have adopted a watch and learn regulatory approach regarding the electronic money industry and the non-banks providing these services.

Protecting consumers from fraud or exploitation by providers with significant market power ensures minimum disclosure and quality standards for consumers who expect confidence in the financial system. Other measures include instituting conduct of business rules,[373] competition policies, ombudsman schemes, minimum disclosure and contracting standards, consumer education surveillance and enforcement measurements. The achievement of mobile financial services facilities' access to payment and banking transactions, especially for areas without established physical bank branches, is important. It may also involve certain risks. The inability of consumers to assess their own risks, such as the loss of their funds, may impair these objectives. Standardisation can enhance transparency and consumers' ability to compare offers and enforce minimum levels of quality. These contingency arrangements should be in place in the case of a technical or operational failure of the mobile payment service.

### 4.7.1 Lack of a cohesive consumer protection regulation

Mobile payments existed before there was a cohesive policy and regulatory framework that had a market-wide consumer protection law or authority. There is currently no specific consumer protection law in Kenya that deals specifically with financial services.[374] Instead, a number of fragmented provisions,[375] guidelines[376] and acts[377] address mobile financial services issues directly and indirectly. In the absence of the above law, transaction disputes are handled according to the contracts between MNOs and their parties, primarily their agents. An amalgam of indirect, but not easily applicable or effective, provisions of telecommunications law relating to telecommunications billing and CBK rules relating to agents guide these issues.[378]

While the Banking Act 1969 gave authority to the CBK to regulate banking activities, including safeguarding the 'interest of consumers', it did not define the specific mandate for consumer protection. Subsequent law has clarified some issues, such as when the Banking Regulations of 2006 prescribed procedures such as the increase of banking and other fees.[379] However, the law leaves preventing unlawful, misleading and comparative advertising and implementing remedy mechanisms to individual banks. The CBK should offer microprudential regulation for mobile payments to address these issues.

The CBK's 2010 'Agent Guidelines'[380] provide direct consumer protection provisions, although these relate more to formalities in the transaction process than any dispute resolution facilities. For example, s9.2 of the 'Agent Guidelines' provides the following minimum requirements:

'i)    Institutions shall establish mechanisms that will enable their customers or users to appropriately identify their agents and the services provided through such agents.

ii)    Agents shall issue receipts for all transactions undertaken through them. Institutions shall provide their agents with equipment that generates receipts or acknowledgements for transactions carried out through agents. In this regard, electronic receipts or acknowledgements are permissible.

ii)    Where an agent acts as a receiver and deliverer of documents, an acknowledgement shall be provided for all documents received or delivered by the agent to or from the customer.

iv)    A channel for communication of customer complaints to the institution shall be provided. Institutions shall provide dedicated customer care telephone lines for lodging complaints by their customers. The customers can also use this telephone line to verify with the institution, the authenticity and identity of the agent, its physical location and the validity of its agent banking business.

v)    Institutions shall establish a complaints mechanism and shall ensure proper communication of this mechanism to their customers.

vi)    All customer complaints shall be addressed within a reasonable time and in any case not later than thirty days from the date of reporting or lodging the complaint with the institution. Institutions shall keep record of all customer complaints and how such complaints are redressed.

vii)    An agent shall have signs that are clearly visible to the public indicating that it is a provider of services of the institution with which it has an agency contract. The agent shall not however represent to the public that it is an institution.

viii)    In the provision of agent banking services, institutions shall use secure systems that ensure customer information confidentiality.

ix)    The customer should be made aware of the fact that he is not supposed to carelessly store his PIN and other critical information or share such information with other parties including agents.

x)    An institution may establish contact centres to facilitate easy communication between a customer and the institution.'[381]

Therefore, Kenya's inherent problem is a lack of coherence in consumer protection and market oversight, related to the split in responsibility between the CCK and the CBK. Having two regulatory regimes for what most consumers perceive as a single product or service can result in different rights and a divergence in protection for personal and small business consumers.[382] Mobile payment users may not fully understand which regulations apply to a payment transaction and how these differ, depending on the payment method and platform used, the parties involved in the payment transaction and the nature of the product purchased. Banks, MNOs and agents not only operate under different regulatory bodies but also operate under different sets of regulations. This creates confusion over consumers' redress rights and to which entity to turn for a payment-related problem.

Further, consumer protection regulation practices do not match the written guidelines, partly because no law establishes the regulations or the authority to regulate the sector. The CBK and the MNOs have operated by asserting that the regulatory structure shall be clarified in time, through the operationalization of a payments systems law.[383] This lack of formality has implications for consumers, who have no regulatory body to which to appeal. As consumers continue to use mobile payments for uses other than for person-to-person payments, and increasingly in the way a bank customer would use a current account, supporting service providers in the mobile payment system are building and deploying new services based on the mobile payments platform.[384] Banks, for example, link physical bank accounts with mobile accounts, with some even enabling providers to link subscribers' funds to their bank accounts; this innovation serves customers but also makes them vulnerable.

### 4.7.2 Protection of consumer funds

Due to their wide and existing customer base, MNOs are well placed to reach customers with affordable financial services. The MNOs' existing customer base, marketing capabilities, physical distribution and infrastructure and experience with high volume/low value transactions makes this possible. While the usual categorisation of payment values defined by a national prudential regulator is high value and low value, which then results in the requisite regulatory focus, a third category, micro-payments, can be added to the broad canvas of payment values, lest its growing importance be quenched in the broad 'low value' definition. When MNOs receive funds from the public, even for payments, rather than for saving, this arguably represents accepting public deposits.[385] Strict prudential requirements and supervision protect deposits in banks,[386] and the loss of funds in the absence of such requirements will create distrust in the payment system, causing serious consequences for public confidence in financial systems.[387] I argue the regulatory agencies should treat MNOs and the funds they receive from the public through mobile payments as deposits, subject to the same oversight as bank deposits,[388] and the same implicit guarantee by governments.[389]

The regulatory gaps allow MNOs to bypass the full range of prudential oversight afforded to banks. Customers increasingly use the money collected by MNOs as a short-term savings mechanism, and MNOs deposited the funds in joint trust accounts at several commercial banks for the benefit of the customers. However, in the event of insolvency, customers have no means to claim trust assets;[390] they have no recourse when and if the bank or an MNO becomes insolvent. Not considering electronically stored value bank to be deposits creates these complexities.[391] The mobile payment system must clarify the status of electronically stored value; regulations require banks to maintain liquid assets as accounts with a prudentially regulated bank, and MNOs have been maintaining them as other 'safe assets', such as government securities, which are not always liquid.[392] This leaves client assets unsecured. While either a safety net or a deposit insurance scheme might offer some protection,[393] I posit that a deposit insurance scheme, where the government implicitly guarantees the protection of consumer funds in accordance with the current regulatory structure, despite the fact it has no legal responsibility, would best serve consumers.

Protecting consumer funds implies ensuring that funds are available to meet customer demands for cashing out electronic value. Such measures typically include restrictions on the use of such funds.[394] There should be a diversification of floats across several financial institutions.[395] Regulators might require MNOs to offer guarantees by way of liquid assets to match the electronic funds available.[396] They might require assets to be isolated and held in a bank account. Kenya's regulators should ensure that funds deposited are done so in prudentially regulated banks, which further ensures that they are safeguarded.[397] These requirements may be more stringent than those imposed on deposit taking financial institutions, which typically must only keep a small portion of total deposits in liquid assets.[398] Regulation should require that trust accounts be safeguarded from institutional risks, though not discussed here. These may involve claims from creditors when bankruptcy occurs. It is suggested that a trust account will be resold and offer safeguards, especially through the fiduciary agreement instituted.[399]

If Safaricom, for example, were to become insolvent, these failings could lead to complications and delay in distribution and place consumer funds at risk of set-off and consequential diminution. This is because the CBK treats Safaricom not as a monopoly, but rather as an entity with multiple dominant positions. Market dominance, which is a stricter concept than market power, is typically defined by two conditions, a relatively high market share, which Safaricom has, and significant barrier to entry into the relevant markets occupied by the dominant firm. The first condition holds in all markets where Safaricom is active. The second may hold in the agent market, but not in the mobile telephony market, due to the CCK's action.

Additionally, MNOs who may be operating on a regional scale, or international scale, may become increasingly interconnected and possibly cause disruptions if they experience problems in the wider financial markets. The channels of risk distribution may be less visible in the mobile money value chain than in traditional banks, which raises the risk. Further, mobile payments have turned into a 'shadow' banking system,[400] undermining government supervision and the comprehensive regulation of traditional banking. Regulation should ensure that in protecting consumer funds, MNOs maintain liquid assets equivalent to the total value of the customer funds collected.[401]

The MNOs' use of a pooled trust account has created the presumption that the MNO is the legal owner of the funds, which makes customer funds vulnerable to creditors. The Deposit Protection Fund Board[402] states that it 'only protects deposits in current accounts savings accounts and fixed deposit accounts.'[403] However, funds held in trust are treated 'as distinct from individually owned accounts, and therefore insured separately'.[404] This however does not offer clarity over whether mobile money is covered under the Deposit Protection Fund Board, as regulators have been reluctant to clarify and define these perimeters.

Regulation of banking activities sometimes includes caps are on interest rates, restrictions on product cross-subsidisation, and regulation of pricing policies. Contracting standards, such as a requirement that agents validate the authenticity of documents or signatures, might also apply to mobile payment schemes.[405] However, these kinds of measures can easily inhibit innovation. Operators and regulators together need to review limitations that may pose unnecessary constraints.

Apart from the insolvency of the MNO or the bank in which the MNO deposited customer funds, illiquidity of either entity threatens consumer funds. Further, technical difficulties such as a lack of connection or a system outage, fraudulent agents, unexpected or unauthorised agents not clearly disclosed to the customers all threaten mobile payment users. Customers whose personal identification numbers have been stolen, wrongfully accessed, shared, or used to conduct unauthorised transactions or for commercial purposes may not be able to use mobile payment systems under the current lack of regulation. The case calls for alternative and complementary measures to protect consumer funds.

MNOs should be compelled by the regulators to protect consumer funds by demanding that they maintain the equivalent of the outstanding electronic value issued in a bank account. This ensures that the funds are maintained on a low risk category. They also should require that MNOs use the funds for purposes other than withdrawals, transfers and cash-in and cash-out services.[406] The same should be required for trust account holders.[407] Liquid assets might be accounts held with prudentially regulated banks, though 'safe assets', such as government securities, although they may not always be as liquid as bank accounts, would also serve.

Although this is a more stringent requirement than deposit taking financial institutions function under, it reflects a fundamental difference among banks, MNOs and their respective business models.[408] This is since banks normally are able to intermediate capital, loaning funds out, which is something that non-banks such as MNOs do not do. However, aside from their telecommunications services, they obtain revenue from transaction charges and distribution of airtime.[409]

The lack of clarification over who owns the funds MNOs hold in trust accounts should lead to increased scrutiny. Since the definition of the deposits is equally unclear, the uncertainty over whether the funds are owned by the customers forming individual accounts, or whether the pooled trust account is held for benefit of the customers as a whole, would result in the prohibition of MNOs from guaranteeing the funds as a security or offering protection against creditors in the case of the MNO's insolvency. The EU E-Money Directive (2009), for instance, requires contracts to state clearly and prominently the conditions of redemption, including any fees, and limits charges on redemption to a few specific circumstances. This would mean ensuring a deposit protection scheme or, in this case, a stored value protection scheme.[410]

Deposit protection schemes play an important role in protecting consumers by providing compensation should an entity such as the agents or MNOs fail to meet its obligations to them.[411] Arguably, consumer protection was the main motivation behind the creation of the original deposit protection scheme. The importance of safeguarding deposits cannot be overstated, as the US model suggests. In the United States, all funds placed in an insured depository institution are considered insured.[412] The US model employs a 'pass-through' protection scheme for each customer, up to the insurance limit.[413] Developed countries typically have deposit protection; the United States, for instance, has characterised stored value funds as deposits and, therefore, clarifies their position in law which requires that deposit insurance covers such deposits.[414] Prudential requirements aim to maintain the integrity of the institution's capital and a certain level of liquidity. They are intended to mitigate credit and liquidity risks and might include minimum capital ratios, capital adequacy measurement systems, reserve requirements or other measures intended to preserve the liquidity of the provider are at the core of deposit protection.

Deposit protection through insurance might be a viable solution, but such a system requires that some entity involved pay premiums, which might ultimately increase the fees customers pay for mobile money services, which may ultimately cause undue burden on the goals of financial inclusion.

Further, the value of pooled accounts might exceed the applicable deposit insurance coverage limits.[415] As mobile value offerings grow in volume and popularity, and as evidence mounts that customers increasingly use e-money schemes as savings vehicles,[416] extending deposit insurance protection at the level of individual customer mobile money balances, or alternatively, raising the cap for pooled accounts, may be necessary. On the other hand, deposit insurance is usually funded by premiums paid by participating financial institutions, which typically pass these costs along to their customers. Thus, inclusion of e-money issuers in a deposit insurance system may make their services slightly more expensive.

MNOs in Kenya currently use this mechanism; the Central Bank of Congo's e-money regulation references the concept as a mechanism to ensure that the mobile payment user can recover their funds in the event of the MNO failure.[417] The risk that mobile money customers will lose the money they have stored in the system is mitigated by the fact that if MNOs do not use the funds,[418] and funds isolation happens, the MNOs funds then become protected from claims by their creditors,[419] but additional regulation is needed.

### 4.7.3 Lack of public and private mechanisms for legal remedies for consumers

The lack of public mechanisms for customers to pursue claims against MNOs contributes to the challenges that oversight over mobile payments presents. In instances where the payments malfunction and mobile payments users experience the risks discussed in Chapter 3,[420] the CCK currently forwards any complaints received from subscribers to the MNO or bank and to the CBK.[421]

As discussed in Chapter 3, system malfunctions cause operational risk.[422] This in turn calls for MNOs to offer private recourse for customers in their use of mobile payments services.[423] The Banking Act CAP 488 allows the CBK to restrict increases in bank charges, and mobile payments may be subject to these restrictions, but the CBK has no enforceable direct oversight over MNOs, and the CCK regulates the pricing of telecommunications voice and data charges, which may or may not apply to mobile payments. The CBK only requires providers to have procedures and capacities to handle and resolve complaints promptly, with reports.[424] The Kenya Information and Communications (Dispute Resolution) Regulations 2010[425] set out the scope of and the guidelines for any disputes[426] between a licence holder and a consumer. However, this piece of legislation appears fragmented.

The Restrictive Trade Practices, Monopolies and Price Control Act of 1989 is the most comprehensive legislation related to competition in Kenya. Although the Act does not empower consumer advocacy organisations to lodge a complaint, nor contain provisions on consumer welfare, the Public Complaints Commission does provide third-party recourse for consumers of public sector services. There are still gaps in mechanisms for consumers, which private actors in the industry can employ without government involvement. Institutions offering mobile payments services operating within a jurisdiction where regulators cannot or prefer not to be involved make these remedies particularly useful. In conclusion, this part has highlighted the challenges Kenya's current approach to regulating mobile payments poses for consumers.

## 4.8 Conclusion

Mobile payments bring multifaceted regulatory challenges. Addressing these challenges requires coordination, and, at best, dialogue between the various industry players in both the public and private sector. The introduction of mobile payments has called into question the strength of regulatory reforms in Kenya, and the speed with which the Kenyan government has considered, reviewed and adopted regulation. The Kenyan government's attempts to open dialogue with the private sector through consultations[427] seek to ensure that MNOs receive the necessary support from government and also evaluate possible new financial services products that affect the integrity of the financial system. Regulatory reform of the payments systems in Kenya will strengthen the operation of mobile payments through enhancing the central administration coordinating and regulating capacity. How to regulate and establish an appropriate regulatory framework remains the most important challenge. This chapter has also examined the regulatory powers of the regulatory authorities and tried to expose their inadequacies due to their institutional structures and their approach. Chapter 6 will discuss how these regulatory bodies should coordinate in order to establish an appropriate regulatory framework for mobile payments.

In summation, this chapter has demonstrated that the Kenya Information and Communications Act 1998, by failing to expressly provide for converged mobile and financial services, or any other type of intrasectoral converged services, leaves a regulatory inadequacy not remedied by the regulation of value added services under the Kenya Information and Communications Regulations. The telecom regulatory framework is inadequate to address mobile financial services. While the CCK has surrendered the regulatory mandate of the converged services to the CBK, the NPSA does not provide adequate provisions for mobile payments. Under the current law, CBK will have to coordinate with CCK has to ensure that the policies on mobile payments are consistent as it develops the regulatory framework.[428]

This need for more regulation in no way diminishes the success of M-Pesa in Kenya. It is the bellwether of transformational innovation and regulatory latitude by a progressive prudential regulator. The rapidity of its evaluation and growth even in the regulatory vacuum left by the lack of a national payments law at the time of its inception demonstrates the need for non-bank participation in the primary provision of payment services. Kenya's mobile payment system provided a rapid enabling of financial inclusion as well as immediate and manifest downstream benefits, with more than 40,000 agent outlets, enhancement of competition in financial services, and a web of interconnected business users whose difficulty getting paid in the past, M-Pesa has remedied.

Users' dependence on M-Pesa as a savings service, although its creators did not conceive it as such, and users at least partially recognise the risks involved, suggests a strong need for a safe store of value. The M-Kesho hybrid system that complements M-Pesa's pure payments regime points to a second generation of usage and users, which in turn extends and enhances access for unbanked people to the formal financial framework.[429] M-Kesho was launched in May 2010. It allows M-Pesa users to transfer their funds into an interest bearing equity bank account, and they, therefore, have access to loans and lines of credit. By August 2010, 455,000 customers had opened accounts, which grew to 718,000 by April 2011. Although activity on these accounts is reportedly low, more and more banks have begun to offer such services through hybrid business models with MNO bank-led services. The CBK will face continuing challenges, not only in developing the regulatory framework for mobile payments, but also in enforcing and implementing the provisions under the NPSA.

Policy-makers and scholars continue to debate how regulation should look. Other developing countries have taken a variety of approaches in their regulation, but Kenya has the opportunity to serve as a benchmark for such regulation, despite the fact that it has been ambiguous and lax to date. While mature and developed markets allow regulators to react to information promptly and to accept market participants' strong role in regulatory matters, mobile payments present a special circumstance, particularly in Kenya, where they have developed faster and more expansively than any other deployment in Africa,[430] and here all other payment systems are immature. Market discipline requires a mature and liberal market, which combats information asymmetry, a great obstacle to market discipline in less mature markets. Therefore CBK has to ensure that the regulatory framework for mobile payments is flexible, transparent, stable and promotes competition. Although CBK has the challenge of establishing its role as the main regulatory authority for mobile payments, as a developing country, Kenya often needs to fulfil other developmental tasks and fulfil other objectives, including the development of efficient payment systems. It is important that regulation avoids pitting these objectives against each other to prioritise the interests of the public.

Thus far, Kenya's main legal contribution the regulatory discussions for mobile payments or mobile financial services in general is the *lacuna* in the definition of a 'deposit'. The efficiency with which MNOs have exploited this loophole indicates inter alia just how critical contextualised legal drafting is, in relation to banking and payments law. While this exploitation, in my view, has had demonstrable public policy benefits, through enabling financial inclusion, it conversely may have caused adverse effects on the Kenyan economy or on the sub-region in the event of systemic failure of the banks or the MNO.

In the future, Kenya may undertake a policy and regulatory legal discourse about implementing mobile payments, introducing mobile payments alongside the establishment of safety and soundness provisions to safeguard user funds, and thereby make a larger contribution to the international body of regulatory approaches to mobile payments.[431] Regular reporting[432] by MNOs on their financial health to the CBK and placement of funds in trust accounts at commercial banks demonstrates that adequate planning, a progressive regulator, alongside technical innovation ensures that there is no systemic impact on the financial system or harm to consumers.

Effective regulation will require coordination and, at best, dialogue between the various industries players in both the public and private sector. This chapter has aimed to show that the introduction of mobile payments has called into question the strength of the CBK as the financial regulator, its regulatory power and its regulatory capacity.[433] It has also brought into question the speed with which regulation is adopted, which is troublingly slow. The Kenyan government has made attempts to open dialogue with the private sector through consultations;[434] however, these consultations have not yet yielded adequate approaches.

Open dialogue should ensure that 'providers receive the necessary support from government and also evaluate possible repercussions of new products to the integrity of the financial system'.[435] Regulatory reforms of the payments systems in Kenya would strengthen the operation of mobile payments through enhancing the central administration's coordinating and regulating capacity. Finding the regulatory approach to mobile payments is a challenge that regulators need to address. Various regulatory instruments exist that seek to resolve some of these challenges; they have not been adequate in their approach. Chapter 5 will therefore discuss how these regulatory bodies should coordinate in order to establish an appropriate regulatory framework for mobile payments.

## Notes

1 Bronwen Morgan and Karen Yeung, An Introduction to Law and Regulation: Text and Materials (Cambridge University Press 2007) 3.
2 Vivienne Lawack-Davids, 'The Legal and Regulatory Framework of Mobile Payments in South Africa: A Trade-Off? Analyses' (2012) 24 *SA Mercantile Law Journal= SA Tydskrif vir Handelsreg* 77.
3 Neil McEvoy, 'Capabilities of Mobile Operators from the Perspective of a Financial Regulator' in GSMA 'Mobile Money for the Unbanked' (Annual Report, July 2009); see also Paul Makin and Consult Hyperion, 'Regulatory Issues Around Mobile Banking' (2010) The Development Dimension ICTs for Development Improving Policy Coherence: Improving Policy Coherence 139; Paul Tucker, 'The Debate on Financial System Resilience: Macroprudential Instruments' 22 (Barclays annual lecture, London, 22 October 2009).
4 See Chapter 3: Financial Stability and Integrity after Financial Inclusion the Mobile Payment Risks.
5 Ibid.
6 Andreas Dombret, 'Resilient Banks – Essential Building Blocks of a Stable Financial System' (2013) <www.bis.org/review/r130925b.pdf> accessed 3 September 2014; financial resilience has been stressed as the ability for a financial system to overcome shocks to its system. This is especially after the Global Financial Crisis. See, Jean-Claude Trichet, 'Financial System Resilience' Systemic Risk: The Dynamics of Modern Financial Systems' (2011) 101; See also Kartik Anand et al., 'A Network Model of Financial System Resilience' (2013) 85 *Journal of Economic Behavior & Organization* 219.
7 See Chapter 2 Section 2.6: the 'mass market' in most developing countries is comprised of low-income, unbanked people who make up the majority of the population; see, Claudia McKay and Mark Pickens, 'Branchless Banking Pricing Analysis' (2010) <www.slideshare.net/CGAP/branchless-banking-pricing-analysis-2010> accessed 3 September 2014; See Chapter 2 Section 2.5. Title Success of Mobile Payment: Financial Inclusion. Page 60.
8 See Chapter 3 Section Titled Inherent Risks to the Payment System.
9 Vivienne Lawack-Davids, 'The Legal and Regulatory Framework of Mobile Payments in South Africa: A Trade-Off? Analyses' (2012) 24 *SA Mercantile Law Journal= SA Tydskrif vir Handelsreg* 77
10 Neil McEvoy, 'Capabilities of Mobile Operators from the Perspective of a Financial Regulator' in GSMA 'Mobile Money for the Unbanked' (Annual Report, July 2009); see also Paul Makin and Consult Hyperion, 'Regulatory Issues Around Mobile Banking' (2010) The Development Dimension ICTs for Development Improving Policy Coherence: Improving Policy Coherence 139; Paul Tucker, 'The Debate on Financial System Resilience: Macroprudential Instruments' 22 (Barclays annual lecture, London, 22 October 2009).
11 Jeremmy Okonjo, *Nature and Impact of Mobile Financial Services on Regulation of Mobile Telecoms in Kenya* (2014) Chapter 1, where convergence has been described as the amalgam of different regulatory authorities with the mobile financial services ecosystem, where the telecommunications industry and the financial services industry are converged to provide mobile payments. See, Colin R. Blackman, 'Convergence Between Telecommunications and Other Media. How Should Regulation Adapt?' (1998) 22 *Telecommunications Policy* 163.

12 I discuss the regulatory authorities under Section 4.2.2.Regulatory Authorities.
13 The objectives of the CCK are different from Central Bank objectives. Communications Authority of Kenya, 'Strategic Plan' <www.cck.go.ke/resc/publica tions/strategic_plan/CCK_3rd_Strategic_Plan_2013_26_11_13.pdf> accessed 3 September 2014; Central Bank of Kenya, <www.cck.go.ke/regulations/down loads/ICT_policy_guidelines_July_2013_FV3_-_5th_July_2013.pdf> accessed 3 September 2014.
14 At the time of writing this chapter, the National Payments Systems Act had not been enacted. However, it has now (as of 2014) been enacted though not enforced. National Payments System Act 2011.
15 The fragmentation of consumer protection, where fragmentation suggests that there is no consolidation in the approach to consumer protection for financial services. See, Andreas Fischer-Lescano and Gunther Teubner, 'Regime-Collisions: the Vain Search for Legal Unity in the Fragmentation of Global Law' (2004) 25(4) *Mich J Int'l L* 999.
16 Agencies that exclusively cater to consumers in the financial system. The Consumer Financial Protection Bureau (CFPB) is an independent agency of the United States government responsible for consumer protection in the financial sector. <www.consumerfinance.gov/> accessed 3 September 2014.
17 See Title Regulatory Overlap on page 56.
18 See Title Regulatory Inertia on page 65.
19 See Title Regulatory Arbitrage on page 59.
20 Todd S. Aagaard, 'Regulatory Overlap, Overlapping Legal Fields, and Statutory Discontinuities' (2011) 29 *Virginia Environmental Law Journal* 237.
21 Stephen G. Breyer, Breaking the Vicious Circle: Toward Effective Risk Regulation (Harvard University Press 1993).
22 The BIS, for example, published five reports on e-money between 1996 and 2001; the ECB (and its predecessor, the European Monetary Institute [EMI], operating between 1994 and 1997) published two reports (1994 and 1998) and a security framework for e-money issuers (2002). The German government amended the German banking law in 1997 requiring e-money issuers to become banks. From Malte Krueger, 'Offshore e-Money Issuers and Monetary Policy' (2001) 6 *First Monday* 10 <http://firstmonday.org/ojs/index.php/fm/article/view/894/803> accessed 3 September 2014.
23 E Gerald Corrigan, 'Are Banks Special?' (1983) Federal Reserve Bank of Minneapolis 1982 <www.minneapolisfed.org/pubs/ar/ar1982a.cfm> accessed 3 September 2014: a discussion on deposit taking institutions should be specifically regarded as banks.
24 Leon Perlman, 'Legal and Regulatory Aspects of Mobile Financial Services' (2012) <http://uir.unisa.ac.za/bitstream/handle/10500/13362/thesis_perlman_lj.pdf? sequence=4> accessed 3 September 2014. Leon states that, 'Any inapplicability of the deposit analogy to a large category of SVPs would mean that utilising bank-type deposit rules and principles for SVPs would be nugatory. Important in this consideration is the nature of the initial contract between the system operators and the user insofar as use of the funds handed over to the system operator or his agent, as well as the legal and prudential nature of the issuer.'
25 See Brian Muthiora, 'Reinventing the Wheel: "Pass Through" Deposit Insurance Coverage for Mobile Money in Kenya' (2014) <www.gsma.com/mobileforde velopment/reinventing-the-wheel-pass-through-deposit-insurance-coverage-for-mobile-money-in-kenya> accessed 3 September 2014.
26 BIS (1996157). To use a helpful taxonomic analogy, the term stored value payments is used in this thesis to describe the 'family' of systems or devices that store value electronically.

27 The CPSS defined 'stored value' products as: 'prepaid payment instruments in which a record of funds owned by or available to the consumer is stored on an electronic device in the consumer's possession, and the amount of stored "value" is increased or decreased, as appropriate, whenever the consumer uses the device to make a purchase or other transaction', Committee on Payment and Settlement Systems (CPSS), 'Security of Electronic Money' (1996) 3 <www.bis.org/publ/cpss18.htm> accessed 3 September 2014. The user simply uses an appropriate device or system to obtain access to the value and associated payment facilities through computer and telecommunications links.

28 Banking Act CAP 488 Laws of Kenya.

29 See Section 4.5.3 Titled The Definition of Deposits Pg. 175

30 Roger McCormick, *Legal Risk in the Financial Markets* (Oxford, Oxford University Press 2010). He discusses legal risk as the risk or loss to an institution which is primarily caused by: (a) a defective transaction; or (b) a claim (including a defence to a claim or a counterclaim) being made or some other event occurring which results in a liability for the institution or other loss (for example, as a result of the termination of a contract); or (c) failing to take appropriate measures to protect assets (for example, intellectual property) owned by the institution; or (d) change in law.

31 See Section 4.6.3, Regulatory Capacity.

32 Stakeholders in the payment system, everyone that has an interest in the payment system as was stated in Kenya Payment System, Framework and Strategy (2004) <www.docin.com/p-433903551.html> accessed 3 September 2014.

33 Section Regulation of Mobile Payments Prior to the National Payment Systems Act 2011.

34 Banking Act, CAP 488 Laws of Kenya.

35 See Section 4.6.3., Regulatory Arbitrage. pg,195.

36 This alludes to a an ideal standard or base model of regulation; J. Luis Guasch and Pablo Spiller, 'The Challenge of Designing and Implementing Effective Regulation: A Normative Approach and an Empirical Evaluation' (2012) The World Bank <http://wwwwds.worldbank.org/external/default/WDSContentServer/WDSP/IB/2012/07/17/000386194_2012071 7015947/Rendered/PDF/710190WP0Publi0ing0and0implementing.pdf> accessed 3 September 2014. See, generally, Bronwen Morgan and Karen Yeung, *An Introduction to Law and Regulation* (Cambridge University Press 2007); Colin Scott, *Regulation in the Age of Governance: the Rise of the Post Regulatory State* (Edward Elgar Publishing 2004).

37 The idea of fragmentation generally comes from the idea of a lack of normative or institutional hierarchy that addresses the regulatory concerns in a structured way; instead, there exists a lack of consolidation of the regulatory instruments which leads to inconsistencies in their application. See, Radha Upadhyaya, 'Analyzing the Sources and Impact of Segmentation in the Banking Sector: a Case Study of Kenya' (PhD, University of London, School of Oriental and African Studies, 2011), where she addresses rather elaborately the state of fragmentation in Kenya's financial services sector regulation. Also fragmentation exists in other areas of law such as in international law as was discussed in Martti Koskenniemi et al., 'Fragmentation of International Law? Postmodern Anxieties' (2002) 15 *Leiden Journal of International Law* 553.

38 Nzomo Mutuku, 'Case for Consolidated Financial Sector Regulation in Kenya' (2008) Retirement Benefits Authority <http://papers.ssrn.com/sol3/papers.cfm?abstract_id=1837354> accessed 3 September 2014.

39 Ibid.

40 Section 4.2. The current regulatory framework looks at Kenya's legal institutional arrangements as a precursor to mobile payments' inception and the regulatory environment through which mobile payments operated.

41 Kenya enacted NPSA in 2011, but public consultations about it began in October 2013, and it became operational on 1 August 2014, although its implementation is still underway.

42 Arnaldo Mauri, 'The Currency Board and the Rise of Banking in East Africa' University of Milan Economics, Business and Statistics Working Paper. The National Payment System Framework Strategy. 2004. Financial services regulation in Kenya is characterised by fragmented or a multiplicity of regulatory authorities that oversee different subsectors of the financial system. I focus specifically on the current regulatory framework in which mobile payments have been operational in advancing my arguments.

43 CBK, 'Payment System in Kenya' (2003) 1 <www.centralbank.go.ke/downloads/nps/nps%20old/psk.pdf> accessed 3 September 2014. Laws relating to the use of cheques are based on English law, primarily the Cheques Act of 1957 and the Bills of Exchange Act 1882.

44 Schedule 1, Central Bank of Kenya Act of 1966, Cap 491 Laws of Kenya; Central Bank of Kenya, 'Introduction to Financial System' <www.centralbank.go.ke/financialsystem/banks/Introduction.aspx> accessed 3 September 2014: Out of the 44 banks, 31 are locally owned, and 13 are owned by foreigners. Out of the 31 local banks, three comprise banks with significant government state corporations shareholding (National Bank of Kenya is 70.6 per cent government owned; Consolidated Bank is 77 per cent government owned; Development Bank of Kenya is 100 per cent government owned); 27 are commercial banks which include Equity Bank, among the largest banks in East Africa.

45 Retirement Benefits Authority, 'Registered Schemes' <www.rba.go.ke/media/docs/schemes/Registered-Schemes.pdf> accessed 3 September 2014.

46 Central Bank of Kenya, 'Deposit Taking Microfinance Institutions' <www.central bank.go.ke/index.php/bank-supervision/microfinance-institutions/14-bank-supervision/83-list-of-licensed-deposit-taking> accessed 3 September 2014: these are Faulu Kenya DTM Ltd; Kenya Women Finance Trust DTM Ltd; Remu DTM Ltd; SMEP DTM Ltd; UWEZO DTM Ltd; Rafiki DTM – with a total of 54 branches nationwide between them. Ndung'u (2009) op cit note 2. In 2007, an estimated 19 per cent of the adult population had access to formal financial services through banks, with 8 per cent served by MFIs and SACCOs. See CGAP (2010b) op cit note 2.

47 The CBK was established in 1966 under the Central Bank Act (Cap 481) 1966. Central Bank of Kenya (CBK), 'Central Bank of Kenya: Background Information' (2011) <http://goo.gl/FnLsy> accessed 3 September 2014.

48 CBK, 'CBK Mandate' (2009) <www.centralbank.go.ke/index.php/cbk-objectives> accessed 3 September 2014.

49 Njuguna Ndung'u, 'Mobile and Agency Banking in Kenya', Address by Prof Njuguna Ndung'u, Governor of the Central Bank of Kenya, at the Technical Cooperation among Developing Countries Programme on 'Mobile and Agency Banking in Kenya' (2013) Kenya School of Monetary Studies <www.bis.org/review/r130515c.pdf?frames=0> accessed 3 September 2014.

50 CBK, 'Oversight of Payment System in Kenya: Policy Framework' (2009) <http://goo.gl/OIu0D> accessed 3 September 2014.

51 CBK (2009) op cit note 43.

52 Leon Perlman in his PhD thesis (n 25) provides the term regulatory *lacuna* as the gaps in regulatory frameworks that present a regulatory dilemma and deems them problematic in the regulation of mobile financial services.

53  This was actually an enabling environment, See Chapter 2, Section 2.4.4. pg 46.
54  Jeremmy Okonjo, 'Chapter 2: the Impact of Convergence of Mobile Telecoms and Financial Services on Regulation of Mobile Telecommunications' (2014) <www.slideshare.net/JeremmyOkonjo/2-chapter-two-impact-of-convergence-of-mobile-financial-services-on-regulation-of-mobile-telecoms-in- kenya> accessed 3 September 2014.
55  Provisions are made for the recognition of electronic transactions in Kenya as part of the Kenya Information and Communications Act, Part VIA.
56  The Constitution of Kenya 2010, <www.kenyalaw.org:8181/exist/kenyalex/act view.xql?actid=Const2010> accessed 3 September 2014.
57  The Central Bank of Kenya Act 1966, amended 2010.
58  Jeremmy Okonjo, (n 55). It is unclear whether payment services providers in the context of mobile payments includes electronic money. However, there is a clear distinction in my view of the two.
59  Leon J Perlman (2012) (n 25); see, John B. Taylor, 'The Monetary Transmission Mechanism: an Empirical Framework' (1995) *The Journal of Economic Perspectives* 11460–11478; and see, François Gianviti, *Current Legal Aspects of Monetary Sovereignty* (2004) <www.imf.org/external/np/leg/sem/2004/cdmfl/eng/gianvi.pdf> accessed 3 September 2014.
60  Such as the European Union government.
61  Ibid., pg. 65.
62  The Federal Reserve of the United States has updated its legislation to include mobile payments under regulation Z that ensures financial integrity, and Nigeria has updated their Payments Systems Law, The Regulatory Framework for Mobile Payments in Nigeria, <www.bu.edu/bucflp/files/2012/01/Regulatory-Framework-for-Mobile-Payment-Systems-in-Nigeria.pdf> accessed 22 September 2014.
63  Committee on Payment Systems, 'Core Principles for Systemically Important Payment Systems' Bank of International Settlements 2001. See also David Sawyer and John Trundle, 'Core Principles for Systemically Important Payment Systems' (2001) 8 *Financial Stability Review* <www.bis.org/cpmi/publ/d43.pdf> accessed 3 September 2014
64  See Chapter 3.
65  The payment services component allows transportation of value along a payment system.
66  The BIS sees this oversight as promoting the smooth functioning of payment systems and to protect the financial system from possible 'domino effects', which may occur when one or more participants in the payment system incurs credit or liquidity problems. The oversight of payment systems is aimed at a given system (e.g., a funds transfer system) rather than at individual participants. See CPSS, 'Payment and Settlement Systems in selected Countries' (2003) <www.bis.org/publ/cpss54.pdf> accessed 3 September 2014; Fraser (1994).
67  Leon J. Perlman (2012) (n 25). Historically, this monopoly oversight and involvement evolved because of disparate mechanisms of payment that led to market inefficiencies and weaknesses in payment, and the need for an efficient mechanism of payments.
68  In 1998, the US Federal Reserve stepped in to preserve the financial markets when it filled a payment void left by the multibillion dollar failure of the Long-Term Capital Management hedge fund. See Kevin Dowd, 'Too Big to Fail? Long-Term Capital Management and the Federal Reserve' (1999) Cato Briefing Paper No 52 <www.cato.org/pubs/briefs/bp52.pdf> accessed 3 September 2014.
69  Although at the time of writing this chapter the Regulatory Authority for Communications was the CCK, this title has changed to the Communications Authority

of Kenya. However, this chapter shall continue to refer to the Authority as the CCK rather than the CAK for fluidity.

70 Africog, 'Cause for Public Concern on the Telkom Privatization and Safari-com IPO' <www.africog.org/reports/Cause%20for%20Public%20Concern%20 over%20safaricom%20IPO.pdf> accessed 3 September 2014.
71 Alice Munyua and Muriuki Mureithi, 'Kenya' (2007) Global Information Society Watch (GISW) 2007 Report www.globaliswatch.org/en/node/500 accessed 3 September 2014.
72 Africog, 'Cause for Public Concern on the Telkom Privatization and Safari-com IPO' <www.africog.org/reports/Cause%20for%20Public%20Concern%20 over%20safaricom%20IPO.pdf> accessed 3 September 2014.
73 Ibid.
74 Committee on Payment and Settlement Systems, 'Policy Issues for Central Banks in Retail Payments' (2003) Bank for International Settlements 1–3.
75 The Central Bank is the financial sector regulator.
76 Through its National Payments Systems Division, though initially very reluc-tantly. See Chapter 4, 4.6.5 The political interference with the collective will to regulate.
77 The development of mobile financial services in general have morphed to include various financial products, such as M-Kopo and M-Kesho.
78 See generally, Michael E. Levine and Jennifer L. Forrence, 'Regulatory Capture, Public Interest, and the Public Agenda: Toward a Synthesis' (1990) *Journal of Law, Economics, & Organization* 167; Joseph E. Stiglitz, *The Role of the State in Financial Markets*, vol 21 (Institute of Economics, Academia Sinica 1993).
79 Oliver James, 'Regulation Inside Government: Public Interest Justifications and Regulatory Failures' (2000) 78 *Public Administration* 327.
80 In fact, for those in Uganda, Rwanda, Tanzania, South Africa and Nigeria, African countries modernising their payments systems to include mobile financial services due to its efficiency and inclusiveness. See, The Africa Competitiveness Report (2013) <www.worldbank.org/content/dam/Worldbank/document/Africa/Report/ africa-competitiveness-report-2013-main-report-web.pdf> accessed 3 September 2014.
81 Central Bank Governor, Njoroge Ndung'u interviewed by Simon Di Castri on the Test and Learn Approach to banking the unbanked. Simone di Castri, 'A Conversation with Professor Njuguna Ndung'u, Governor of the Central Bank of Kenya, on the critical policy issues around mobile money' (2013) <www.gsma. com/mobilefordevelopment/a-conversation-with-professor-njuguna-ndungu-governor-of-the-central-bank-of-kenya-on-the-critical-policy-issues-around-mobile-money> accessed 3 September 2014.
82 At the time of writing this thesis, the law was enacted but was not enforced and was not in effect.
83 See Part II, Overall Regulatory Challenges for the Regulatory Authorities in Reg-ulating Mobile Payments. Regulatory Capacity.
84 This overregulation would create a rigid market, stifling flexibility of operation and development.
85 Robert Baldwin, Martin Cave and Martin Lodge, *Understanding Regulation: Theory, Strategy, and Practice* (Oxford University Press 2011) 415.
86 Antonio Estache and Liam Wren-Lewis, 'Toward a Theory of Regulation for Developing Countries: Following Jean-Jacques Laffont's Lead' (2009) *Journal of Economic Literature* 729; Jean-Jacques Laffont, *Regulation and Development* (Cambridge University Press 2005).
87 Ibid at 84, one of the key aspects is how to deal with populations that are unlikely or unwilling to pay for services rendered especially in electricity.

88  See Levine and Forrence (n 78); Ernesto Dal Bó, 'Regulatory Capture: a Review' (2006) 22 *Oxford Review of Economic Policy* 203.

89  The Ministry of Finance and the Ministry of Information Communication and Technology, <www.govermentofkenya.com> accessed 3 September 2014.

90  See, Committee on Payment and Settlement Systems Secretariat, 'The Contribution of Payments Systems to Financial Stability' (2000) *Bank for International Settlements*.

91  Ibid., n 39, Mutuku (2008)

92  Central Bank of Kenya, 'Role of National Payment Systems' <www.centralbank. go.ke/index.php/role-of-national-payment-systems> accessed 3 September 2014. The Central Bank's overall objective as provided under Section 4 A (i)d of the Central Bank of Kenya Act is to formulate and implement such policies as to best promote the establishment, regulation and supervision of efficient, effective payment, clearing and settlement systems. Available at Central Bank of Kenya, <www.cbk.co.ke> accessed 3 September 2014.

93  Central Bank of Kenya Act 1966.

94  'National Payment Systems in Kenya' (2003) published by the Central Bank of Kenya.

95  The National Payment Systems Division was created for these purposes.

96  See Mutuku (2008) (n 39); Francis Mwega, 'The Competitiveness and Efficiency of the Financial Services Sector in Africa: A Case Study of Kenya' (2011) 23 *African Development Review* 44.; Simon P. Nkeri, 'The Case for Consolidated Regulation of Financial Conglomerates in Kenya' (2014)

97  'Implications for Central Banks of the Development of Electronic Money' Bank for International Settlements See, 'Innovations in Retail Payments and the BIS Statistics on Payment and Settlement Systems' (2008) *IFC Bulletin* 31.

98  Ibid., Marc Hollanders.

99  Ibid. This acceptability of risks means that not all risks can be prevented or mitigated as all payment systems are inherently risky. See Chapter 3, Inherent Risks in the Payment System.

100  See Chapter 3.

101  See Chapter 3.

102  See Chapter 2, Section 2.5, Success of Mobile Payments: Financial Inclusion. Tommaso Paedoa- Schioppa, 'Policy Issues for Central Banks in Retail Payments (2003) Committee on Payment and Settlement Systems (n 58). I also extensively discuss the relationship between financial stability and the payment system.

103  Harry Leinonen, 'Developments in Retail Payment Systems' (2001) Bank for International Settlements Information Press & Library Services CH-4002 Basel, Switzerland 61.

104  Regulatory strategies, see Anthony Ogus, 'Rethinking Self-regulation' (1995) 15(1) *Oxford Journal of Legal Studies* 97.

105  The CPPS recommends an efficient and mature market for the industry to be able to develop retail payments systems on its own accord. See Paedoa-Schioppa (2003) (n 58) 13–15. However, MNOs cannot be assessed as mature markets, since their introduction into the Kenyan telecommunications market and their efficiency is debatable. See Chapter 3, Section on Operational Risks.

106  Ibid.

107  See Chapter 3.

108  Objectives of the CBK under Section 4 of the Central Bank Act 1966.

109  See Chapter 4 on Section Regulatory Capacity. See also Rosa M. Lastra, *Central Banking and Banking Regulation* (Financial Markets Group, London School of Economics and Political Science 1996) where the argument was put forth that the central banks in developing countries are frequently the only organisations

that can be referred to due to a lack of an independent financial services regulator such as the PRA in the UK.

110 See Part III, Challenges in the Enforcement of National Payment Systems Act 2011.

111 Julian R. Franks, Stephen M. Schaefer and Michael D. Staunton, 'The Direct and Compliance Costs of Financial Regulation' (1997) 21 *Journal of Banking & Finance* 1547.

112 See section on the theoretical considerations in regulating mobile payments, titled Market Discipline page, Anthony I. Ogus, *Regulation: Legal Form and Economic Theory*, vol 152 (Clarendon Press 1994); See also, Baldwin, Cave and Lodge (2011) (n 87).

113 This term was used by Njuguna Ndungu the Central Bank Governor, in his interview with Simone Di Castri (2013) (n 83).

114 The Consumer Financial Protection Bureau in the United States provides an appropriate regime in which public and private mechanisms for accountability can be sought by consumers, unlike the Consumer Protection Act 2012 in Kenya that does not assess the right of consumers who use financial services.

115 See Chapter 2, Section Enabling Environment of Mobile Payments, Lack of a Regulatory Framework, page, 47.

116 The first such public consultation was called on 18 October 2013, seven years after the inception of mobile payments.

117 Without transparency, a haphazard regulatory framework may be instituted.

118 There is no established convention for the designation of 'developed' and 'developing' countries or areas in the United Nations system. United Nations, 'Composition of Macro Geographical (Continental) Region' (2013) <http://unstats.un.org/unsd/methods/m49/m49regin.htm#ftnc> accessed 3 September 2014. The designations 'developed' and 'developing' are intended for statistical convenience and do not necessarily express a judgment about the stage reached by a particular country or area in the development process; also see, United Nations, 'United Nations Statistics Division: Standard Country and Area Codes Classifications (M49)' (2012) <http://unstats.un.org/unsd/methods/m49/m49.htm> accessed 3 September 2014.

119 The term 'legal transplant' was coined by scholar Alan Watson to indicate the moving of a rule or a system of law from one country to another as maintained by Watson, transplantation is the most fertile source of legal development. Alan Watson, *Legal Transplants: An Approach to Comparative Law* (University of Georgia Press 1974); Alan Watson, *Legal Transplants: An Approach to Comparative Law* (2nd edn, University of Georgia Press 1993).

120 Investment climate advisory services of the World Bank Group, 'Better Regulation for Growth Governance Frameworks and Tools for Effective Regulatory Reform Regulatory Capacity Review of Kenya' (2010) <www.wbginvestmentclimate.org/uploads/Kenya.pdf> accessed 3 September 2014.

121 Eugene Cotran, 'The Development and Reform of the Law in Kenya' (1983) 27 *Journal of African Law* 42, 42–61.

122 Holger Spamann, 'Contemporary Legal Transplants – Legal Families and the Diffusion of (Corporate) Law' (2009) *Brigham Young University Law Review* 6, 1813

123 The current constitution was adopted in 1963 and amended in 1999. Kenya has been involved in a constitutional review process for the last three years, with the population having rejected the latest amendments in a referendum in 2007

124 Article 3 of the Constitution of Kenya.

125 Decrees may be issued under the name of the president, but they have to be submitted to Parliament for ratification at its next session.

126  Richard L. Abel, 'Customary Laws of Wrongs in Kenya: An Essay in Research Method' (1969) *The American Journal of Comparative Law* 573.

127  Yash Ghai, 'Law, Development and African Scholarship' (1987) 50 *The Modern Law Review* 750.

128  Niall Hayes and Chris Westrup, 'Context and the Processes of ICT for Development' (2012) 22 *Information and Organization* 23; Alliance for Financial Inclusion, 'Enabling Mobile Money Transfer: The Central Bank of Kenya's Treatment of M-PESA' (2010) <www.afi-global.org/en/phoca-publications-case-studies> accessed 3 September 2014. At the inception of M-PESA in Kenya in 2007, Safaricom lobbied the CBK and the CCK for authorisation to provide mobile money transfer services, without a regulatory framework. The CCK's reluctance to step in as a primary regulator was probably due to its unfamiliarity with the new converged product. The CBK has hinged on its macroprudential regulatory mandate under Section 3 of the Central Bank of Kenya Act to issue negative authorisation to the provision of mobile financial services by MNOs. This is by way of issuance of letters of no objection.

129  These capacity constraints include the lack of unified financial regulation and the fragmentation of the legislation as articulated by Mutuku (2008) (n 39).

130  Financial Sector Regulation and Reforms in Emerging Markets Hayes and Westrup. Hayes, N. and C. Westrup (2012), 'Context and the Processes of ICT for Development', Information and Organization.

131  Jillian Hossein, Colin Kirkpatrick and David Parker, 'Creating the Conditions for International Business Expansion: The Impact of Regulation on Economic Growth in Developing Countries – a Cross-Country Analysis' (2003) <http://ageconsearch.umn.edu/handle/30554> accessed 3 September 2014.

132  Bede C. Opata, 'Transplantation and Evolution of Legal Regulation of Interconnection Arrangements in the Nigeria Telecommunications Sector' (2011) 14 *Int'l J Comm L & Pol'y* 1, also this phenomenon shall further be discussed in Chapter 5: Mobile Payments Regulation an Appropriate Approach.

133  This dichotomy between 'innovations versus regulation' has been previously discussed in Chapter 1; it is also described as the Regulatory Dilemma by Leon Perlman in Legal Aspects of Mobile Financial.

134  See Chapter 2. The enabling regulatory environment has been used in various literature on mobile payments to describe the conducive conditions that have allowed mobile payments in Kenya to prosper, those have not been restrictive. This is also discussed in the first chapter as an altogether enabling environment which has contributed to mobile payment success in Kenya.

135  Antonio Estache and Liam Wren Lewis, *Toward a Theory of Regulation for Developing Countries* (American Economic Association 2009).

136  Baldwin, Cave and Lodge (2011) (n 87).

137  Ismael Levergne, 'Mobile Payment Regulation – the Regulator's Role' (2012) <www.gfg-group.com/mobile-payments/2012/08/mobile-payment-regulation-the-regulators-role/> accessed 3 September 2014.

138  Ibid.

139  Safaricom has to send audit reports to the CBK on a monthly basis.

140  The Kenya Communications Act 2 of 1998, *Kenya Gazette Supplement* No 64, 9 November 1998 at 219–220, available at <http://goo.gl/98dpL> accessed 3 September 2014. For a critical analysis of the Act, see Rebecca Wanjiku, 'Kenya Communications Amendment Act (2009): Progressive or Retrogressive?' (2009) <www.apc.org/en/system/files/CICEWAKenya20090908_EN.pdf> accessed 3 September 2014.

141  Kenya Communications (Amendment) Act 1 of 2009 <www.cck.go.ke/> accessed 3 September 2014. The Kenya Communications Act 2 of 1998 is now known as the Kenya Information and Communications Act 2 of 1998.

142 Perlman, (2012) although the Ministries were renamed after the 2013 General Election in 2013.

143 Ibid.

144 Ibid., pg. 99.

145 Ibid., pg. 144

146 Ibid., pg. 144, See also, Communications Commission of Kenya (CCK), 'Market Structure – Telecommunications: Unified Licensing Framework' (2011) <www.cck.go.ke/licensing/telecoms/market.html> accessed 3 September 2014.

147 Jeremmy Okonjo, 'Impact of Convergence of Mobile Financial Services on regulation of Mobile Telecoms in Kenya' (2014) <www.slideshare.net/JeremmyOkonjo/2-chapter-two-impact-of-convergence-of-mobile-financial-services-on-regulation-of-mobile-telecoms-in-kenya> accessed 3 September 2014; Monica Kerrets, 'ICT Regulation and Policy at a Crossroads: a Case Study of the Licensing Process in Kenya' (2004). The courts have also appreciated the nature of telecommunications services as public goods. For example, in 'Observer Publications Limited v Campbell Mickey Mathew and Others' (2001) 10 *BHRC* 252, a case from the Commonwealth Caribbean, dealt with constitutional provisions relating to freedom of expression similar to those of the Constitution of Kenya of 1969, the Privy Council held that 'The airwaves are public property whose use has to be regulated and rationed in the general interest.'

148 Jenny C. Aker and Isaac M. Mbiti, 'Mobile Phones and Economic Development in Africa' (2010) Working Paper 211 <www.cgdev.org/files/1424175_file_Aker_Mobile_wp211_FINAL.pdf> accessed 3 September 2014.

149 Licensing powers are vested and operationalised by Sections 5 and 25 of the Kenyan Information and Communications Act, Cap 411A, Laws of Kenya.

150 CCK's total estimated income for the year 2012/2013 is Kshs. 6.22 billion. See Communications Commission of Kenya, 'Annual Report Financial Year 2011/12' (2013) <www.marsgroupkenya.org/documents/documents/11776/> accessed 3 September 2014.

151 Leon Perlman, 'Legal and Regulatory Aspects of Mobile Financial Services' (2012) <http://uir.unisa.ac.za/bitstream/handle/10500/13362/thesis_perlman_lj.pdf?sequence=4> accessed 3 September 2014.

152 Ismael Lavergne, 'Mobile Payment Regulation, The Regulators Role' <www.gfg-group.com/mobile-payments/2012/08/> accessed 3 September 2014.

153 Ben Sihanya, 'Infotainment and Cyber Law in Africa: regulatory benchmarks for the third Millennium' (2000) Bernard Sihanya (2000) "Infotainment and Cyber law in Africa: Regulatory Benchmarks for the Third Millennium," 10 Transnational Law and Contemporary Problems, pp. 583–640 suggests that licensing allocation should be based on an applicant's ability to deliver services.

154 Statutory frameworks for competition, especially by way of licensing, are integral to the realisation of the freedoms of speech, expression and the media, under Articles 33 and 34 of the Constitution.

155 Jeremy Okonjo (2014) (supra note 154); Ivan Mortimer-Schutts, 'The Regulatory Implications of Mobile and Financial Services Convergence' (2007) in 'The Transformational Potential of M-Transactions: Moving the Debate Forward' (2007) The Policy Paper Series No. 6 <www.vodafone.com/content/dam/vodafone/about/public_policy/policy_papers/public_policy_series_6.pdf> accessed 3 September 2014.

156 Market restriction regulatory policies as an impediment to freedoms of speech are considered.

157 See James Bilodeaeau, William Hoffman, and Sjoerd Nikkelen, 'Findings from the Mobile Financial Services Development Report' (2011) the Capco Institute Journal of Financial Transformation.

158 Section 23(2)(b) of the Kenya Information and Communications Act provides that the Commission shall 'maintain and promote effective competition between persons engaged in commercial activities connected with Telecommunication services in Kenya in order to ensure efficiency and economy in the provision of such services and to promote research and development in relation thereto'.

159 Ibid.

160 James Bilodeaeau, William Hoffman, and Sjoerd Nikkelen, 'Findings from the Mobile Financial Services Development Report' (2011) the Capco Institute Journal of Financial Transformation.

161 Communications Commission of Kenya, 'Annual Report Financial Year 2008/09' (2010) <www.marsgroupkenya.org/documents/documents/11776/> accessed 3 September 2014.

162 Ibid.

163 PricewaterhouseCoopers, 'Telecoms in Africa: Innovative and Inspiring' (2012) 17(1) *Communications Review* 100

164 Mike Nxele and Thankom Arun, 'Regulatory Impact on the Development of the Telecommunications Sector in East Africa: a Case Study of Kenya' (2005) Working Paper Series No 99 <http://econpapers.repec.org/RePEc:ags:idpmcr:30598> accessed 3 September 2014.

165 Andrew Crockett, 'Market Discipline and Financial Stability' 26 Journal of Banking & Finance 977. See the balance of market discipline in bank regulation 'In International Seminar- the Breakdown of Public &Private Law Dichotomy in Commercial and Financial Law (n208) 81.103–105

166 Notes on Regulation of Branchless Banking in Kenya – GSMA 2007 <www.gsma.com/mobilefordevelopment/wpcontent/uploads/2012/06/kenyanotesonregulationbranchlessbanking2007.pdf> accessed 3 September 2014.

167 Ibid.

168 Ibid., pg. 169. In its August 2004 strategy paper on the Kenya payment system, the CBK stated that it 'is encouraging the population to move to non-cash payment instruments such as payment cards and electronic money.' Kenya Payment System (Framework and Strategy) (2004) (n 23) vii, which further alludes to the lax approach the CBK initially adopted.

169 CGAP, 'Notes on Regulation of Branchless Banking' (2012) <www.gsma.com/mobilefordevelopment/wpcontent/uploads/2012/06/kenyanotesonregulationbranchlessbanking2007.pdf> accessed 3 September 2014.

170 Broadly speaking the space in which mobile payments operate. Colin Scott, 'Analysing regulatory space: fragmented resources and institutional design' (2001) in Maurice Sunkin (ed), *Public Law* (Sweet and Maxwell, 2014) 329–353.

171 The Banking Act 1989 (Cap 488).

172 Prior to the Banking Act of 1969, banking in Kenya was regulated under a piece of legislation from the colonial era, namely, the Banking Ordinance. The 1969 Act allowed the minister of Finance to license banks and non-bank financial institutions. It also gave the CBK the responsibility of inspecting all financial institutions. The Banking (Amendment) Act 1985 changed the licensing regime, such that the CBK did so with the minister's approval. A series of bank failures in Kenya led to the Deposit Protection Fund (DPF) in 1986. For a comparative and historical perspective on banking in East Africa, see Arnaldo Mauri, 'The Currency Board and the Rise of Banking in East Africa' (2007) Working Paper No 10 <http://econpapers.repec.org/paper/milwpdepa/2007-10.htm> accessed 3 September 2014.

173 Perlman (2012) (n 25).

174 Banking Act, Section 2 – Kenya Law Resource Centre, 'Statutory definitions of a bank' <www.kenyalawresourcecenter.org/2011/07/statutory-definitions-of-bank.htm> accessed 3 September 2014.

175 Current account means an account maintained by a bank for, and in the name of or in a name designated by, a customer of the bank into which money is paid by or for the benefit of such customer and on which cheques and other bills of exchange may be drawn by, and transfers and other banking transactions made on the instructions of, the customer. Banking Act, Section 2.

176 Ibid.

177 Banking Act 1989, Section 3.

178 Ragnar Gudmundsson, Kethi Ngoka-Kisinguh and Maureen T. Odongo, 'The Role of Capital Requirements on Bank Competition and Stability: The Case of the Kenyan Banking Industry' (2013) <www.kba.co.ke/workingpaperseries/img/pdf/Working_Paper_WPS_05_12[2].pdf> accessed 3 September 2014.

179 'CGAP Annual Report 2007' (2007) <www.cgap.org/sites/default/files/CGAP-Annual-Report-Dec-2007.pdf> accessed 3 September 2014.

180 National Payment Systems Bill at the time in 2009.

181 Rhys Bollen, 'Recent Developments in Mobile Banking and Payments' (2009) Journal of International Banking Law and Regulation 454; Alan L. Tyree, *Banking Law in Australia* (Butterworths 1998).

182 In the seventeenth century, when merchants turned to goldsmiths to provide, or 'deposit', their valuables for safekeeping and pecuniary advantage, Henry D. Macleod, *The Theory and Practice of Banking*, vol 1 (Longmans, Green, Reader, & Dyer 1866 2012) <http://books.google.co.uk/books/about/The_Theory_and_Practice_of_Banking.html?id=JKkyAQAAMAAJ> accessed 3 September 2014.

183 The law merchant (lex mercatoria).

184 Ibid.

185 Humphrey et al (1996) (n 1).

186 See Shelagh Heffernan, Modern Banking in Theory and Practice (John Wiley and Sons 2003) at 15; Richard Apostolik, Christopher Donohue and Peter Went, Foundations of Banking Risk: An Overview of Banking, Banking Risks, and Risk-Based Banking Regulation (Wiley Finance 2009) at 5.

187 Claudio E. Borio and Renato Filosa, 'The Changing Borders of Banking: Trends and Implications' (1994) BIS Working Paper No 23 <http://papers.ssrn.com/sol3/papers.cfm?abstract_id=868431> accessed 3 September 2014.

188 See FNB Connect, a division of FNB Bank that offers fixed and mobile services to anyone, not only to bank customers.

189 Perlman suggests that just as in Salmon J in *Woods* v *Martins Bank* (1959) 1 QB 55 at 56 said: '[T]he limits of a banker's business cannot be laid down as a matter of law. The nature of such business must in case be a matter of fact, and, accordingly cannot be treated as if it were a matter of pure law. What may have been true of the Bank of Montreal in 1918 is not necessarily true of Martins Bank in 1958.'

190 Joan Wadsley and Graham Penn, *Law Relating to Domestic Banking* (2nd ed., Sweet and Maxwell 2000) 91.

191 Ibid., pg. 89.

192 Cynthia Merritt, 'Mobile Money Transfer Services: The Next Phase in the Evolution of Person-to- Person Payments' (2011) 5 *Journal of Payments Strategy & Systems* 143; See also Maria Stephens and Lisa Dawson, 'A Risk-Based Approach to Regulatory Policy and Mobile Financial Services' (2011) Federal Reserve Bank of Atlanta, Americas Center <www.frbatlanta.org/documents/news/conferences/> accessed 3 September 2014.

193 Ibid. Cynthia Merritt, 'Mobile Money Transfer Services: The Next Phase in the Evolution of Person-to- Person Payments' (2011) 5 *Journal of Payments Strategy & Systems* 143.

194 The relationships that are created beyond the traditional core activities of intermediation, such as investment advice and safe storage of value, can be described
as *sui generis*.

195 See, for example, the Australian case Commissioners of the State Savings Bank
of Victoria v Permewan Wright and Co Ltd (1914) 19 CLR 457 (hereafter
Permewan) where on the issue of the 'business of banking', Issacs J (at 470,
471) said that: 'The essential characteristics of the business of banking . . . may
be described as the collection of money by receiving deposits on loan, repayable
when and as expressly or impliedly agreed upon, and the utilisation of the money
so collected by lending it again in such sums as are required.' As Tyree points
out, this 'reservoir' definition does not require current accounts or payment
facilities. Further, the purported 'bank' was not acting as a 'banker' since it neither allowed funds to be drawn upon by cheque nor did it collect cheques. See
Alan Tyree, 'The Business of Banking' <http://austlii.edu.au/~alan/business-
of-banking.html> accessed 3 September 2014.

196 E. P. Ellinger, E. Lomnicka and R. J. A. Hooley, *Ellinger's Modern Banking Law*
(5th ed., Oxford University Press 2011) 69.

197 Ibid., pg. 62.

198 Additionally, common law views of banking and what is termed the 'business
of banking' are based on judicial decisions, the evolution of business processes
and the influence of related statutes which are constantly changing due to external factors. Leon Perlman (2012) (supra note 25); Sandra Joireman, 'Inherited Legal Systems and Effective Rule of Law: Africa and the Colonial Legacy'
(2001) 39(4) Journal of Modern African Studies 571.

199 As Schulze correctly points out, because of the multifaceted nature of banking,
banking law depends on the application of various fields of law and a large number of other pieces of legislation that apply indirectly to banking law.

200 The post-colonial period provided the opportunity for states to adopt their own
legislation; however, the adoption of colonial legal regimes was commonplace.

201 Financial intermediation, See, Ross Levine, Norman Loayza and Thorsten Beck,
'Financial Intermediation and Growth: Causality and Causes' (2000) 46 Journal
of Monetary Economics 31.

202 See, William S. Holdsworth, *A History of English Law*, vol 1 (Methuen 1922);
Maximilian J. Hall, *Banking Regulation and Supervision: A Comparative Study
of the UK, USA and Japan* (E. Elgar 1993).

203 Robert Chorley, *Law of Banking* (6th edn, Sweet and Maxwell 1974) at 23.

204 Others indicate that core services which banks are said traditionally to provide
are deposit collection, payment services and loan underwriting. See Richard
Apostolik, Christopher Donohue and Peter Went, *Foundations of Banking Risk:
An Overview of Banking, Banking Risks, and Risk-Based Banking Regulation*,
vol 507 (Wiley 2009). See also Rhys Bollen, 'What is a Deposit (And Why Does
It Matter)' (2006) 13 eLaw J.

205 While statutory definitions may buttress the common law definitions, the common law definition has been criticised as being overly restrictive when it hones in
on precise mechanisms; see Eliahu Ellinger, Eva Lomnicka and Richard Hooley,
'Ellinger's Modern Banking' (Oxford University Press 2006) at 73.

206 Borio and Filosa (1994) (n 187).

207 Alan Tyree, 'The Business of Banking' (2008) <http://austlii.edu.au/~alan/
business-of-banking.html> accessed 3 September 2014; Benjamin Geva, *Bank
Collections and Payment Transactions: A Comparative Legal Analysis* (Oxford
University Press 2001).

208 Ibid.

209 Ana Carvajal et al., *The Perimeter of Financial Regulation* (International Monetary Fund 2009). See also AAMC Task Force on Financial Conflicts of Interest

in Clinical Research, 'Protecting Subjects, Preserving Trust, Promoting Progress II: Principles and Recommendations for Oversight of an Institution's Financial Interests in Human Subjects Research' 78 Academic Medicine 237; also, Louis De Koker, 'Identifying and Managing Low Money Laundering Risk: Perspectives on FATF's Risk-based Guidance' (2009) 16 Journal of Financial Crime 334.

210 Similarly, see in relation to the effect of e-money on the business of banking and the traditional core activities, W. G. Schulze, 'Smart Cards and E-Money: New Developments Bring New Problems' (2004) 16(4) *SA Mercantile Law Journal* at 712.

211 Section 16(3) says that for the purposes of Section 16(2) money is paid on terms which are able to be referred to the provision of property or services or to the giving of security if, and only if, it is paid by way of advance or part payment under a contract for the sale, hire or other provisions of property or services, and is repayable only in the event that the property is, or services are not, in fact sold, hired or otherwise provided; if it is paid by way of security for the performance of a contract or by way of security in respect of loss which may result from the non-performance of a contract; or it is paid by way of security for the delivery up or return of any property whether in a particular state of repair or otherwise. In terms of Section 16(4), a 'deposit' does not include a sum paid by the Central Bank or by an institution or the persons mentioned in Section 54 or a sum which is paid by a person to an associate of that person.

212 According to the Banking Act 1969 Amended (2009).

213 To determine whether deposits are accepted only on particular occasions, the CBK looks at the frequency of those occasions and to any characteristics distinguishing them from each other; Section 16(8) Banking Act.

214 Section 16(6) of the Banking Act 1989.

215 Banking Act 1989, Section 2 – Interpretation 'Current Account'.

216 Intermediation is a term used by the CBK to describe this process. See, for example, Gerald Nyaoma, 'Mobile Payments regulatory Framework Perspectives in Kenya' (2010) <www.efina.org.ng/media-centre/events/workshops/mobile-payments-regulatory-framework-dissemination- workshop/forcedownload/91> accessed 3 September 2014; Gerald Nyaoma, 'Regulating Mobile Money: the Case of M-PESA' (2009) <www.afi-global.org/sites/default/files/publications/GPF_Gerald_Nyaoma.pdf> accessed 3 September 2014.

217 To determine whether deposits are accepted only on particular occasions, the CBK looks at the frequency of those occasions and to any characteristics distinguishing them from each other; see Section 16(8) of the Banking Act.

218 AFI's Mobile Financial Services Working Group, 'Mobile Financial Services: Mobile-enabled Cross- border Payments' (2008) Alliance for Financial Inclusion. See also Mark Pickens, David Porteous and Sarah Rotman, 'Banking the Poor via G2P payments' (2007) 58 Focus Note; Ananda Fanon and Ismail Ateya, 'A Preliminary M-Payment Model for M-Commerce in Kenya' (2008) <www.strathmore.edu/pdf/ictc-08/m-payment.pdf> accessed 3 September 2014.

219 Kenya Law Resource Centre, 'Statutory Definitions of a Bank' <www.kenyalawresourcecenter.org/2011/07/statutory-definitions-of-bank.htm> accessed 3 September 2014.

220 To determine whether deposits are accepted only on particular occasions, the CBK looks at the frequency of those occasions and to any characteristics distinguishing them from each other; see Section 16(8) of the Banking Act.

221 AFI (2010a) op cit note 2 at 4 ; see also Mark Pickens, David Porteous and Sarah Rotman (2007) (n 222); Fanon and Ateya (2008) (n 222).

222 Safaricom (2011a).

223 See criteria by CBK in Nyaoma (2010) (n 220).

224 Risks brought on due to the exposure from mobile payments agents as discussed in Chapter 3: Multi-layered Analysis of the Risks at Every Level of the Mobile Payments Ecosystems.
225 Hugh Rockoff, 'The Free Banking Era: A Reexamination' (1974) *Journal of Money, Credit and Banking* 141.
226 Protecting Customer Funds in Transformational Branchless Banking, CGAP (2007) (supra note 186) op cit note 2 at 5.
227 It is not clear whether the funds from this trust company are invested by banks; however, all interests earned are used as part of Safaricom's corporate social responsibility.
228 A commercial bank in Kenya that holds the mobile payments funds from M-Pesa operations.
229 Ignacio Mas and Amolo Ng'weno, 'Three Keys to M-PESA's Success: Branding, Channel Management and Pricing' (2010) <http://papers.ssrn.com/sol3/papers.cfm?abstract_id=1593387> accessed 3 September 2014.
230 It did, however, recently open up the opportunity to earn interest using a conventional bank account in an agreement with Equity Bank. Their M-Kesho scheme is a full savings account issued by Equity Bank, but marketed as an 'M-Pesa Equity account'. M-Kesho accounts pay interest, but they do not have a limit on account balances and are linked to limited emergency credit and insurance facilities. Unlike its regular equity account holders who can only transact at the bank's 140 branches, Equity's M-Kesho customers will be able to transact at any of the 17,000 retail outlets that accept M-Pesa. 'M-KESHO in Kenya: A New Step for M-PESA and Mobile Banking' <www.financialaccess. org/blog/2010/05/m-kesho-kenya- new-step-m-pesa-and-mobile-banking> accessed 28 September 2014
231 CGAP, 'Update on Regulation of Branchless Banking in Kenya' (2010) <www. cgap.org/sites/default/files/CGAP-Regulation-of-Branchless-Banking-in-Kenya-Jan-2010.pdf> accessed 3 September 2014; see also, Eliahu P. Ellinger, Eva Lomnicka and Christopher Hare, *Ellinger's Modern Banking Law* (Oxford University Press 2011).
232 Ibid, Commercial Bank of Africa and Kenya Commercial Bank.
233 CGAP, 'Notes on Regulation of Branchless Banking in Kenya' (2012) CGAP Focus Note <www.gsma.com/mobilefordevelopment/wpcontent/uploads/2012/06/kenyanotesonregulationbranchlessbanking2007.pdf > accessed 3 September 2014.
234 At the time of writing this chapter, there was no payment systems act.
235 The CBK says that an enabling approach requires purposeful and continued engagement to understand and facilitate innovations that can improve financial inclusion. See Nyaoma (2010) (n 220).
236 Daily Nation, 'Michuki: Probe Cash Transfer' (2008) <www.nation.co.ke/News/-/1056/500454/-/u0kd67/-/index.html> accessed 3 September 2014.
237 Ignacio Mas and Amolo Ng'weno (2010) (n 233).
238 Ibid. Although this figure has increased exponentially as the metamorphosis of M-Pesa has advanced to encompass various needs, the average transaction continues to increase and the figures should not be seen as minimal.
239 Geva (2001) (n 211) 61; S v Kearney 1964 (2) SA 495 (A) at 503.
240 Foley v Hill (1848) 2 HL C 28 at 45 (hereafter Foley).
241 As per Lord Cottenham LC. In Scotland, the relationship was described by MacKay L. in *Royal Bank of Scotland* v *Skinner* 1931 SLT 382 at 384, OH as such: 'After some fluctuation of opinion, it is now well settled that the relationship of customer and banker is neither a relation of principal and agent nor a relation of a fiduciary nature, trust, or the like, but a simple relation – it may be one-sided, or it may be two-sided – of creditor – debtor. The banker is not, in

the general case, the custodian of money. When money is paid in, despite the popular belief, it is simply consumed by the banker, who gives an obligation of equivalent amount.'

242 Ibid., note 230.

243 Consumer protection issues will be discussed in Part III of this chapter.

244 Alan L. Tyree, *Banking Law in Australia* (Butterworths 1990); Tyree (2008) (n 205) 17. In the Australian case of Australian Independent Distributors Ltd v Winter (1964) 112 CLR 443 (for example, the court held that the society was not carrying on the business of banking when it lent to its members for the purpose of acquiring land or buildings). In fact, none of the society's money was used for making loans.

245 Eliahu P. Ellinger, Eva Lomnicka and Christopher Hare, *Ellinger's Modern Banking Law* (Oxford University Press 2011).

246 Ibid.

247 Borio and Filosa (1994) (supra note 187).

248 Denning J in UDT.

249 Brad Pasanek and Simone Polillo, Beyond Liquidity: The Metaphor of Money in Financial Crisis (Routledge 2013) 117.

250 Julia Elyachar, 'Next Practices: Knowledge, Infrastructure, and Public Goods at the Bottom of the Pyramid' (2010) 24 Public Culture 109. The question was raised as to whether payments infrastructure should be treated as a '*bien commun*' public good.

251 Catia Batista, Felix Simione and Pedro C. Vicente, 'International Experiences of Mobile Banking Regulation' (2012).

252 Ibid.

253 Mobile Money Association of India (MMAI) and GSMA Submission to the Reserve Bank of India's (RBI) Committee on Comprehensive Financial Services for Small Businesses and Low-Income Households. MMAI/GSMA, 'Mobile Money: the Opposition for India' (2013) <www.gsma.com/mobilefordevelopment/wp-content/uploads/2013/12/MMAI-GSMA-on-Mobile-Money-in-India-for-RBI-Financial-Inclusion-Committee_Dec13.pdf> accessed 3 September 2014.

254 See the proposed ruling made by the US Department of the Treasury's FinCEN indicating that they wish to rename 'stored value' as 'prepaid access' and define that term in order to address regulatory gaps that they say have resulted from the proliferation of prepaid innovations, since the original Federal Reserve Board rules were formulated, because if these gaps are not addressed, they believe there is increased risk for the use of prepaid access as a means to further ML. For the proposed rules and their rationale, see also William Jack, Tavneet Suri and Robert Townsend, 'Monetary Theory and Electronic Money: Reflections on the Kenyan Experience' (2010) 96(1) Economic Quarterly at 84, available from <www.richmondfed.org/publications/research/economic_quarterly/2010/q1/pdf/townsend.pdf> accessed 3 September 2014. This effective parallel currency has triggered concerns amongst national governments and central bankers that these new paradigms may *inter alia* provide loopholes that may frustrate global efforts to combat ML and TF.

255 As in South Africa, agency-related risks are not regulated separately. Common law principles of agency make any bank or non-bank using retail agents liable for their agents' actions. Rules on AML/CFT do not apply, because existing provisions have a loophole – they apply only to banks.

256 In the meantime, the risks presented by Safaricom's M-Pesa mobile payments service are, at least from a practical perspective, significantly mitigated by the involvement of the United Kingdom's Department for International Development, which co-financed the initiative's pilot phase.

257 Rosa M. Lastra and Heba Shams, 'Public Accountability in the Financial Sector', in Eilis Ferran and Charles A. E. Goodhart (eds), *Regulating Financial Services and Markets in the 21st Century* (Hart Publishing, 2001) 165–188, at 170–71.

258 Brian Muthiora, 'Reinventing the Wheel: "Pass Through" Deposit Insurance coverage for Mobile Money in Kenya' (2014) <www.gsma.com/mobileforde velopment/reinventing-the-wheel-pass-through-deposit-insurance-coverage-for-mobile-money-in-kenya> accessed 3 September 2014.

259 Ibid.

260 These funds are reportedly not reinvested by the banks, however this remains unclear.

261 Kenya Deposit Insurance Act 2012.

262 Ibid, 257.

263 As explained in Chapter 2, Section 2.3.4. Page. 29.

264 Timothy Lyman, Gautam Ivatury and Stefan Staschen, 'Use of Agents in Branchless Banking for the Poor: Rewards, Risks, and Regulation' (2006) 38 Focus Note [page?].

265 Ibid., pg. 189.

266 Ibid.

267 Safaricom <www.safaricom.co.ke/> accessed 3 September 2014.

268 Which therefore poses a legal challenge in its regulation as agents are often confused with agency banking or third party outsourcing as Leon Perlman suggests. See, Leon Perlman, 'Legal and Regulatory Aspects of Mobile Financial Services' (PhD, University of South Africa 2012).

269 A traditional 'street-side' business that deals with its customers face to face in an office or store that the business owns or rents. The local grocery store and the corner bank are examples of 'brick and mortar' institutions. Brick and mortar businesses can find it difficult to compete with web-based businesses, because the latter usually have lower operating costs and greater flexibility.

270 This will also be referred to as 'float'

271 'Mobile Banking: Agents as Mediators' | CGAP <www.cgap.org/blog/mobile-banking-agents- mediators? accessed 28 September 2014.

272 Section 8(1) of Banking Act Cap 488.

273 The Banking Act 1995 <www.imolin.org/doc/amlid/Kenya_Banking%20 Act%201995.pdf> accessed 3 September 2014. Banking Act, Section 2 – Inter pretation. This may affect the functioning of agents.

274 CGAP (2007) (supra note 186) op cit note 2 at 7.

275 Ibid.

276 Specifically through the, 'Guideline on Agent Banking' (2000) <www.bu.edu/ bucflp/files/2012/01/Guideline-on-Agent-Banking-CBKPG15.pdf> accessed 3 September 2014. See also African Development Bank Group, 'Fostering Financial Inclusion with Mobile Banking' (2013) <www.afdb.org/en/news-and-events/article/ fostering-financial-inclusion-with-mobile-banking-12125/> accessed 3 September 2014.

277 CGAP, 'M-KESHO in Kenya' (2010) <www.gsma.com/mobilefordevelopment/ m-kesho-in-kenya> accessed 3 September 2014; Central Bank of Kenya, 'CBK/ PG/15: Guidelines on Agent Banking' (2010) <www.bb.org.bd/aboutus/ regulationguideline/psd/agentbanking_banks_v13.pdf> accessed 3 September 2014. The guidelines define an agent as 'an entity that has been contracted by an institution and approved by the Central Bank to provide the services of the institution on behalf of the institution in the manner specified in this Guideline'. It also defines an 'outlet' as being 'an agent's place of business directly responsible to the Head Office, used for carrying out a commercial activity of the agent but does not include a mobile unit'. See, 'Guideline on the Appointment

and Operations of Third Party Agents' <www.bu.edu/bucflp/files/2012/01/Deposit-Taking-Microfinance-Circular-No.-1- Guideline-on-the-Appointment-and-Operations-of-Third-Party-Agents-by-DTMs-consumer-protection-related.pdf> accessed 28 September 2014.

278  Ibid. See Chapter 2, The Enabling Environment for Mobile Payments. Page 29.

279  Safaricom (2011) figures as provided in 2011 from the Safaricom website <www.safaricom.co.ke> accessed 2 November 2011. Cash agents get incentives for registering customers and a share of commission on remittances so as to compensate them for being bypassed for the purchase of airtime voucher recharges by subscribers.

280  Safaricom list the following as the duties of an agent: register M-Pesa customers; deposit cash into registered customers' M-Pesa accounts; process cash withdrawals for registered M-Pesa customers; process cash withdrawals for non-registered M-Pesa customers; customer education compliance with Safaricom AML & KYC policy; compliance with Safaricom business practices; and branding of their outlets as per provided guideline.

281  Safaricom, <www.safaricom.co.ke> accessed 3 September 2014.

282  CGAP (2007) (supra note 186).

283  CBK (2010) (supra note 134).

284  Section 2 of the Banking Act 1989 as amended.

285  This includes interest-bearing accounts.

286  Banks that could not have the same type of loose affiliation as banking agents such as those used in MFS are now able to do so within the parameters of the CBK 'Agent Guidelines' issued in 2010 in terms of the Banking Act.

287  Ibid.

288  Denise Dias and Kate McKee, 'Protecting Branchless Banking Consumers' (2010) <www.cgap.org/publications/protecting-branchless-banking-consumers> accessed 3 September 2014.

289  Joy Malala, Interview with Mercy Buku, 'An Interview With Senior Manager Money Laundering Reporting At Safaricom' (2014).

290  Ibid.

291  BIS, 'Financial Sector Regulation for Growth, Equity and Stability' (2012) BIS Papers No 62 <www.bis.org/publ/bppdf/bispap62.pdf> accessed 3 September 2014.

292  Ibid.

293  The Communications Commission of Kenya, for example, recently issued substantial consumer protection regulations with implications for mobile payment services (Kenya Gazette, 23 April 2010).

294  Bill Maurer, Taylor C. Nelms and Stephen C. Rea, "Bridges to Cash': Channelling Agency in Mobile Money' (2013) 19 Journal of the Royal Anthropological Institute 52.

295  The principle of accountability is explored in Chapter 5.

296  Safaricom Ltd has one with M-Pesa agents.

297  For instance, it should not evade or avoid responsibility in instances where agents access customers' information and withdrawals are made from these accounts.

298  CGAP, Focus Note, 'Banking through Networks of Retail Agent' (2008) <www.gsma.com/mobilefordevelopment/wp-content/uploads/2012/06/fn47_d_24.pdf> accessed 3 September 2014. This may trigger liquidity risks, as assessed in Chapter 3.

299  An agent business can be set up so that neither the customer nor the bank needs to incur settlement risk.

300  Most Kenyan banks now provide liquidity as super agents.

301  See Chapter 3.

302 This vetting process is done through the special arrangement and agreement they have with their respective MNOs. For instance, Safaricom has AML M-Pesa agent requirements. Safaricom, 'M-PESA Agent Requirements' (2010) <www.safaricom.co.ke/images/Downloads/Resources_Downloads/m- pesa_agent_requirements_-_for_external_use.pdf> accessed 3 September 2014.

303 This agreement is called the service level agreement.

304 For a general overview of the agent ecosystem, see also Mark Pickens, 'Understanding What Drives Profits for Agents: M-pesa' (2009) <www.experientia.com/blog/understanding-what-drives-profits-for-agents-m-pesa/>[22 September 2014.

305 Colin Blackman (1998) (n 11) 170.

306 Raymond U. Akwule, 'Telecommunications in Kenya: Development and policy issues' (1992) 16(7) Telecommunications policy 603–611.

307 PwC, 'Telecommunications Industry: Overview of the Sector in Kenya' (2009) <www.pwc.com/ke/en/industries/telecommunications.jhtml%3E> accessed 3 September 2014.

308 Telkom Kenya, 'History of Telkom Kenya' (2011) <www.telkom.co.ke/index.php?option=com_content&view=article&id=60&Itemid=95> accessed 3 September 2014.

309 Ibid., this listing was done in May 2008.

310 Ibid., which was also achieved in November 2008.

311 See Chapter 3, 3.3. The Need for an Appropriate Regulatory Approach through the Examination of the Pre-Conditions to a Safe and Sound Payment System page. 71.

312 Baldwin, Cave and Lodge (2011) (n 90). See also the importance of Safaricom to the general economy creates a regulatory challenge in that it creates amongst regulators and industry stakeholders the need to remove regulatory barriers that facilitates gains for all involved. See also, Tony Prosser, *Nationalised Industries and Public Control: Legal, Constitutional and Political Issues* (Blackwell 1986), where Tony Prosser analyses the links between public law and the study of politics and administration.

313 Jeffrey Carmichael and Michael Pomerleano, *The Development and Regulation of Non-bank Financial Institutions* (World Bank Publications 2002); Clive Briault, 'The Rationale for a Single National Financial Services Regulator' (2000) Co-sponsored by the European Commission and the World Bank (A European Borrowers Network Initiative) 211.

314 CBK licensing guidelines are informed by very different legislative and policy considerations, as compared to CCK guidelines. See Chapter 3 for an in depth discussion of the regulatory philosophies of the two regulators.

315 The WTO's instruments such as Articles II and III of the Trade Related Investment Measures (TRIMs) and the Trade Related Aspects of Intellectual Property and Services (TRIPS) emphasise that cyberspace and infotainment business ought to be liberalized.

316 Alliance for Financial Inclusion (2010) (supra note 134).

317 International Telecommunications Union, '11th Global Symposium for Regulators: Armenia City, Columbia: Chairman's report' (2011) <www.itu.int/ITU- D/treg/Events/Seminars/GSR/GSR11/pdf/GSR11_Chairmanreport_en.pdf> accessed 3 September 2014.

318 Instances of regulatory overlap are dealt with administratively and politically, at the cabinet level, consultations, rather than through legal structures.

319 This coordination of functions shall be explained in Chapter 5 in the discussion of the themes around the regulatory approach to mobile payments.

320 The Supreme Court in Re The Matter of the Interim Independent Electoral Commission (2011) Constitutional *Application No. 2* (unreported) underscored

the importance of independent state organs to cooperate with each other in discharging their mandates.

321 Nzomo Mutuku (2008) (supra note 40).

322 Ibid.

323 Martha Garcia-Murillo and Ian MacInnes, 'The Impact of Technological Convergence on the Regulation of ICT Industries' (2002) 5(1) International Journal on Media Management 57–67.

324 Jérôme Bezzina and Mostafa Terrab, 'Impacts of New Technologies in Regulatory Regimes: an Introduction' (2005) The World Bank <www.dirsi.net/files/documentos%20varios/research/impact_of_new_technologies_on_regulatory_regimes.pdf> accessed 3 September 2014.

325 Ibid.

326 Atul K. Shah, 'Regulatory Arbitrage Through Financial Innovation' (1997) 10(1) Accounting, Auditing & Accountability Journal 85–104. The author refers to regulatory arbitrage as 'creative compliance'. He notes that while creative compliance may not be illegal, it undermines the spirit of regulation and makes the regulatory framework appear weak and ineffective.

327 See Jeremmy Okonjo (2014) (supra note 56).

328 Ibid.

329 Ibid.

330 See Consultative Group to Assist the Poor, 'Notes on Regulation of Branchless Banking in Kenya' (2007) <www.cgap.org/p/site/c/template.rc/1.26.1480/> accessed 3 September 2014. Consultations were held between both the CBK and the CCK, without assigning regulatory roles. However, the CBK under Section 3 of the Central Bank of Kenya Act and was facilitated by way of a no objection letter.

331 International Telecommunications Union (2011) (n 323). See also, Alliance for Financial Inclusion. (2010 www.afi-global.org/) (n 134).

332 Ibid.

333 Loretta Michaels, 'Better than Cash: Kenya Mobile Money Market Assessment' (2011) USAID <http://nethope.org/assets/uploads/Kenya-Mobile-Money-Assessment.pdf> accessed 3 September 2014.

334 See CGAP, 'Notes on Regulation of Branchless Banking in Kenya' (2007) <www.cgap.org/sites/default/files/CGAP-Regulation-of-Branchless-Banking-in-Kenya-Jan-2010.pdf> accessed 3 September 2014.

335 Anat R. Admati and Martin Hellwig, 'Good Banking Regulation Needs Clear Focus, Sensible Tools, and Political Will' (2011) Working Paper <www.gsb.stanford.edu/sites/default/files/research/documents/AdmatiHellwig GoodReg021412.pdf> accessed 3 September 2014.

336 Ibid.

337 Anat R. Admati and Martin Hellwig (2011) (n 341).

338 Global Financial Crises of 2007–2008.

339 Consultative Group to Assist the Poor (2010) This CGAP focus note includes a tool to help regulators start assessing consumer protection concerns in their own markets and options to address them.

340 Christopher Leonard, 'Client Assets and Money in the Post-Lehman World' November, 2010 www.bingham.com/Publications/Files/2011/10/Client-Assets-and-Money-in-the-Post-Lehman-World> accessed 28 September 2014.

341 Ibid.

342 See for example: United Kingdom, 'Financial Services and Markets Act 2000: Chapter 8', The National Archives <www.legislation.gov.uk/ukpga/2000/8/pdfs/ukpga_20000008_en.pdf.> accessed 14 May 2014; 'Financial Services Act 2012', The National Archives <www.legislation.gov.uk/ukpga/2012/21/pdfs/ukpga_20120021_en.pdf.> accessed 17 May 2014.

343 Brian Muthiora, 'Reinventing the Wheel: "Pass Through" Deposit Insurance coverage for Mobile Money in Kenya' <www.gsma.com/mobilefordevelop ment/reinventing-the-wheel-pass-through-deposit-insurance-coverage-for-mobile-money-in-kenya>. See also, Samuel G. Hanson, Anil K. Kashyap and Jeremy C. Stein, 'A Macroprudential Approach to Financial Regulation' (2011) Journal of Economic Perspectives 3.

344 Giesela Ruhl, 'Consumer Protection in Choice of Law' (2011) 44 Cornell International Law Journal. <www.lawschool.cornell.edu/research/ILJ/upload/Ruhl-final.pdf> accessed 28 September 2014; Hugh Beale, *Inequality of Bargaining Power* (Jstor 1986), (1986) 6 Oxford Journal of Legal Studies 123; John Kenneth Galbraith, *The New Industrial State* (Princeton University Press 1971) 213–220; Friedrich Kessler, 'Contracts of Adhesion: Some Thoughts About Freedom of Contact' (1943) 43 *COLUM. L. REV.* 629, 632, 640–641 (1943); Spencer N. Thal, 'The Inequality of Bargaining Power Doctrine: The Problem of Defining Contractual Unfairness' 8 Oxford Journal of Legal Studies.

345 Peter Cartwright, 'The Vulnerable Consumer of Financial Services: Law Policy and Regulation' [2011] Research Paper – Nottingham University of Business School; T. Wilhelmsson, 'The Informed Consumer v the Vulnerable Consumer in European Unfair Commercial Practices Law – a Comment' in G. Howells, A. Nordhausen, D. Parry and C. Twigg-Flesner (eds), *Yearbook of Consumer Law* (Ashgate 2007) 211 at 213.

346 Ibid.

347 Giesela Ruhl, 'Consumer Protection in Choice of Law' (2011) 44 Cornell International Law Journal 569 <www.lawschool.cornell.edu/research/ILJ/upload/Ruhl-final.pdf>

348 Schaffer Haupt, and Alan Schwartz, 'Legal Implications of Imperfect Information in Consumer Markets', (1995) 151 Journal of Institutional & Theoretical Economics 31, 35–36 (1995) (F.R.G?.); Fernando Gomez Pomar and Nuna Garupa, Max Weber Lecture: 'The Economic Approach to European Consumer Protection Law' (21 November 2007).

349 Ibid., at 260.

350 Ibid.

351 Peter Cartwright, 'Law, Theory, and Policy in the UK, <UK http://bilder.buecher.de/zusatz/23/23331/23331195_inha_1.pdf> accessed 28 August 2014

352 Ibid.

353 'Global Survey on Consumer Protection and Financial Literacy' < http://responsiblefinance.worldbank.org/~/media/GIAWB/FL/Documents/Publications/Global-Consumer-Protection-and-Financial-Literacy-results-brief.pdf>30 September 2014 Alliance for Financial Inclusion (2010), 'The 2010 AFI Survey Report on Financial Inclusion Policy in Developing Countries'

354 A situation in which one party in a transaction has more or superior information compared to another. In this situation, Safaricom or any other MNO is considered to have more information than its consumers due to it not being a public entity, but a private company with strict non-disclosure practices.

355 Annual Report from Safaricom. <www.safaricom.co.ke> accessed 12 July 2014.

356 IRA (Insurance Regulatory Authority). The Insurance Regulatory Authority of Kenya is the sole authority charged with regulation and supervision of the insurance industry. It ensures compliance by insurance/reinsurance companies, protects consumers and promotes a high degree of security for policyholders.

357 Consumer Protection Diagnostic Study, FSD Kenya, <www.fsdkenya.org/pdf_documents/11–02–22_Consumer_diagnostic_study.pdf> accessed 30 July 2015. See also, Bankable Frontier Associates LLC (2010), 'Enabling Mobile Money Transfer – The Central Bank of Kenya's Treatment of M-PESA', Alliance for Financial Inclusion.

358 The market-leading MNO.
359 Here the term 'providers' will also be used to mean MNOs as is used in the legislation.
360 'Consumer Protection Regulation in Low-Access Environment Opportunities to promote Responsible Finance' <www.cgap.org/sites/default/files/CGAP-Focus-Note-Consumer-Protection-Regulation-in-Low-Access-Environments-Opportunities-to-Promote-Responsible-Finance-Feb- 2010.pdf> accessed 28 September 2014; Laura Brix and Katharine McKee, 'Consumer Protection Regulation in Low-access Environments: Opportunities to Promote Responsible Finance' 60 Focus Note <www.ruralfinance.org/fileadmin/templates/rflc/documents/74560_Focus_Note_60_en.pdf> accessed 14 March 2014.
361 Sue Rutledge, 'Improving Protection in Financial Services for Russian Consumers' (2009) <http://aisel.aisnet.org/cais/vol27/iss1/29> accessed June 2013, Shalini Chandra, Shirish C. Srivastava and Yin-Leng Theng, 'Evaluating the Role of Trust in Consumer Adoption of Mobile Payment Systems: An Empirical Analysis' 27 Communications of the Association for Information Systems<http://aisel.aisnet.org/cais/vol27/iss1/29> accessed June 2013.
362 Sue Rutledge, 'Improving Protection in Financial Services for Russian Consumers' (2009) <http://aisel.aisnet.org/cais/vol27/iss1/29> accessed June 2013.
363 Susan Rutledge,'Consumer Protection and Financial Literacy: Lessons from Nine Country Studies'. (2010) <http://siteresources.worldbank.org/CROATIAEXTN/Resources/3012441272903536699/Importance_vol1.pdf> accessed 28 September 2014.
364 Ibid.
365 Geraint G. Howells and Stephen Weatherill, *Consumer Protection Law* (Ashgate Publishing Ltd. 2005).
366 Connie Prater, 'Going Mobile? Link Payments to Credit Cards for Best Protection' 2012, www.foxbusiness.com/personal-finance/2011/04/21/going-mobile-link-payments-credit-cards-best-protection/> accessed 28 September 2014.
367 Harmonisation here refers to the need for a consolidation of legislation due to the fragmentation that existed before the Consumer Protection Act. Clive Briault, *The Rationale for a Single National Financial Services Regulator*, vol 2 (Financial Services Authority 1999).
368 Mark MacCarthy and Gail Hillebrand, 'Mobile Payments Need Strong Consumer Protections' *American Banker Tuesday*, 10 August 2010 <http://defendyourdollars.org/posts/211 mobile_payments_need_strong_consumer_protections> accessed 28 September 2014.
369 Information asymmetry creates an imbalance of power in transactions which can sometimes cause a market failure resulting from moral hazard, and information monopoly. Most commonly, information asymmetries are studied in the context of principal – agent problems. John O. Ledyard, 'market failure'" *The New Palgrave Dictionary of Economics* (2nd edn, Palgrave Macmillan 2008).
370 Ibid supra note John O. Ledyard.
371 Maria Chirati, Mulaguti, 'Access to Finance, Retail Payments and an Enabling Legal Environment' (2013) <www.uncitral.org/pdf/english/colloquia/microfinance-2013/1601/MC_Malaguti_January_16.pdf> accessed 28 September 2014.
372 Biagio Bossone and Massimo Cirasino, 'The Oversight of the Payments Systems: a Framework for the Development and Governance of Payment Systems in Emerging Economies' July 2001, The World Bank and CEMLA.
373 Similar to the conduct of business rules of the financial conduct authorities.
374 Although the Consumer Protection Act 2012 does not address the needs of users of financial services.

375 Section 3 of the Communications Act 2012 allows the CCK to resolve disputes between a consumer and a service provider; a service provider and another service provider; or any other persons as may be prescribed under the Act. This may ostensibly bring M-Pesa under the jurisdiction of the CCK if there is any dispute as to charges, billing or general loss of value in the prepaid stored value account.

376 CBK Agent Guidelines.

377 Ibid at 383 and the Competition Act 2012.

378 Ibid.

379 David Asher, 'Kenya Financial Consumer Protection – Slidshare' www.slide share.net/Daniel_Asher/kenya-financial-consumer-protection accessed 12 September 2014.

380 CBK (2010) <www.bu.edu/bucflp/files/2012/01/Guideline-on-Agent-Banking-CBKPG15.pdf> accessed 28 September 2014.

381 The Reserve Bank of Fiji has adapted these guidelines in their prescription of Agency Guidelines <www.reservebank.gov.fj/docs2/Banking%20Supervision%20Policy%20Statement%20No%2018-Agent%20Banking%20Guidelines%201.pdf> accessed 24 June 2014.

382 The government's latest thinking on consumer credit reform www.nortonrose fulbright.com/knowledge/publications/33932/the-governments-latest-thinking-on-consumer-credit-reform accessed 25 June 2014.

383 'Consumer Protection Diagnostic Study', Kenya (2011) <www.fsdkenya.org/pdf_documents/11-02-22_Consumer_diagnostic_study.pdf>. At the time of writing this chapter, this clarification was not forecasted.

384 Examples include KOPOKOPO LTD, a service that provides a low-cost software service for mobile money repayment mechanisms for small and medium sized enterprises.

385 As discussed, which is an activity almost always reserved for prudentially regulated financial institutions, such as commercial banks. 'CGAP Nonbank E-Money Issuers' www.cgap.org/publications/nonbank-e-money-issuers%3E. accessed 30 July 2014.

386 The term 'bank' as used in this chapter refers to any supervised and prudentially regulated financial services institution that is commonly, but not always, a bank.

387 Denise Dias Katherine Mckees, 'Protecting Branchless Banking Consumers: Policy Objectives and Regulatory Options' <http://siteresources.worldbank.org/FINANCIALSECTOR/Resources/PReadingProtectingBranchless.pdf> No 64 September 2010.

388 'Consumer Protection Diagnostic Study: Kenya, Financial Sector Deepening'. January 2011 Simone di Castri and others, 'Consumer Protection Diagnostic Study: Financial Consumer Protection in Kenya' SSRN Journal.

389 Ibid.

390 Geoffrey Irungu, January 2014, Business Daily, The Daily Nation Kenya, 'Banks Raise Alarm over Mobile Cash Deposit Insurance – Money' <www.busi nessdailyafrica.com/mobile-cash-deposit-insurance/-/539552/2157770/-/dgm4ojz/-/index.html%3E> accessed 28 September 2014.

391 Ibid.

392 'International Experiences of Mobile Banking Regulation – IGC' www.theigc. org/sites/default/files/Batista%20and%20Vicenter. Safe assets 'deposit' provide challenges in the regulation of mobile payments because of their legal ambiguity definitions and their ambiguity.

393 This assessment would be after a proper definition of what the electronically stored value is and what banks would consider it to be, thus making it easier to offer the same protection as they would other legally defined 'deposits'.

394 Requirements that such funds be placed in their entirety in bank accounts or government debt.

395 Mobile Financial Services: Basic Terminology (2013) www.afiglobal.org/sites/default/files/publications/mfswg_gl_1_basic_terminology_finalnewnew_pdf. Michael Tarazi and Paul Breloff, 'Nonbank E-Money Issuers: Regulatory Approaches to Protecting Customer Funds' 63 Focus Note <www.cgap.org/gm/ document-1.9.45715/FN_63_Rev.pdf> accessed 13 September 2013.
396 Simon di Castri, 'Mobile Money: Enabling Regulatory Solutions' [2013] GSMA London United Kingdom <www.gsma.com/mobilefordevelopment/wp-content/uploads/2013/02/MMU-Enabling-Regulatory-Solutions-di-Castri-2013.pdf> accessed 28 September 2014.
397 Ring-fencing and Safeguard of Customer Money' www.gsma.com/mobilefordevelopment/programmes/mobile-money-for-the-unbanked/safeguard-of-customer-money. Slightly different approaches have been taken by regulators which, rather than requiring the entire e-money float to be held in a bank, have allowed it to be invested in low-risk securities such as government bonds.
398 Tarazi and Breloff Simone Di Castri, 'Mobile Money: Enabling Regulatory Solutions' GSMA, London, United Kingdom <http://www gsma com/mobilefordevelopment/wp-content/uploads/2013/02/MMU-Enabling-Regulatory-Solutions-di-Castri-2013 pdf> 'Customer funds are usually pooled and held by the bank(s) in the name of the issuer'.
399 Trust is a common law concept; in Congo, mechanisms are put in place to for consumers to recover their funds in the event of a provider failure.
400 This phrase has been used on several occasions to define the parallel, informal banking system that mobile payments have afforded.
401 Supra note, Batista, Simione and Vicente, 'International Experiences of Mobile Banking Regulation – IGC'. That is the total value of electronic value issued and outstanding, also known as the 'e-float'.
402 DPFB is a corporation established under Section 36 of the Banking Act, Chapter 488 of the Laws of Kenya as a deposit insurance scheme to provide cover for depositors and act as a liquidator of failed member institutions <www.centralbank.go.ke/index.php/deposit-protection-fund> accessed 28 September 2014.
403 Ibid.
404 Deposit Protection Fund – Central Bank of Kenya <www.centralbank.go.ke/index.php/deposit-protection-fund>
405 'The Transformational Potential of M–Transactions' www.vodafone.com/content/dam/vodafone/about/public_policy/policy_papers/public_policy_series_6.pdf. Moving the debate forward The Policy Paper Series, Number 6, July 2007.
406 Ibid at Dias and McKee (n 300).
407 The float, being the total value of electronic value issued and possibly outstanding.
408 Michael Tarazi and Paul Breloff, 'Nonbank E-Money Issuers: Regulatory Approaches to Protecting Customer Funds' (2010). 63 Focus Note <www.gsma.com/mobilefordevelopment/wp-content/uploads/2013/09/fn63rev.pdf> accessed 28 September 2014.
409 Ibid.
410 Dias and McKee 2010.
411 'Payment, Clearing and Settlement Systems in the CPSS Countries' <www.bis.org/publ/cpss105.pdf> accessed 20 October 2013.
412 Di Castri 2013.
413 Ibid.
414 The Federal Deposit Insurance Corporation (FDIC) is a United States government corporation operating as an independent agency created by the Banking Act of 1933.
415 Batista, Simione and Vicente 2012 supra note.

416 In the Philippines, an estimated 10 per cent of unbanked users save an average of US$31 (one-quarter of their family savings) in the form of e-money (Pickens 2009). In addition, nearly a third of banked customers in Kibera, Kenya, keep a balance in their M-PESA. See Morawczynski and Pickens (2009).

417 Banque Centrale du Congo, Instruction n.24/2011. www.legifrance.gouv.fr/affichTexte.do?cidTexte=JORFTEXT000000821047&dateTexte=.

418 Financial intermediation is business conducted or services offered by a financial intermediary (typically a bank, but also a non-bank financial institution) that accepts money from individuals or entities with capital surpluses and then lends it (directly through loans or indirectly through capital markets) to individuals or entities with capital deficits to earn a profit.

419 Through the 'Pass through' guarantee offered in the US model that the Kenyan regulators may adopt.

420 United Nations Conference on Trade and Development, 'Mobile Money for Business Development in the East African Community: a comparative study of existing platforms and regulations' (2012) <http://unctad.org/en/Publica tionsLibrary/dtlstict2012d2_en.pdf> accessed 3 September 2014.

421 Ibid.

422 See Chapter 3 3.4.1.4. Operational Risk 88.

423 UNCTAD (2012) (supra note 350).

424 Gerald Nyaoma, 'Mobile Payments regulatory Framework Perspectives in Kenya' (2010) <www.efina.org.ng/media-centre/events/workshops/mobile-payments-regulatory-framework-dissemination-workshop/forcedownload/91> accessed 3 September 2014.

425 Kenya Information and Communication Dispute Resolution Regulations (2010) <www.cck.go.ke/regulations/downloads/Kenya_Information_and_Communica-tion_Dispute_Resolution_Regulations_2010.pdf > accessed 3 September 2014.

426 Section 2 of the Kenya Information and Communications (Dispute Resolu-tion) Regulations defines 'dispute' as any matter that is in contention between a licensee and another, a consumer and a licensee, where one or both parties is aggrieved by the conduct of the other and the parties have failed to reach an amicable resolution after due effort has been made.

427 The Central Bank of Kenya began consultations for its draft regulation for the National Payment Systems Bill. Consultation is an essential part of regulatory accountability. Central Bank of Kenya, 'Public Consultations: National Payment Systems Draft Regulation' (2012) <www.centralbank.go.ke/index.php/public-consultations> accessed 3 September 2014.

428 Since the CCK regulates the institutions that provide mobile payments, MNOs, and the financial institutions regulated by the CBK.

429 See Mas and Radcliffe (2010).

430 Efforts to scale up mobile payments in other countries such as Tanzania have not enjoyed similar success.

431 A discussion explained in this chapter and offered as a risk in Chapter 3.

432 Financial Reporting Centre in Kenya, MNOs are required to report all inci-dences of fraud as was articulated during the interview with Mercy Buku, Joy Malala, Interview with Mercy Buku, 'An Interview with Senior Manager Money Laundering Reporting at Safaricom' (2014).

433 Regulatory capacity has been discussed in Part II of this chapter.

434 The Central Bank of Kenya began consultations for its draft regulation for the National Payment Systems Bill. Consultation is an essential part of regulatory accountability. CBK (2012)

435 Mwangi Kimenyi and Njuguna Ndung'u, 'Expanding the Financial Services Frontier: Lessons from Mobile Phone Banking in Kenya' (2009) <www.brook ings.edu/~/media/Files/rc/articles/2009/1016_mobile_phone_kenya_kime nyi/1016_mobile_phone_kenya_kimenyi.pdf> accessed 3 September 2014.

# Bibliography

Aagaard, Todd S., 'Regulatory Overlap, Overlapping Legal Fields, and Statutory Discontinuities' (2011) 29 *Virginia Environmental Law Journal* 237.

AAMC Task Force on Financial Conflicts of Interest in Clinical Research, 'Protecting Subjects, Preserving Trust, Promoting Progress II: Principles and Recommendations for Oversight of an Institution's Financial Interests in Human Subjects Research' 78 *Academic Medicine* 237.

Abel, Richard L., 'Customary Laws of Wrongs in Kenya: An Essay in Research Method' (1969) *The American Journal of Comparative Law* 573.

Admati, Anat R. and Martin Hellwig, 'Good Banking Regulation Needs Clear Focus, Sensible Tools, and Political Will' (2011) Working Paper <www.gsb.stanford.edu/sites/default/files/research/documents/AdmatiHellwigGoodReg021412.pdf> accessed 3 September 2014.

AFI's Mobile Financial Services Working Group, 'Mobile Financial Services: Mobile-Enabled Cross-Border Payments' (2008) *Alliance for Financial Inclusion*.

The Africa Competitiveness Report (2013) <www.worldbank.org/content/dam/Worldbank/document/Africa/Report/africa-competitiveness-report-2013-main-report-web.pdf> accessed 3 September 2014.

African Development Bank Group, 'Fostering Financial Inclusion with Mobile Banking' (2013) <www.afdb.org/en/news-and-events/article/fostering-financial-inclusion-with-mobile-banking-12125/>accessed on 3 September 2014.

Africog, 'Cause for Public Concern on the Telkom Privatization and Safaricom IPO' <www.africog.org/reports/Cause%20for%20Public%20Concern%20over%20safaricom%20IPO.pdf> accessed 3 September 2014.

Aker, Jenny C. and Isaac M. Mbiti, 'Mobile Phones and Economic Development in Africa' (2010) Working Paper 211 <www.cgdev.org/files/1424175_file_Aker_Mobile_wp211_FINAL.pdf> accessed 3 September 2014.

Alliance for Financial Inclusion, 'Enabling Mobile Money Transfer: The Central Bank of Kenya's Treatment of M-PESA' (2010) <www.afi-global.org/en/phoca-publications-case-studies> accessed 3 September 2014.

Akwule, Raymond U., 'Telecommunications in Kenya: Development and Policy Issues' (1992) 16(7) *Telecommunications Policy* 603–611.

Apostolik, Richard, Christopher Donohue and Peter Went, *Foundations of Banking Risk: An Overview of Banking, Banking Risks, and Risk-Based Banking Regulation*, vol 507 (Wiley 2009).

Asher, David, 'Kenya Financial Consumer Protection – Slidshare' www.slideshare.net/Daniel_Asher/kenya-financial-consumer-protection accessed 12 September 2014.

*Australian Independent Distributors Ltd* v *Winter* (1964) 112 CLR 443

Baldwin, Robert, Martin Cave and Martin Lodge, *Understanding Regulation: Theory, Strategy, and Practice* (Oxford University Press 2011) 415.

Banking Act, Section 2 – Kenya Law Resource Centre, 'Statutory definitions of a bank' <www.kenyalawresourcecenter.org/2011/07/statutory-definitions-of-bank.htm> accessed 3 September 2014.

The Banking Act 1995 <www.imolin.org/doc/amlid/Kenya_Banking%20Act%201995.pdf> accessed 3 September 2014.

Batista, Catia, Felix Simione and Pedro C Vicente, 'International Experiences of Mobile Banking Regulation' (2012)

Beale, Hugh, *Inequality of Bargaining Power* (Jstor 1986), (1986) 6 *Oxford Journal of Legal Studies* 123.

Bezzina, Jérôme and Mostafa Terrab, 'Impacts of New Technologies in Regulatory Regimes: An Introduction' (2005) *The World Bank* <www.dirsi.net/files/docu mentos%20varios/research/impact_of_new_technologies_on_regulato *ry_regimes. pdf*> accessed 3 September 2014.

Bilodeaeau, James, William Hoffman, and Sjoerd Nikkelen, 'Findings from the Mobile Financial Services Development Report' (2011) *The Capco Institute Journal of Financial Transformation.*

BIS, 'Financial Sector Regulation for Growth, Equity and Stability' (2012) BIS Papers No 62 <www.bis.org/publ/bppdf/bispap62.pdf> accessed 3 September 2014.

Blackman, Colin R., 'Convergence Between Telecommunications and Other Media. How Should Regulation Adapt?' (1998) 22 *Telecommunications Policy* 163.

Bollen, Rhys, 'Recent Developments in Mobile Banking and Payments' (2009) *Journal of International Banking Law and Regulation* 454; Tyree, Alan L., *Banking Law in Australia* (Butterworths 1998).

Bollen, Rhys, 'What Is a Deposit (and Why Does It Matter)' (2006) 13 *eLaw J.*

Borio, Claudio E. and Renato Filosa, 'The Changing Borders of Banking: Trends and Implications' (1994) BIS Working Paper No 23 <http://papers.ssrn.com/sol3/papers.cfm?abstract_id=868431> accessed 3 September 2014.

Bossone, Biagio and Massimo Cirasino, 'The Oversight of the Payments Systems: A Framework for the Development and Governance of Payment Systems in Emerging Economies' July 2001, The World Similar to the Financial Conduct Authorities, Conduct of Business rules.

Breyer, Stephen G., *Breaking the Vicious Circle: Toward Effective Risk Regulation* (Harvard University Press 1993).

Briault, Clive, 'The Rationale for a Single National Financial Services Regulator' (2000) Co-Sponsored by the European Commission and the World Bank (A European Borrowers Network Initiative) 211.

Briault, Clive, *The Rationale for a Single National Financial Services Regulator*, vol 2 (Financial Services Authority 1999).

Brix, Laura and Katharine McKee, 'Consumer Protection Regulation in Low-access Environments: Opportunities to Promote Responsible Finance' 60 *Focus Note* <www.ruralfinance.org/fileadmin/templates/rflc/documents/74560_Focus_Note_60_en.pdf> accessed on 14 March 2014.

Carmichael, Jeffrey and Michael Pomerleano, *The Development and Regulation of Non-Bank Financial Institutions* (World Bank Publications 2002).

Cartwright, Peter, 'Law, Theory, and Policy in the UK, <UK http://bilder.buecher.de/zusatz/23/23331/23331195_inha_1.pdf> accessed 28 August.

Cartwright, Peter, 'The Vulnerable Consumer of Financial Services: Law Policy and Regulation' (2011) *Research Paper – Nottingham University of Business School.*

Carvajal, Ana et al., *The Perimeter of Financial Regulation* (International Monetary Fund 2009).

Castri, Simon di, 'Mobile Money: Enabling Regulatory Solutions' [2013] GSMA London United Kingdom Enabling Regulatory Solutions <www.gsma.com/mobilefordevelopment/wp-content/uploads/2013/02/MMU-Enabling-Regulatory-Solutions-di-Castri-2013.pdf> accessed 28 September 2014.

Castri, Simone di, 'A Conversation with Professor Njuguna Ndung'u, Governor of the Central Bank of Kenya, on the Critical Policy Issues Around Mobile Money' (2013) <www.gsma.com/mobilefordevelopment/a-conversation-with-professor-njuguna-ndungu-governor-of-the-central-bank-of-kenya-on-the-critical-policy-issues-around-mobile- money> accessed 3 September 2014.

CBK (2010) <www.bu.edu/bucflp/files/2012/01/Guideline-on-Agent-Banking-CBKPG15.pdf> accessed 28 September 2014.

CBK, 'CBK Mandate' (2009) <www.centralbank.go.ke/index.php/cbk-objectives> accessed 3 September 2014.

CBK, 'Oversight of Payment System in Kenya: Policy Framework' (2009) <http://goo.gl/OIu0D> accessed 3 September 2014.

CBK, 'Payment System in Kenya' (2003) <www.centralbank.go.ke/downloads/nps/nps%20old/psk.pdf> accessed 3 September 2014.

Central Bank of Kenya, 'Background Information' (2011) <http://goo.gl/FnLsy> accessed 3 September 2014.

Central Bank of Kenya, 'CBK/PG/15: Guidelines on Agent Banking' (2010) <www.bb.org.bd/aboutus/regulationguideline/psd/agentbanking_banks_v13.pdf> accessed 3 September 2014.

Central Bank of Kenya, 'Deposit Taking Microfinance Institutions' <www.central bank.go.ke/index.php/bank-supervision/microfinance-institutions/14-bank-supervision/83-list-of-licensed-deposit-taking> accessed 3 September 2014.

Central Bank of Kenya, 'Role of National Payment Systems' <www.centralbank.go.ke/index.php/role-of-national-payment-systems> accessed 3 September 2014.

CGAP, 'M-KESHO in Kenya' (2010) <www.gsma.com/mobilefordevelopment/m-kesho-in-kenya> accessed 3 September 2014

CGAP, 'Notes on Regulation of Branchless Banking in Kenya' (2007) <www.cgap.org/sites/default/files/CGAP-Regulation-of-Branchless-Banking-in-Kenya-Jan-2010.pdf> accessed 3 September 2014.

CGAP, 'Notes on Regulation of Branchless Banking in Kenya' (2012) *CGAP Focus Note* <www.gsma.com/mobilefordevelopment/wpcontent/uploads/2012/06/kenyanotesonregulation branchlessbanking2007.pdf > accessed 3 September 2014.

CGAP, 'Update on Regulation of Branchless Banking in Kenya' (2010) <www.cgap.org/sites/default/files/CGAP-Regulation-of-Branchless-Banking-in-Kenya-Jan-2010.pdf> accessed 3 September 2014.

CGAP, Focus Note, 'Banking through Networks of Retail Agent' (2008) <www.gsma.com/mobilefordevelopment/wp-content/uploads/2012/06/fn47_d_24.pdf> accessed 3 September 2014. This may trigger liquidity risks as is assessed in Chapter 3.

'CGAP Annual Report 2007' (2007) <www.cgap.org/sites/default/files/CGAP-Annual-Report-Dec-2007.pdf> accessed 3 September 2014.

'CGAP Nonbank E-Money Issuers' www.cgap.org/publications/nonbank-e-money-issuers%3E. accessed 30 July 2014.

Chandra, Shalini, Shirish C. Srivastava and Yin-Leng Theng, 'Evaluating the Role of Trust in Consumer Adoption of Mobile Payment Systems: An Empirical Analysis' 27 *Communications of the Association for Information Systems* <http://aisel.aisnet.org/cais/vol27/iss1/29> accessed June 2013.

Chirati, Maria, Mulaguti, 'Access to Finance, Retail Payments and an Enabling Legal Environment' (2013) <www.uncitral.org/pdf/english/colloquia/microfinance-2013/1601/MC_Malaguti_January_16.pdf> accessed 28 September 2014.

Chorley, Robert, *Law of Banking* (6th edn, Sweet and Maxwell 1974) at 23.

*Commissioners of the State Savings Bank of Victoria* v *Permewan Wright and Co Ltd* (1914) 19 CLR 457

Committee on Payment and Settlement Systems (CPSS), 'Security of Electronic Money' (1996) 3 <www.bis.org/publ/cpss18.htm> accessed 3 September 2014.

Committee on Payment and Settlement Systems, 'Policy Issues for Central Banks in Retail Payments' (2003) *Bank for International Settlements* 1–3.

Committee on Payment and Settlement Systems Secretariat, 'The Contribution of Payments Systems to Financial Stability' (2000) Bank for International Settlements.

Committee on Payment Systems, 'Core Principles for Systemically Important Payment Systems' Bank of International Settlements 2001.

Communications Commission of Kenya (CCK), 'Market Structure – Telecommunications: Unified Licensing Framework' (2011) <www.cck.go.ke/licensing/telecoms/market.html> accessed 3 September 2014.

Communications Commission of Kenya, 'Annual Report Financial Year 2011/12' (2013) <www.marsgroupkenya.org/documents/documents/11776/> accessed 3 September 2014.

Communications Commission of Kenya, 'Annual Report Financial Year 2008/09' (2010) <www.marsgroupkenya.org/documents/documents/11776/> accessed 3 September 2014.

The Constitution of Kenya (2010) <www.kenyalaw.org:8181/exist/kenyalex/actview.xql?actid=Const2010> accessed 3 September 2014.

Consultative Group to Assist the Poor, 'Notes on Regulation of Branchless Banking in Kenya' (2007) <www.cgap.org/p/site/c/template.rc/1.26.1480/> accessed 3 September 2014.

'Consumer Protection Diagnostic Study: Kenya, Financial Sector Deepening'. January 2011 Simone di Castri and others, 'Consumer Protection Diagnostic Study: Financial Consumer Protection in Kenya' SSRN Journal.

'Consumer Protection Diagnostic Study', Kenya (2011) <www.fsdkenya.org/pdf_documents/11-02-22_Consumer_diagnostic_study.pdf>.

'Consumer Protection Regulation in Low-Access Environment Opportunities to promote Responsible Finance' <www.cgap.org/sites/default/files/CGAP-Focus-Note-Consumer-Protection-Regulation-in-Low-Access-Environments-Opportunities-to-Promote-Responsible-Finance-Feb- 2010.pdf> accessed 28 September 2014.

Corrigan, E. Gerald, 'Are Banks Special?' (1983) *Federal Reserve Bank of Minneapolis* 1982<www.minneapolisfed.org/pubs/ar/ar1982a.cfm> accessed 3 September 2014.

CPSS, 'Payment and Settlement Systems in selected Countries' (2003) <www.bis.org/publ/cpss54.pdf> accessed 3 September 2014

Crockett, Andrew, 'Market Discipline and Financial Stability' 26 *Journal of Banking & Finance* 977. Notes on Regulation of Branchless Banking in Kenya – GSMA2007 <www.gsma.com/mobilefordevelopment/wpcontent/uploads/2012/06/kenyanotesonregulationbranchlessbanking2007.pdf> accessed 3 September 2014.

Daily Nation, 'Michuki: Probe Cash Transfer' (2008) < www.nation.co.ke/News/-/1056/500454/-/u0kd67/-/index.html> accessed 3 September 2014.

Dal Bó, Ernesto, 'Regulatory Capture: a Review' (2006) 22 *Oxford Review of Economic Policy* 203.

Deposit Protection Fund – Central Bank of Kenya <www.centralbank.go.ke/index.php/deposit- protection-fund>

Dias, Denise and Kate McKee, 'Protecting Branchless Banking Consumers' (2010) <www.cgap.org/publications/protecting-branchless-banking-consumers> accessed 3 September 2014.

Dombret, Andreas, 'Resilient Banks – Essential Building Blocks of a Stable Financial System' (2013) <www.bis.org/review/r130925b.pdf> accessed 3 September 2014

Dowd, Kevin, 'Too Big to Fail? Long-Term Capital Management and the Federal Reserve' (1999) Cato Briefing Paper No 52 <www.cato.org/pubs/briefs/bp52. pdf> accessed 3 September 2014.

Ellinger, Eliahu P., Eva Lomnicka and Christopher Hare, *Ellinger's Modern Banking Law* (Oxford University Press 2011).

Ellinger, Eliahu, Eva Lomnicka and Richard Hooley, *Ellinger's Modern Banking* (Oxford University Press 2006).

Elyachar, Julia, 'Next Practices: Knowledge, Infrastructure, and Public Goods at the Bottom of the Pyramid' (2010) 24 *Public Culture* 109.

Estache, Antonio and Liam Wren Lewis, *Toward a Theory of Regulation for Developing Countries* (American Economic Association 2009).

Estache, Antonio and Liam Wren-Lewis, 'Toward a Theory of Regulation for Developing Countries: Following Jean-Jacques Laffont's Lead' (2009) *Journal of Economic Literature* 729; Jean-Jacques Laffont, *Regulation and Development* (Cambridge University Press 2005).

Fanon, Ananda and Ismail Ateya, 'A Preliminary M-Payment Model for M-Commerce in Kenya' (2008) <www.strathmore.edu/pdf/ictc-08/m-payment.pdf> accessed 3 September 2014.

Fischer-Lescano, Andreas and Gunther Teubner, 'Regime-Collisions: The Vain Search for Legal Unity in the Fragmentation of Global Law' (2004) 25(4) *Mich J Int'l L* 999.

*Foley v Hill* [1848] 2 HL C 28 at 45 (hereafter *Foley*).

Fraser (1994).

Galbraith, John Kenneth, *The New Industrial State* (1971).

Garcia-Murillo, Martha and Ian MacInnes, 'The Impact of Technological Convergence on the Regulation of ICT Industries' (2002) 5(1) *International Journal on Media Management* 57–67.

Geva, Benjamin, 'Bank Collections and Payment Transactions: A Comparative Legal Analysis' (Oxford University Press 2001)

Ghai, Yash, 'Law, Development and African Scholarship' (1987) 50 *The Modern Law Review* 750.

Gianviti, François, *Current Legal Aspects of Monetary Sovereignty* (2004) <www.imf. org/external/np/leg/sem/2004/cdmfl/eng/gianvi.pdf> accessed 3 September 2014.

'The Government's Latest Thinking on Consumer Credit Reform' www.nortonrosefulbright.com/knowledge/publications/33932/the-governments-latest-thinking-on-consumer-credit-reform accessed 25 June 2014.

Guasch, J. Luis and Pablo Spiller, 'The Challenge of Designing and Implementing Effective Regulation: A Normative Approach and an Empirical Evaluation' (2012) *The World Bank* <http://wwwwds.worldbank.org/external/default/WDSContentServer/WDSP/IB/2012/07/17/000386194_2012071 7015947/Rendered/PDF/710190WP0Publi0ing0and0implementing.pdf> accessed 3 September 2014.

Gudmundsson, Ragnar, Kethi Ngoka-Kisinguh and Maureen T. Odongo, 'The Role of Capital Requirements on Bank Competition and Stability: The Case of the Kenyan Banking Industry' (2013) <www.kba.co.ke/workingpaperseries/img/pdf/Working_Paper_WPS_05_12[2].pdf> accessed 3 September 2014.

'Guideline on Agent Banking' (2000) <www.bu.edu/bucflp/files/2012/01/Guideline-on-Agent-Banking-CBKPG15.pdf> accessed 3 September 2014.

'Guideline on the Appointment and Operations of Third Party Agents' <www.bu.edu/bucflp/files/2012/01/Deposit-Taking-Microfinance-Circular-No.-1-Guideline-on-the-Appointment-and-Operations-of-Third-Party-Agents-by-DTMs-consumer-protection- related.pdf> accessed 28 September 2014.

Hall, Maximilian J., *Banking Regulation and Supervision: A Comparative Study of the UK, USA and Japan* (E. Elgar 1993).

Hanson, Samuel G., Anil K. Kashyap and Jeremy C. Stein, 'A Macroprudential Approach to Financial Regulation' (2011) *Journal of Economic Perspectives* 3; Ruhl, Giesela, 'Consumer Protection in Choice of Law' (2011) 44 *Cornell International Law Journal* <www.lawschool.cornell.edu/research/ILJ/upload/Ruhl-final.pdf> accessed 28 September 2014.

Haupt, Schaffer, and Alan Schwartz, 'Legal Implications of Imperfect Information in Consumer Markets', (1995) 151 *Journal of Institutional & Theoretical Economics* 31, 35–36 (1995) (F.R.G?.)

Hayes, Niall and Chris Westrup, 'Context and the Processes of ICT for Development' (2012) 22 *Information and Organization* 23

Heffernan, Shelagh, *Modern Banking in Theory and Practice* (John Wiley and Sons 2003) at 15.

Holdsworth, William S., *A History of English Law*, vol. 1 (Methuen 1922).

Hossein, Jillian, Colin Kirkpatrick and David Parker, 'Creating the Conditions for International Business Expansion: The Impact of Regulation on Economic Growth in Developing Countries – a Cross-Country Analysis' (2003) <http://agecon search.umn.edu/handle/30554> accessed 3 September 2014.

Howells, Geraint G. and Stephen Weatherill, *Consumer Protection Law* (Ashgate Publishing Ltd. 2005).

'International Experiences of Mobile Banking Regulation – IGC' www.theigc.org/sites/default/files/Batista%20and%20Vicenter.

International Telecommunications Union, '11th Global Symposium for Regulators: Armenia City, Columbia: Chairman's Report' (2011) <www.itu.int/ITU-D/treg/Events/Seminars/GSR/GSR11/pdf/GSR11_Chairmanreport_en.pdf> accessed 3 September 2014.

'Introduction to Financial System' <www.centralbank.go.ke/financial *system/banks/Introduction.aspx*> accessed 3 September 2014.

Irungu, Geoffrey, 'Banks Raise Alarm over Mobile Cash Deposit Insurance – Money' *Business Daily, The Daily Nation Kenya* (January 2014) <www.businessdailyafrica.com/mobile-cash-deposit- insurance/-/539552/2157770/-/dgm4ojz/-/index.html%3E> accessed 28 September 2014.

Jack, William, Tavneet Suri and Robert Townsend, 'Monetary Theory and Electronic Money: Reflections on the Kenyan Experience' (2010) 96(1) *Economic Quarterly* 84, <www.richmondfed.org/publications/research/economic_quarterly/2010/q1/pdf/townsend.pdf> accessed 3 September 2014

James, Oliver, 'Regulation Inside Government: Public Interest Justifications and Regulatory Failures' (2000) 78 *Public Administration* 327.

Kartik Anand et al., 'A Network Model of Financial System Resilience' (2013) 85 *Journal of Economic Behavior & Organization* 219.

Kenya' (2014) <www.gsma.com/mobilefordevelopment/reinventing-the-wheel-pass-through-deposit-insurance-coverage-for-mobile-money-in-kenya> accessed 3 September 2014.

The Kenya Communications Act 2 of 1998, *Kenya Gazette Supplement* No. 64, 9 November 1998 at 219–220, <http://goo.gl/98dpL> accessed 3 September 2014.

Kenya Communications (Amendment) Act 1 of 2009 <www.cck.go.ke/> accessed 3 September 2014.

Kenya Information and Communication Dispute Resolution Regulations (2010) <www.cck.go.ke/regulations/downloads/Kenya_Information_and_Communica tion_Dispute_Re solution_Regulations_2010.pdf > accessed 3 September 2014.

Kenya Law Resource Centre, 'Statutory Definitions of a Bank' <www.kenyalawre sourcecenter.org/2011/07/statutory-definitions-of-bank.htm> accessed 3 September 2014.

Kenya Payment System, Framework and Strategy (2004) <www.docin.com/p-433903551.html> accessed 3 September 2014.

Kerrets, Monica, 'ICT Regulation and Policy at a Crossroads: A Case Study of the Licensing Process in Kenya' (2004)

Kessler, Friedrich, 'Contracts of Adhesion: Some Thoughts About Freedom of Contact' (1943) 43 *COLUM. L. REV.* 629, 632, 640–641 (1943)

Kimenyi, Mwangi and Njuguna Ndung'u, 'Expanding the Financial Services Frontier: Lessons from Mobile Phone Banking in Kenya'(2009) <www.brookings.edu/~/media/Files/rc/articles/2009/1016_mobile_phone_kenya_kimenyi/1016_mobile_ phone_kenya_kimenyi.pdf> accessed 3 September.

Koker, Louis De, 'Identifying and Managing Low Money Laundering Risk: Perspectives on FATF's Risk-based Guidance' (2009) 16 *Journal of Financial Crime* 334.

Koskenniemi, Martti et al., 'Fragmentation of International Law? Postmodern Anxieties' (2002) 15 *Leiden Journal of International Law* 553.

Krueger, Malte, 'Offshore E-Money Issuers and Monetary Policy' (2001) 6 *First Monday* 10 <http://firstmonday.org/ojs/index.php/fm/article/view/894/803> accessed 3 September 2014.

Lastra, Rosa M. and Heba Shams, 'Public Accountability in the Financial Sector', in Eilis Ferran and Charles A. E. Goodhart (eds), *Regulating Financial Services and Markets in the 21st Century* (Hart Publishing, 2001) 165–188.

Lavergne, Ismael, 'Mobile Payment Regulation, the Regulators Role' <www.gfg-group.com/mobile-payments/2012/08/> accessed 3 September 2014.

Lawack-Davids, Vivienne, 'The Legal and Regulatory Framework of Mobile Payments in South Africa: A Trade-Off? Analyses' (2012) 24 *SA Mercantile Law Journal= SA Tydskrif vir Handelsreg* 77.

Lawack-Davids, Vivienne, 'The Legal and Regulatory Framework of Mobile Payments in South Africa: A Trade-Off? Analyses' (2012) 24 *SA Mercantile Law Journal= SA Tydskrif vir Handelsreg* 77.

Ledyard, John O, 'Market failure' *The New Palgrave Dictionary of Economics* (2nd edn, 2008).

Leonard, Christopher, 'Client Assets and Money in the Post-Lehman World' November, 2010 www.bingham.com/Publications/Files/2011/10/Client-Assets-and-Money-in-the-Post-Lehman-World> accessed 28 September 2014 <www.legislation.gov. uk/ukpga/2000/8/pdfs/ukpga_20000008_en.pdf.> accessed 14 May 2014; 'Financial Services Act 2012.

Levergne, Ismael, 'Mobile Payment Regulation – the Regulator's Role' (2012) <www.gfg-group.com/mobile-payments/2012/08/mobile-payment-regulation-the-regulators-role/> accessed 3 September 2014.

Levine, Michael E. and Jennifer L. Forrence, 'Regulatory Capture, Public Interest, and the Public Agenda: Toward a Synthesis' (1990) *Journal of Law, Economics, & Organization* 167; Joseph E. Stiglitz, *The Role of the State in Financial Markets*, vol 21 (Institute of Economics, Academia Sinica 1993).

Lyman, Timothy, Gautam Ivatury and Stefan Staschen, 'Use of Agents in Branchless Banking for the Poor: Rewards, Risks, and Regulation' (2006) 38 *Focus Note* [page?].

MacCarthy, Mark and Gail Hillebrand, 'Mobile Payments Need Strong Consumer Protections' *American Banker Tuesday*, 10 August 2010 <http://defendyour dollars.org/posts/211mobile_payments_need_strong_consumer_protections> accessed 28 September 2014.

Macleod, Henry D., *The Theory and Practice of Banking*, vol. 1 (Longmans, Green, Reader, & Dyer18662012) <http://books.google.co.uk/books/about/The_ Theory_and_Practice_of_Banking.html?id=JKkyAQAAMAAJ> accessed 3 September 2014.

Makin, Paul and Consult Hyperion, 'Regulatory Issues Around Mobile Banking' (2010) *The Development Dimension ICTs for Development Improving Policy Coherence: Improving Policy Coherence* 139.

Malala, Joy, Interview with Mercy Buku, 'An Interview with Senior Manager Money Laundering Reporting at Safaricom' (2014).

Mas, Ignacio and Amolo Ng'weno, 'Three Keys to M-PESA's Success: Branding, Channel Management and Pricing' (2010) <http://papers.ssrn.com/sol3/papers. cfm?abstract_id=1593387> accessed 3 September 2014.

Maurer, Bill, Taylor C. Nelms and Stephen C. Rea, '"Bridges to Cash": Channelling Agency in Mobile Money' (2013) 19 *Journal of the Royal Anthropological Institute* 52.

Mauri, Arnaldo, 'The Currency Board and the Rise of Banking in East Africa' (2004) University of Milan Economics, Business and Statistics Working Paper. The National Payment System Framework Strategy.

Mauri, Arnaldo, 'The Currency Board and the Rise of Banking in East Africa' (2007) Working Paper No 10 <http://econpapers.repec.org/paper/milwpdepa/2007-10. htm> accessed 3 September 2014.

McCormick, Roger, *Legal Risk in the Financial Markets* (Oxford University Press 2010).

McEvoy, Neil, 'Capabilities of Mobile Operators from the Perspective of a Financial Regulator' in GSMA 'Mobile Money for the Unbanked' (Annual Report, July 2009).

McKay, Claudia and Mark Pickens, 'Branchless Banking Pricing Analysis' (2010) <www.slideshare.net/CGAP/branchless-banking-pricing-analysis-2010> accessed 3 September 2014.

Mckees, Denise Dias Katherine, 'Protecting Branchless Banking Consumers: Policy Objectives and Regulatory Options' <http://siteresources.worldbank.org/ FINANCIALSECTOR/Resources/PReadingProtectingBranchless.pdf> No 64 September 2010.

Merritt, Cynthia, 'Mobile Money Transfer Services: The Next Phase in the Evolution of Person-to- Person Payments' (2011) 5 *Journal of Payments Strategy & Systems* 143.

Michaels, Loretta, 'Better Than Cash: Kenya Mobile Money Market Assessment' (2011) *USAID* <http://nethope.org/assets/uploads/Kenya-Mobile-Money-Assess ment.pdf> accessed 3 September 2014.

The Ministry of Finance and the Ministry of Information Communication and Technology, <www.govermentofkenya.com> accessed 3 September 2014.

'M-KESHO in Kenya: A New Step for M-PESA and Mobile Banking' <www.financialac cess.org/blog/2010/05/m-kesho-kenya- new-step-m-pesa-and-mobile-banking> accessed 28 September 2014.

Mobile Financial Services: Basic Terminology (2013) <www.afiglobal.org/sites/default/files/publications/mfswg_gl_1_basic_terminology_finalnewnew_pdf>.

Mobile Money Association of India (MMAI) and GSMA Submission to the Reserve Bank of India's (RBI) Committee on Comprehensive Financial Services for Small Businesses and Low-Income Households. MMAI/GSMA, 'Mobile Money: The Opposition for India (2013) <www.gsma.com/mobilefordevelopment/wp-con tent/uploads/2013/12/MMAI-GSMA-on-Mobile-Money-in-India-for-RBI-Financial-Inclusion-Committee_Dec13.pdf> accessed 3 September 2014.

Morawczynski and Pickens (2009). Banque Centrale du Congo, Instructionn. 24/2011. www.legifrance.gouv.fr/affichTexte.do?cidTexte=JORFTEXT0000008 21047&dateTexte=.

Morgan, Bronwen and Karen Yeung, *An Introduction to Law and Regulation* (Cambridge University Press 2007) 3

Mortimer-Schutts, Ivan, 'The Regulatory Implications of Mobile and Financial Services Convergence' in *The Transformational Potential of M-Transactions: Moving the Debate Forward* (2007) The Policy Paper Series No. 6 <www.vodafone.com/content/dam/vodafone/about/public_policy/policy_papers/public_policy_series_6.pdf> accessed 3 September 2014.

Munyua, Alice and Muriuki Mureithi, 'Kenya' (2007) Global Information Society Watch (GISW) 2007 Report www.globaliswatch.org/en/node/500 accessed 3 September 2014.

Muthiora, Brian, 'Reinventing the Wheel: "Pass Through" Deposit Insurance Coverage for Mobile Money in Kenya' (2014) <www.gsma.com/mobileforde velopment/reinventing-the-wheel-pass-through-deposit-insurance-coverage-for-mobile-money-in-kenya> accessed 3 September 2014.

Mwega, Francis, 'The Competitiveness and Efficiency of the Financial Services Sector in Africa: A Case Study of Kenya' (2011) 23 *African Development Review* 44.

Mutuku, Nzomo, 'Case for Consolidated Financial Sector Regulation in Kenya' (2008) *Retirement Benefits Authority* <http://papers.ssrn.com/sol3/papers.cfm?abstract_id=1837354> accessed 3 September 2014.

The National Archives <www.legislation.gov.uk/ukpga/2012/21/pdfs/ukpga_2012 0021_en.pdf.> accessed 17 May 2014.

Ndung'u, Njuguna, 'Mobile and Agency Banking in Kenya', Address by Prof Njuguna Ndung'u, Governor of the Central Bank of Kenya, at the Technical Cooperation among Developing Countries Programme on 'Mobile and Agency Banking in Kenya' (2013) Kenya School of Monetary Studies <www.bis.org/review/r130515c.pdf?frames=0> accessed 3 September 2014.

Nkeri, Simon P., 'The Case for Consolidated Regulation of Financial Conglomerates in Kenya' (2014)

'Notes on Regulation of Branchless Banking' (2012) <www.gsma.com/mobileforde velopment/wpcontent/uploads/2012/06/kenyanotesonregulationbranchlessban king2007.pdf> accessed 3 September 2014.

Nxele, Mike and Thankom Arun, 'Regulatory Impact on the Development of the Telecommunications Sector in East Africa: a Case Study of Kenya' (2005) Working Paper Series No 99 <http://econpapers.repec.org/RePEc:ags:idpmcr:30598> accessed 3 September 2014.

Nyaoma, Gerald, 'Mobile Payments Regulatory Framework Perspectives in Kenya' (2010) <www.efina.org.ng/media-centre/events/workshops/mobile-payments-regulatory-framework-dissemination- workshop/forcedownload/91> accessed 3 September 2014.

Nyaoma, Gerald, 'Regulating Mobile Money: The Case of M-PESA' (2009) <www.afiglobal.org/sites/default/files/publications/GPF_Gerald_Nyaoma.pdf> accessed 3 September 2014.

Okonjo, Jeremmy, 'Chapter 2: the Impact of Convergence of Mobile Telecoms and Financial Services on Regulation of Mobile Telecommunications' (2014) <www.slideshare.net/JeremmyOkonjo/2-chapter-two-impact-of-convergence-of-mobile-financial-services-on-regulation-of-mobile-telecoms-in-kenya> accessed 3 September 2014.

Okonjo, Jeremmy, 'Impact of Convergence of Mobile Financial Services on regulation of Mobile Telecoms in Kenya' (2014) <www.slideshare.net/JeremmyOkonjo/2-chapter-two-impact-of-convergence-of-mobile-financial-services-on-regulation-of-mobile-telecoms-in-kenya> accessed 3 September 2014.

Okonjo, Jeremmy, *Nature and Impact of Mobile Financial Services on Regulation of Mobile Telecoms in Kenya* (2014).

Opata, Bede C., 'Transplantation and Evolution of Legal Regulation of Interconnection Arrangements in the Nigeria Telecommunications Sector' (2011) 14 *Int'l J Comm L & Policy* 1.

Pasanek, Brad and Simone Polillo, *Beyond Liquidity: The Metaphor of Money in Financial Crisis* (Routledge 2013) 117.

'Payment, Clearing and Settlement Systems in the CPSS Countries' <www.bis.org/publ/cpss105.pdf> accessed 20 October 2013.

Perlman, Leon J., 'Legal and Regulatory Aspects of Mobile Financial Services' (2012) <http://uir.unisa.ac.za/bitstream/handle/10500/13362/thesis_perlman_lj.pdf?sequence=4> accessed 3 September 2014.

Perlman, Leon, 'Legal and Regulatory Aspects of Mobile Financial Services' (PhD, University of South Africa 2012).

Pickens, Mark, 'Understanding What Drives Profits for Agents: M-pesa' (2009) <www.experientia.com/blog/understanding-what-drives-profits-for-agents-mpesa/> accessed on 22 September 2014.

Pickens, Mark, David Porteous and Sarah Rotman, 'Banking the Poor via G2P payments' (2007) 58 *Focus Note*.

Pomar, Fernando Gomez and Nuna Garupa, Max Weber Lecture: 'The Economic Approach to European Consumer Protection Law' (21 November 2007).

Prater, Connie, 'Going Mobile? Link Payments to Credit Cards for Best Protection' 2012, www.foxbusiness.com/personal-finance/2011/04/21/going-mobile-link-payments-credit-cards-best-protection/> accessed 28 September 2014.

PricewaterhouseCoopers, 'Telecoms in Africa: Innovative and Inspiring' (2012) 17(1) *Communications Review* 100.

Prosser, Tony, *Nationalised Industries and Public Control: Legal, Constitutional and Political Issues* (Blackwell 1986)

PwC, 'Telecommunications Industry: Overview of the Sector in Kenya' (2009) <www.pwc.com/ke/en/industries/telecommunications.jhtml%3E> accessed 3 September 2014.

'The Regulatory Framework for Mobile Payments in Nigeria', <www.bu.edu/bucflp/files/2012/01/Regulatory-Framework-for-Mobile-Payment-Systems-in-Nigeria.pdf> accessed 22 September 2014.

'The Reserve Bank of Fiji guidelines in their prescription of Agency Guidelines' <www.reservebank.gov.fj/docs2/Banking%20Supervision%20Policy%20Statement%20No%201 8-Agent%20Banking%20Guidelines%201.pdf> accessed 24 June 2014.

Re The Matter of the Interim Independent Electoral Commission [2011] Constitutional Application No. 2 (unreported)

Retirement Benefits Authority, 'Registered Schemes' <www.rba.go.ke/media/docs/schemes/Registered-Schemes.pdf> accessed 3 September 2014.

'Ring-Fencing and Safeguard of Customer Money' www.gsma.com/mobilefordevelopment/programmes/mobile-money-for-the-unbanked/safeguard-of-customer-money.

Rockoff, Hugh, 'The Free Banking Era: A Reexamination' (1974) *Journal of Money, Credit and Banking* 141

Ruhl, Giesela, 'Consumer Protection in Choice of Law' (2011) 44 *Cornell International Law Journal* 569 <www.lawschool.cornell.edu/research/ILJ/upload/Ruhl-final.pdf>

Rutledge, Sue, 'Improving Protection in Financial Services for Russian Consumers' (2009) <http://aisel.aisnet.org/cais/vol27/iss1/29> accessed June 2013.

Rutledge, Sue, 'Improving Protection in Financial Services for Russian Consumers' (2009)

Rutledge, Susan, 'Consumer Protection and Financial Literacy: Lessons from Nine Country Studies'. (2010) <http://siteresources.worldbank.org/CROATIAEXTN/Resources/3012441272903536699/Importance_vol1.pdf> accessed 28 September 2014.

*S v Kearney* 1964 (2) SA 495 (A) at 503.

Safaricom <www.safaricom.co.ke/> accessed 3 September 2014.

Safaricom, 'M-PESA Agent Requirements' (2010) <www.safaricom.co.ke/images/Downloads/Resources_Downloads/m-pesa_agent_requirements_-_for_external_use.pdf> accessed 3 September 2014.

Safaricom, <www.safaricom.co.ke> accessed 3 September 2014.

Sawyer, David and John Trundle, 'Core Principles for Systemically Important Payment Systems' (2001) 8 *Financial Stability Review* <www.bis.org/cpmi/publ/d43.pdf> accessed 3 September 2014.

Schulze, W.G., 'Smart Cards and E-Money: New Developments Bring New Problems' (2004) 16(4) *SA Mercantile Law Journal* 712.

Scott, Colin, *Regulation in the Age of Governance: the Rise of the Post Regulatory State* (Edward Elgar Publishing 2004).

Section Regulation of Mobile Payments Prior to the National Payment Systems Act 2011.

Shah, Atul K., 'Regulatory Arbitrage Through Financial Innovation' (1997) 10(1) *Accounting, Auditing & Accountability Journal* 85–104.

Stephens, Maria and Lisa Dawson, 'A Risk- Based Approach to Regulatory Policy and Mobile Financial Services' (2011) *Federal Reserve Bank of Atlanta*, Americas Center <www.frbatlanta.org/documents/news/conferences/> accessed 3 September 2014.

Tarazi and Breloff Simone Di Castri, 'Mobile Money: Enabling Regulatory Solutions' GSMA, London, United Kingdom <www.gsma.com/mobilefordevelopment/wp-content/uploads/2013/02/MMU-Enabling-Regulatory-Solutions-di-Castri-2013 pdf>

Tarazi, Michael and Paul Breloff, 'Nonbank E-Money Issuers: Regulatory Approaches to Protecting Customer Funds' 63 *Focus Note* <www.cgap.org/gm/ docu

Tarazi, Michael and Paul Breloff, 'Nonbank E-Money Issuers: Regulatory Approaches to Protecting Customer Funds' (2010) 63 *Focus Note* <www.gsma.com/mobilefordevelopment/wp-content/uploads/2013/09/fn63rev.pdf> accessed 28 September 2014.

Taylor, John B., 'The Monetary Transmission Mechanism: an Empirical Framework' (1995) *The Journal of Economic Perspectives* 11460–11478.

Telkom Kenya, 'History of Telkom Kenya' (2011) <www.telkom.co.ke/index.php?option=com_content&view=article&id=60&Itemid=95> accessed 3 September 2014.

Thal, Spencer N., 'The Inequality of Bargaining Power Doctrine: The Problem Of Defining Contractual Unfairness' 8 *Oxford Journal of Legal Studies*.

'The Transformational Potential of M – Transactions' www.vodafone.com/content/dam/vodafone/about/public_policy/policy_papers/public_policy_series_6.pdf.

Trichet, Jean-Claude, 'Financial System Resilience' Systemic Risk: The Dynamics of Modern Financial Systems' (2011) 101; See also Kartik Anand et al., 'A Network Model of Financial System Resilience'.

Tucker, Paul, 'The Debate on Financial System Resilience: Macroprudential Instruments' 22 (Barclays annual lecture, London, 22 October 2009).

Tyree, Alan L., *Banking Law in Australia* (Butterworths 1990); Tyree (2008) (n 205) 17.

Tyree, Alan, 'The Business of Banking' (2008) <http://austlii.edu.au/~alan/business-of-banking.html> accessed 3 September 2014

United Nations Conference on Trade and Development, 'Mobile Money for Business Development in the East African Community: A Comparative Study of Existing Platforms and Regulations' (2012) <http://unctad.org/en/PublicationsLibrary/dtlstict2012d2_en.pdf> accessed 3 September 2014.

Upadhyaya, Radha, 'Analyzing the Sources and Impact of Segmentation in the Banking Sector: a Case Study of Kenya' (PhD, University of London, School of Oriental and African Studies, 2011)

Wadsley, Joan and Graham Penn, *Law Relating to Domestic Banking* (2nd edn, Sweet and Maxwell 2000) 91.

Wanjiku, Rebecca, 'Kenya Communications Amendment Act (2009): Progressive or Retrogressive?' (2009) <www.apc.org/en/system/files/CICEWAKenya 20090908_EN.pdf> accessed 3 September 2014.

Wilhelmsson, T., 'The Informed Consumer v the Vulnerable Consumer in European Unfair Commercial Practices Law – a Comment' in G. Howells, A. Nordhausen, D. Parry and C. Twigg-Flesner (eds), *Yearbook of Consumer Law* (Ashgate 2007) 211 at 213.

<www.cck.go.ke/regulations/downloads/ICT_policy_guidelines_July_2013_FV3_-_5th_July_2013.pdf> accessed 3 September 2014.

<www.cck.go.ke/resc/publications/strategic_plan/CCK_3rd_Strategic_Plan_2013_26_11_13.pdf>accessed 3 September 2014; Central Bank of Kenya.

# 5 Themes around the appropriate regulatory framework for mobile payments systems

## 5.1 Introduction

Mobile payments deserve special regulation because of their specific system design and because, like other emerging payments systems,[1] mobile payments have shown the potential to be systemically important.[2] This systemic importance is manifested within its system, affecting the MNOs' institutional structure and the stakeholders involved, including the agents and the financial services they provide. Chapter 4 demonstrated that the challenge of regulating rapidly changing technologies and environments is that regulations are not enforced as fast as technological innovations are introduced, which creates a regulatory dilemma where regulators have to balance the need to enable innovation, while at the same time guarantee the safety and soundness of the financial system.

Thus, where unregulated services such as mobile payments are introduced, the concern that they may stifle innovation persists.[3] Consequently, establishing an appropriate regulatory framework for mobile payments by regulators should be at the crux of any payment system reform, especially one that is financially inclusive. Not simply because a regulatory framework would clarify the regulators' objectives in this converged environment, but also because, post-financial inclusion, mobile payments have brought forth regulatory challenges that have not been addressed by regulation.

The preceding chapters have discussed the overarching legal and regulatory challenges that mobile payments present.[4] They have done so by discussing and highlighting the regulatory environment that enabled mobile payments to succeed in the context of the challenges of post-financial inclusion that these new payments have presented. Through an examination of the post-financial inclusion issues, challenges that have not piqued the interest of regulators and the literature at large have drawn the attention to the fragmented regulatory framework within the financial services sector in Kenya and the lack of adequate financial consumer protection mechanisms due to the fact that, consumer risk has now been distributed to the now 'banked' population. Thus, how best to approach the regulation of mobile payments, following the risks and challenges discussed in Chapters 3 and 4 remains a pertinent question, especially in the so-called post-financial inclusion era in Kenya.

Mobile payments have provided a unique chance to reconsider existing regulatory structures in order to develop an appropriate regulatory strategy, in the hope of effecting a regulatory framework that would ensure an adequate safety net for mobile payments users.[5] This chapter proposes an appropriate regulatory approach for mobile payments by discussing the regulatory themes that would best suit the approach that should be adopted and the issues that regulators should be mindful of when enforcing and implementing this regulation. This chapter also answers the final research question[6] about which reforms should be implemented in the current regulatory framework to adequately oversee mobile payments. This enables us to draw conclusions about how an appropriate regulatory framework should address the challenges in the current regulatory framework, while at the same time building an enabling environment for the growth of innovation in the payments systems with sensitivity to financial inclusion. This further suggests that the Kenyan regulatory framework would have to balance the competing interests of the mobile financial services stakeholders, whose main objectives would be to increase their profits through new financial services products. They would also have to consider adopting a balanced approach that addresses industry development by driving national and global development and consequently increasing financial inclusion.

## 5.2 The considerations in prescribing appropriate financial services regulation for mobile payments

In the aftermath of the Global Financial Crisis, assigning appropriate regulation has been revisited,[7] since previous models had failed to work and the need for improved regulation was necessary. What was highlighted at least from a systemic point of view was that the interconnection across sectors, products and regions contributed to the financial crisis and these cannot be ignored. Furthermore regulatory reform has been a 'response to widespread perceptions of inadequacy of existing systems' and the weak application and implementation of the sound regulatory frameworks.[8] All this was in light of finding an ultimate regulatory environment that would prevent market abuse, while maintaining financial sector soundness. The regulatory reforms were aimed at limiting moral hazard and the concept of 'too big to fail' that guaranteed insolvent financial institutions that 'lenders of last resort' would be insured. This assignment is quite similar, in the examination of an appropriate regulatory framework for mobile payments. Additionally, an examination of a macroprudential approach to mobile payments is suggested, since it has been argued that the causes of the GFC were due to a weak application of microprudential approaches to regulation.[9]

Mobile payments and their success in Kenya have precipitated an environment in which MNOs may be considered institutions that are too big to fail, and their collapse or insolvency may have systemic effects for the payments system.[10] It has been reiterated during the discussion of post-financial inclusion that this could have catastrophic effects if such a case were to happen. Hence, the assessment of an appropriate regulatory framework for mobile payments requires an evaluation of certain benchmarks in deciding whether the regulation is good, acceptable or in need of reform.[11]

These benchmarks are described as 'principles of good regulation',[12] where Baldwin[13] asserts that there should be key tests that should be performed before reaching an evaluation on what good regulation should be, or is appropriate in a particular case, as the quest for 'good' regulation varies from country to country.[14] This study has throughout prescribed 'appropriate' regulation deliberately, as developing countries merit a different approach to their regulatory processes, or rather in the prescription of their regulation. This is because previous regulatory strategies and supervision measures are becoming outdated, and new approaches and techniques now need urgent consideration. Although the rationale for and principles of financial regulation are not fundamentally different in developing countries, it led Baldwin to ask whether developing countries were 'special'.[15]

Relevant to this discussion are the institutional components that are regarded as problematic when regulating in developing countries.[16] These components include, limited capacity[17] where the state structure as well as the internal resources of the state are often regarded as being too limited to stand up to well-resourced private interests, in this case Safaricom, the most successful firm deploying M-Pesa. Also to be included are limited commitment or, as discussed in Chapter 4, the lack of political will to regulate[18] and the fact that there needs to be a limiting of the discretion in regulatory and political decision-making, and finally limited accountability, where governments face limited demands for transparency, which means that their decisions are relatively free from challenge.[19]

Therefore, the examination of appropriate regulation requires the discussion of the regulatory principles.[20] This section will assess the regulatory principles in the regulation of mobile payments. This study identifies the principles as they were used by the Better Regulations Task Force 2005[21] and then includes the specific principles that are unique to both developing country perspectives and, more importantly, to mobile payments. These principles are: proportionality, accountability, transparency and consistency. I include the examination of state objectives such as consumer and investor protection, the promotion of competition, financial stability, regulation and supervision and finally, the unique design of the regulated entity based mainly on the legal status of the entity, in this case the MNO: whether it is an institution-based approach, or on the activities it performs, a functional-based approach and the governance structure of the oversight function, as additional and distinctive criteria for appropriate regulation in Kenya's context. Consequently, an appropriate regulatory framework should be one that enables mobile money, creates an open and level playing field that nurtures competition and innovation and influences the value schemes of both banks and MNOs. This environment should also enable and enhance investments and let providers focus on refining operations and promoting customer adoption.[22]

### 5.2.1 *Proportionality*

Proportionality requires that the legal and regulatory framework should not be excessively restrictive and arduous in relation to the possible issues it is designed to tackle. Proportionality also suggests that any such inconsistencies are recognised and resolved in accordance with a country's overall priorities, which should achieve an appropriate balance.[23] However, public policy objectives may not always accommodate the need for a proportionate regulatory approach. This is because developing countries' objective of encouraging inclusion may override the need for stability and safety and soundness of the financial system.

Consequently, regulatory proportionality includes laws and regulations which enable the viable development of financial services through mobile phones and balance the cost of regulation both to the institutions and the regulator with its benefits.[24] Furthermore, there should be an assurance that any burden or constraint that is imposed should be proportionate to the benefits.[25] A consideration of the costs to firms and consumers is usually an indication of how proportionate an imposition of a regulation would be. Cost benefit analysis would be necessary for the proposed regulatory requirements, and regulators should only intervene when necessary. In the case of mobile payments, the risks outlined in Chapter 3 present a justification for intervention and the compliance costs would be passed on to the MNOs. These risks, in particular integrity risks, fraud and loss of funds, far outweigh the cost of compliance by MNOs, and the enforcement regimes should be proportionate to the risks posed.

Thus, the establishment of an appropriate regulatory framework for mobile payments should provide a balance between technological innovations on the one hand, and safeguard against the unique risks of the ever-evolving mobile money ecosystem on the other. Since MNOs are not regulated by financial regulators, but rather the telecoms regulator, the CCK, the proportionality of mobile payments regulation as related to the associated unique risks should also be considered. A good regulatory approach should, on the one hand, balance the need for stability and safety and soundness of the payments system and the financial system as whole, and on the other hand be flexible and neutral and accommodate various ways for the stakeholders to meet compliance requirements.[26] This brings into focus how regulatory objectives by the regulator should be advanced, as proportionality also hinges on the careful balance of any policy objectives the state may have, such as financial inclusion. Proportionality requires balance when regulatory objectives clash, as can be expected where previously autonomous regulatory domains converge. For instance, where the objective of private firms is profit, that of the telecoms regulator, the CCK, is to issue industry standards, and these may often be at odds with the regulatory objectives of the government of Kenya, for instance, in the provision of an enabling environment for mobile payments to reduce cash dominance in the economy and its associated risks, thereby further advancing financial inclusion.

In so doing, regulatory proportionality would require that regulators issue regulation that fosters, rather than inhibits, innovation in association with regulated activities, such as by allowing scope for different means of compliance, so that market participants are not unduly restricted from launching new financial products and services.

### 5.2.2 Transparency

As a prerequisite for good governance and sound financial regulation,[27] transparency offers information about existing conditions so decisions and actions are made accessible, viable and understandable.[28] The allocation of resources is enabled through transparency, as it ensures that market players have adequate resources to identify risks and to distinguish one firm's, or one country's, circumstances from another.[29] Transparency helps to inform markets of accurate information, thereby helping to stabilise markets during times of uncertainty and also contributing to the effectiveness of announced policies.[30] Better policy options are encouraged through transparency, which aids the reduction of the incidence of arbitrary decisions in regulatory implementation.[31] The importance of transparency to the regulatory policy agenda emanates from the many causes of regulatory failures.[32] These failures include regulatory capture and bias towards focussed benefits, 'inadequate information in the public sector, rigidity, market uncertainty and inability to understand policy risk and a lack of accountability'.[33]

Transparency would allow market participants to garner sufficient information to enable them to make sound judgments.[34] It also requires that the CBK, as the main regulatory authority for mobile payments, should inform the public that regulatory choices have been taken to encourage administrative discretion and deter corruption.[35] The CBK as the main regulatory authority for mobile payments should gather information and documents and disseminate them to all parties concerned. This central body disseminating the relevant information must ensure timely and accurate distribution. The CBK should be able to exercise its discretion as to which information to disseminate.[36] To encourage the use of mobile payments by market participants and consumers, the relationship between relevant authorities has to be transparent. Policies announced by the CBK and the CCK can reduce uncertainties about policy intentions.[37]

They will also restrain the authorities from misleading the public and consumers. Public consultations are key regulatory tools employed to improve transparency. The CBK, in their efforts to formulate and operationalise the NPSA, only called for one public consultation.[38] It may be debatable as to whether citizens or the industry at large were informed, as it was only possible for industry experts to comment, which highlights a slight flaw in the efforts for transparency and calls into question the efficacy of the NPSA 2011. It is important that consultation should take place before the proposals are developed so that stakeholders' views and expertise are taken into account. The regulated should be aware of their obligations, while being given the opportunity to comply.

Trade, competition and investment are also encouraged through transparency of the regulatory system to limit undue influences by special interests.[39] It reinforces the legitimacy and fairness of regulatory process, but it is not easy to establish in practice, especially in the framework of developing countries such as Kenya. Transparency involves a wide range of practices, including standardised processes. These would include consultations with the public in clear language when drafting publication codification. It should also be easy to find and understand the implementation and appeal processes, which should be predictable and consistent – something the CBK failed to do, perhaps due to both internal and external pressure in a 'rush to regulate' mobile payments.[40]

All guarantees should be made clear through transparency, and all stakeholders of financial products and services should be made fully aware of their responsibilities. This certainly may be a difficult criteria to fulfil, which further adds to the complexities that financial regulation in developing countries face, especially post-financial inclusion.[41] Hence, the CBK in establishing an appropriate regulation for mobile payments should clarify their position and communicate these clarifications to interested parties, in this case MNOs, agents and consumers. Transparency is also closely linked to the need for accountability, which the next section discusses.[42] Providing the public with adequate information ensures that all stakeholders are provided with the opportunity to comment or contribute to the best quality regulation that emerges. This ensures that the resulting regulation should be the best possible.[43] Too big to fail institutions that create a moral hazard, as a result of public perception and the imprimatur of the government, would hamper the quest for transparency and that all guarantees are made explicit. Transparency is the key instrument in preventing market abuse, including insider dealing[44] and market manipulation,[45] money laundering, terrorism financing and corruption.[46]

Transparency also ensures that the regulatory strategy of disclosure is effected and enforced. Disclosure rules usually prohibit the supply of false or misleading information, and so decrease information asymmetry and offer some protection to consumers, as they allow consumers to make decisions on the acceptability of the processes involved in the production of goods and the services they are offered. This strategy provides a mode of regulation that is not heavily interventionist.[47] A mandatory disclosure may occur whereby MNOs must reveal certain important information, such as pricing or quality of services to the public. Disclosure regulation may also involve the supply of information to the public directly through the CBK the assigned regulator or the CCK, the specific telecoms regulator.[48]

Disclosure through transparency increases publicly available information; it enables market actors to make informed investment decisions and thus improves market efficiency. However, the customer profiles of mobile payment users, who have been described as low-income earners, previously unbanked and financially illiterate, may not always use the information properly or may merely fail to understand this information. This would require Kenyan regulators to adequately and precisely ensure that all information is disseminated in a manner that is accessible to all segments of the population. Transparency is also applied in the enforcement of the regulatory framework,[49] as it is normally considered paramount in order to indicate to the regulatory community that regulation is implemented consistently and proportionally.[50]

### 5.2.3 Accountability

An appropriate regulatory framework would have to ensure accountability as one of its key components. Accountability is closely linked to the concept of transparency. Furthermore, the quest to find the core of accountability is likely to be plagued by the plurality of interests and ideas that surround this concept.[51] Colin Scott defines regulatory accountability as 'the duty to give account for one's actions to some other person or body'.[52] Accountability is more often associated with reporting duties, whereas transparency offers visibility, such as the publication of all intentions to regulate or for procurement contracts and what would be regarded as public discretion.[53] A further definition of accountability is 'a liability to reveal, to explain, and to justify what one does; how one discharges responsibilities, financial or other, whose several origins may be political, constitutional, hierarchical or contractual'.[54] This principle would compel the regulatory framework in Kenya to state who is accountable for what and to whom: a question that is always asked when discussing accountability as a regulatory principle. In this instance, the question lingers within the mobile payments system framework, with different stakeholders and sectoral regulators, where CBK is the financial regulator and CCK is the industry regulator, that have to be accountable for their actions and decisions. This is because accountability by regulators illustrates their power in two respects: they affect the outcomes for financial firms, and they can have a significant impact on consumer welfare.[55]

This precipitates the more accurate questions, 'who regulates the regulators' or who regulators are accountable to and how this accountability is achieved.[56] This forms an important aspect in determining and conceptualising an appropriate regulatory approach, because, as stated earlier, accountability is the need to justify and accept responsibility for the decisions taken based on the objectives.

Therefore, appropriate regulation should allocate responsibility that has to be upheld by either the CBK or the CCK as the regulators of mobile payments. This responsibility requires ex post oversight of the actions of one institution by another institution.[57] Accountability also ensures that there is a certain discipline in ensuring that the authorities are answerable to the general public and market participants, such as agents and consumers, regarding the decision that they have made.[58] A better-informed public will also strengthen the credibility and public understanding of the issues in question.[59]

For instance, as discussed in Chapter 4, holding agents liable for their actions and inactions provides an opportunity for accountability by the MNO and CBK, at large as the regulator. Accountability would manifest itself in how providers assume legal liability for the actions of agents, especially in their discharge of the agent agreements between the MNOs and agents. Accountability requires that regulators should be able to justify their actions and decisions and be subject to public scrutiny.[60] Draft regulations should be published, and all those affected in the industry should be informed prior to decisions being made. This provides that regulators are required to establish clear standards and criteria against which they are accountable; these requirements include accessibility, fairness and the need for effective complaint and appeal procedures.

This accountability is extended to public servants and government officials.[61] Regulatory authorities should be concerned about the applicability of the regulations they frame. All stakeholders should therefore be able to know who is accountable by recognising who is the authority. This may be complicated, particularly in converged industries such as mobile payments.[62] This usually aids in the implementation of policies or regulation, as they are then easily amended. In answering who is accountable, in this case with the MNO as the regulated party, the MNO would be accountable to the CBK for mobile payments and to the CCK for telecommunications. However, the CBK would need to be accountable to another institution for its regulatory approach. As each authority has its own specific roles and objectives to meet, there must be clear coordination among the authorities to clarify their roles. Only when the functions are clear can each authority be made accountable for its actions. Furthermore, central banks may have statutory independence, but they do not have policy independence,[63] which imposes limits on their accountability, since they may have immunity over lawsuits from citizens.[64]

Accountability also needs to be appropriate for the resources of the country, or the regulators more specifically, and for the effective pursuit of the regulatory objectives.[65] In this case, the regulated party would be the MNO; as control is exercised by certain institutions, the competence of these institutions in specialty areas may also be called into question.[66] Accountability would call for a clearly explained process as to how final decisions are determined. This would ensure that criteria are maintained so they can be judged. Since accountability is closely linked with transparency,[67] accountability would call for well-publicised, accessible, fair and effective complaints and appeals procedures. The aspect of accountability that asks, 'accountable to who' means that regulators, and possibly enforcers, should have clear lines of accountability to the parliament as well as to the public.[68] Where accountability imposes discipline on regulators, transparency, on the other hand, enhances the quality of accountability by installing corporation amongst regulators and calling on them to justify their decisions.[69]

Accountability is a duty that has to be upheld by each authority.[70] As each authority has its own specific roles and objectives to meet, there must be clear coordination among the authorities to clarify their roles. Only when the functions are clear can each authority be made accountable for its actions. A better-informed public will also strengthen the credibility and public understanding of the issues in question.[71] Accountability in financial regulation also calls for regulatory agencies to operate independently of sectional interests. This also calls for the CBK to implement a regulatory structure that is accountable to its stakeholders and subject to audit.[72]

Although accountability attracts universal support due to its position in protecting the interests of the public, it may have certain limits.[73] As Lastra states, 'too much independence may lead to the creation of a state within a state, while too much accountability threatens the effectiveness of independence and therefore an optimal trade-off between independence and accountability must be attained'.[74]

## 5.2.4 Consistency

Closing gaps and inconsistencies, as discussed in Chapter 4,[75] should involve all areas, including policies, legal framework and approval and monitoring of mobile payments schemes in Kenya. It is paramount to avoid gaps and inconsistencies in order to be free from ill effects and damaging uncertainties.[76] Mobile payments, established as a retail payment instruments, are continuously developing. The CBK may meet challenges in keeping up with the changing conditions such as, in particular, the technical innovations and changing profiles of market participation. If these changing circumstances are not recognised, the CBK may find gaps and inconsistencies in information related to the development of mobile payments.

Cooperation between the CBK and other authorities in the sharing of information may narrow gaps and inconsistencies, thereby maintaining financial stability and certainty, which are also important in maintaining trust and integrity in the payments system. This avoidance is also necessary because it ensures that the CBK can identify the rights and responsibilities of all parties, such as the functions of the MNO holding the platform for mobile payments. It may be difficult to conceive a consistent regulatory framework, especially for a retail payment services framework. Regulation should therefore be predictable in order to offer stability and certainty to those being regulated, which would call for a consistent application of regulation across the country.[77]

## 5.2.5 Balancing the objectives of the state

Appropriate regulation should be able to balance the objectives of the state and the need for regulation, where the objectives include protecting consumers and safeguarding the payments system. Since mobile payments have reflected the national conditions, the economic goals through the financial inclusion agenda and the different socio-economic and political circumstances, as well as the level of infrastructure development in Kenya's financial system, then all these factors should be considered in order to effect appropriate regulation. These considerations are paramount because they are the reason that only mobile payments have managed to be successful in Kenya, since the infrastructure and enabling environment varies from country to country. As a result, solutions which have been effective to achieve national goals in one country may not always be so in another. Objectives are to resolve the market and maintain financial stability.[78]

The state should extend its mandate on the competitive concerns at the retail level. This approach ensures that competitive concerns, such as interoperability amongst MNOs, are adequately addressed, while also limiting ex ante regulation to those areas where the benefits to consumers cannot be achieved using ex post regulation.[79] This further calls for periodic assessment of competitive conditions in the market place. Time and resources would have to be allocated to reviewing and revising the targeted ex ante regulation[80] to avoid stifling innovation and ensuring that a balance is met so that the interests of consumers and the long-term benefits of financial inclusion are met.[81]

As reiterated, an enabling environment for mobile payments is optimal, especially in reducing cash dominance in the economy. The reduction of cash dominance is an objective of governments because of the risks involved.[82] It should also include a specification of minimum technical and business requirements for various participants in the mobile payments system.[83]

### 5.2.6 *The design of the non-bank payment provider*

It is important that appropriate regulation for mobile payments should take into account the need to accommodate market innovation.[84] This would require that the regulation should be neutral and avoid favouring particular business models over any other, as it is likely to distort the market's competitive process.[85] Additionally, the design of the non-bank payment provider suggests that while the MNO requires technical expertise, regulators should aim to have technology neutral rules in order to maintain their longevity. This is evident in industries that, for instance, are overly reliant on new technologies. Although this presents a challenge due to the fact that technology often, as has been demonstrated by mobile payments, post-dates regulation, an appropriate regulatory framework would ensure that new regulations instituted remain meaningful and useful for an extended period.

Regimes are more likely to be sustainable where they are designed around the behaviour they are trying to manage and are as neutral as possible about the mechanisms and technologies involved.[86] One commentator noted, 'as nature abhors a vacuum, so do regulators'.[87] In our view, the presence of a regulator with supervision and enforcement powers is an important part of any effective regulatory regime for payment services. We assume that for each of the regulatory models discussed in this and the following chapter, a regulatory agency of some sort would be involved. Regulatory regimes are not generally self-executing. They tend to need a regulator to supervise and enforce conduct of business rules. Relying on private citizens or competitors without sufficient expertise and incentive to take action is unlikely to be a fully effective enforcement strategy. Law enforcement is a public good – it is likely to be undersupplied by private actors in a free market system. An efficiency or competition protection regime is generally accepted as justifiable and necessary for payment services. Product disclosure is discussed below. Minimum fair play rules are also needed. As discussed in

Sections 3.3 and 5.2 above, they include prohibitions on misleading, deceptive, unconscionable and harassing conduct.

Traditional regulation of financial institutions has been mainly based on the institutional capacity rather than the business undertaken.[88] This has led to a gap in the distinction between institutional and functional regulation. Hence, the regulation of parties has ultimately indicated that their core business was also regulated. These distinctions are apparent in regulating banks whose business is banking; however, due to the merging of industries due to technology, the institutional structure of supervision has thus become a major issue of policy debate.[89] Nevertheless, a contrast between functional and institutional regulation and institutions based on objectives or market failure has the potential to be misguided, as they serve different purposes. This is because usually, institutions, not functions, fail. However, with the advent of technology, functions are likely to fail; therefore, on the one hand institutions should be regulated for safety and soundness, while functions would have to be periodically assessed for functionality and for the mitigation of operational risks. Furthermore, functional regulation involves regulating how institutions conduct the various aspects of their business (conduct of business) and how they behave within their industry.[90]

In summation, what constitutes good regulation may be difficult to establish and is a matter that is inevitably subject to contention. Adapting regulations which effectively regulate services such as mobile payments is an important factor to consider. However, before attempting to disseminate this, it is important to discuss the various modalities of regulation. An appreciation of the sphere of regulation is necessary, especially in the telecoms sector, as there needs to be consideration of the various regulatory actors and their tools or powers, which were extensively discussed in Chapter 4.

The role of the CBK as the state actor and the role of non-state actors have to be considered in establishing regulatory frameworks. Several authors have contended that regulation is not merely the action of the state to set prescriptive rules backed by sanctions, and have attempted a conceptual understanding of the spheres of regulatory influence. For example, Lessig and others, writing on privacy issues within the information industry, have contributed to this discourse by suggesting frameworks for classifying various sources of regulatory power.[91]

## 5.3 The CBK's approach in regulating mobile payments

The CBK's is said to have recently instituted a functional as opposed to an institutional approach to regulating mobile payments,[92] since the development of technology has transcended national boundaries and exposed consumers to a myriad of providers. It is increasingly difficult for regulators to block out all unlicensed services providers and suggestions have been made that consumers should become better equipped to exert market discipline on MNOs. It is questionable whether regulators, particularly, central banks, are prepared to let market discipline be the main monitor of financial regulation.[93]

The CBK's 'Test and Learn' approach to regulation has been publicised by the Governor of the CBK, Njuguna Ndung'u.[94] Njuguna has reiterated the government's desire not to stifle innovation in the payments industry. This reaffirms the influence of political policy on regulation.[95] In this approach, the governor states that regulators should 'think beyond the conventional brick and mortar delivery channels to enhance financial inclusion'.[96] This assertion has reinforced the CBK's approach which has been to 'embrace technological innovations and provide a supportive policy environment to nurture the growth of mobile financial services in a safe manner.'[97] Their risk assessment strategy was to carry out pilot tests before inception which would 'curb the risks of failures'.[98] He further highlighted the limits to a risk-based approach by stating that 'it was important to avoid the fear of the unknown since an extreme risk-averse attitude can lead to corner solutions'. However this approach may be seen as too lax, as a risk-based approach to regulating mobile payments would be appropriate.

The CBK also applied a regulatory approach that would aim to 'balance innovation and stability'. The governor acknowledges that a 'proactive regulatory environment is critical in ensuring a balance between access and stability'. He justifies this, since regulatory processes post-date innovation, this delay stifles innovation, hence slowing the market dynamism which undermines access.[99] This shows that the strategic policy choice that Kenya adopts is to allow technological innovations, albeit under prudential monitoring so as to ensure financial integrity.[100] This involves the discharge of its role in ensuring that innovations do not result in risks to the markets' stability. Their approach also included enabling a competitive environment that would attract private sector investors into the mobile financial services sub-sectors and ensure that the market is open to competition. The CBK also aimed at eliminating barriers to entry and creating an enabling legal environment,[101] as it recognized the potential for financial inclusion if a competitive supply of mobile financial services products are provided.[102] The CBK also highlighted the need for 'better regulation rather than more regulation' in efforts to ensure that regulatory regimes do not stifle innovations. The 'better' regulatory framework would have the ability to readily identify weaknesses and emerging vulnerabilities, to analyse and price risks appropriately, to provide appropriate incentives and penalties to induce prudent behaviours in the market and to encourage innovations while developing strong institutions.

## 5.4 Themes round the regulation of mobile payments

The themes and regulatory strategies[103] that should be employed in the appropriate regulation of mobile payments have to encapsulate specific interests: in my view, the safety and soundness of the payments system and of the financial systems as whole, paying special attention to the needs of consumers. There are various instruments that states can use to regulate directly.[104] However, choosing the right strategy for regulation is important while considering Kenya's regulatory capacity,[105] as it is a developing country,[106] its resources and the influence it possesses.[107] Kenya further needs to assess the right regulatory strategy in order to achieve its objectives, such as the safety and soundness of the payment system and the efficiency and stability of the financial system as a whole.[108]

In Kenya, mobile payments have been very successful, as reiterated through the introduction of M-Pesa.[109] There is no doubt that there needs to be an appropriate regulatory framework for mobile payments based on the risks discussed in Chapter 3 and the challenges examined in Parts I through III in Chapter 4. However, Kenya has chosen to develop its regulatory framework, solely entrusting the Central Bank of Kenya with this task. Since mobile payments are relatively new to the payments system, the challenge however is in its enforcement and implementation. It is hence important to consider a number of regulatory theories to evaluate the normative basis of Kenya's approach in the regulation of mobile payments.

It is extremely early to conclude whether the CBK has successfully implemented its regulatory oversight through the NSPA on mobile payments without jeopardising their further development, since the Act is not fully operational; moreover, whether the CBK has the committed intent to regulate since the lacuna in the current regulatory framework has been the main catalyst for its proliferation.[110] It is also premature to consider whether, upon the actualisation of the Act by the CBK, the industry would change accordingly. It is necessary therefore to consider the rationales and implications that the regulatory policies may have in view of the theories of regulation and the expected outcomes

### 5.4.1 Risk-based approach to the regulation of mobile payments

The call for risk-based regulation, in efforts to minimise both the inherent payment systems risks and the unique mobile payment system risks, appears to be an appropriate approach lauded amongst regulatory authorities.[111] The core of risk-based regulation, as universally understood, is the prioritising of regulatory actions in accordance with an assessment of risks that parties will present to the regulatory body achieving its objectives.[112] The normative rationale is that the risk-based approach hinges on the fact that attempts to minimise adverse governance outcomes to nil tend to be inefficient, since they can be unduly costly to achieve, perversely create other risks such as political risk, or distract attention from more serious problems.[113] This would seem to mean that regulators should target regulation where the most harm is expected.

Regulatory reforms have increasingly put forward risk-based strategies in efforts to manage their resources.[114] Risk-based regulation 'in its idealized form, offers an evidence-based means of targeting the use of resources and of prioritizing attention to the highest risks in accordance with a transparent, systematic and defensible framework'.[115] A further prompting to re-examine the implementation challenges of risk-based regulation comes in the wake of the 2007–2009 credit crisis and stems from the widespread perception that risk-based regulation, at least in the UK, signally failed to protect consumers and the public from the catastrophic failure of the banking system.[116]

A risk-based regulatory framework for mobile payments would ensure that the focus is on risks and not on rules. This focus compels the regulators, in this case the CBK, to focus on identifying the risks that they are seeking to manage and not the rules they have to enforce. In this case, the unique mobile payment risks which this thesis identified in Chapter 3 would be of paramount concern to the regulators. A risk-based approach would also require the CBK to explicitly select the frameworks of analysis through which they would be regulating.

A risk-based regulatory approach would involve an assessment of the hazard or adverse event and the likelihood of it occurring. As discussed in Chapter 3, inherent risks arising from the nature of mobile payments would require an adoption of a risk-based approach to regulation. The CBK would have to regulate in a way that is responsive to the regulated firm's behaviours, attitude and culture, which, as Julia Black states, are the optimal institutional environments that are required for a responsive risk-based approach, perhaps through the adoption of a nuanced risk-based regulatory approach. This approach requires that strategies should use effective targeting of enforcement resources on the basis of assessments of the risks to which regulated firms are exposed.[117]

In this study, I have examined risk as a justification for regulation, not particularly governmental regulation, but by other sectorial regulators, such as the CCK. Risk as examined in Chapter 3 was used to 'determine the boundaries of the state's legitimate intervention in society' by solidifying the CBKs role to manage risk. A risk-based approach ensures that the state's balance of objectives such as financial inclusion and integrity centres on all AML/CFT considerations within the mobile payment system. Furthermore, a risk-based approach aligns itself with the proportionality principle, which means attaining 'the right balance between risks and benefits by tailoring regulation to mitigate the risk of the product without imposing an undue regulatory burden that could stifle innovation'.[118] A risk-based approach is seen as being critical for countries building inclusive formal financial systems and increasing financial access for the unbanked and under banked.[119] This has also been articulated by the FATF, which stressed the need for the application of its guidance to new payment methods that would focus on the implementation of AML/CFT measures.[120] These measures have additionally called for the application of a risk mitigation process which essentially underpins a risk-based approach, through the application of simplified CDD which would thus encourage financial inclusion.

A risk-based approach to mobile payments would ensure that the implementation of AML/CFT measures is effective.[121] In Kenya, the risk-based approach has been institutionally endorsed most emphatically after the advent of mobile payments.[122] Regulation is a form of risk management both within and beyond the state and is therefore becoming a benchmark for good governance for organisations.[123] Risk provides an important role in regulation or at least the examination of risk as shown in Chapter 3.

It provides an object of regulation, it justifies regulation and it also constitutes and frames regulatory organisations and procedures through framing accountability relationships.[124] It is with this in mind that regulators are now adopting risk-based measures in efforts to maintain their reputations.[125]

However, risk-based regulation, though appropriate in certain circumstances, may not be appropriate in determining the best way to approach the regulation of mobile payments. Therefore, what implications do these criticisms have in the regulation of mobile payments in Kenya? Among the limits of risk-based regulation is that it is problem-based, and regulators should seek to anticipate problems and deal with them.[126] A risk-based approach also requires that regulators identify the risk while trying to achieve its objectives. This shows that regulators would have to focus on the risks they deem more important, leading to many other issues being missed. Another challenge, which is quite pertinent in this context, is the organisational difficulty for risk-based regulators when their regulatory powers are shared with other regulatory authorities, in this case, the CBK and the CCK.[127] It should therefore be seen as a control strategy that has to be combined with other control strategies for it to be effective.[128] However, these difficulties are outweighed by the costs of regulatory failure for the mobile payments system.

### 5.4.2 *Self-regulation and enforced regulation*

Self-regulation, also referred to as consensus, is a term used to incorporate a broad array of regulatory arrangements that may vary along the 'degree of formality with which those arrangements are established and enforced, the extent to which the self-regulatory body exerts exclusive or monopoly control over the regulated activity and the level at which behaviour is regulated'.[129] Self-regulation may be preferred over state regulation, since MNOs would be able to use their expertise more widely, particularly in regulation of technical issues.[130] Self-regulatory bodies provide regulation that is flexible and rapidly able to adapt to market conditions, such as technological or economic changes as opposed to state centric regulations. Kenya provides a classic example where state regulation may be an impediment to the development of an appropriate regulatory framework. The CCK's regulations for instance, must be approved by parliamentary committees.[131] Additionally, self-regulation ensures that the costs of state regulation are reduced as the regulatory burden is lowered.[132] Similarly, state regulation, though costly, may be reduced to accommodate appeals from the self-regulatory bodies, allowing MNOs to act without interference from the state.[133]

Consequently, self-regulation provides a conducive environment for MNOs and their operation of mobile payments, especially due to the increase of new business models and technological advanced services.[134] Julia Black states that there are sources of confusion in the discussion of self-regulation.[135] What is meant by 'self', what is meant by 'regulation', and 'what is the nature of the state's involvement?' She argues that the term 'self' is used to mean two different things: self as in individual, and self as in collective.[136]

Thus the term 'self-regulation', is used to describe the disciplining of one's own conduct by oneself,[137] regulation tailored to the circumstances of particular firms,[138] and regulation by a collective group of the conduct of its members or others.[139] The definition of regulation varies from the 'command and control' model of regulation, to regulation by the market,[140] to voluntary decisions of each individual to control their own behaviour. Finally, the term can be used to imply no relationship with the state at all, or to describe a particular, corporatist arrangement.[141] Black argues that the essence of self-regulation is a process of collective government and that the term 'self' is used to describe a collective. 'Self-regulation' designates parties acting together, performing a regulatory function in respect of themselves and others who accept their authority.[142] As such, it should be distinguished from what may be termed individualised regulation. The two may co-exist, but they are analytically distinct and raise significantly different public law issues. Individualised regulation is regulation tailored to the individual firm. Ayers and Braithwaite's 'enforced self-regulation' is an example of such individualised regulation, as is Ogus's 'consensual' self-regulation. Individualised regulation may exist within a self-regulatory framework,[143] or a statutory one.[144] No particular relationship with the state is implied by the term 'self-regulation'.

This interpretation contrasts with some of the corporatist or neo-corporatist approaches which see self-regulation as simply a species of the genus corporatism. Broadly, we can identify four types of possible relationships: mandated self-regulation, in which a collective group, an industry or profession for example, is required or designated by the government to formulate and enforce norms within a framework defined by the government, usually in broad terms; sanctioned self-regulation, in which the collective group itself formulates the regulation, which is then subjected to government approval;[145] coerced self-regulation, in which the industry itself formulates and imposes regulation but in response to threats by the government that if it does not, the government will impose statutory regulation;[146] and voluntary self-regulation, where there is no active state involvement, direct or indirect, in promoting or mandating self-regulation.

Further, self-regulation may vary not only in its relationship with the state but in the nature of its participants (which may be solely members of the collective or may be outsiders); its structure (there may be a separate agency or it may be a cartel); its enforcement (it may enforce its own norms or it may rely on individuals to enforce); and its rule type (its rules may be of legislative, contractual or no legal status, be general or specific, vague or precise, simple or complex).[147]

Where a regulated activity requires technical expertise and knowledge, self-regulation would be appropriate. This is because the industry would have superior informational capacities, rendering it more efficacious.[148] For instance, the MNOs under the CCK should be able to self-regulate due to their highly specialised industry. This involves the regulated entities developing a system of rules that monitor and enforce against its own members. Enforced self-regulation occurs when it is subject to a form of governmental structuring or oversight supervision.[149] Consequently, self-regulation pulls the state's mandate in regulating institutions against the legal structure and interest of private firms.[150]

### 5.4.2 Command and control

Baldwin et al.[151] assert that the essence of command and control regulation is the exercise of influence by imposing standards backed by criminal sanctions.[152]

Therefore, in the telecommunications context, the CCK[153] may bring criminal prosecutions against MNOs who breach telecommunications regulation. The force of law is used here to prohibit certain forms of conduct, to demand some positive actions or to lay down conditions for entry into a sector, for example, through licensing.[154] Regulations should be equipped with rule-making powers and standard setting by government departments through either primary or secondary legislation and then enforced by regulatory bureaucracies.[155] Command and control involves licensing to process and screen entry into any activity, to control not only the quality of service or the manner of production but also the allocation of resources, products or commodities and prices charged to consumers or profits made by enterprises.[156]

### 5.4.3 Incentive-based regimes

This regulatory strategy works on the basis that the regulator imposes incentives or penalties to influence the behaviour of industry players, MNOs and agents.[157] Regulation by means of economic incentives might be thought to offer an escape from highly restrictive command and control regimes.[158] Baldwin states that according to the incentives approach, the potential mischief causer can be induced to behave in accordance with public interest by the state or a regulator imposing negative or positive taxes or deploying grants and subsidies from the public.[159] The advantages of this have been argued to be the relatively low levels of regulatory discretion required because financial punishments or rewards operate automatically once they have been established.[160] This strategy is also seen to be cheaper to administrate[161] and to involve light burdens of information collection and compliance costs which may be appropriate for Kenya as a developing country.

Furthermore, an incentive-based regulatory strategy is an important strategy as it enhances communication, while providing a regulated environment in which they can influence the way regulation is designed to operate in the marketplace.[162] This ensures that the regulator would have to depend on the MNOs to provide it with the knowledge so as best to regulate the activities within its mandate. This process is especially utilised when 'rules' are being negotiated and forums and committees are set up to gather and disseminate best practice and provide mutually acceptable 'rules' to govern such activities.

Whilst such a relationship could raise the concern of regulatory capture[163] because of the bargaining power wielded by the regulated, the process provides an environment of mutual responsibility which can, in the majority of occasions, outweigh such concerns. The use of an incentive-based approach would, as Grabosky gives cautious encouragement to the use of incentives as they could reduce the burden of regulation.[164] Incentives generally provide positive inducements to cooperate with the regulator rather than negative penalties, such as disqualification or market disclosure. For example, incentives range from grants and subsidies to favourable administrative considerations.[165] Regulatory holidays are another incentive, whereby an organisation is relieved from inspections because of its 'good track record' in compliance with regulatory requirements.

Incentive-based schemes compel parties to come clean with compliance failures which have been identified by the institution itself. This action maintains the trust relationship between the regulator, the CBK or the CCK and the regulated MNO. It also supports the view that most firms do accept regulation and supervision as a form of financial control where the reputation of the institution could be adversely affected if non-compliance is publicised. Furthermore, it highlights the importance of self-regulation in an environment where even the most compliant institutions can get it wrong. Ultimately disclosing non-compliance provides the regulated with the possibility of a lesser sanction or, in some cases, no punishment at all, because there is no evidence of complacency or dishonesty.

### 5.4.4 Market discipline and direct action

Market discipline suggests the creation of an incentive structure that encourages the market to take safer and sounder actions.[166] Market discipline is when part of the risk in a particular industry is allocated to the stakeholders in the market who monitor the activities of the market.[167] For instance, in the banking industry, the stakeholders sanction the banks by withdrawing investments or causing reputational loss when imprudent activities of the bank are detected, thus encouraging banks to manage prudently with sound investment decisions. In the case of mobile payments, this would be directed towards either the commission in its mandates over MNOs or to consumer protection. The regulator can also use their direct resources to achieve desired results by taking direct action.[168] This is seen as plausible as direct action ensures that public money is used in the furtherance of democratically established objectives. This also mimics the deterrence-based approach, which is centred on the imposition of sanctions and retribution.[169]

The deterrence-based approach is centred on the imposition of sanctions and retribution. In this light, deterrence could be construed as a mechanism for ensuring compliance by negative means. This is in contrast to a compliance-based approach, which may discourage non-compliance by placing attention on the threat of adverse consequences that can arise from a criminal prosecution or imposition of a punitive civil sanction. The deterrence-based approach is in this respect more reactive, as it assigns regulatory resources to detecting infringements of the law so that penalties can be successfully applied. According to Reiss, a regulatory strategy based on deterrence would consider the imposition of a penalty as a positive sign of success.[170] The choice of sanction is also dependent upon the seriousness of the breach or offence. This suggests that a broad range of both non-punitive and punitive sanctions is needed to address the varying degrees of culpability that can underpin non-compliance. Ayres and Braithwaite have set out the choice of sanctions in a pyramid with the most serious sanctions at the top.[171]

### 5.4.5 Rights and liabilities

Instead of imposing certain rules or standards on the industry, legislation could allocate rights to the public to encourage socially desirable behaviour.[172] When this is the case, the industry that provides the product would be deterred from providing goods or services which are not based on the allocation of rights.

### 5.4.6 Procedural dimension of regulation

The procedural dimension of regulation permits the regulator to have a certain degree of discretion in line with the informal agreement of the stakeholders. This power would be provided on the basis that the regulator would undertake ad hoc problem solving. Regulation is policy oriented and follows the overall policy framework of the government. Along the procedural dimension, even if the country followed the principle that basic legal rules have to be established by legislation, administrative rules, decrees and informal guidance often prevail.[173] In this situation, the industries have to adapt their business activities to a more discretionary law.[174] Under the NPSA, the CBK has categorised mobile payments systems. Law cannot simply be transplanted[175] without due consideration for the relevant economic framework within which it operates. The argument of the evolutionary approach is that it has been driven by new insights, in some cases by a veritable paradigm change or by the importation of outside, foreign rules and principles.

The development of payment systems is an evolving process and there should be very little resistance or debate on whether to regulate mobile payments. The decision to regulate mobile payments, I argue, has been to protect consumers and that this financial service should not be left to freely develop by the market. I also question whether the CBK, in maintaining prudential oversight through the provision of conduct of business requirements, has the expertise, resources and capacity for such a task. With the government's policy for financial inclusion, the CBK is in a strong position to adopt this policy.

### 5.4.7 Competition laws

Competition laws offer a direct means through which regulation can be channelled. This ensures that the market provides adequate services to consumers and the public.[176] Such laws can be used to control market behaviour so as to prevent anti-competitive or unfair practices such as predatory pricing by dominant operators.[177] This would be appropriate in consideration of Safaricom, the leading MNO's market dominance in the provision of mobile payments in the telecommunications industry provides an example of competition law being used instead of classical command and control regulation. Kenya's only sectoral regulator in the telecommunications industry is the CCK, which has specific rules for its operation; however, competition laws have not been clarified for the provision of mobile financial services, especially on pricing policies.

At the time of M-Pesa's inception, Kenya's competition law[178] did not contain explicit provisions on consumer protection. Although favoured by most stakeholders, the actual need for comprehensive consumer legislation was still the subject of debate. The debate was whether to combine competition policy and consumer protection into one authority. Obviously, the protection of consumers against deceptive and fraudulent behaviour by sellers has strong links to competition policy; consumers need protection from the exploitive tendencies of large corporations, as large enterprises abuse their dominant powers over consumers by selling at monopoly prices and by imposing unfavourable terms of trade. In fact, there are strong reasons for believing that less mature regional markets are often more vulnerable to anti-competitive practices.

Although this thesis will not delve into issues on interoperability, as the concept is still developing within the industry,[179] the Competition Authority of Kenya[180] would be involved. Interconnection[181] allows users of one MNO to communicate with users of another MNO to allow access to services provides by either MNOs.[182] Interoperability is defined as, 'the ability of communication systems, units or elements to provide services and to accept services from other systems, units or forces and to use the services exchanged to enable them operate effectively together'.[183]

Though interoperability may be a technological issue in this respect, this thesis highlights that it is a regulatory one. Interoperability allows for the interconnection of various MNOs and offers great benefits for consumers.[184] This is because various consumers can be reached through this method.[185] Interoperability also enables problems to be captured and prevents inept placement of repetitive or insufficient networks.[186] Due to the benefits of financial inclusion, this presents an opportunity for both the CBK and the CCK to work in cohesion in developing a sustainable environment post-financial inclusion as developing a sound interoperability approach would greatly benefit the industry. Furthermore, since interconnection promotes competition in the market,[187] it would challenge dominant MNOs.[188] Safaricom's dominance is partly due to the lack of interoperability within the industry.[189] This section has argued that interoperability poses both a legal and a regulatory challenge that merits an examination. The CCK has the mandate to regulate interconnection and interoperability of mobile payments. This is because mobile payments fall outside the ambit of banking services, which creates uncertainty in its regulation. These transactions could also fall within the jurisdiction of the CCK, as provided under Section 83C of the Kenya Information and Communications Act 2013.[190]

## 5.5 Enforcement of the appropriate mobile payments regulation

Enforcement is essential once the regulators have established their objectives.[191] Those objectives are then advanced through accomplishing the five tasks Julia Black sets out: detecting undesirable or non-compliant behaviour; responding to that behaviour by developing tools and strategies; enforcing those tools and strategies on the ground; assessing their success or failure, through an impact analysis and modifying approaches accordingly.[192] Formulation of a regulatory framework involves three stages: the enactment of enabling legislation; the creation of regulatory administrations and rules and imposing the rules on persons or institutions sought to be influenced and controlled; and enforcement.[193] Incisive enforcement can resolve design defects in regulatory mechanisms, and ill-enforcement can undermine well-designed regulations.[194] Proper enforcement of legislation to regulate mobile payment systems should require using discretion in applying the provisions to the legislation and being selective in order to solve the practical problems. However, failure to identify and deal with the breaches of the rules and regulations through excessive discretion can reduce the legislation and regulatory framework to a paper exercise.[195] While perfect compliance is neither likely[196] nor practical, bringing the matter of a violation to prosecution[197] involves huge expenses, so imposing fines is the most reasonable approach to violations; nonetheless, enforcement must not be so lax as to be useless. Therefore, the proper enforcement of any appropriate regulatory approach for mobile payments depends on the successful harmonisation of the regulatory functions and powers of the two regulatory authorities.

### 5.5.1 *Harmonization between the CBK and the CCK*

The development of mobile payment and mobile financial services in general, and its rapid acceptance, has led to the creation of various financial products which employ the mobile phone as a means to reach potential customers.[198] However, this success, as I reiterate, should be managed so as to avoid catastrophic results as a consequence of its overreliance. As the previous chapters have examined, the regulatory framework for mobile payments in Kenya is set to become a relative structure based on the notion of state-led economic development and the need to increase economic growth through financial inclusion. While the application of greater market discipline in financial regulation in the future is highly likely, for the time being, it seems that the policy of government-led mobile payment development indicates that CBK, as the main regulatory authority, will take an active role in both the promotion and regulation of mobile money and payments. In ensuring the legitimacy of such broad regulation, the CBK's functions and objectives should be clarified and agreed among all participants.

Harmonisation between the central bank and other regulatory authorities with interests in mobile payments is not new and has been recognised as vital.[199] This study intentionally focuses on the harmonisation between the CBK and the CCK as the relationships with other authorities such as the Competition Authority of Kenya, for instance, would warrant an extensive exploration, which is beyond the scope of this study.

Harmonisation would acknowledge the CCK as the telecoms regulatory authority to which the MNOs are accountable. Mobile financial services or the use of mobile-based technology to offer financial services will continue to develop and evolve.[200] This harmonisation would involve the sharing of information based on regular liaison.

The harmonisation of functions would involve the exchange of information and expertise, policy coordination and mutual assistance to facilitate and make forward-looking arrangements for further development.[201] The areas of coordination would have to be around policies for mobile money. These policies would include the mechanisms on approval and monitoring and broader issues such as the development of mobile money. At present, policies on mobile money have not been assigned by either the CBK or the CCK, and as such, the CBK has to keep abreast with the policy development of the CCK. Since the CCK licenses the MNOs, policy harmonisation would become all the more vital since the CCK approves the entry of new MNOs. Since Kenya's policy has not explicitly stated whether non-financial institutions can enter the market and develop mobile money schemes, coordination is required to create a level playing field among MNOs that provide mobile payments.

Presently, there is a lack of coordination between the CCK and the CBK. However, instituting a memorandum of understanding between the two regulatory authorities would clarify the regulatory challenges, such as regulatory overlaps, as a result of this new integrated environment. The development of retail payments systems, particularly mobile payments, is complicated and has consequently highlighted the inefficiencies of the current regulatory framework for adopting new payments systems. These inefficiencies are, however, not unique to Kenya, as even developed countries are struggling to grapple with the adoption of mobile payments.[202]

These challenges have highlighted the fact that the laws of payment systems are complex and confusing and cause uncertainties.[203] This is due to, as reiterated, the hybrid nature of mobile payments systems. Regulators therefore need to consider the fact that mobile payments and mobile financial services are still developing and the laws relating to them cannot be comprehensive and have to be enhanced with time, as was stated in SIPS, that although sound legal underpinnings are very important, absolute legal certainty is seldom achievable.[204] However, this should not deter authorities from seeking to establish a sound legal basis for payment systems, but rather a more clear understanding of the laws and their applicability to mobile payments should be established. Therefore, harmonisation between the CBK and the CCK should be encouraged.

The developments of retail payments in general is complicated, and it is even more complicated for mobile payments in developing countries, such as Kenya, where most consumers have been reliant on cash.[205] The complication arises from the fact that MNOs and the users of retail payments have the impression that laws of payment systems are complex and confusing, causing uncertainties due to their hybrid nature.[206]

In order to provide clarity to all parties affected by the development of mobile payments, the substance of the legislation, enshrined in the National Payments Systems Act, has to be understood by all parties in the mobile payments ecosystem. All parties have to appreciate that since the framework of mobile payments is still developing, the laws relating to them cannot be comprehensive and have to be enhanced with time. It has been stated in SIPS that although sound legal underpinnings are very important, absolute legal certainty is seldom achievable.[207]

Central banks and their involvement in retail payments cannot be underestimated.[208] Financial stability relies on the efficiency and stability of a country's retail payment systems.[209] In recent years, many countries have been more explicit in their efforts to include payment systems as part of their agenda for the overall development of the financial market. Other countries, for instance, have established specific boards within their regulatory framework to deal with payments.[210] Canada, for example, has explicitly enacted specific legislation on payment systems.[211]

Many developed countries have also made efforts to establish cooperation among relevant government authorities, which have interests in payment issues. Formal cooperation between government authorities has been established to ensure the smooth and continuing development of payment systems.[212] Kenya has followed suit and made the development of payment systems a priority. The recently enacted National Payment Systems Act has been amended to include objectives of the CBK in defining its responsibility to ensure the efficiency of payment systems. This has been seen as an effort by the CBK to ensure public confidence in the legal foundation built for payment systems.

It is important that the CBK continues to monitor the policy related to mobile payments, as mobile money schemes will continue to develop, and it must ensure that the regulatory framework on mobile payments considers all other mobile money schemes. The enhancement of mobile payments systems has been recognised as important for the whole development of payment systems, and the CBK's interest in ensuring the efficiency and development of retail payment instruments is not new.

In the CBK's role as the main regulatory authority, it has to ensure that cooperation exists among parties that have interests in mobile payments or mobile money schemes. This is to ensure the continuing development of all mobile money products. The Central Bank's objectives cannot be achieved if there is negligence in the roles and functions of other authorities affecting mobile payment issues.

The harmonisation between the CBK and CCK has to be formalised in order for it to be recognised by all parties concerned. Despite the fact that the CCK regulates the institution and the CBK the function, any new law should provide for clear separate powers and clarity on the roles and functions has to be established and understood by each regulatory authority. Therefore, the execution of a memorandum of understanding may promote harmonisation between the two regulators to enhance understanding. To ensure the continuing development of the regulatory framework as mobile payments progress, the roles and functions of the authorities involved have first to be defined. Further cooperation cannot be established if existing responsibilities are not first agreed upon.

Moreover, the execution of the MoUs will promote transparency, which assists MNOs and consumers in understanding the roles and functions of the authorities involved, which will also lead to a better understanding on the existing regulatory framework of mobile payments in Kenya. This transparency will enhance consumer confidence, which would lead to greater financial inclusion by having MoUs, which not only define the responsibilities of the authorities but also the agreement to review and to provide solutions in the event of disputes, which may fulfil the consumer protection objective.

The MoU should be seen as the first step taken by the CBK in ensuring a workable regulatory framework for mobile payments, thus enhancing the acceptance and development of mobile money schemes. This would also ensure and enhance the commitment between the CBK and the CCK in performing their complementary regulatory functions. It is unclear at present whether the proposal, National Payment System Act of 2011, provides the possibility of harmonisation of functions between the CBK and the CCK for mobile payments. Although CBK is the main regulator, the CCK's functions cannot entirely be removed. The current fragmented framework has not been practical.

### 5.5.2 Justification for regulatory harmonisation between the CBK and the CCK

The harmonisation between the CBK and the CCK should be encouraged to attain the policy objectives previously discussed. It is recommended that for retail payments, the common goals that central banks and sectoral regulatory authorities should have are to address the legal and regulatory impediments to market development and innovation, to foster competitive market conditions and behaviours and to support the development of effective standards and infrastructure arrangement.[213] This can be precipitated through different types of cooperation. Firstly through the cooperation between the CBK and the CCK and through the CBK and other non-regulatory authorities such as a Consumer Protection Agency, which should be in line with the public interest.

The cost to each party in the mobile payment system is a justification for the coordination of functions, since MNOs have large networks that involve a billing relationship with their customers. At the same time, traditional banking functions involve cash management risk controls as part of their core business.[214]

Information sharing is an important aspect of establishing an appropriate approach for regulating mobile payments. This would involve the information sharing between the CBK and the CCK in reporting of any misconduct or market changes. This would enhance knowledge of the mobile payments schemes or any other mobile financial services in operation. Such knowledge would enable effective regulation. Successful monitoring of the schemes would also depend on how comprehensively the regulatory authorities understand the structure of the scheme in operation – specifically, in a situation where there may be joint regulatory functions between the CBK and the CCK, such as in licensing, as effective implementation of regulatory functions under separate legislation, may only be achieved through information sharing.[215] The information shared should not be limited to specific information for the purpose of regulating and monitoring the mobile payments themselves, but rather should include information on the organisational structure of each authority (both the CBK and the CCK) through an established and enhanced arrangement such as an MoU. This is because institutional structures change over time. Furthermore, different types of information are needed based on the legal and regulatory regime and the specific objectives within which the authorities operate. For instance, the CCK's objectives are markedly different from those of the CBK.

Information sharing is important between CBK and CCK to enhance knowledge of the electronic money schemes in operation. Such knowledge would enable effective regulation and supervision of mobile payments. Successful monitoring of the schemes would also depend on how comprehensively the regulatory authorities understand the structure of the scheme in operation. Specifically, in a situation where there may be joint regulatory functions between the CBK and the CCK, effective implementation of regulatory functions under separate legislation may only be achieved through information sharing. Information shared among the authorities involved may not be limited to specific information for the purpose of regulating and monitoring retail payment products but also to information on the organisational structure of each authority. The procedure of information sharing among the authorities involved has to be established. Information sharing arrangements should be in compliance with the legal foundation.[216] Continuous enhancement of the arrangement is important because the structure of any of the authorities could be altered over time. There are several types of information needed in order to secure an effective regulatory framework for mobile payments, of whose objectives within which the authorities operate. Currently, the MNOs have the widest range of information on mobile money, which the CBK does not, and effective regulation has been hampered by a lack of information sharing.

Therefore, the CBK needs to ensure that it has the widest range of information on mobile payments. This is because the CBK as the main financial regulator would appreciate that all those involved in the sharing of information may have valuable insights or information. This information would need to be shared with MNOs and the CCK, whose main mandate is the operation of MNOs. The regulation of mobile payments in a multi-sector or often fragmented regulatory environment calls for a new overarching and all-encompassing regulatory framework. Coordination should thus be institutionalised where information is shared between the regulators.

## 5.6 Conclusion

In conclusion, the successful implementation of an appropriate regulatory framework needs legislation that carefully balances innovation, and financial stability, the protection of consumers and the integrity of the financial system.[217] Kenya is lauded as the bellwether of the development of mobile payments, and its eventual success provides an opportunity to serve as an adequate template for other developing countries attempting to adopt inclusive financial services. Mobile payments have brought into focus the re-examination of the importance of retail payments and their core role in each country's overall financial stability.[218] Since mobile payments regulation has developed differently in different jurisdictions, as a result of country specific factors,[219] the regulatory approaches may not effectively be replicated in other countries. Furthermore, each country adopting mobile payments, or any mobile financial services, may not yield the same success that Kenya has had, since all countries are at a different stage of development.

Furthermore, as has been demonstrated, national regulations may not always fit a global marketplace[220] as legal transplantation in legal drafting that is common place in developing countries would not be fit for purpose. However, the harmonisation of standards[221] for mobile payments, which are now globally being accepted, would encourage cross-border remittances to be safe and secure.[222] Simply importing another country's regulatory system without modification for the target country's regulatory culture or environment as well as infrastructure banking and legal structures, business practices, culture and needs could lead to a suboptimal system.[223]

Central Banks play an important role in the development of retail payment systems, especially in developing countries where their regulatory capacities may not always accommodate innovative services that post-date their current regulatory frameworks.[224] In recent years, many countries have been more explicit in their effort to include payment systems as part of their agendas. For the overall development of the financial market in Kenya, the involvement of mobile payments and its significance to the overall stability of the financial system has not been examined in the depth that it should be, partly because of its nascent nature and the regulatory environment that mobile payments have developed. Other developed countries[225] have made efforts to establish coordination among their regulatory authorities that oversee payment system issues where cooperation has been established to ensure the smooth and continuing development of payment systems, especially where non-banks are involved.

Kenya should therefore follow suit in making mobile payments a priority. The NPSA should be amended to include the objectives of the CBK in defining its responsibility in ensuring the efficiency of mobile payment systems. Through the establishment of the NPSA, the CBK has made efforts to ensure public confidence in the legal foundation built for payment systems despite its deficiencies. Therefore, it is necessary that the CBK should continue to monitor the policy related to mobile payments. The CBK is best placed in its role as the main regulatory authority to ensure that cooperation exists between the mobile payment stakeholders, the MNO, consumers and agents. This is so that the continuing development of the product is ensured and the CBKs objectives are achieved. This is specifically important as the current regulatory framework for mobile payment in Kenya unintentionally already provides a possible cross-regulatory function between two separate authorities under different laws. It is the formalisation of this cooperation between the CBK and the CCK that should be fostered in order to establish an appropriate regulatory framework for all the stakeholders concerned. The fragmentation of the regulatory mandates and laws, as discussed in Chapter 4, has proven challenging, as the separate powers do not offer clarity in their roles and functions under both the CBK and the CCK.

Therefore, the placement of the MoU may promote a better understanding of these two separate regulatory authorities to foster better understanding of their mandates. This would further continuing development of the regulatory framework of mobile payments and enhance the roles and functions that would offer clarification to consumers and reduce information asymmetries and increase public confidence in the mobile payment system and foster better adoption and increase financial inclusion. A MoU would establish a clear and well-defined regulatory framework for mobile payments. In order to augment the commitment between the CBK and CCK in performing their cross regulatory functions, the cooperation between the regulatory authorities may be established through legislation to replace the MoU. The CCK would have to consider the possibility of excluding its regulatory powers on mobile payments under the NPSA based on the CBK's current extensive regulatory provisions. Even though the KPCA provides wide powers to CCK, a fragmented regulatory framework may not be practical, especially for mobile payments which are still developing. For electronic money especially, which is still developing, a clear regulatory framework based on a single regulatory authority may be desirable.

Whether a risk-based approach is used, it is true that no established regulatory approach is fool proof or encompasses the most effective form. It is further true that each accommodates certain aspects of the regulated entity: risk-based for risk, and principle-based for standards setting that would guide how institutions act. It is extremely early to conclude whether the CBK has successfully implemented its regulatory oversight through the National Payment System Act 2011, which integrates the regulation of mobile payments.

In the long run, the most effective regulatory framework that will promote mobile payments should be guided by risk management, and safeguarding of funds, and it should be one that balances the needs to enhance stability and promote innovation. It should also incorporate policy objectives which should focus on consumer protection and the clear definition of stored value in order to lay an enabling regulatory framework for other innovative peer-to-peer payments systems, such as Bitcoin, which is slowly becoming prevalent in Kenya.[226] Regulation of mobile payments should be participatory and effective.[227]

Two theories of regulation of industry are widely held: positive theories of regulation and normative theories of regulation.[228] Positive theories of regulation examine why regulation occurs,[229] while normative theories of regulation are based on a theory of market failure.[230] Famed economist Stiglitz notes that regulation begins with a simple question: why is regulation needed and followed, and why do markets by themselves not suffice? Then, if there is to be government intervention, why does it take the form of regulations?[231] Some would see the need for regulation[232] as a response to market failure, others as the need to provide the groundwork for growth and consistency.

M-Pesa's success, as reiterated in the previous chapters, has shown that there needs to be an appropriate regulatory framework for mobile payments. In Kenya, mobile payments have been very successful, as discussed through the introduction of M-Pesa.[233] There is no doubt that there needs to be an appropriate regulatory framework for mobile payments based on the risks discussed in Chapter 3 and the challenges examined in Chapter 4. However, Kenya has chosen to develop its regulatory framework by solely entrusting the CBK with this task in regulating mobile payments. Since mobile payments are relatively new to the payments system, the challenge however is in enforcement and implementation. It is hence important to consider a number of regulatory theories to evaluate the normative basis of Kenya's approach in the regulation of mobile payments.

The Act is not fully operational; moreover, it remains to be seen whether the CBK has the committed intent to regulate, since the lacuna in the current regulatory framework has been the main catalyst for its proliferation.[234] It is also premature to consider whether upon the implementation of the Act by CBK, the industry would change accordingly. It is necessary therefore to consider the rationales and implications that the regulatory policies may have in view of the theories and themes around regulation of mobile payments and the expected outcomes and consequently the appropriate regulatory framework which this chapter discusses.

## Notes

1 Such as electronic payments and peer to peer payments such as Bitcoin. See Satoshi Nakamoto, 'Bitcoin: A Peer-to-Peer Electronic Cash System' (2008) 28 <http://bitcoin.org/bitcoin.pdf> accessed 26 September 2014.
2 Systemically important institution has been discussed in Chapter 3: The Mobile Payment Risks.
3 James E. Prieger, 'Regulation, Innovation, and the Introduction of New Telecommunications Services' (2002) 84 Review of Economics and Statistics Working Papers 00–8 <www.mitpressjournals.org/doi/pdf/10.1162/003465302760556512> accessed 26 September 2014.
4 Chapters 3 and 4 have discussed the post-financial inclusion regulatory challenges surrounding mobile payments systems.
5 Mondato, 'Mobile Payment Regulation' (2014) <http://mondato.com/about/expertise/mobile-payment-regulation/> accessed 26 September 2014.
6 See Chapter 1, Secondary Questions.
7 Literature following the GFC is extensive. See, John Raymond LaBrosse, Rodrigo Olivares-Caminal and Dalvinder Singh, *Financial Crisis Containment and government Guarantees* (Edward Elgar 2013); Steven L. Schwarcz, 'Understanding the Subprime Financial Crisis' (2009) 60 *S.C. L. REV.* 549, 561–62 (quoting Steven L. Schwarcz, 'Protecting Financial Markets: Lessons from the Subprime Mortgage Meltdown' (2008) 93 *MINN. L. REV.* 373, 406.
8 Stavros B. Thomadakis, 'What Makes Good Regulation?' (2007) IFAC Council Seminar <www.ifac.org/sites/default/files/downloads/30th_anniversary_Thomadakis_Pres_Nov_07.pdf> accessed 26 September 2014.
9 Samuel G. Hanson, Anil K. Kashyap and Jeremy C. Stein, 'A Macroprudential Approach to Financial Regulation' (2011) *Journal of Economic Perspectives* 169.
10 This is because there is an interconnectivity between the services they provide and the role they play in the payments system.
11 Robert Baldwin and Christopher McCrudden, *Regulation and Public Law* (London Oxford 1987); Jon.Stern, 'The Evaluation of Regulatory Agencies' in Robert Baldwin, Martin Cave and Martin Lodge (eds), *The Oxford Handbook of Regulation* (Oxford University Press 2010).
12 Better Regulation Task Force, *Principles of Good Regulation* (Weidenfeld and Nicolson 2003), where the principles were described as Proportionality, Accountability, Consistency, Transparency and Targeting.
13 Robert Baldwin, Martin Cave and Martin Lodge, *Understanding Regulation: Theory, Strategy, and Practice* (Oxford University Press 2011) 25.

14 The evaluation of good regulation is relative. Better Regulation Task Force (BRTF), Principles of Good Regulation (BRTF 2003)

15 Robert Baldwin, Martin Cave, and Martin Lodge. *Understanding Regulation: Theory, Strategy, and Practice* (Oxford University Press 2012) 410.

16 Jean J. Laffont, *Regulation and Development* (Cambridge University Press 2005); Antonio Estache and Liam Wren-Lewis, 'On the Theory of Evidence on Regulation of Network Industries in Developing Countries' (2010) *Oxford Handbook of Regulation* 376–378

17 Regulatory capacity as discussed in Chapter 4.

18 Chapter 4, Section: Lack of Political Will to Regulate. Anat R. Admati and Martin Hellwig, 'Good Banking Regulation Needs Clear Focus, Sensible Tools, and Political Will.' (2011) <www.gsb.stanford.edu/sites/default/files/research/documents/AdmatiHellwigGoodReg021412.pdf> accessed 26 September 2014.

19 Antonio Estache and Liam Wren-Lewis, 'Toward a Theory of Regulation for Developing Countries: Following Jean-Jacques Laffont's Lead' (2009) *Journal of Economic Literature* 729–770.

20 These principles are internationally recognised as the benchmark for 'good regulation', See, Andrew Crockett et al, 'The Fundamental Principles of Financial Regulation' (2009) *Geneva Reports on the World Economy* 11.

21 Better Regulation Task Force (BRTF), Principles of Good Regulation (BRTF 2003).

22 GSMA, 'Mobile Money' (2013) <www.gsma.com/mobilefordevelopment/wp-content/uploads/2013/02/MMU-Enabling-Regulatory-Solutions-di-Castri-2013.pdf> accessed 26 September 2014.

23 Committee on Payment and Settlement Systems and the World Bank 2007.

24 James Bilodeau, William Hoffman, Sjoerd Nikkelen, 'The Seven Pillars of Mobile Financial Services Development' (2012) Ch 1.1 <http://reports.weforum.org/mobile-financial-services-development-2011/content/pdf/01-part-1/wef-mfsd-chapter-1–1.pdf> accessed 26 September 2014.

25 This additionally finds that proportionate regulation should seek to find out why there is restricted access for people to financial services

26 James Bilodeau, William Hoffman, Sjoerd Nikkelen, 'The Seven Pillars of Mobile Financial Services Development' (2012)

27 Ibid.

28 See BIS, 'Report of the Working Group on Transparency and Accountability' (1998) <www.bis.org/publ/othp01b.pdf> accessed 26 September 2014.

29 Ibid. Information is the essence of a perfect market. See for example, Joseph Stiglitz and Amar Bhattacharya, 'Underpinning for a Stable and Equitable Global Financial System: From Old Debates to a New Paradigm' (1999) 11th Annual Bank Conference on Development Economics on 28–30 April 1999 <http://www0.gsb.columbia.edu/faculty/jstiglitz/download/2000_Underpinnings_of_a_Stable_and_Equitable.pdf> accessed 26 September 2014.

30 Gil Mehrez and Daniel Kaufmann, 'Transparency, Liberalization, and Financial Crisis' (2000) World Bank Policy Research Working Paper 2286 <http://papers.ssrn.com/sol3/papers.cfm?abstract_id=258976> accessed 26 September 2014.

31 Jin-Guk Kim, Tae-Yun Kim and Junsok Yang, 'Regulatory Transparency: What We Learned in Korea' (2010) <http://unpan1.un.org/intradoc/groups/public/documents/APCITY/UNPAN014177.pdf> accessed 26 September 2014.

32 Ibid.

33 Scott H. Jacobs, 'The Second Generation of Regulatory Reforms' (1999) *OECD Public Management Service* <www.imf.org/external/pubs/ft/seminar/1999/reforms/jacobs.htm> accessed 26 September 2014; OECD, 'First Workshop of the APEC-OECD Co-Operative Initiative' (2001) <www.oecd.org/Regreform/Regulatory-Policy/2506438.pdf> accessed 26 September 2014.

34 'First Workshop of the APEC-OECD Co-Operative Initiative' (2001) <www. oecd.org/Regreform/Regulatory-Policy/2506438.pdf> accessed 26 September 2014.
35 Ibid.
36 BIS, 'Report of the Working Group on Transparency and Accountability' (1998) 98 <www.bis.org/publ/othp01b.pdf> accessed 26 September 2014
37 Ibid.
38 Central Bank of Kenya, 'Call for Public Consultations on the National Payments Draft Regulations' (2013) <www.centralbank.go.ke/index.php/2012-09-21-11-44-41/public-consultations> accessed 26 September 2014.
39 Financial System Inquiry Final Report (Wallis Report), 'Philosophy of Financial Regulation' (1997) <www.fsi.treasury.gov.au/content/downloads/FinalReport/chapt05.doc> accessed 26 September 2014.
40 Christen, Robert Peck, and Richard Rosenberg. *The Rush to Regulate: Legal Frameworks for Microfinance*. Consultative group to assist the poorest (CGAP), 2000.
41 Ibid.
42 Stavros B. Thomadakis, 'What Makes Good Regulation' (2007) *IFAC Council Seminar* <www.ifac.org/sites/default/files/downloads/30th_anniversary_Thomadakis_Pres_Nov_07.pdf> accessed 26 September 2014.
43 Ibid.
44 Capital Markets Act Cap 485A.
45 Ibid.
46 United Nations Office on Drugs and Crime, 'United Nations Convention against Corruption' (2003) <www.unodc.org/documents/treaties/UNCAC/Publications/Convention/08-50026_E.pdf> accessed 26 September 2014, names transparency as one of the building blocks of anti-corruption policies
47 Karen Yeung, 'Government by Publicity Management: Sunlight or Spin?' (2005) *Public Law* 360.
48 Anat R. Admati and Paul Pfleiderer, 'Forcing Firms to Talk: Financial Disclosure Regulation and Externalities' (2000) 13 *Review of Financial Studies* 479.
49 Andrew Haynes and Deborah Sabalot, 'Butterworths Financial Services Law Guide (Butterworths 1997).
50 Dalvinder Singh, 'Enforcement Methods and Sanctions in Banking Regulation and Supervision' (2002) 4(4) *International and Comparative Corporate Law Journal* 307–343.
51 Martin Lodge and Lindsay Stirton, 'Accountability in the Regulatory State' in Robert Baldwin, Martin Cave, Martin Lodge (eds), *The Oxford Handbook of Regulation* (Oxford University Press 2010) 353.
52 Colin Scott, 'Accountability in the Regulatory State' (2000) 27(1) *Journal of Law and Society* 38–60 <http://acmd.com.bd/Presentation/Salehuddin,%20 2013,%20Transparency%20and%20accountability.pdf> accessed 26 September 2014.
53 Ibid.; Odhiambo-Mbai, 'Public Service Accountability and Governance in Kenya since Independence' (2003) 8(1) *African Journal of Political Science* 116.
54 Bruce L. Smith and D. C. Hague (eds), *The Dilemma of Accountability in Modern Government: Independence Versus Control* (Palgrave Macmillan 1971); E. L. Normanton, 'Public Accountability and Audit: A Reconnaissance' (1971) in Bruce L. Smith and D. C. Hague (eds), *The Dilemma of Accountability in Modern Government: Independence versus Control* (Macmillan, 1971).
55 Charles Goodhart, Philipp Hartmann, David T. Llewellyn, Liliana Rojas-Suarez and Steven Weisbrod, *Financial Regulation: Why, How and Where Now?* (Routledge 2013) 68.

56 Julia Black, 'Constitutionalizing Self-Regulation' (1996) 59 *Modern Law Review* 24.
57 Bronwen Morgan, and Karen Yeung. *An Introduction to Law and Regulation* (Cambridge University Press 2007) 228; P. Birkinshaw, 'Decision-Making and its Control in the Administrative Process – an Overview' in Patrick McAuslan and John McEldowney (eds), *Law, Legitimacy and the Constitution* (Sweet and Maxwell 1985) 152.
58 Claudio Borio, 'Implementing the Macroprudential Approach to Financial Regulation and Supervision' in Christopher J. Green, Eric J. Pentecost and Thomas G. Weyman-Jones (eds), The Financial Crisis and the Regulation of Finance (Edward Elgar 2009).
59 Rosa M. Lastra, 'Governance Structure for Financial Regulation and Supervision in Europe' (2003) 10 *Colum. J. Eur. L.* 49.
60 Georgina Lawrence, 'Who Regulates the Regulators?' (2002) CRI Occasional Paper 16 <http://teambath.bath.ac.uk/management/cri/pubpdf/Occasional_Papers/16_Lawrence.pdf> accessed 26 September 2014.
61 BRTF, 'Principles of Good Regulation' (2003) <http://webarchive.national-archives.gov.uk/20100407162704/http:/archive.cabinetoffice.gov.uk/brc/upload/assets/www.brc.gov.uk/principlesleaflet.pdf> accessed 26 September 2014.
62 Martin Lodge, *Accountability and Transparency in Regulation: Critiques, Doctrines and Instruments* (Edward Elgar 2004); Cosmo Graham, 'Is there a Crisis in Regulatory Accountability?' in Robert Baldwin, Colin Scott and Christopher Hood (eds), *A Reader on Regulation* (Oxford University Press 1998) 471.
63 See, Alberto Alesina, and Lawrence H. Summers, 'Central Bank Independence and Macroeconomic Performance: Some Comparative Evidence' (1993) *Journal of Money, Credit and Banking* 151–162.
64 Sylvester C. W. Eijffinger and Marco Hoeberichts, 'Central Bank Accountability and Transparency: Theory and Some Evidence' (2002) 5(1) *International Finance* 73–96.
65 Ibid.; see also, Cosmo Graham (1998) (n 62). See, Christopher Crowe and Ellen E. Meade, 'Central Bank Independence and Transparency: Evolution and Effectiveness' (2008) 24(4) *European Journal of Political Economy* 763–777.
66 Ibid. Cosmo Graham (1998) (n 62)
67 It was argued that transparency is essential to accountability. For example, legislature needs information about the policy actions and the rationale for the policy if it is to hold the central bank accountable. See L. H. Meyer, 'Comparative Central Banking and the Politics of Monetary Policy' (2001) Paper by Member of the Board of Governors of the United States Federal Reserve System at the National Association for Business Economics Seminar on Monetary Policy and the Markets in Washington DC on 21 May 2001 <www.bis.org/publ/qtrpdf/r_qt1403.pdf> accessed 26 September 2014; Laurence H. Meyer, 'Comparative Central Banking and the Politics of Monetary Policy' (2001) 36 *Business Economics* 43.
68 BRTF (2003) (n 61).
69 BIS (1998) (n 37).
70 Ibid (vii–viii.)
71 Ibid.
72 Deepti George, 'Australia's Regulatory Principles and the Licensing of Providers' (2014) IFMR Finance Foundation <www.ifmr.co.in/blog/2012/02/21/australia%E2%80%99s-regulatory-principles-and-the-licensing-of-providers/> accessed 26 September 2014.
73 Ibid.
74 Rosa M. Lastra, *Central Banking and Banking Regulation* (Financial Markets Group, London School of Economics and Political Science, 1996) 58–59.
75 See Chapter 4 Regulatory Gaps, 194, Overlaps195, Inconsistencies Arbitrage 197.

76  Since the development of mobile financial services hinges on technological advancements, it is quite difficult to predict how the market will develop, since this may simply be a new form of a technology boom waiting to burst. See Charles Poor Kindleberger *Manias* Panics *and Crashes* (6th ed.), Palgrave Macmillan 2010.

77  'Principles of Good Regulation' The National Archives, http://webarchive. nationalarchives.gov.uk/20100407162704/http:/archive.cabinetoffice.gov. uk/brc/upload/assets/www.brc.gov.uk/principlesleaflet.pdf accessed September 28, 2014.

78  ICT Regulation Toolkit, 'Why Regulate?' (2014) <www.ictregulationtoolkit.org/6.2> accessed 26 September 2014.

79  Ibid.

80  Steven L. Schwarcz, 'Ex Ante versus Ex Post Approaches to Financial Regulation – Friday January 28, 2011' (2011) 15 *Chap. L. Rev.* 257. The author states that regulation that targets bad conduct before it occurs is deemed ex ante, whereas regulation that targets bad conduct after it occurs is deemed ex post. Therefore, bad conduct will be deterred if targeted with appropriate regulation.

81  Ibid.

82  Central Bank of Nigeria, 'Regulatory Framework for Mobile Payments Services in Nigeria' <www.cenbank.org/OUT/CIRCULARS/BOD/2009/REGULA TORY%20FRAMEWORK%2 0%20FOR%20MOBILE%20PAYMENTS%20SER VICES%20IN%20NIGERIA.PDF> accessed 26 September 2014.

83  ICT Regulation Toolkit (2014) (n 78).

84  Mark E. Budnitz, 'Stored Value Cards and the Consumer: The Need for Regulation' (1996) 46 *American University Law Review* 1027.

85  Simon L. Lelieveldt, 'The Electronic Future of Cash: How to Regulate Electronic Cash – an Overview of Regulatory Issues and Strategies' (1997) 46 *American University Law Review* 1163 at 1166–1167; Brian Smith and Ramsey Wilson, 'The Electronic Future of Cash: How Best to Guide the Evolution of Electronic Currency Law' (1997) 46 *The American Undergraduate Law Review* 1105

86  Bert-Jaap Koops, 'Should ICT Regulation Be Technology-Neutral?' 9 in Bert-Jaap Koops, Miriam Lips, Corien Prins & Maurice Schellekens (eds), *Starting Points for ICT Regulation. Deconstructing Prevalent Policy One- Liners IT & Law Series* (TMC Asser Press 2006) 77.

87  Judith Rinearson, 'Regulation of Electronic Stored Value Payment Products Issued by Non-Banks under State "Money Transmitter" Licensing Laws' (2002) 58 *The Business Lawyer* 317, at 321.

88  Narendra Jadhav, 'Single versus Multiple Regulator' <www.drnarendrajadhav. info/drnjadhav_web_files/speeches/Single%20versus%20Multiple%20Regulator. pdf> accessed September 29, 2014

89  Ibid.

90  David T. Llewellyn, 'Institutional Structure of Financial Regulation and Supervision: The Basic Issues' (2006) <http://siteresources.worldbank.org/INTTOP CONF6/Resources/2057292–1162909660809/F2FlemmingLlewellyn.pdf> accessed 26 September 2014

91  'Financial Supervision in the New Millennium'. Speech by Mr Koh Yong Guan, Managing Director, MAS at the Millennium Law Conference <www.mas. gov.sg/news-and-publications/speeches-and-monetary-policy-statements/ speeches/2000/financial-supervision-in-the-new-millennium-10-apr-2000. aspx> accessed 29 September 2014.

92  'Mobile Money for the Unbanked' GSMA, New Regulatory Framework for e-Money Issuers in Kenya www.technologybanker.com/regulations-compliance/ new-regulatory-framework-for-e-money-issuers-in-kenya accessed 29 September 2014. David Llewellyn (2006) (n 90).

93 Maria J. Nieto, 'Reflections on the Regulatory Approach to E-Finance' (2001) BIS Paper No 7 <www.bis.org/publ/bppdf/bispap07j.pdf> accessed 26 September 2014.

94 Simone di Castri, 'A Conversation with Professor Njuguna Ndung'u, Governor of the Central Bank of Kenya, on the critical policy issues around mobile money' (2013) GSMA <www.gsma.com/mobilefordevelopment/a-conversation-with-professor-njuguna-ndungu-governor-of-the-central-bank-of-kenya-on-the-critical-policy-issues-around-mobile-money> accessed 26 September 2014.

95 Ibid.

96 Ibid.

97 Ibid.

98 Ibid.

99 Ibid.

100 Ibid.

101 Where the lack of specific regulation inherently provided an enabling environment as stated in Chapter 2, which would ultimately encourage increased domestic and foreign investments

102 Simone di Castri (2013) (n 94).

103 Strategies are needed in the regulation of various aspects of a country. Either through self-regulation, through state oversight or through delegation of third parties, such as public interest groups like consumer protection advocates. See Neil Gunningham, Peter N. Grabosky and Darren Sinclair, *Smart Regulation: Designing Environmental Policy*, vol 514 (Clarendon Press, 1998). See also Neil Gunningham and Darren Sinclair, *Designing Smart Regulation* (1998) <www.oecd.org/environment/outreach/33947759.pdf> accessed 26 September 2014.

104 Neil Gunningham, Peter N. Grabosky and Darren Sinclair, Smart Regulation: Designing Environmental Policy, vol 514 (Clarendon Press, 1998).

105 The expression 'regulatory capacity', or 'regulatory capability', is used in the analysis of institutional endowment in less developed economies. The World Bank Group and the continental Development Banks, as well as other development-related institutions, use the term 'regulatory capacity' in their projects.

106 Jean J. Laffont, 'Enforcement Regulation Development' (2003) 12(2) *Journal of African Economics* 193–211.

107 Robert Baldwin, Martin Cave and Martin Lodge, *Understanding Regulation* (1st edn, Oxford University Press 2012) 105.

108 Section 4 of the Central Bank Act CAP 488 1989

109 See Chapter 2, Section 2.5. Page 59.

110 See Chapter 2, Section 2.3., the Success of Mobile Payments.

111 Samuel G. Hanson, Anil K. Kashyap, and Jeremy C. Stein, 'A Macroprudential Approach to Financial Regulation' (2011) *Journal of Economic Perspectives* 3–28.

112 Julia Black, 'The Emergence of Risk Based Regulation and the New Public Risk Management in the United Kingdom' (2005) *Public Law* 512: Julia Black, 'Risk Based Regulation: Choices Practices and Lessons being Learnt (2010) <www.oecd-ilibrary.org/risk-and-regulatory-policy_5kmmx4x7ksnr.pdf;jsessionid=9i6cngkl507c3.x-oecd-live-02?contentType=%2fns%2fOECDBook%2c%2fns%2fStatisticalPublication%2c%2fns%2fBook&itemId=%2fcontent%2fbook%2f9789264082939- en&mimeType=application%2fpdf&containerItemId=%2fcontent%2fserial%2f19900481&accessItemIds> accessed 26 September 2014; Julia Black, 'Role of Risk in Regulatory Processes' in Robert Baldwin, Martin Cave, Martin Lodge (eds), *The Oxford Handbook of Regulation* (Oxford University Press 2010) 353.

113 Robert J. MacCoun, 'The Costs and Benefits of Letting Juries Punish Corporations: Comment on Viscusi' (2000) <http://scholarship.law.berkeley.edu/cgi/viewcontent.cgi?article=3096&context=facpubs> accessed 26 September 2014.

'Risk and the Limits of Governance: Exploring Varied Patterns <www.kcl.ac.uk/sspp/departments/geography/people/academic/rothstein/2013-Rothstein-Borraz-Huber.pdf>accessed 29 September 2014.

114 Henry Rothstein, Phil Irving, Terry Walden, and Roger Yearsley, 'The Risks of Risk-Based Regulation: Insights from the Environmental Policy Domain' (2006) 32(8) *Environment International* 1056–1065. Julia Black, 'The Emergence of Risk-based Regulation and the New Public Risk Management in the United Kingdom' (2005) *Public Law* 512–548.

115 LETR | Legal Education and Training Review, <http://letr.org.uk/the-report/chapter-3/the- changing-regulatory-landscape/index.html> accessed 29 September 2014.

116 Robert Baldwin and Julia Black, 'Really Responsive Regulation' (2008) 71 *The Modern Law Review*. The evidence is mixed regarding the culpabilities of risk-based regulation, as banks in Australia and Canada, whose regulators have well-developed systems of risk-based regulation, fared far better than those in other Western countries, suggesting that the causes of regulatory failure were more complex than are accounted for by the existence of a risk-based system of supervision

117 'Risk-based regulation' has a range of meanings. See Julia Black, *Rules and Regulators* (Oxford University Press 1997).

118 FATF, 'Guidance for a Risk-Based Approach: Prepaid Cards, Mobile Payments and Internet-Based Payment Services' (2013) <www.fatf-gafi.org/media/fatf/documents/recommendations/Guidance-RBA-NPPS.pdf> accessed 26 September 2014. Also see G20 Principle 8 on Proportionality: Build a policy and regulatory framework that is proportionate with the risks and benefits involved in such innovative products and services and is based on an understanding of the gaps and barriers in existing regulation.

119 Ibid.

120 Ibid.

121 Central Banking Events, 'AML & CFT: Implementing a Risk Based Framework' (2014) <http://events.centralbanking.com/windsor/static/how-to-implement-a-risk-based-framework-for-aml-and-cft> accessed 26 September 2014.

122 Maria C. Stephens, 'Promoting Responsible Financial Inclusion: a Risk-based Approach to Supporting Mobile Financial Services Expansion' (2011) 27 *Banking and Finance Law Review* 329.

123 Michael Power, 'Organized Uncertainty: Designing a World of Risk Management' (2008) <www.frbatlanta.org/documents/news/conferences/11consumer_banking_stephens.pdf> accessed 26 September 2014.

124 Julia Black, 'Role of Risk in Regulatory Processes' (2010) in Robert Baldwin, Martin Cave, Martin Lodge (eds), *The Oxford Handbook of Regulation* (Oxford University Press 2010) 303.

125 Henry Rothstein, Phil Irving, Terry Walden, and Roger Yearsley (2006) (n 125); Julia Black (2005) (n 123).

126 Julia Black, The development of risk based regulation in financial services just 'modelling through' page 156. Julia Black and Robert Baldwin, 'When Risk Based Regulation Aims Low: Approaches and Challenges' (2012) *Regulation & Governance* 2 is 2 [vol number?], 137–164.

127 Julia Black, 'Decentring Regulation: the Role of Regulation and Self-Regulation in a Post Regulatory World' (2001) 54 *Current Legal Problems* 103–146.

128 Robert Baldwin and Martin Cave, Understanding Regulation Theory Strategy and Practice (2nd edn, Oxford University Press 2012) 295.

129 Morgan and Yeung (2007) (n 58) 93.

130 Jeremy Okanjo, 'Chapter 3: Designing a Telecoms Regulatory Framework for Converged Mobile Financial Services in Kenya' (2014) <www.slideshare.net/JeremmyOkonjo/3-chapter-three-designing-a-telecoms-regulatory-framework-

for-converged-mobile-financial-services-in-kenya> accessed 26 September 2014. However, this is not always the result in establishing self-regulation. In the media industry in Kenya, for example, the media has been accused of 'lacking the will, intellectual leadership and capacity to address the diversity of legal, policy and regulatory challenges facing them. Their desultory handling of media laws and regulation is indicative of its lack of commitment to address critical issues facing the sector radically and speedily.' See Peter Oriare, Rosemary Okello-Orlale, Wilson Ugangu, 'The Media We Want: the Kenya media vulnerabilities study' (2008) <http://library.fes.de/pdf-files/bueros/kenia/07887.pdf> accessed 26 September 2014.

131 Such as the Committee on Energy, Communication and Information, and the Committee on Delegated Legislation, Section 34(1) of the Interpretations and General Provisions Act, Cap 2, Laws of Kenya.

132 The World Bank, 'Doing Business in Kenya 2012' (2012) <www.doingbusiness.org/~/media/GIAWB/Doing%20Business/Documents/Subnational-Reports/DB12-Sub-Kenya.pdf> accessed 26 September 2014. The burden of regulatory compliance for Kenyan companies is particularly heavy, for example, in tax compliance. Globally, Kenya stands at 166 in the ranking of 183 economies on the ease of paying taxes. On average, Kenyan firms make 41 tax payments a year, spend 393 hours a year filing, preparing and paying taxes and pay total taxes amounting to 33.1 per cent of profit.

133 Fran Quigley, 'Growing Political Will from the Grassroots: How Social Movement Principles Can Reverse the Dismal Legacy of Rule of Law Interventions' (2009) <http://papers.ssrn.com/sol3/papers.cfm?abstract_id=1748612> accessed 26 September 2014; Connie N. Houghton, 'Access to Justice and the Rule of law in Kenya' (2006) <www.kenyalaw.org/kl/index.php?id=1934> accessed 26 September 2014.

134 Currently, there are no telecoms regulations specific to mobile financial services. Aside from the provisions of Section 83C of the Kenya Information and Communications Act, which touch on electronic transactions, the CCK does not exercise a direct regulatory role.

135 Julia Black, 'Constitutionalising Self-Regulation' (2011) 59 *The Modern Law Review* 24.

136 Simona Rodriquez, 'Self-Regulation as a Regulatory Strategy: The Italian Legal Framework' (2007) <www.utrechtlawreview.org/index.php/ulr/article/download/URN%3ANBN%3ANL%3AUI%3A10–1–101070/51> accessed 26 September 2014.

137 A definition frequently used in financial services regulation by both regulators and the regulated.

138 Ayers and Braithwaite's 'enforced self-regulation' is an example as is Ogus's 'consensual self-regulation' (op cir n 7). An example in practice is the UK system of health and safety regulation.

139 See for example, Alan Page, 'Self-Regulation: The Constitutional Dimension' (1986) 49 *Modern Law Review* 141.

140 See, Market Discipline below. An example is Ogus's first model of competitive self-regulation, unconstrained market competition (in which a firm adopts standards of product quality in response to consumer demand and which may incorporate industry wide practices) and some forms of his second model, independent agency-assisted competition, in which an agency accredits or certifies the quality of the product and accreditation is sought by the firm for competitive purposes (e.g., kitemarks). Competition may also develop between accrediting regimes. Ogus, 7

141 Wolfgang Streeck and Philippe C. Schmitter, 'Community, Market, State and Associations? The Prospective Contribution of Interest Governance to Social Order' (1985) 1(2) *European Sociological Review* 119; Patrick Birkinshaw,

*Government by Moonlight: The Hybrid Parts of the State* (Routledge, 1990) 3; Cosmo Graham, 'Self-Regulation' in Genevra Richardson and Hazel Genn, *Administrative Law and Government Action* (Oxford University Press, 1995).
142 Simona Rodriquez (2007).
143 Such as the Bank of International Settlements' system for the regulation of risk exposure of international banking firms.
144 Such as the UKs health and safety laws.
145 Robert Baldwin and Christopher McCrudden, *Regulation and Public Law* (Weidenfeld and Nicholson 1987).
146 Ibid.
147 Julia Black, 'Which Arrow? Rule Type and Regulatory Policy' (1995) *Public Law* 94.
148 Ibid.
149 John Braithwaite, 'Enforced Self-regulation: A New Strategy for Corporate Crime Control' (1982) 80(7) *Michigan Law Review* 1466; Neil Gunningham and Joseph Rees, 'Industry Self-regulation: an Institutional Perspective' (2002) 19 *Law & Policy* 363; Virginia Haufler, *A Public Role for the Private Sector: Industry Self- regulation in a Global Economy* (Carnegie Endowment 2013).
150 Ibid. John Braithwaite, 'Enforced Self-regulation: A New Strategy for Corporate Crime Control' (1982) 80(7) *Michigan Law Review* 1466
151 Baldwin, Cave and Lodge (2011) (n 14) 106.
152 Regulatory strategies in general use, see Stephen G. Breyer, *Regulation and its Reform* (Harvard University Press 2009) 8; Neil Gunningham, Peter Grabosky and Darran Sinclair, *Smart Regulation: Designing Environmental Policy* (Oxford University Press 1998). Also see command and control alternatives, Robert Baldwin, Regulation after 'command and control' 65; Keith Hawkins, *The Human Face of Law: Essays in Honour of Donald Harris* (Clarendon Press 1997); Thinking made easy, 'Government as regulator of business' <http://ivy thesis.typepad.com/term_paper_topics/2009/06/government-as-regulator-of-business.html> accessed 26 September 2014.
153 Communications Commission of Kenya.
154 The CBK and the CCK both have licensing powers or are rather licensing authorities.
155 Ibid., at 51. Page 106.
156 Ibid.
157 Ibid., at page 111.
158 Terence Daintith, 'The Techniques of Government' in Jeffrey Jowell and Dawn Oliver, *The Changing Constitution* (3rd edn, Clarendon Press 1994).
159 Ibid.
160 Peter N. Grabosky, 'Regulation by Reward: On the Use of Incentives as Regulatory Instruments' (1995) 17 *Law & Policy* 257.
161 William J. Baumol, 'On Taxation and the Control of Externalities' (1972) *The American Economic Review* 307.
162 K. Hawkins and J. M. Thomas (eds), *Enforcing Regulation* (1st edn, Springer 1983) 32.
163 Jean-Jacques Laffont, and Jean Tirole, 'The Politics of Government Decision-making: A Theory of Regulatory Capture' (1991) *Quarterly Journal of Economics* 1089–1127.
164 Peter N. Grabosky (1995) (n 160).
165 Ibid.
166 Andrew Crockett (2009) (n 21)
167 Ibid.
168 Baldwin, Robert Baldwin, Martin Cave and Martin Lodge (2011) (n 14) 121.

169 Dalvinder Singh, 'Enforcement Methods and Sanctions in Banking Regulation and Supervision' (2002) 4(4) *International and Comparative Corporate Law Journal* 307–343.

170 Albert J. Reiss, 'Consequences of Compliance and Deterrence Models of Law Enforcement for the Exercise of Police Discretion' (1984) *Law and Contemporary Problems* 83–122.

171 Ian Ayres and John Braithwaite, *Responsive Regulation* (1st edn, Oxford University Press 1992).

172 Shakeb Afsah, Benoit Laplante, David Wheeler, 'Regulation in the Information Age' (1997) <http://siteresources.worldbank.org/NIPRINT/Resources/Regulation InTheInformationAge.pdf> accessed 26 September 2014.

173 Ibid at note 171.

174 Ibid at note 171.

175 Legal transplantation has previously been discussed in this chapter in Part II. The term 'legal transplant' was coined by scholar Alan Watson to indicate the moving of a rule or a system of law from one country to another; as maintained by Watson, transplantation is the most fertile source of legal development. Alan Watson, *Legal Transplants: An Approach to Comparative Law* (2nd edn, University of Georgia Press 1993).

176 Richard Whish and David Bailey, *Competition Law* (Oxford University Press 2012) Ch 23.

177 John Vickers, 'Abuse of Market Power' (2005) 115 *The Economic Journal* F244.

178 The Competition Law Act 2012 was recently enacted.

179 This may be subject to future research, as it provides a regulatory challenge in the mobile payment context that is worth exploring.

180 Competition Authority of Kenya was instituted in 2012, Competition Authority of Kenya, 'About Us' <www.cak.go.ke/> accessed 26 September 2014.

181 The physical and logical linking of telecommunication networks used by the same or different service licensees.

182 Section 2 of the Kenya Information and Communications (Interconnection and Provision of Fixed Links, Access and Facilities) Regulations, 2010. Where, for example, interconnection of mobile network operator infrastructure allows subscribers of Safaricom to call, text, and receive calls and texts from Airtel network subscribers.

183 Jeremy Okonjo, 'Convergence of Mobile and Financial Services Implications for Regulation of Mobile Telecoms in Kenya' (2014) <www.slideshare.net/ JeremmyOkonjo/convergence-of-mobile-and-financial-services-implications-for-regulation-of-mobile-telecoms> accessed 26 September 2014. Section 2 of the Kenya Information and Communications (Interconnection and Provision of Fixed Links, Access and Facilities) Regulations, 2010. For example, interoperability of Safaricom's and Airtel's mobile financial service platforms would allow subscribers of M-Pesa to send and receive money from ZAP, respectively.

184 Chukwudiebube Bede Opata, 'Looking Towards Europe: Regulation of Dominance in Nigerian Telecommunications' SSRN Journal.

185 John Buckley, Telecommunications Regulation (IET 2003).

186 Ivan Mortimer-Schutts, 'The Regulatory Implications of Mobile and Financial Services Convergence' (2007) in The Transformational Potential of M-Transactions: moving the debate forward (2007) The Policy Paper Series 6 <www.vodafone. com/content/dam/vodafone/about/public_policy/policy_papers/public_ policy_series_6.pdf> accessed 26 September 2014.

187 Bede C. Opata, 'Transplantation and Evolution of Legal Regulation of Interconnection Arrangements in the Nigerian Telecommunications Sector' (2011) <www. researchgate.net/publicliterature.PublicPublicationPromoRequestFulltext.

signup.html?publicationUid=256033593&ev=su_pub_req> accessed 26 September 2014. The author notes that this might be beneficial to sector incumbents at the onset of liberalisation, as they have all existing subscribers, but prohibitive of new entry.

188 William H. Melody, 'Interconnection: Cornerstone of Competition' in William Melody (ed), *Telecom Reform: Principles, Policies and Regulatory Practices* (Technical University of Denmark 1997) 441–450.

189 Communications Commission of Kenya, 'Annual report financial year 2010/11' (2012) <www.ca.go.ke/images//downloads/PUBLICATIONS/ANNUAL-REPORTS/Annual%20Report%20for%20the%20Financial%20Year%202010–2011.pdf> accessed 26 September 2014.

190 Section 83C of the Kenya Information and Communications Act gives the Communications Commission of Kenya the mandate to, *inter alia*, develop sound frameworks to minimise the incidence of forged electronic records and fraud in electronic commerce and other electronic transactions.

191 Joanna Gray and Jenny Hamilton, Implementing Financial Regulation: Theory and Practice (John Wiley & Sons Ltd 2006) 33.

192 Julia Black and Robert Baldwin (2008) (page 145).

193 Ibid.

194 Ibid.

195 Ibid.

196 Ibid.

197 Ibid.

198 As discussed, M-Kopo and M-Kesho.

199 Committee on Payments and Settlement Systems, 'Policy Issues for Central Banks in Retail Payments' (2003) 14–15 <www.bis.org/cpmi/publ/d52.pdf> accessed 26 September 2014.

200 Mugambi Mutegi, 'Equity Bank Goes for Special SIM Cards for Its Mobile Money Service' *The Business Daily* (2014) <www.businessdailyafrica.com/Corporate-News/Equity-to-issue-mobile-money-customers-with-special-SIM-cards/-/539550/2329906/-/f6qtws/-/index.html> accessed 26 September 2014.

201 Robert M. Axelrod, The Evolution of Cooperation (1st edn, Basic Books 2006).

202 The US Regulatory Landscape For Mobile Payments, Summary Report of Meeting between Mobile Payments Industry Workgroup and Federal and State Regulators on April 24, 2012 www.frbatlanta.org/documents/rprf/rprf_pubs/120730_wp.pdf accessed 29 September 2013.

203 See Board of Governors of the Federal Reserve System, 'Staff Study 175 – The Future of Retail Electronic Payments Systems: Industry Interviews and Analysis' (2002) <www.federalreserve.gov/pubs/staffstudies/2000-present/ss175.pdf> accessed 26 September 2014.

204 Core Principle I of SIPS available at, BIS, 'Core Principles for Systemically Important Payment Systems' (2001) <www.bis.org/cpmi/publ/d43.pdf> accessed 26 September 2014.

205 Kenya has acknowledged that innovations affect the development of payment systems. The development of payment instruments like mobile payments is considered important for financial inclusion.

206 Board of Governors of the Federal Reserve System (2002) (n 204).

207 See Paragraph 7.1.3 of the background discussion under Core Principle I of SIPS; BIS (2001) (n 205).

208 Ibid.

209 BIS, 'Policy Issues for Central Banks in Retail Payments' (2003) 11 <www.bis.org/cpmi/publ/d52.pdf> accessed 26 September 2014.

210 Australia, for instance, established a payment systems board specifically to accommodate issues related to payment systems and their development. The Payment Systems Board's responsibilities and powers are wide and cover four separate pieces of legislation. These are the Reserve Bank of Australia Act 1959, the Payment Systems (Regulations) Act 1998, the Payment Systems and Netting Act 1998 and the Cheques Act 1986. See Reserve Bank of Australia, 'Payments Policy – Payment Systems Board' <www.rba.gov.au/payments-system/policy-framework/psb-board.html> accessed 26 September 2014. See The Parliament of the Commonwealth of Australia House of Representatives, 'Explanatory Memorandum of the Payment Systems (Regulations) Bill 1998' <www.comlaw.gov.au/GenericErrorPage.aspx?aspxerrorpath=/Details/C2011B00065/b9c1b5a3-6253-401c-859a-59c67990917f> accessed 26 September 2014.

211 As early as 1996, Canada enacted the Payment Clearing and Settlement Act to give the Bank of Canada responsibility for the oversight of payments and other clearing and settlement systems for the purpose of controlling systemic risk. For example, one of the powers of the Bank of Canada under the Act is to designate payment systems that have the potential to create systemic risk. These payment systems, which are designated, will be regulated on a continuing basis. See Bank of Canada, 'Oversight of Payments and Other Clearing and Settlement Systems' <http://news.gc.ca/web/article-en.do?nid=601299> accessed 26 September 2014.

212 Ibid. For example, in Canada, to avoid and to minimise duplication between the Bank of Canada, which has responsibilities under the Payment and Clearing Settlement Act, and the Minister of Finance, who has functions under the Canadian Payments Act, a statutory body called the Payment Advisory Committee was formed.

213 International Remittances: Policy Issues from a Central Bank <http://siteresources.worldbank.org/Extpaymentremmittance/Resources/FRBJackWalton.pdf> accessed 29 September 2014).

214 Marc Bourreau and Marianne Verdier, 'Cooperation for Innovation in Payment Systems: the Case of Mobile Payments' (2010) Communications & Stratagies <www.thefreelibrary.com/Cooperation+for+innovation+in+payment+systems%3a+the+case+of+mobile . . . . -a0239090194> accessed 26 September 2014.

215 See BIS, 'Framework for Supervisory Information Sharing Paper' (1999) <www.bis.org/publ/bcbs47c5.pdf> accessed 26 September 2014.

216 Ibid.

217 Ibid.

218 BIS (2003) (n 202) 11.

219 See 'Chapter 2: On an Elaborate Discussion on the Enabling Environment of Mobile Payments in Kenya'; Ignacio Mas and Dan Radcliffe, 'Mobile Payments go Viral: M-PESA in Kenya' (2010) <http://siteresources.worldbank.org/AFRICAEXT/Resources/258643-1271798012256/M-PESA_Kenya.pdf> accessed 26 September 2014. These factors include existing regulations and constitutional frameworks, market competition and segmentation, political climate and stability and international obligations.

220 Each country has a different regulatory culture, and different countries may have different developmental goals that may not necessarily reflect the need for regulation or similar regulation.

221 IAIS, 'Core Principles for Effective Banking Supervision' (2011) <www.iaisweb.org/index.cfm?pageID=39> accessed 26 September 2014.

222 Which is also a phrase from the Better Regulation Task Force UK 2005.

223 Robert H. Keppler, 'Transforming Payment Systems: The Building Blocks and the World Bank's Role' (1999) World Bank/Federal Reserve of New York

(FRBNY) Seminar 13–16 April 1999; Fernando Montes- Negret and Robert Keppler, 'Project Design for Payment Systems' (1995) FPD Note No. 37
<http://info.worldbank.org/etools/docs/library/155862/paymentsys
tems2003/pdf/Montes_Keppler.pdf> accessed 26 September 2014.

224  www.wantinews.com/news-8162076-Central-Bank:-the-overall-stability-of-the-
financial-system-has-accumulated-some-industries-risk.htm accessed 29 September 2014.

225  Countries such as Tanzania, Uganda Malawi and South American countries.

226  BitPesa, 'Send Money to Kenya Cheaper and Faster with BitPesa, it's Easy'
(2014) <www.bitpesa.co/> accessed 26 September 2014.

227  Zorayda R. B. Andam and Christian G. P. Castillo, 'Regulating Communications
in a Converging Environment: Technology, Markets and Dilemmas (2004) 79
*Philippine Law Journal* 392.

228  Robert W. Hahn, 'Theories of Regulation and Deregulation: A Critical Appraisal'
(2006) accessed 26 September 2014; Public Utility Research Center, 'Theories
of Regulation' (2011) accessed 26 September 2014; Joseph E. Stiglitz, 'Government Failure vs Market Failure: Principles of Regulation' (2009) 2<http://
academiccommons.columbia.edu/download/fedora_content/download/
ac:126998/CONTENT/JES.Govt.Failure.Mkt.Failure.pdf> accessed 26 September 2014; Johan den Hertog, 'General Theories of Regulation' (1999)
<http://goo.gl/8QjYD> accessed 26 September 2014.

229  Theories of Regulation <http://regulationbodyofknowledge.org/general-
concepts/theories-of- regulation/> accessed 29 September 2014. Public Utility
Research Center (2011) 9; Johan den Hertog (1999) 9.

230  Ibid.

231  Joseph E. Stiglitz, 'Government Failure vs Market Failure: Principles of Regulation' (2009) 2<http://academiccommons.columbia.edu/download/fedora_
content/download/ac:126998/CONTENT/JES.Govt.Failure.Mkt.Failure.
pdf> accessed 26 September 2014.

232  Regulation can be taken to mean the employment of legal instruments for the implementation of social- economic policy objectives. See Johan den Hertog (1999) 9.

233  See Chapter 2, Section 2.5, Page 59. Joy Malala, ''Consumer Protection for
Mobile Payments in Kenya: An Examination of the Fragmented Legislation
and the Complexities It Presents for Mobile Payments' (2014) Kenya Bankers
Association, Centre for Research on Financial Markets and Policy Working
Paper Series No 7 <www.kba.co.ke/workingpaperseries/img/pdf/Working%20
Paper%20WPS-07–13.pdf> accessed 3 September 2014.

234  See Chapter 2, Section 2.3, the Success of Mobile Payments, Page 38.

# Bibliography

Admati, Anat R. and Martin Hellwig, 'Good Banking Regulation Needs Clear Focus,
Sensible Tools and Political Will.' (2011) <www.gsb.stanford.edu/sites/default/
files/research/documents/AdmatiHellwigGoodReg021412.pdf> accessed 26 September 2014.

Admati, Anat R. and Paul Pfleiderer, 'Forcing Firms to Talk: Financial Disclosure
Regulation and Externalities' (2000) 13 *Review of Financial Studies* 479.

Afsah, Shakeb, Benoit Laplante, David Wheeler, 'Regulation in the Information Age'
(1997) <http://siteresources.worldbank.org/NIPRINT/Resources/Regulation
InTheInformationAge.pdf> accessed 26 September 2014.

Alesina, Alberto, and Lawrence H. Summers, 'Central Bank Independence and Macroeconomic Performance: Some Comparative Evidence' (1993) *Journal of Money,
Credit and Banking* 151–162.

Andam, Zorayda R. B. and Castillo, Christian G. P., 'Regulating Communications in a Converging Environment: Technology, Markets and Dilemmas (2004) 79 *Philippine Law Journal* 392.

Axelrod, Robert M., *The Evolution of Cooperation* (1st edn, Basic Books 2006).

Baldwin, Robert and Christopher McCrudden, *Regulation and Public Law* (Weidenfeld an Julia Black, 'Which Arrow? Rule Type and Regulatory Policy' (1995) *Public Law*.

Baldwin, Robert and Martin Cave, *Understanding Regulation Theory Strategy and Practice* (2nd edn, Oxford University Press 2012).

Baldwin, Robert Baldwin, Martin Cave and Martin Lodge (2011) (n 14)

Baldwin, Robert, Martin Cave and Martin Lodge, *Understanding Regulation* (1st edn, Oxford University Press 2012) 105.

Baldwin, Robert, Martin Cave, and Martin Lodge. *Understanding Regulation: Theory, Strategy, and Practice* (Oxford University Press 2012) 410.

Bank of Canada, 'Oversight of Payments and Other Clearing and Settlement Systems' <http://news.gc.ca/web/article-en.do?nid=601299> accessed 26 September 2014.

Baumol, William J., 'On Taxation and the Control of Externalities' (1972) *The American Economic Review* 307.

BetterRegulationTaskForce(BRTF),*PrinciplesofGoodRegulation*(BRTF2003).GSMA, 'Mobile Money' (2013) <www.gsma.com/mobilefordevelopment/wp-content/uploads/2013/02/MMU-Enabling-Regulatory-Solutions-di-Castri-2013.pdf> accessed 26 September 2014.

Bilodeau, James, William Hoffman, Sjoerd Nikkelen, 'The Seven Pillars of Mobile Financial Services Development' (2012) Ch 1.1 <http://reports.weforum.org/mobile-financial-services-development-2011/content/pdf/01-part-1/wef-mfsd-chapter-1–1.pdf> accessed 26 September 2014.

Bilodeau, James, William Hoffman, Sjoerd Nikkelen, 'The Seven Pillars of Mobile Financial Services Development' (2012)

Birkinshaw, Patrick, *Government by Moonlight: The Hybrid Parts of the Stare* (Routledge, 1990) 3

Graham, Cosmo, 'Self-Regulation' in Genevra Richardson and Hazel Genn, *Administrative Law and Government Action* (Oxford University Press, 1995).

Birkinshaw, P., 'Decision-Making and Its Control in the Administrative Process – an Overview' in Patrick McAuslan and John McEldowney (eds), *Law, Legitimacy and the Constitution* (Sweet and Maxwell 1985) 152.

BIS, 'Framework for Supervisory Information Sharing Paper' (1999) <www.bis.org/publ/bcbs47c5.pdf> accessed 26 September 2014.

BIS, 'Policy Issues for Central Banks in Retail Payments' (2003) <www.bis.org/cpmi/publ/d52.pdf> accessed 26 September 2014.

BIS, 'Report of the Working Group on Transparency and Accountability' (1998) <www.bis.org/publ/othp01b.pdf> accessed 26 September 2014.

BIS, 'Report of the Working Group on Transparency and Accountability' (1998) 98 <www.bis.org/publ/othp01b.pdf> accessed 26 September 2014.

BitPesa, 'Send Money to Kenya Cheaper and Faster with BitPesa, It's Easy' (2014) <www.bitpesa.co/> accessed 26 September 2014.

Black, Julia and Robert Baldwin, 'When Risk Based Regulation Aims Low: Approaches and Challenges' (2012) *Regulation & Governance* 2 is 2 vol number?], 137–164.

Black, Julia, 'Constitutionalizing Self-Regulation' (1996) 59 *Modern Law Review 24.*

Black, Julia, 'Decentring Regulation: the Role of Regulation and Self-Regulation in a Post Regulatory World' (2001) 54 *Current Legal Problems* 103–146.

Black, Julia, 'Risk Based Regulation: Choices Practices and Lessons Being Learnt (2010) <www.oecd-ilibrary.org/risk-andregulatoypolicy_5kmmx4x7ksnr.pdf;jsessionid=9i6 cngkl507c3.x-oecd-live-02?contentType=%2fns%2fOECDBook%2c%2fns %2fStatisticalPublication%2c%2fns%2fBook&itemId=%2fcontent%2fbook %2f9789264082939- en&mimeType=application%2fpdf&containerItemId=%2fco ntent%2fserial%2f19900481&accessItemIds> accessed 26 September 2014

Black, Julia, 'Role of Risk in Regulatory Processes' (2010) in Robert Baldwin, Martin Cave, Martin Lodge (eds), *The Oxford Handbook of Regulation* (Oxford University Press 2010) 303.

Black, Julia, 'Role of Risk in Regulatory Processes' in Robert Baldwin, Martin Cave, Martin Lodge (eds), *The Oxford Handbook of Regulation* (Oxford University Press 2010) 353.

Black, Julia, 'The Emergence of Risk-based Regulation and the New Public Risk Management in the United Kingdom' (2005) *Public Law* 512–548.

Black, Julia, *Rules and Regulators* (Oxford University Press 1997). FATF, 'Guidance for a Risk-Based Approach: Prepaid Cards, Mobile Payments and Internet-Based Payment Services' (2013) <www.fatf-gafi.org/media/fatf/documents/recommen dations/Guidance-RBA-NPPS.pdf> accessed 26 September 2014.

Black, Julia., 'Constitutionalising Self-Regulation' (2011) 59 *The Modern Law Review* 24.

Board of Governors of the Federal Reserve System, 'Staff Study 175 – The Future of Retail Electronic Payments Systems: Industry Interviews and Analysis' (2002) <www. federalreserve.gov/pubs/staffstudies/2000-present/ss175.pdf> accessed 26 September 2014.

Borio, Claudio, 'Implementing the Macroprudential Approach to Financial Regulation and Supervision' in Christopher J. Green, Eric J. Pentecost and Thomas G. Weyman-Jones (eds), *The Financial Crisis and the Regulation of Finance* (Edward Elgar 2009).

Bourreau, Marc and Marianne Verdier, 'Cooperation for Innovation in Payment Systems: the Case of Mobile Payments' (2010) Communications & Stratagies<www. thefreelibrary.com/Cooperation+for+innovation+in+payment+systems%3a+the+ca se+o f+mobile. . . -a0239090194> accessed 26 September 2014.

Braithwaite, John, 'Enforced Self-regulation: A New Strategy for Corporate Crime Control' (1982) 80(7) *Michigan Law Review* 1466.

Braithwaite, John, 'Enforced Self-regulation: A New Strategy for Corporate Crime Control' (1982) 80(7) *Michigan Law review* 1466d Nicholson 1987.

BRTF, 'Principles of Good Regulation' (2003) <http://webarchive.nationalarchives. gov.uk/20100407162704/http:/archive.cabinetoffice.gov.uk/brc/u     pload/ assets/www.brc.gov.uk/principlesleaflet.pdf> accessed 26 September 2014.

Budnitz, Mark E., 'Stored Value Cards and the Consumer: The Need for Regulation' (1996) 46 *American University Law Review* 1027.

Castri, Simone di, 'A Conversation with Professor Njuguna Ndung'u, Governor of the Central Bank of Kenya, on the Critical Policy Issues Around Mobile Money' (2013)

Central Bank of Kenya, 'Call for Public Consultations on the National Payments Draft Regulations' (2013) <www.centralbank.go.ke/index.php/2012-09-21-11-44-41/ public-consultations> accessed 26 September 2014.

Central Bank of Nigeria, 'Regulatory Framework for Mobile Payments Services in Nigeria' <www.cenbank.org/OUT/CIRCULARS/BOD/2009/REGULATORY%20 FRAMEWORK%2    0%20FOR%20MOBILE%20PAYMENTS%20SERVICES%20 IN%20NIGERIA.PDF> accessed 26 September 2014.

Central Banking Events, 'AML & CFT: Implementing a Risk Based Framework' (2014) <http://events.centralbanking.com/windsor/static/how-to-implement-a-risk-based-framework-for-aml-and-cft> accessed 26 September 2014.

Christen, Robert Peck, and Richard Rosenberg. *The Rush to Regulate: Legal Frameworks for Microfinance*. Consultative group to assist the poorest (CGAP), 2000.

Committee on Energy, Communication and Information, and the Committee on Delegated Legislation, Section 34(1) of the Interpretations and General Provisions Act, Cap 2, Laws of Kenya.

Committee on Payments and Settlement Systems, 'Policy Issues for Central Banks in Retail Payments' (2003) 14–15 <www.bis.org/cpmi/publ/d52.pdf> accessed 26 September 2014.

Communications Commission of Kenya, 'Annual report financial year 2010/11' (2012) <www.ca.go.ke/images//downloads/PUBLICATIONS/ANNUALREPORTS/Annual%20Report%20for%20the%20Financial%20Year%202010–2011.pdf> accessed 26 September 2014.

Core Principle I of SIPS available at, BIS, 'Core Principles for Systemically Important Payment Systems' (2001) <www.bis.org/cpmi/publ/d43.pdf> accessed 26 September 2014.

Crockett, Andrew et al., 'The Fundamental Principles of Financial Regulation' (2009) *Geneva Reports on the World Economy* 11.

Daintith, Terence, 'The Techniques of Government' in Jeffrey Jowell and Dawn Oliver, *The Changing Constitution* (3rd edn, Clarendon Press 1994).

Eijffinger, Sylvester C. W. and Marco Hoeberichts, 'Central Bank Accountability and Transparency: Theory and Some Evidence' (2002) 5(1) *International Finance* 73–96. 'Independence and Transparency: Evolution and Effectiveness' (2008) 24(4) *European Journal of Political Economy* 763–777.

Estache, Antonio and Liam Wren-Lewis, 'Toward a Theory of Regulation for Developing Countries: Following Jean-Jacques Laffont's Lead' (2009) *Journal of Economic Literature* 729–770.

'Financial Supervision in the New Millennium'. Speech by Mr Koh Yong Guan, Managing Director, MAS at the Millennium Law Conference <www.mas.gov.sg/news-and-publications/speeches-and-monetary-policy-statements/speeches/2000/financial-supervision-in-the-new-millennium – 10-apr- 2000.aspx> accessed 29 September 2014.

Financial System Inquiry Final Report (Wallis Report), 'Philosophy of Financial Regulation' (1997) <www.fsi.treasury.gov.au/content/downloads/FinalReport/chapt05.doc> accessed 26 September 2014.

'First Workshop of the APEC-OECD Co-Operative Initiative' (2001) <www.oecd.org/Regreform/Regulatory-Policy/2506438.pdf> accessed 26 September 2014.

George, Deepti, 'Australia's Regulatory Principles and the Licensing of Providers' (2014).

Goodhart, Charles, Philipp Hartmann, David T. Llewellyn, Liliana Rojas-Suarez and Steven Weisbrod, *Financial Regulation: Why, How and Where Now?* (Routledge 2013) 68.

Grabosky, Peter N., 'Regulation by Reward: On the Use of Incentives as Regulatory Instruments' (1995) *17 Law & Policy* 257.

GSMA<www.gsma.com/mobilefordevelopment/a-conversation-with-professor-njuguna-ndungu-governor-of-the-central-bank-of-kenya-on-the-critical-policy-issues-around-mobile-money> accessed 26 September 2014.

Gunningham, Neil and Darren Sinclair, Designing Smart Regulation (1998) <http://www.oecd.org/env/outreach/33947759.pdf> accessed 26 September 2014.

Gunningham, Neil and Joseph Rees, 'Industry Self-Regulation: An Institutional Perspective' (2002) 19 *Law & Policy* 363.

Gunningham, Neil, Grabosky, Peter N. and Darren Sinclair, *Smart Regulation: Designing Environmental Policy*, vol 514 (Clarendon Press, 1998). See also Gunningham and Darren Sinclair, *Designing Smart Regulation*.

Gunningham, Neil, Peter N. Grabosky and Darren Sinclair, *Smart Regulation: Designing Environmental Policy*, vol 514 (Clarendon Press, 1998)

Hahn, Robert W., 'Theories of Regulation and Deregulation: A Critical Appraisal' (2006) accessed 26 September 2014; Public Utility Research Center, 'Theories of Regulation' (2011) accessed 26 September 2014.

Hanson, Samuel G., Anil K. Kashyap, and Jeremy C. Stein, 'A Macroprudential Approach to Financial Regulation' (2011) *Journal of Economic Perspectives* 3–28. Julia Black, 'The Emergence of Risk Based Regulation and the New Public Risk Management in the United Kingdom' (2005) *Public Law* 512.

Haufler, Virginia, *A Public Role for the Private Sector: Industry Self-Regulation in a Global Economy* (Carnegie Endowment 2013).

Hawkins, K. and Thomas, J. M. (eds), *Enforcing Regulation* (1st edn, Springer 1983) 32.

Haynes, Andrew and Deborah Sabalot, *Butterworths Financial Services Law Guide* (Butterworths 1997).

Hertog, Johan den, 'General Theories of Regulation' (1999) <http://goo.gl/8QjYD> accessed 26 September 2014.

Houghton, Connie N., 'Access to Justice and the Rule of law in Kenya' (2006) <www.kenyalaw.org/kl/index.php?id=1934> accessed 26 September 2014.

IAIS, 'Core Principles for Effective Banking Supervision' (2011)<www.iaisweb.org/index.cfm?pageID=39> accessed 26 September 2014.

ICT Regulation Toolkit, 'Why Regulate?' (2014) <www.ictregulationtoolkit.org/6.2> accessed 26 September 2014.

IFMR Finance Foundation <www.ifmr.co.in/blog/2012/02/21/australia%E2%80%99s-regulatory-principles- and-the-licensing-of-providers/> accessed 26 September 2014.

International Remittances: Policy Issues from a Central Bank <http://siteresources.worldbank.org/Extpaymentremmittance/Resources/FRBJackWalton.pdf> accessed 29 September 2014).

Jacobs, Scott H., 'The Second Generation of Regulatory Reforms' (1999) *OECD Public ManagementService* <www.imf.org/external/pubs/ft/seminar/1999/reforms/jacobs.htm> accessed 26 September 2014.

Jadhav, Narendra, 'Single Versus Multiple Regulator' <www.drnarendrajadhav.info/drnjadhav_web_files/speeches/Single%20versus%20Multiple%20 Regulator.pdf> accessed September 29, 2014.

John Buckley, Telecommunications Regulation (IET 2003).

Keppler, Robert H., 'Transforming Payment Systems: The Building Blocks and the World Bank's Role' (1999) World Bank/Federal Reserve of New York (FRBNY) Seminar 13–16 April 1999; Montes- Negret, Fernando and Robert Keppler, 'Project Design for Payment Systems' (1995) FPD Note No. 37 <http://info.worldbank.org/etools/docs/library/155862/paymentsystems2003/pdf/Montes_Keppler.pdf> accessed 26 September 2014.

Kim, Jin-Guk, Tae-Yun Kim and Junsok Yang, 'Regulatory Transparency: What We Learned in Korea' (2010) <http://unpan1.un.org/intradoc/groups/public/documents/APCITY/UNPAN 14177.pdf> accessed 26 September 2014.

Koops, Bert-Jaap, 'Should ICT Regulation Be Technology-Neutral?' in Bert-Jaap Koops, Miriam Lips, Corien Prins & Maurice Schellekens (eds), *Starting Points for ICT Regulation. Deconstructing Prevalent Policy One- Liners IT & Law Series* (TMC Asser Press 2006) 77.

Laffont, Jean J., 'Enforcement Regulation Development' (2003) 12(2) *Journal of African Economics* 193–211.

Laffont, Jean J., *Regulation and Development* (Cambridge University Press 2005); Estache, Antonio and Liam Wren-Lewis, 'On the Theory of Evidence on Regulation of Network Industries in Developing Countries' (2010) *Oxford Handbook of Regulation* 376–378.

Laffont, Jean-Jacques, and Jean Tirole, 'The Politics of Government Decision-making: A Theory of Regulatory Capture' (1991) *Quarterly Journal of Economics* 1089–1127.

Lastra, Rosa M., 'Governance Structure for Financial Regulation and Supervision in Europe' (2003) 10 *Colum. J. Eur. L.* 49.

Lastra, Rosa M., *Central Banking and Banking Regulation* (Financial Markets Group, London School of Economics and Political Science, 1996) 58–59.

Lawrence, Georgina, 'Who Regulates the Regulators?' (2002) CRI Occasional Paper 16 <http://teambath.bath.ac.uk/management/cri/pubpdf/Occasional_Papers/16_Lawrence.pdf> accessed 26 September 2014.

Lelieveldt, Simon L., 'The Electronic Future of Cash: How to Regulate Electronic Cash – an Overview of Regulatory Issues and Strategies' (1997) 46 *American University Law Review* 1163.

LETR | Legal Education and Training Review, <http://letr.org.uk/the-report/chapter-3/the- changing-regulatory-landscape/index.html> accessed 29 September 2014.

Llewellyn, David T., 'Institutional Structure of Financial Regulation and Supervision: The Basic Issues' (2006) <http://siteresources.worldbank.org/INTTOP CONF6/Resources/2057292–1162909660809/F2FlemmingLlewellyn.pdf> accessed 26 September 2014.

Lodge, Martin and Lindsay Stirton, 'Accountability in the Regulatory State' in Robert Baldwin, Martin Cave, Martin Lodge (eds), *The Oxford Handbook of Regulation* (Oxford University Press 2010) 353.

Lodge, Martin, *Accountability and Transparency in Regulation: Critiques, Doctrines and Instruments* (Edward Elgar 2004)

Graham, Cosmo, 'Is There a Crisis in Regulatory Accountability?' in Robert Baldwin, Colin Scott and Christopher Hood (eds), *A Reader on Regulation* (Oxford University Press 1998) 471.

MacCoun, Robert J., 'The Costs and Benefits of Letting Juries Punish Corporations: Comment on Viscusi' (2000) <http://scholarship.law.berkeley.edu/cgi/viewcontent.cgi?article=3096&context=facpubs> accessed 26 September 2014.

Malala, Joy, 'Consumer Protection for Mobile Payments in Kenya: An Examination of the Fragmented Legislation and the Complexities It Presents for Mobile Payments' (2014) Kenya Bankers Association, Centre for Research on Financial Markets and Policy Working Paper Series No <www.kba.co.ke/workingpaperseries/img/pdf/Working%20Paper%20WPS-07–13.pdf> accessed 3 September 2014

Mehrez, Gil and Daniel Kaufmann, 'Transparency, Liberalization, and Financial Crisis' (2000) World Bank Policy Research Working Paper 2286 <http://papers.ssrn.com/sol3/papers.cfm?abstract_id=258976> accessed 26 September 2014.

Melody, William H., 'Interconnection: Cornerstone of Competition' in William Melody (ed), *Telecom Reform: Principles, Policies and Regulatory Practices* (Technical University of Denmark 1997) 441–450.

'Mobile Money for the Unbanked' GSMA, New Regulatory Framework for e-Money Issuers in Kenya www.technologybanker.com/regulations-compliance/new-reg ulatory-framework-for-e-money-issuers-in-kenya accessed 29 September 2014. David Llewellyn (2006) (n 90).

Morgan, Bronwen and Karen Yeung. *An Introduction to Law and Regulation* (Cambridge University Press 2007) 228

Mortimer-Schutts, Ivan, 'The Regulatory Implications of Mobile and Financial Services Convergence' in *The Transformational Potential of M-Transactions: Moving the Debate Forward* (2007) The Policy Paper Series 6 <www.vodafone.com/content/dam/vodafone/about/public_policy/policy_papers/public_policy_series_6. pdf> accessed 26 September 2014.

Mutegi, Mugambi, 'Equity Bank Goes for Special SIM Cards for Its Mobile Money Service' *The Business Daily* (2014) <www.businessdailyafrica.com/Corporate-News/Equity-to-issue-mobile-money- customers-with-special-SIM-cards/-/539550/23 29906/-/f6qtws/-/index.html> accessed 26 September 2014.

Nieto, Maria J., 'Reflections on the Regulatory Approach to E-Finance' (2001) BIS Paper No 7 <www.bis.org/publ/bppdf/bispap07j.pdf> accessed 26 September 2014.

Odhiambo-Mbai, C. 'Public Service Accountability and Governance in Kenya since Independence' (2003) 8(1) *African Journal of Political Science* [page?].

OECD, 'First Workshop of the APEC-OECD Co-Operative Initiative' (2001)<www. oecd.org/Regreform/Regulatory-Policy/2506438.pdf> accessed 26 September 2014.

Okonjo, Jeremy, 'Convergence of Mobile and Financial Services Implications for Regulation of Mobile Telecoms in Kenya' (2014) <www.slideshare.net/Jerem myOkonjo/convergence-of-mobile-and- financial-services-implications-for-regula tion-of-mobile-telecoms> accessed 26 September 2014.

Opata, Bede C., 'Transplantation and Evolution of Legal Regulation of Interconnection Arrangements in the Nigerian Telecommunications Sector' (2011) <www. researchgate.net/publicliterature.PublicPublicationPromoRequestFulltext.signup. html?publicationUid=256033593&ev=su_pub_req> accessed 26 September 2014.

Opata, Chukwudiebube Bede, 'Looking Towards Europe: Regulation of Dominance in Nigerian Telecommunications' *SSRN Journal.*

Oriare, Peter, Rosemary Okello-Orlale, Wilson Ugangu, 'The Media We Want: The Kenya Media Vulnerabilities Study' (2008) <http://library.fes.de/pdf- files/bueros/kenia/07887.pdf> accessed 26 September 2014.

Page, Alan, 'Self-Regulation: The Constitutional Dimension' (1986) 49 *Modern Law Review* 141; Streeck, Wolfgang and Philippe C. Schmitter, 'Community, Market, State and Associations? The Prospective Contribution of Interest Governance to Social Order' (1985) 1(2) *European Sociological Review.*

The Parliament of the Commonwealth of Australia House of Representatives, 'Explanatory Memorandum of the Payment Systems (Regulations) Bill 1998' <www. comlaw.gov.au/GenericErrorPage.aspx?aspxerrorpath=/Details/C2011B00065/b9c1b5a3-6253-401c-859a-59c67990917f> accessed 26 September 2014.

Power, Michael, 'Organized Uncertainty: Designing a World of Risk Management' (2008) <www.frbatlanta.org/documents/news/conferences/11consumer_bank ing_stephens.pdf> accessed 26 September 2014.

'Principles of Good Regulation' The National Archives, <http://webarchive.nation alarchives.gov.uk/20100407162704/http:/archive.cabinetoffice.gov.uk/brc/ upload/assets/www.brc.gov.uk/principlesleaflet.pdf accessed September 28, 2014.

Quigley, Fran, 'Growing Political Will from the Grassroots: How Social Movement Principles Can Reverse the Dismal Legacy of Rule of Law Interventions' (2009) <http://papers.ssrn.com/sol3/papers.cfm?abstract_id=1748612> accessed 26 September 2014.

Reiss, Albert J., 'Consequences of Compliance and Deterrence Models of Law Enforcement of Richard Whish and David Bailey' in *Competition Law* (Oxford University Press 2012) Ch 23.

Reserve Bank of Australia, 'Payments Policy – Payment Systems Board' <www.rba. gov.au/payments-system/policy-framework/psb-board.html> accessed 26 September 2014.

Rinearson, Judith, 'Regulation of Electronic Stored Value Payment Products Issued by Non-Banks under State "Money Transmitter" Licensing Laws' (2002) 58 *The Business Lawyer* 317, at 321.

'RisE and the Limits of Governance: Exploring Varied Patterns <www.kcl.ac.uk/ sspp/departments/geography/people/academic/rothstein/2013-Rothstein-Borraz-Huber.pdf> accessed 29 September 2014.

Rodriquez, Simona, 'Self-Regulation as a Regulatory Strategy: The Italian Legal Framework' (2007) <www.utrechtlawreview.org/index.php/ulr/article/down load/URN%3ANBN%3ANL%3AUI% 3A10–1–101070/51> accessed 26 September 2014.

Rothstein, Henry, Phil Irving, Terry Walden, and Roger Yearsley, 'The Risks of Risk-Based Regulation: Insights from the Environmental Policy Domain' (2006) 32(8) *Environment International* 1056–1065.

Schwarcz, Steven L., 'Ex Ante versus Ex Post Approaches to Financial Regulation – Friday January 28, 2011' (2011) 15 *Chap. L. Rev.* 257.

Scott, Colin, 'Accountability in the Regulatory State' (2000) 27(1) *Journal of Law and Society* 38–60 <http://acmd.com.bd/Presentation/Salehuddin,%202013,%20 Transparency%20and%20accountability.pdf> accessed 26 September 2014.

Singh, Dalvinder, 'Enforcement Methods and Sanctions in Banking Regulation and Supervision' (2002) 4(4) *International and Comparative Corporate Law Journal* 307–343.

Singh, Dalvinder, 'Enforcement Methods and Sanctions in Banking Regulation and Supervision' (2002) 4(4) *International and Comparative Corporate Law Journal* 307–343. Ayres, Ian and John Braithwaite, *Responsive Regulation* (1st edn, Oxford University Press 1992).

Smith, Brian and Ramsey Wilson, 'The Electronic Future of Cash: How Best to Guide the Evolution of Electronic Currency Law' (1997) 46 *The American Undergraduate Law Review* 1105.

Smith, Bruce L. and D. C. Hague (eds), *The Dilemma of Accountability in Modern Government: Independence Versus Control* (Macmillan 1971); Normanton, E. L., 'Public Accountability and Audit: A Reconnaissance' (1971) in Bruce L. Smith and D. C. Hague (eds), *The Dilemma of Accountability in Modern Government: Independence versus Control* (Palgrave Macmillan, 1971).

Stephens, Maria C., 'Promoting Responsible Financial Inclusion: A Risk-Based Approach to Supporting Mobile Financial Services Expansion' (2011) 27 *Banking and Finance Law Review* 329.

Stiglitz, Joseph and Amar Bhattacharya, 'Underpinning for a Stable and Equitable Global Financial System: From Old Debates to a New Paradigm' (1999) 11th Annual Bank Conference on Development Economics on 28–30 April 1999 <http://www0.gsb.columbia.edu/faculty/jstiglitz/download/2000_Underpinnings_of_a_Stable_and_Eq uitable.pdf> accessed 26 September 2014.

Stiglitz, Joseph E, 'Government Failure vs Market Failure: Principles of Regulation' (2009) 2<http://academiccommons.columbia.edu/download/fedora_content/download/ac:126998/CONTEN T/JES.Govt.Failure.Mkt.Failure.pdf> accessed 26 September 2014

Stiglitz, Joseph E., 'Government Failure vs Market Failure: Principles of Regulation' (2009) <http://academiccommons.columbia.edu/download/fedora_content/download/ac:126998/CONTEN T/JES.Govt.Failure.Mkt.Failure.pdf> accessed 26 September 2014

Summary Report of Meeting between Mobile Payments Industry Workgroup and Federal and State Regulators on April 24, 2012 www.frbatlanta.org/documents/rprf/rprf_pubs/120730_wp.pdf accessed 29 September 2013.

Theories of Regulation <http://regulationbodyofknowledge.org/general-concepts/theories-of- regulation/> accessed 29 September 2014. Public Utility Research Center (2011) 9; Johan den Hertog (1999) 9.

Thomadakis, Stavros B., 'What Makes Good Regulation' (2007) IFAC Council Seminar <www.ifac.org/sites/default/files/downloads/30th_anniversary_Thomadakis_Pres_Nov_07.pdf> accessed 26 September 2014.

United Nations Office on Drugs and Crime, 'United Nations Convention against Corruption' (2003) <www.unodc.org/documents/treaties/UNCAC/Publications/Convention/08-50026_E.pdf> accessed 26 September 2014

Vickers, John, 'Abuse of Market Power' (2005) 115 *The Economic Journal* F244. or the Exercise Competition Authority of Kenya was instituted in 2012, Competition Authority of Kenya, 'About Us' <www.cak.go.ke/> accessed 26 September 2014.

Watson, Alan, *Legal Transplants: An Approach to Comparative Law* (2nd edn, University of Georgia Press 1993).

The World Bank, 'Doing Business in Kenya 2012' (2012) <www.doingbusiness.org/~/media/GIAWB/Doing%20Business/Documents/Subnational- Reports/DB12-Sub-Kenya.pdf> accessed 26 September 2014.

<www.wantinews.com/news-8162076-Central-Bank:-the-overall-stability-of-the-financial- system-has-accumulated-some-industries-risk.htm> accessed 29 September 2014.

Yeung, Karen, 'Government by Publicity Management: Sunlight or Spin?' (2005) *Public Law* 360.

# 6 Conclusion

## 6.1 Introduction

The motivation for the exploration of this study began in 2008, just at the advent of mobile money technology and the beginning of what has revolutionised not only the payment industry in Kenya but also the shift in the economic and financial development. This success developed with much admiration and applause, rightfully so, as the benefits that financially inclusive technology has and will continue to have has been heralded, not just in Kenya but also in many developing countries. The reach and possibilities that mobile payments and other mobile financial services have to offer are anticipated with great promise and hope. The ability for mobile payments to develop in spite of a regulatory framework demonstrates the success of and the need for non-bank participation in the primary provision of payment services.

This is because mobile payments have managed to bring Kenyans, despite the lack of institutional, regulatory capacities and advanced infrastructures, into international focus as the model example for financial inclusion that circumvents the global digital divide. Nevertheless, the more mobile money developed and began to entrench itself in the Kenyan society, a shift emerged, where regulators, pundits and critics alike began to examine the costs against the benefits of mobile payments. This debate continues and has not been within the scope of this study. What was evident, however, was the lack of focus on the post-financial inclusion issues which comprised the unique risks introduced by mobile payments – the regulatory challenges in dealing with financially inclusive services and the design of an appropriate regulatory framework that safeguards the payment systems and the financial system as a whole. What this study contributes is a foundational start to these themes: financial inclusion through innovative financial services and the emergent regulatory issues post-financial inclusion, the approach that the regulators took in balancing its objectives, while at the same time allowing a market-led environment for mobile financial services.

## 6.2 Chapter summaries

Chapter 2 explored the research question of why an examination of Kenya's mobile payments system, in particular, was important. It contextualised mobile payments in Kenya by offering a historical context for the introduction of M-Pesa into Kenya's national payments system. It showed the success of M-Pesa as a key driver for lifting people out of poverty through its inclusive capacity, and it also assessed the important placement in Kenya's retail payments market. It also showed that the Central Bank of Kenya had recognised the potential economic benefit of financial inclusion and, although it had initially not included it in its development agendas, by default, created an enabling environment for its advancement by not having a regulatory framework to begin with for payments systems.

This chapter also showed that an enabling environment is essential in scaling up financially inclusive financial products, especially in a developing country. These enabling factors were exclusively typical to Kenya and contributed to its success. It also highlighted the fact that while mobile payments initially started as a seed product, their success was in part due to the specific country profile discussed. Through this, emergent regulatory challenges post-financial inclusion arise such as ensuring the maintenance of financial stability from the introduction of new participants into the formal financial sphere. The immeasurable benefits of financial inclusion through mobile payments were explored, such as the efficacy of transactions, savings and investments through the various financial service products developed.

Chapter 3 addressed the research question 'what are the risks created by mobile payments to the financial system in Kenya and what are the specific risks to consumers as a result of a lack of an adequate regulatory framework?' This assessment was made in the context of financial inclusion, which despite its benefits, has major costs to any financial system. The newly financially included, the new risks created and the institutions that operate in these newly expanded markets as a result of mobile financial services were highlighted through a multi-layered analysis of the risks at each level of the mobile payment system. These risks, which were not initially assessed by regulators, show that, just as in the recent Global Financial Crisis, policy-makers endorsed marketing to subprime borrowers as a means of financial inclusion, and regulators cannot overlook the risks introduced through financial inclusion.

The extensive growth[1] of mobile payments in Kenya makes this imperative; with the unintended[2] benefit of increasing the public's involvement[3] in the formal financial system and by including savings accounts in the banks, consequently extending systemic risk exposure,[4] it has converted widely distributed consumer risk into a concentrated systemic risk.[5] These unique risks arise as a result of the unique design and placement of mobile payments where the involvement of non-bank institutions without the clarification necessary in the legal framework further spreads the risks. These uncertainties are sure to lead to incorrect perceptions of exposures to potential losses as a result of insufficient information or asymmetric information of the financially included.

The most vulnerable stakeholders are exposed to risks they may not recognise, either through perceived risks or risks to retail payments. Risks that affect consumers are not readily addressed, even in the form of guidelines that spell out the nature and types of risks involved.[6] It also established that as mobile financial services continue to develop and begin to offer services that offer credit, such as M-Kopo,[7] this over-extension of credit has the potential to affect the quality of the credit portfolio of banks and financial institutions and could instigate financial fragility and, consequently, instability. This position may be further aggravated by regulatory or governmental forbearance which has the potential to impair the credit culture amongst the newly included. The weak enforcement of prudential regulations by the regulators may be as a result of political pressure on the regulatory authorities.[8] This offered a justification for special regulatory oversight for mobile payments as Kenya continues to become a cashless society that relies on mobile payments, which have become the centre of the settlement process. It was also established that the stability of a financial system relies on the soundness of institutions, the stability of markets, the absence of turbulence[9] and minimal volatility and pointed out the difficulty of achieving these through individual private actions and unfettered market forces alone. In addition to the public sector's role in fostering financial stability as opposed to private collective action, making way for the private sector to achieve an optimum result on its own to take a proactive role is necessary to achieve the full private and social benefits of finance.

To create the required regulatory framework requires a discussion of the preconditions of a safe and sound payment system first, as such an assessment is paramount. This should occur either through the examination of macroprudential or microprudential requirements. Regulators need to have complementary policy objectives that strike a balance between strict KYC controls and lax regulation. Given the lack of compromise between financial inclusion and financial integrity, payment systems such as mobile payments have a significant role in enhancing systemic risk, as they have become a significant component of the national payment system of Kenya, and therefore have the potential to generate and transmit systemic disturbances to the financial sector.[10]

Chapter 4 also highlights the inadequacies of legal drafting in Kenya, which served as the main catalyst for the proliferation of mobile payments. It also highlighted the reluctance by regulators to correct gaps in the regulation due to a lack of industry understanding and weak application of the existing regulation. As there exists multiple regulatory oversight, it also established that there should be dialogue and coordination between the various industry regulators and parties to ensure that the providers receive the necessary support from government and also to evaluate possible repercussions of new products to the integrity of the financial system. It also suggested that the telecom regulatory framework is inadequate to address mobile financial services. While the CCK has surrendered the regulatory mandate of the converged services to the CBK, the NPSA does not provide adequate provisions for mobile payments. Under the current law, the CBK will have to coordinate with the CCK to ensure that the policies on mobile payments are consistent whilst it implements a more fitting regulatory framework.[11] This, as stated, would strengthen the regulatory capacity for reforms within Kenya to act and respond to changes in the market, since how to regulate and establish and appropriate regulatory framework remains the most important challenge.

Chapter 5 addressed the final research question, 'what reforms should be implemented in the current regulatory framework to adequately oversee mobile payments?' After the exploration of the regulatory challenges, this chapter discussed the themes around the regulatory approach to mobile payments, by proposing the need for reforms within the current framework. It establishes that the need for more regulation in no way diminishes the success of M-Pesa in Kenya, but rather, regulation should not always be seen as a stifling factor or a cost to the resources, since better regulation as was stressed by the CBK governor would be more appropriate. Regulation that takes into consideration the principles of 'good' regulation should provide an adequate framework for mobile payments. As Kenya demonstrated, the rapidity of and growth even in the regulatory vacuum left by the lack of a national payments law at the time of its inception shows the need for non-bank participation in the primary provision of payment services. Kenya's mobile payment system provided a rapid enabling of financial inclusion as well as immediate and manifest downstream benefits, with more than 40,000 agent outlets, enhancement of competition in financial services, and a web of interconnected business users whose difficulty getting paid in the past has been remedied by M-Pesa. The CBK will face continuing challenges, not only in developing the regulatory framework for mobile payments but also in enforcing and implementing the provisions under the NPSA.

Policy-makers and scholars continue to debate how regulation should look. Other developing countries have taken a variety of approaches in their regulation, but Kenya has the opportunity to serve as a benchmark for such regulation, despite the fact that it has been unclear in its approach. While mature and developed markets allow regulators to react to information promptly and accept market participants' strong role in regulatory matters, mobile payments present a special circumstance, particularly in Kenya, where the system has developed faster and more expansively than any other deployment in Africa,[12] and here all other payment systems are immature. Market discipline requires a mature and liberal market, which combats information asymmetry, a great obstacle to market discipline in less mature markets. Therefore, the CBK has to ensure that the regulatory framework for mobile payments is flexible, transparent and stable and promotes competition. Although the CBK has the challenge of establishing its roles as the main regulatory authority for mobile payments, as a developing country, Kenya often needs to fulfil other developmental tasks and fulfil other objectives, such as increased economic growth, fulfilling its Millennium Development Goals and financial inclusion. It is important that regulation avoids pitting these objectives against each other to prioritise the interests of the public. Thus far, Kenya's only legal contribution to the body of regulation of mobile payments and mobile financial services in general is a seemingly visible lacuna in the definition of a deposit. The way in which the mobile payment industry has exploited this loophole indicates inter alia just how critical contextualised legal drafting is, in relation to these emerging financial services. This exploitation had demonstrable public policy benefits, but in another time or context, it could have caused adverse effects on the Kenyan economy or on the sub-region in the event of systemic failure of the banks or the MNO.

Chapter 5 further examined the theories around the appropriate regulatory approach for mobile payments. Mobile payments have brought into focus the re-examination of the importance of retail payments and their core role in each country's overall financial stability.[13] This highlighted the importance of the central banks in the development of retail payment systems, especially in developing countries,[14] where their regulatory capacities may not always accommodate innovative services that post-date their current regulatory frameworks. In recent years, many countries have been more explicit in their effort to include payment systems as part of their agendas. For the overall development of the financial market in Kenya, the involvement of mobile payments and its significance to the overall stability of the financial system has not been examined in the depth that it should be, partly because of its nascent nature and the regulatory environment in which mobile payments have developed. Other developed countries[15] have made efforts to establish coordination among their regulatory authorities that oversee payment system issues, and cooperation has been established to ensure the smooth and continuing development of payment systems, especially where non-banks are involved. Kenya should, therefore, follow suit in making mobile payments a priority.

Other countries can learn valuable lessons from the Kenyan experience; however, each country must devise its own payment system. Simply importing another country's system without adjusting for the target country's geography, infrastructure, banking and legal structures, business practices, culture and needs could lead to a suboptimal system.[16] It also established that while no regulatory approach offers full guarantees, there should be adequate safeguards against risks, and each should be carefully assessed. In the long run, the most effective regulatory framework to promote mobile payments should be guided by risk management and safeguarding of funds, and one that balances the needs to enhance stability and promote innovation. It should also incorporate policy objectives which should focus on consumer protection and the clear definition of stored value in order to lay an enabling regulatory framework for other innovative peer-to-peer payments systems, such as Bitcoin, which is slowly becoming prevalent in Kenya.[17]

## 6.3 Future research

As a possible foundational study in this field in Kenya, this work has touched partially on the law and financial inclusion, the financial regulation agenda, and the theoretical underpinnings to regulation in converged environments. There still remains other aspects that warrant an exploration which were beyond the scope of this study, for example, interoperability and the implementation framework of the National Payment System Act 2011. A possible limitation of this thesis is that it is primarily a study of a single economy. The choice was consciously made with these facts in mind, motivated by the acknowledged need for financial sector deepening in Kenya, and in light of the fact that mobile financial services in Africa are still developing. This raises the valid argument that its findings may not necessarily be relevant to other jurisdictions. Furthermore, Kenya has appeared to be the standard and bellwether of mobile payments' success and therefore, any comparisons to other jurisdictions would not have yielded many results. Considering these limitations, this thesis does not argue that it encompasses all the relevant issues involved in mobile payments. The scarcity of research and literature on either the substantive content or the examination of the regulatory issues underlines the originality of this study.

### 6.3.1 Interoperability

Interoperability, which this thesis did not delve into, as it may be subject to future research, provides a regulatory challenge in the mobile payment context. The Competition Authority of Kenya[18] would be involved. Interconnection[19] allows users of one MNO to communicate with users of another MNO to allow access to services provides by either MNOs.[20]

Interoperability, on the other hand, allows 'the ability of communication systems, units or elements to provide services and to accept services from other systems, units or forces, and to use the services exchanged to enable them operate effectively together'.[21] Though interoperability may be a technological issue in this respect, this thesis argues that it is a regulatory one. This is because interoperability provides a consumer benefit[22] by offering a better competitive network.[23] Interoperability also allows externalities to be highlighted and the filtering of ineffective networks.[24] This precipitates further examination as to who would have to oversee this and how would legislation on interconnection look.[25] Interconnection promotes competition in the market.[26] In market structures where there is one dominant MNO, new subscribers tend to prefer the significant market player (SMP) over other lesser players. Safaricom, which boasts a 65 per cent market share, has benefitted from this new subscriber pattern.[27] This is because subscribers derive the benefit of connecting to a wider number of people at once.[28] This is called the 'network effect', which subsequently breeds market monopolies.[29] Hence, competition is encouraged when a new entrant's customers can receive traffic from or originate traffic to any other user within a marketplace. Competition is also encouraged when a new entrant can supply network services to a wider population of customers than the limited number who are directly connected as its own customers.[30]

### 6.3.2 Implementation of the National Payment Systems Act

It is extremely early to conclude whether CBK has successfully implemented its regulatory oversight through the National Payment System Act 2011, which integrates the regulation of mobile payments. Implementation also provides an aspect on which future research would be based. In the future, Kenya may undertake a policy and regulatory legal discourse about implementing mobile payments, introducing mobile payments alongside the establishment of safety and soundness provisions to safeguard user funds, thereby making a larger contribution to the international body of approaches to mobile payments.[31] Regular reporting[32] by MNOs on their financial health to the CBK and placement of funds in trust accounts at commercial banks demonstrates that adequate planning, a progressive regulator, alongside technical innovation ensures that there is no systemic impact on the financial system or harm to consumers.

Due to the cutting edge nature of this study, which seemed to race against the country developments in its analysis, this would have to be done in assessing how the CBK would proscribe, enforce and implement the National Payments Systems Act 2011. Payments systems innovation has greatly influenced the country's development ethic and, as stated in Chapter 5, each country that is looking to adopt mobile payments as an inclusive tool is at a different development stage and would therefore need to look at how it has worked in other countries before adopting mobile payments. Therefore, inquiry into these dynamics would expand the standard of local knowledge on how mobile payments and national development unite. There is also a need to build a national baseline of empirical data on all aspects of the mobile payments system. Collaborative work between researchers and the CBK in Kenya would yield valuable information that would form a critical first-line database for more robust empirical studies. More importantly, it would inform policy-makers seeking to evaluate public policy choices and in their allocation of resources that would enhance beneficial objectives (2014).

## 6.4 Conclusion

What this study has achieved is to create a baseline framework for future explorations of the multidimensional nature of mobile payments by offering a foundational perspective on the development of mobile payments from its inception to eventual regulation. Given that Kenya presents the most successful employment of mobile payments, it is particularly crucial that future work in the legal and institutional mechanics for the growth and development of inclusive financial services be employed with a retrospective approach. Therefore, there needs to be a dedicated early stage financial inclusion programme for Kenya, especially one rooted in research and development. It also aims to correct and expose some assumptions about developing countries' perspectives on inclusive technology by asserting that advanced models of establishing advanced financial systems do not have to use brick and mortar models and that the orthodox views of development can now be challenged and bypassed through the use of technology, but only that sustained through safe and sound frameworks, in this case, appropriate regulatory frameworks. This work has only considered one aspect of mobile payments, the regulatory challenges arising post-financial inclusion; other aspects that remain unexplored to complete the knowledge and 'baseline' for Kenya's mobile financial services are interoperability and ensuring a level playing field within the MNOs to effectively sustain the upward trend of financial inclusion. It would also adequately complement future research to examine, retrospectively, the effects of any future legislation that would seek to remedy the challenges highlighted in this thesis. Therefore, continuing on the basis that this is a foundational study on the regulatory issues surrounding mobile payments in Kenya, it seems fitting that the outcomes of this study's evaluations be translated into a series of law and policy implications through the emergent issues surrounding inclusive financial services.

## Notes

1　Chapter 2 described the proliferation and success of M-PESA in Kenya.
2　As in Chapter 2, 'unintended' here reflects the fact that mobile payments through M-PESA were introduced with a micro-financial aim and the shift from its originally intended use to a major payment system has become financially inclusive.
3　This public involvement refers to the large population of the unbanked as described in Chapter 2, into the financial realm.
4　The 'intermediaries' here are the commercial banks and financial institutions: banks, building societies credit unions financial advisers or brokers insurance companies' collective investment schemes, pension funds.
5　Mobile Financial Services Risk Matrix, <http://mobile-financial.com/blog/mobile-financial-services-risk-matrix> accessed 26 September 2014.
6　Maria C. Stephens, 'Promoting Responsible Financial Inclusion: A Risk-Based Approach to Supporting Mobile Financial Services Expansion' (2012) 27 *Banking and Finance Law Review*.
7　Ibid.
8　Patrick Honohan, *Banking System Failures in Developing and Transition Countries* (1st edn, Bank for International Settlements 1997). Honohan describes forbearance as the Achilles heel of any regulatory system where regulatory forbearance may be attributed to regulatory capture or result from regulators' fear that disclosure of distress in banks may have adverse effects on their reputations.
9　Garry J. Schinasi, 'Defining Financial Stability and Establishing a Framework to Safeguard It' (2011) 15 Central Banking, Analysis, and Economic Policies Book Series. International Monetary Fund <www.imf.org/external/pubs/ft/wp/2004/wp04187.pdf> accessed 22 September 2014).
10　Ryan Hahn, 'Payment Systems and Systemic Risk' (2008) *The World Bank* <http://blogs.worldbank.org/psd/payment-systems-and-systemic-risk> accessed 3 September 2014.
11　Since the CCK regulates the institutions that provide mobile payments, MNOs, and the financial institutions regulated by the CBK.
12　Efforts to scale up mobile payments in other countries such as Tanzania have not enjoyed similar success.
13　See 'Policy Issues for Central Banks in Retail Payments' 2003 (n 17) 11.
14　www.wantinews.com/news-8162076-Central-Bank:-the-overall-stability-of-the-financial-system-has-accumulated-some-industries-risk.htm accessed 20 September 2014.
15　Countries such as Tanzania, Uganda Malawi and South American countries.
16　R. H. Keppler, 1999, 'Transforming Payment Systems: The Building Blocks and the World Bank's Role, World Bank/Federal Reserve of New York' (FRBNY). Seminar held at FRBNY 13–16 April 1999; F. Montes-Negret and R. Keppler, 'Project Design for Payment Systems', March 1995, Public Project for the Private Sector, FPD Note No 37, The World Bank.
17　www.bitpesa.co/ > accessed 29 September 2014.
18　Competition Authority of Kenya was instituted in 2012, Competition Authority of Kenya, 'About Us' <www.cak.go.ke/> accessed 26 September 2014.
19　The physical and logical linking of telecommunication networks used by the same or different service licensees.
20　Section 2 of the Kenya Information and Communications (Interconnection and Provision of Fixed Links, Access and Facilities) Regulations, 2010. For example, interconnection of mobile network operator infrastructure allows subscribers of Safaricom to call, text, and receive calls and texts from Airtel network subscribers.
21　Jeremy Okonjo, 'Convergence of Mobile and Financial Services Implications for Regulation of Mobile Telecoms in Kenya' (2014) <www.slideshare.net/

JeremmyOkonjo/convergence-of-mobile-and-financial-services-implications-for-regulation-of-mobile-telecoms> accessed 26 September 2014. Section 2 of the Kenya Information and Communications (Interconnection and Provision of Fixed Links, Access and Facilities) Regulations 2010. For example, interoperability of Safaricom's and Airtel's mobile financial service platforms would allow subscribers of M-Pesa to send and receive money from ZAP, respectively.

22  John Buckley, Telecommunications Regulation (IET 2003).

23  Chukwudiebube Bede Opata, 'Looking Towards Europe: Regulation of Dominance in Nigerian Telecommunications' SSRN Journal.

24  Ivan Mortimer-Schutts, 'The Regulatory Implications of Mobile and Financial Services Convergence' in *The Transformational Potential of M-Transactions: Moving the Debate Forward* (2007) The Policy Paper Series 6 <www.vodafone.com/content/dam/vodafone/about/public_policy/policy_papers/public_policy_series_6.pdf> accessed 26 September 2014.

25  Joshua Goldstein, 'Embracing "Open Access" in East Africa: A Common Internet Infrastructure Policy Agenda for Human Security and Economic Development' (2008) 19 *Journal of Public and International Affairs* 139–150. The author noted that 'governments and incumbent telecom companies in East Africa are unmotivated to change this status quo because they currently form a cartel that profits from the rent-seeking activities of limited competition and closed access'. See also, Mark Okuttah, 'Telcos lock horns over sharing of infrastructure' *Business Daily* (22 May 2013) <www.businessdailyafrica.com/Telcos- lock-horns-over-sharing-of-infrastructure/-/1248928/1859780/-/2qxqnt/-/index.html> accessed 26 September 2014.

26  William H. Melody, 'Interconnection: Cornerstone of Competition' in William Melody (ed), *Telecom Reform: Principles, Policies and Regulatory Practices* (Technical University of Denmark 1997) 441–450.

27  Communications Commission of Kenya, 'Annual report financial year 2010/11' (2012) <www.ca.go.ke/images//downloads/PUBLICATIONS/ANNUALREPORTS/Annual%20Repo        rt%20for%20the%20Financial%20Year%202010–2011.pdf> accessed 26 September 2014.

28  Bede C. Opata, 'Transplantation and Evolution of Legal Regulation of Interconnection Arrangements in the Nigerian Telecommunications Sector' (2011) <www.researchgate.net/publicliterature.PublicPublicationPromoRequestFulltext.signup.html?publicationUid=256033593&ev=su_pub_req> accessed 26 September 2014. The author notes that this might be beneficial to sector incumbents at the onset of liberalisation, as they have all existing subscribers but are prohibitive of new entry.

29  Ivan Mortimer-Schutts (2007)

30  Ibid.

31  A discussion explained in this chapter and offered as a risk in Chapter 3.

32  The Financial Reporting Centre www.fpc.co.ke MNOs are required to report all incidences of fraud as was articulated during the interview with Mercy Buku; Joy Malala, Interview with Mercy Buku, 'An Interview with Senior Manager Money Laundering Reporting at Safaricom'.

# Bibliography

Arrangements in the Nigerian Telecommunications Sector' (2011) <www.research gate.net/publicliterature.PublicPublicationPromoRequestFulltext.signup. html?publ icationUid=256033593&ev=su_pub_req> accessed 26 September 2014.

Communications Commission of Kenya, 'Annual report financial year 2010/11' (2012) <www.ca.go.ke/images//downloads/PUBLICATIONS/ANNUALREPORTS/

Annual%20Repo rt%20for%20the%20Financial%20Year%202010–2011.pdf> accessed 26 September 2014.

Goldstein, Joshua, 'Embracing "Open Access" in East Africa: A Common Internet Infrastructure Policy Agenda for Human Security and Economic Development' (2008) 19 *Journal of Public and International Affairs* 139–150.

Hahn, Ryan, 'Payment Systems and Systemic Risk' (2008) *The World Bank* <http://blogs. worldbank.org/psd/payment-systems-and-systemic-risk> accessed 3 September 2014.

Honohan, Patrick, *Banking System Failures in Developing and Transition Countries* (1st edn, Bank for International Settlements 1997)

Keppler, R. H., 1999, 'Transforming Payment Systems: The Building Blocks and the World Bank's Role, World Bank/Federal Reserve of New York' (FRBNY). Seminar held at FRBNY 13–16 April 1999.

Melody, William H., 'Interconnection: Cornerstone of Competition' in William Melody (ed), *Telecom Reform: Principles, Policies and Regulatory Practices* (Technical University of Denmark 1997) 441–450.

Mobile Financial Services Risk Matrix, <http://mobile-financial.com/blog/mobile-financial-services- risk-matrix> accessed 26 September 2014.

Montes-Negret, F. and R. Keppler, 'Project Design for Payment Systems', March 1995, Public Project for the Private Sector, FPD Note No 37, The World Bank.

Mortimer-Schutts, Ivan, 'The Regulatory Implications of Mobile and Financial Services Convergence' in *The Transformational Potential of M-Transactions: Moving the Debate Forward* (2007) The Policy Paper Series 6 <www.vodafone.com/con tent/dam/vodafone/about/public_policy/policy_papers/public_policy_series_6. pdf> accessed 26 September 2014.

Okonjo, Jeremy, 'Convergence of Mobile and Financial Services Implications for Regulation of Mobile Telecoms in Kenya' (2014) <www.slideshare.net/Jerem myOkonjo/convergence-of-mobile-and- financial-services-implications-for-regula tion-of-mobile-telecoms> accessed 26 September 2014.

Okuttah, Mark, 'Telcos Lock Horns Over Sharing of Infrastructure' *Business Daily* (22 May 2013) <www.businessdailyafrica.com/Telcos- lock-horns-over-sharing-of-infrastructure/-/1248928/1859780/-/2qxqnt/-/index.html> accessed 26 September 2014.

Opata, Bede C., 'Transplantation and Evolution of Legal Regulation of InterconnectionOpata, Chukwudiebube Bede, 'Looking Towards Europe: Regulation of Dominance in Nigerian Telecommunications' *SSRN Journal*.

Schinasi, Garry J., 'Defining Financial Stability and Establishing a Framework to Safeguard It' (2011) 15 *Central Banking, Analysis, and Economic Policies* Book Series. International Monetary Fund <www.imf.org/external/pubs/ft/wp/2004/ wp04187.pdf> accessed 22 September 2014).

Stephens, Maria C., 'Promoting Responsible Financial Inclusion: A Risk-Based Approach To Supporting Mobile Financial Services Expansion' (2012) 27 *Banking and Finance Law Review*.

<www.wantinews.com/news-8162076-Central-Bank:-the-overall-stability-of-the-financial-system-has-accumulated-some-industries-risk.htm> accessed 20 September 2014.

# Index